ISLAND SUSTAINABILITY

CHALLENGES AND OPPORTUNITIES FOR OKINAWA AND OTHER PACIFIC ISLANDS IN A GLOBALIZED WORLD

Hiroshi Kakazu

Trafford
PUBLISHING®

 www.trafford.com

North America & international
toll-free: 1 888 232 4444 (USA & Canada)
phone: 250 383 6864 ♦ fax: 812 355 4082

CONTENTS

TABLES AND FIGURES

Tables

Figures

PREFACE

This volume is devoted to island sustainability with a focus on the small island prefecture of Okinawa, located at the southwestern edge of Japan. I was raised in Okinawa. Although I have spent a good deal of time in various places outside of Okinawa, I have always returned home. *Nissology* (island studies in Greek), coined by my long-standing friend, Grant McCall, is my life's work. I have published several books on the subject, including the *Sustainable Development of Small Island Economies* (Westview Press, 1994) which has been heavily cited by *nissologists*. The publication of the book was well-timed because the first meeting of the International Small Island Studies Association (ISISA), which I organized, was held in Okinawa in June 1994, centered on the appropriate theme of *"island matters, islands matter."* The ISISA (www.geol.utas.edu.au/isisa) is now a major international forum for island study. Since the establishment of the ISISA, various island-related organizations, studies program and journals have emerged, including the Japan Society of Island Studies (JSIS) of which I have been serving as president since 2005. In 2003, the University of Prince Edward Island in Canada launched a groundbreaking graduate program in island studies, offering an MA in island studies.

Why have small islands attracted so many researchers in recent years? One explanation may be that researchers who have been marginalized in mainstream international academic forums for many years began to assert their identity as islanders. Another explanation may stem from the uniqueness and illusiveness of islands as an object of scientific investigation. According to Baldacchino (2007), an avid *nissologist* at Canada's Institute of Island Studies, there are 180,498 inhabited islands with about 2% and 10% of the World's land area and total population respectively. But their characteristics are vastly different from island to island as is discussed in this volume. For instance, the Japanese islands named

Takara Jima (Treasure Island) and *Akuseki To* (Evil Stone Island) are located side by side. Their names demonstrate the commonly-held but contradictory images of islands as both paradise and hell or closure (prison) and openness (utopia). Because of the illusiveness of islands, including their definition and characteristics, mainstream, disciplined scientists have ignored "islandness" as a minor factor from their investigation. It is also true that an approach to island studies requires what Gunner Myrdal called a "multi- or trans-disciplinary approach" which is more complex than the conventional approach of scientific discovery. Yet I have to admit that *nissology* has still a long way to go before full academic recognition:

> *Island studies is very much about the implications of permeable borders. The small, remote and insular also suggest marginality, being on the edge, being out of sight and so out of mind, situations which can expose the weakness of mainstream ideas, orthodoxies and received wisdoms, while fomenting alternatives to the status quo. Any dominant paradigm is supposedly weakest at its periphery (Baldacchino, 2007).*

Okinawa, the birthplace of *nissology* and Japan's only small island prefecture, embraces all aspects of small, remote island characteristics, including geography, history, economy and culture. Okinawa hosted the third and fourth Pacific Leaders Meeting (PALM) which preceded the Pacific Islands Academic Summits in 2003 and 2006 respectively. Heads of fourteen independent and self-governing Pacific Island countries participated in PALM, which discussed education, tourism, the environment and economic development. PALM adopted "the Okinawa Initiative on Regional Development Strategies for a More Prosperous and Safer Pacific." This initiative emphasized the important role of Okinawa in spearheading and coordinating development and educational relationships among the Pacific islands: "Okinawa shares many common development issues with the Pacific island countries/regions including their small size, isolation, fragmentation, resource limitation and fragility, and vulnerability to natural disasters and outside economic and political impacts beyond their control. As such Okinawa's situation and experiences can be very useful in terms of developing appropriate models for sustainable island development in this region" (Ministry of Foreign Affairs, 2003).

This study intends to respond to the challenges and opportunities raised in the PALM Okinawa Initiative. The contents of this volume are revised versions of presentations made at various forums and meetings in recent years, including the ISISA conferences in Kinmen and Maui islands, meetings of the JSIS, workshops at Hawaii's East-West Center, Hong Kong Colloquium on small island culture and research initiatives, the International Scientific Council for Island Development (UNESCO-IN-SULA), the Japan Society of International Economics (JSIE), the International Geographers Union (IGU) in Taipei, Islands of the World IX Okinawa Pre-conference, the Hanoi Forum on Higher Education, a workshop on Taiwan-Okinawa Relations organized by the Taiwan Research Institute of Waseda University and Taipei's Academia Sinica, and a keynote speech at the Regional World Summit on the Information Society (WSIS) held at the United Nations University in Tokyo.

The ten chapters in this book focus on socio-economic issues and prospects of small Pacific islands with a particular focus on Okinawa's sustainable economic development. Chapter 1 deals with socio-economic characteristics and development issues of Pacific islands. Chapter 2 discusses issues and opportunities for small islands in a globalizing world. Chapter 3 covers the networking of island societies focusing on the Pacific islands and Okinawa. Chapter 4 introduces Japan's diversified remote island policies, plans and their recent performance. Chapter 5 covers the state of agriculture in the Pacific islands and its future role in sustainable development. Chapter 6 focuses on Okinawa's successful melon fly eradication project which opened up new frontiers for island agriculture. Chapter 7 offers a somewhat unconventional approach to Taiwan-Okinawa networking from an emerging perspective of economic partnership agreements. Chapter 8 is on sustainable island tourism focusing on Okinawa. A new concept of social carrying capacity is proposed. Chapter 9 presents Okinawa's unique *champuru* culture. The final chapter charts Okinawa's challenges and opportunities toward sustainable development. Although the focus is on Okinawa, analytical methods and visions presented in this final chapter will provide food for thought for many similar island societies.

This volume is a product of collaborative endeavors among my supporters as well as critical commentators on my original writings. I am particularly grateful to the many individual members of ISISA, UNESCO-INSULA, JSIS and JSIE who directly and indirectly made comments and suggestions on my earlier drafts. I also wish to extend my thanks to my former colleagues and students at the International University of Japan (IUJ), Nagoya University, Nihon University and the University of the Ryukyus who shared with me their experiences and inner thoughts with regard to the complex issues of islands' sustainability. I owe a special debt to Dr. Gay Satsuma of the University of Hawaii who not only proofread the entire manuscript, but her valuable editorial comments and suggestions also helped make this volume readable. Thanks are also extended to Dr. John Purves of the University of the Ryukyus for his comments and suggestions on the earlier draft. Needless to say, none of them are responsible for any shortcomings in this work.

NOTES

Baldacchino, G. (2007), p.6.
Ministry of Foreign Affairs (2003), p.3.

REFERENCES

Baldacchino, G. (ed.). 2007. *A World of Islands*. Malta: Published by the Institute of Island Studies of Prince Edward Island.

Kakazu, H. 1994. *Sustainable Development of Small Island Economies*. Boulder: Westview Press.

Ministry of Foreign Affairs. 2003. *The Pacific Leaders Meeting Between Japan and Members of the Pacific Islands Forum. The Okinawa Initiative: Regional (Development) Strategy for a More Prosperous and Safer Pacific*. Okinawa, May 16-17, Tokyo.

Chapter 1

ISLANDS CHARACTERISTICS
AND SUSTAINABILITY

INTRODUCTION

When discussing the socio-economic development of small island economies, one is always troubled as to the definition and measurement of island. According to *The Encyclopedia Britannica*, an island is "a piece of land completely surrounded by water." It is smaller than the size of Australia (7,686,843 sq km), which is the smallest continent in the world, and larger than a rock. According to this definition, Greenland is the largest island followed by New Guinea, Borneo, Madagascar, Baffin, Sumatra, Japan's Honshu (mainland), Victoria, Great Britain and Ellesmere if we list the ten largest islands (see Kakazu, 1994; Royle, 2007 and Dahl, 2007 for the latest definitions and classification of islands). Being an island itself does not necessarily imply a small economy. Japan for instance, the second largest economy in the world in terms of GDP, is a typical island country. In this volume, we define "small islands" as those with a total population of under 1.5 million (Commonwealth Secretariat, 1997).

According to the Global Shoreline Database (www.ngdc.noaa.gov/mgg/ shorelines/ gshhs.html), there are 180,498 islands with a population of 550 million or 10% of the world's total population in 2006. Although these islands occupy only 2% of the Earth's surface area, they account for 22% of the U.N. seats (Baldacchino, 2007). Information with regard to the number of islands and their populations is incomplete, out of date, and to a large degree inaccurate. The UNITAR Study (Rappapor and Therattil, 1971) lists ninety-six small states and territories with less than one million population and makes a distinction between thirty-nine mainland territories and fifty-seven islands or island groups. Of the small island states and territories, twenty are in the Pacific, seventeen in the Caribbean, eleven in the Atlantic Ocean, eight in the Indian Ocean, and two in the Mediterranean Sea. The small Pacific islands, which this investigation focuses upon are not only the most numerous, but the most scattered and varied islands in the world.

Unique development problems arise when the island is associated with its smallness as well as isolation which has significant socio-economic consequences. The problems of small economies will be intensified if they are located far from their major markets such as the South Pacific and Ryukyu Islands on which this study focuses. This is why the United Nations (1975) has identified "geographically disadvantaged developing island countries" along with "least developed" and "land-locked" developing countries as being in need of special attention.

Smallness can be defined in terms of the physical size (land area), population and GNP (or GDP), or a combination of these variables as attempted by Kakazu (1994), depending upon the purpose of the analysis. Kuznets (1960) used a population of ten million as the economically significant dividing line between small and large economies. Most of the arguments, however, favor using the concept of national income as the most appropriate one to measure the size of an economy, particularly in the discussion of "diseconomies" of small-scale production in small countries, and the derivative arguments concerning instability and trade dependence in small nations. If we want to see smallness in terms of current productive capacity, GNP or GDP best serves the purpose.

Shand's (1979) systematic classification of the islands in the South Pacific and Indian Ocean in terms of "small," "very small," and "micro" categories, however, demonstrates that a small population in general corresponds to a small land area and also to a small GDP. Of course, as Shand warns, these size indicators are more or less arbitrary and there will be no economically significant cut-off point for "small," "very small," and "micro." However, by using these size indicators, we may be able to identify their stage of economic development as well as the similarity in their development problems. If we take into consideration other factors, such as "isolation," "migration," and "external sources of income," the usefulness of such classification may greatly enhanced.

GENERAL CHARACTERISTICS OF ISLAND SOCIETIES

Keeping in mind again that "smallness" is a relative and not absolute idea, the general characteristics, merits and demerits of small islands from the standpoints of socio-economic development can be summarized in the following (FIGURE 1-1). Remoteness, oceanic and smallness are the most distinguishable characteristics of any island society.

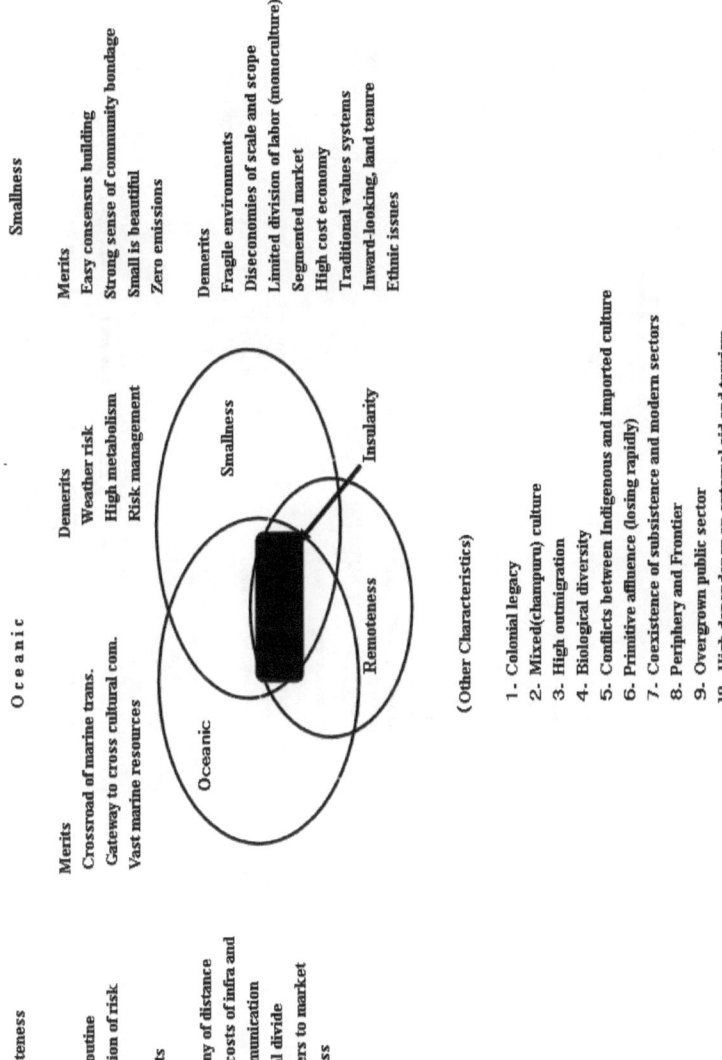

Remoteness

Merits
Non-routine
Aversion of risk

Demerits
Tyranny of distance
High costs of infra and communication
Digital divide
Barriers to market access

Oceanic

Merits
Crossroad of marine trans.
Gateway to cross cultural com.
Vast marine resources

Demerits
Weather risk
High metabolism
Risk management

Smallness

Merits
Easy consensus building
Strong sense of community bondage
Small is beautiful
Zero emissions

Demerits
Fragile environments
Diseconomies of scale and scope
Limited division of labor (monoculture)
Segmented market
High cost economy
Traditional values systems
Inward-looking, land tenure
Ethnic issues

(Other Characteristics)

1. Colonial legacy
2. Mixed(champuru) culture
3. High outmigration
4. Biological diversity
5. Conflicts between Indigenous and imported culture
6. Primitive affluence (losing rapidly)
7. Coexistence of subsistence and modern sectors
8. Periphery and Frontier
9. Overgrown public sector
10. High dependency on external aid and and tourism

Source: Kakazu, H. (2007).

FIGURE 1-1. Main Socio-Economic Characteristics of Small Island Societies.

17

Two development issues preventing the economic growth are the following:

(1) Their overall economic activities are less diversified and more specialized than large economies due mainly to their narrow range of human and non-human economic resources and markets. The narrow resource base and domestic market, coupled with high transport costs, severely limit what Kindleberger (1968) calls the "capacity of transformation" of the economies. All Pacific Island Forum (PIF) countries, except Papua New Guinea (PNG), have populations of less than a million (TABLE1-1). The island of Niue has only 2,000 residents.

TABLE 1-1. Main Indicators of the Pacific Island Countries and Regions, 2005

Countries/Regions	Population (000s persons)	Land Area (km²)	EEZ (000s km²)	Per Capita Income (US$)	Major Sources of Income	Political Status (Date of Independence)
(MELANESIA)						
P N G	5,800	462,840		500	Mining/lumber/agri./tourism	Independence (1975)
FIJI	840	18,272	1,290	2,240	Sugar/gourmet/remittances	Independence (1970)
SOLOMON IS.	521	27,540		560	Agriculture/fish/transfers (aid)	Independence (1978)
VANUATS	213	240		1,180	Tourism/transfers/US bases	Independence (1965)
(POLYNESIA)						
SAMOA	171	12,200		1,440	Agriculture/fish/transfers (aid)	Independence (1962)
TONGA	102	2,850		1,440	Agri./tourism/transfers (aid)	Independence (1970)
COOK IS.	20	488	629	7,550	Tourism/transfers (aid)	SGFA with New Zealand (1965)
TUVALU	11	21		1,350	Exports of phosphate/agri.	Independence (1978)
NIUE	2	26		1,100	Agri./transfers (aid)	SGFA with New Zealand (1974)
(MICRONESIA)						
KIRIBATI	104	718		860	Agri./tourism/transfers (aid)	Independence (1970)
FSM	108	717	2,978	2,070	Agri./tourism/transfers (aid)	Independence (1979)
MARSHALL IS.	61	701		2,710	Agri./tourism/transfers (aid)	Independence (1986)
PALAU	21	181	2,131	5,740	Agri./tourism/transfers (aid)	Independence (1986)
NAURU	10	101		3,740	Agri./tourism/transfers (aid)	Independence (1968)
P I F TOTAL	7,984	526,895				
(REFERENCES)						
GUAM	170	541	218	21,000	Tourism/transfers/US bases	Unincorporated Territory of the US
CNMI	80	471	1,823	12,500	Tourism/transfers (aid)	Commonwealth (US)
HAWAII	1,275	16,757	?	30,589	Tourism/US bases	A State of the US
NEW CALEDONIA	216	19,103	1,740	15,000	Tourism/transfers aid/nickel	Overseas Territory of France
OKINAWA	1,368	2,274	?	21,148	Tourism/transfers/US bases	Japan's Prefecture

Notes: CNMI = Commonwealth of Northern Mariana Islands.
EEZ = Exclusive Economic Zone (200 miles from all shorelines).
FSM = Federated States of Micronesia.
SGFA = Self-Governing Free Association.
Per capita incomes are 2002–2004.

Sources: Latest data compiled by H. Kakazu from the Websites of ADB, CIA, State and Prefectural governments of Hawaii and Okinawa.

(2) Because of the small domestic market, there are not many policy options

available for economic development. Thus, owing to the constant population pressure on the limited arable land and the "revolution of rising expectations," almost all small island countries had to open up their economies to the world markets. A small country or island often had a relatively large foreign trade not only because of her limited production resources, but also because "she has a larger frontier in proportion to her area than a larger country of the same shape" (Marshall, 1968). Because of their small size, they tend to be price-takers instead of price-makers. The degree of openness to or dependency on the world markets is customarily measured by the trade to GDP ratio. The smallest trade (exports + imports) to GDP ratio was 47% in 2000 for Kiribati. For economies such as Fiji and PNG, the ratio is nearly 90%.

Although these trade data are rather outdated, the picture has not changed significantly in recent years. Considering the fact that the trade to GDP for large island economies such as Indonesia and the Philippines is typically less than 30%, we can see how these small economies are vitally dependent upon foreign trade. This dependency creates economic instability and vulnerability.

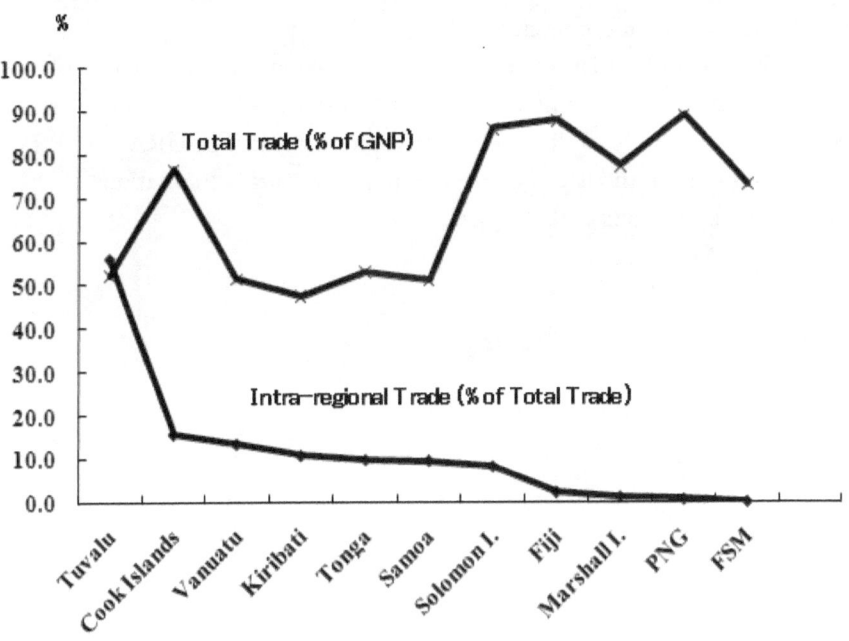

Source: Calculated from ADB Key Indicators (2002).

FIGURE 1-2. Intra-regional Trade among the Pacific Islands Forum Countries: 2000.

FIGURE1-2 also shows intra-regional trade flows among the Pacific Islands which account for only 2% of regions' total trade. PNG and the Federated States of Micronesia (FSM) have virtually no trade record with their neighboring island countries. The poor trade interrelationships among the regional countries are a natural outcome of the meager complimentarity of their economic activities. Economic diversification within the South Pacific Forum (SPF) countries is the most important prerequisite for achieving an economically viable regionalism which has been a much discussed subject for many years.

(3) It is a well-known fact that small island economies with limited resources and markets do not necessarily mean low per capita income economies. On the contrary, they are richer than most big developing economies (see Armstrong and Read, 2000 for an in-depth study on the issue). Per capita incomes of Hawaii and Okinawa are higher than the average per capita income of the OECD countries. According to the latest *Economist's* special report (February 24th 2007), the Caribbean islands of Bermuda, Cayman and the British Virgin Islands enjoy the highest per capita income in the world with booming offshore banking businesses. As is discussed latter in this book, banking and networking businesses are typical high-value added, future-oriented "footloose service industries" which fit into the environments of islands climate.

In the case of Okinawa's outlying islands, economic size in terms of the size of population, which roughly corresponds to the size of land resource and GDP, seems related inversely to the level of per capita income (FIGURE 1-3). Per capita income is higher in the islands that have popular tourist destinations or that specialize in cash products such as sugar.

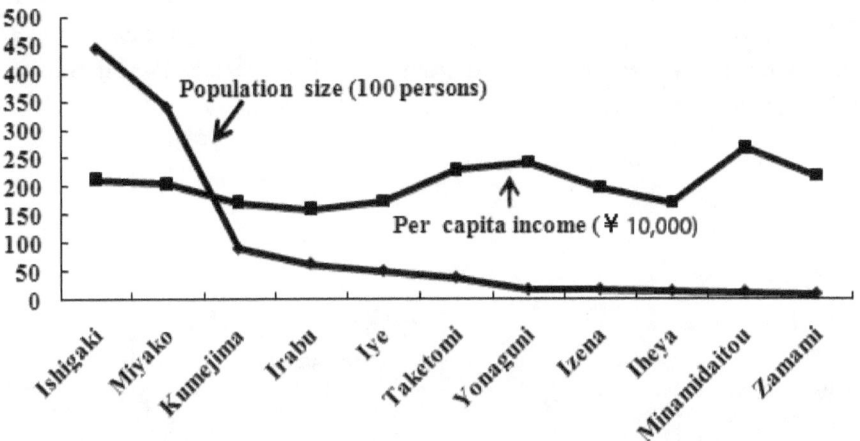

100 persons; ¥ 10,000

Population size (100 persons)

Per capita income (¥ 10,000)

Ishigaki Miyako Kumejima Irabu Iye Taketomi Yonaguni Izena Iheya Minamidaitou Zamami

Source: Okinawa Prefectural Government.

FIGURE 1-3. Economic Size and Per Capita Incomes of Okinawa's Islands: 2004.

(3) As a direct result of the narrow range of their resource base and production conditions, small island economies depend upon a few primary products for their export earnings, while importing a wide range of consumer as well as capital goods. One export commodity, such as fish in American Samoa and copra in Kiribati and Tokelau, accounts for nearly all of their export incomes.

The exports of these island economies are also characterized by their high geographical concentration. This characteristic may be easily inferred from the fact that island countries, whose politico-economic ties with former colonial governments are still strong, produce more or less similar primary products in relatively small quantities that can never influence the world market. The large percentages of South Pacific exports are directed towards a few developed countries. Nearly all exports of Niue and Cook Islands are directed to New Zealand, as are imports of American Samoa to the United States. Nearly sixty per cent of exports in French Polynesia and New Caledonia are destined for their sovereign country, France. Imports also tend to be geographically concentrated, but they are more diversified than exports. The dependency on a few export products and markets not only makes these island economies vulnerable to the fluctuations of world markets, but they are also susceptible to natural hazards such as cyclones, typhoons, floods, drought, and disease.

(4) Most of the small island economies have been suffering from chronic deficits in trade balances which have largely been financed by growing inflows of

remittances, Official Development Assistance (ODA), and tourism incomes (FIG-URE 1-4 and FIGURE 1-5). ODA flows more than offset the trade deficits of Solomon Islands and Marshall Islands. I should note, however, that "while financial aid from abroad can make the economy of the small islands more prosperous, there is no question it comes at the heavy cost of the island's lost autonomy and independence on the part of the island's residents" (Kanemitsu, 2005).

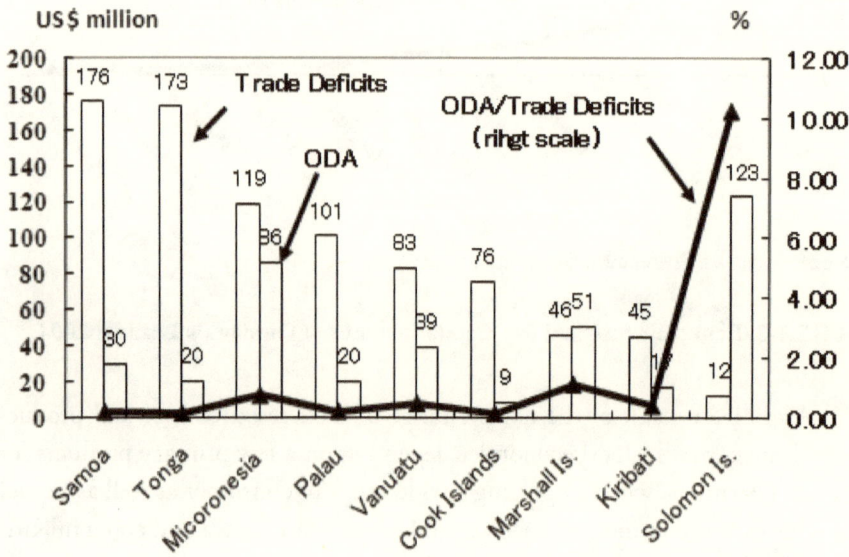

Source: ADB, *Key Indicators* (2006).

FIGURE 1-4. Financing Trade Deficits by ODA for Selected Pacific Islands: 2005.

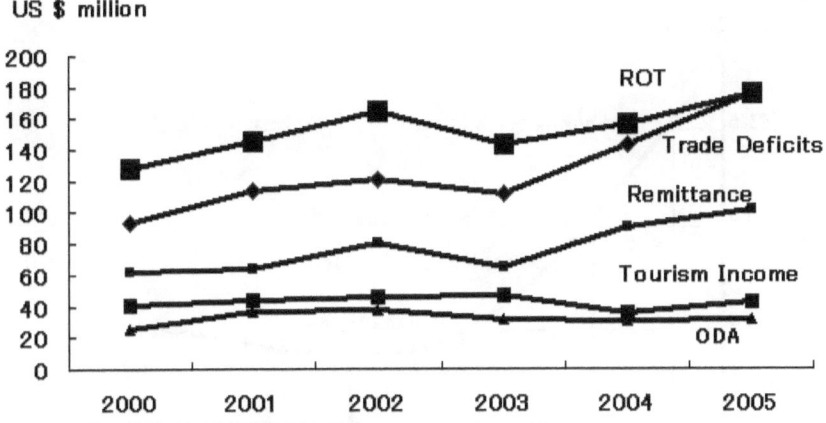

US $ million

Note: ROT = Remittances + ODA + Tourism Income.
Source: ADB, *Key Indicators* (2006).

FIGURE 1-5. Samoa's Main Sources of Financing Trade Deficits.

In addition to ODA, tourism income and remittances from emigrated workers or families are considered to be the major sources of income to be used to pay for imports as is typically illustrated by the case of Samoa (FIGURE 1-5). These three external sources have just covered the deficit in 2005.

(5) Small island economies suffer from diseconomies of scale in production, investment, consumption, transportation, education, and administrative services. The problem of diseconomies of scale becomes intensified when the island countries or territories are fragmented into "mini" islands and are located far from large foreign markets. In the South Pacific, Fiji alone consists of nearly 100 inhabited islands, and most of the South Pacific islands are located more than 1,000 km from the nearest continent.

The problem of diseconomies of scale is probably the most discussed subject in the development of small island economies. Yet, except for some fragmentary evidence, there has been no systematic empirical study on the subject. This author once calculated the scale effect of unit cost in generating electricity in the islands of Okinawa. The unit cost curve for generating electricity decreases dramatically as the size of the islands in terms of population increases (FIGURE 1-6). The costs of generating electricity per hour in neighboring small islands and Miyako & Yaeyama Islands are more than 196% and 58% higher respectively than Okinawa Island which accounts for 87 % of the total population of Okinawa Prefecture.

Unit Cost
Per 1 KW/H (yen)

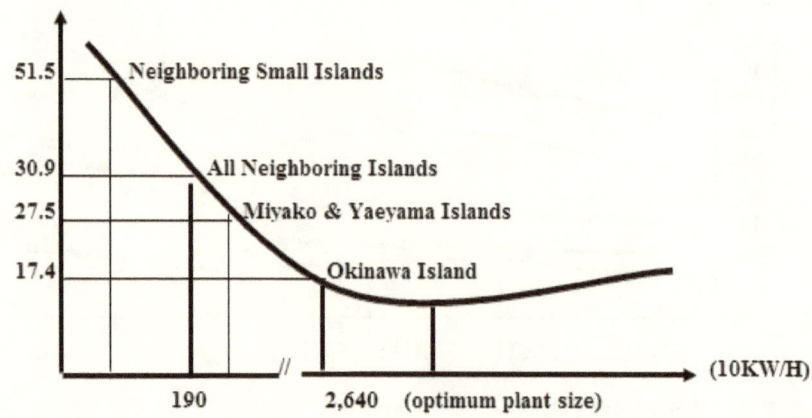

51.5 — Neighboring Small Islands

30.9 — All Neighboring Islands

27.5 — Miyako & Yaeyama Islands

17.4 — Okinawa Island

190   2,640   (optimum plant size)   (10KW/H)

Source and notes, see Kakazu (1994).

FIGURE 1-6. Unit Cost Curve for Generating Electricity in the Islands of Okinawa: 1980.

(6) The heavy burden of transportation costs may be the single most important barrier to the socioeconomic development of small islands. The UNESC Report (1974) states that the problem of transportation is not only the high cost of shipping resulting from extremely small-scale operations, but also the irregularity of supply which leads, even in the absence of any balance of payments constraints on imports, to periodic shortages and erratic price movements.

(7) Many small island economies have experienced more population growth and urbanization than other developing economies, which have aggravated the problems of unemployment. The increasing population pressure on the limited land is reflected in the rising population density for most of the countries in the South Pacific.

One of the striking features of small island economies is a persistent net migration to the neighboring mainland which helps to ease population pressure. The Cook Islands and Niue, for example, recorded depopulation during the past decade due to a substantial net migration to New Zealand. Out-migration is particularly important in island countries or territories with a population of below 150,000 inhabitants. Despite continuous outflows of labor force, there is ample evidence of a serious unemployment problem in most South Pacific countries, though unemployment statistics are available for only a few of the countries and are often difficult to interpret because of inadequate data.

(8) Because of their smallness, remoteness and openness, island economies have shaped distinctive industrial structure (TABLE 1-2). Commodities producing sectors such as agriculture and manufacturing have declined as global competi-

tion accelerates, while the service sectors such as tourism, government, labor and offshore banking have gained strength. Relatively large economies in the South Pacific such as Fiji, Tonga and Vanuatu still maintain large agricultural sectors due largely to protective measures and sizable subsistence sectors. The goods producing sectors (agriculture and manufacturing) of Hawaii and Okinawa have shrunk rapidly because both economies have exhausted all their subsistence agriculture and manufacturing sectors under the constant pressure of global competition.

TABLE 1-2. Industrial Structure of Selected Island Economies
(% of Gross Domestic Products)

	Population (1000)		Agriculture		Manufactuirng		Services	
	1990	2005	1990	2005	1990	2005	1990	2005
Cook Islands	17.0	20.2	21.2	12.8	3.9	3.7	73.8	81.1
Fiji	737.0	846.1	22.2	14.5	12.7	15.0	60.4	65.6
Hawaii	1,108.0	1,275.0	1.2	1.0	2.8	1.6	96.0	97.4
Kiribati	72.3	91.9	18.6	10.1	1.2	0.7	73.8	77.6
Marshall Is.	46.2	63.6	13.9	10.4	1.2	4.5	70.1	69.1
Okinawa	1,222.0	1,361.0	3.0	1.9	5.8	4.7	80.3	89.5
Palau	15.1	19.9	8.1	3.1	0.9	0.4	82.2	76.9
Samoa	160.3	183.3	23.0	13.1	19.6	14.6	48.7	60.9
Tonga	96.4	101.9	34.7	28.5	6.0	4.8	51.7	60.2
Tuvalu	9.0	10.4	25.6	16.6	3.1	3.7	59.9	73.4
Vanuatu	147.3	218.0	20.7	15.0	5.5	3.6	67.0	76.8

Notes: Agriculture includes all primary incomes; Services include all tertiary incomes.

Sources: ADB, *Key Indicators*; *State of Hawaii Data Book*; *Okinawa Statistical Yearbook*.

(9) Most Pacific island economies are hybrids, or dual systems, where the monetary sector co-exists with a substantial subsistence sector (this topic will be fully discussed in Chapter 5). Walsh (1975) suggests that a wide-range of subsistence socio-economic activities are regarded as a semi-permanent feature of Pacific island society, and policy makers should operate within this term of reference.

Because of such diversified subsistence income generating activities which cannot be easily accounted in formal income statistics, there are wide discrepancies between market-valued per capita income and purchasing power parity (PPP) estimates (FIGURE 1-7). Tonga's per capita income in terms of PPP for instance is more than 6 times higher than its nominal (foreign exchange) income. It can be said that the wider the gap between market measure and PPP, the relatively larger the subsistence sector.

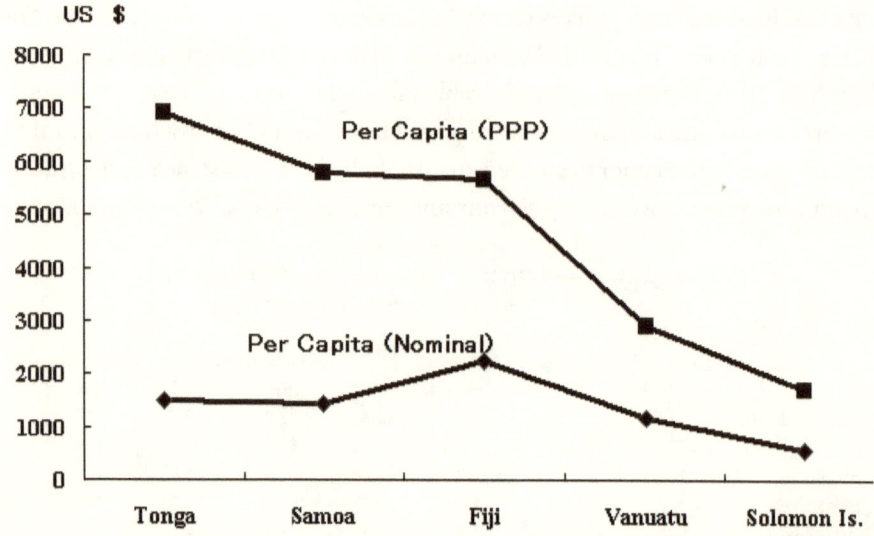

US $

Per Capita (PPP)

Per Capita (Nominal)

Tonga   Samoa   Fiji   Vanuatu   Solomon Is.

Notes: PPP = In terms of purchasing power parity.
Nominal = In terms of nominal exchange rate.

Source: World Bank, World Development Indicators.

FIGURE 1-7. Relative Size of the Subsistence Sectors Measured in Terms
of Per Capita Incomes: 2005.

The theory of comparative advantage has better served for large economies where alternative resources for exports can more easily be developed than small ones. For very small economies of the South Pacific, the exhaustion of non-renewable exportable resources means the complete collapse of external trade and return to a subsistence economy. There is a good possibility that the return to the subsistence economy will result in a lower level of production than the level of pre-trade due to the possible loss of traditional subsistence skills and other subsistence resources. The collapse case of small, resource-rich island economies and possible policy implications are fully discussed in Chapter 5.

(10) Another characteristic of island economies, which is more or less related to the aforementioned problems, is their heavy dependence on government activities as a major source of income, employment, and probably as a symbol of social prestige for employment status. It is astonishing to know that the government expenditures in the Cook Islands, Niue, and Samoa account for more than 80 per cent of their respective gross national products. Government involvement in private commerce has crowded out private enterprise while drawing resources away

from the provision of public services which are so necessary for growth of private enterprise. Poor property rights to land, insecurity of debt contracts, unsustainable budget deficits, and political and policy instability have all raised the risk premium on investment, resulting in high grading of investment opportunities.

(11) Some small island countries are also dependent on the monetary authorities of industrial countries in the sense that they do not have an independent currency and/or do not follow autonomous monetary policies. We should also note that one or more large multinational corporations dominate foreign trade in a number of small island economies. The policies and decisions of these companies have a determining influence on the island's development. These characteristics are a vestige of the colonial heritage of other developing countries. Specialization in a few primary export products in the South Pacific has been intensified both by colonial economic policies and new demands created through imported goods. There is a very interesting study on "Colonialism and Modern Income: Islands as Natural Experiments" (Feyrer and Sacerdote, 2006). After examining the long run effects of colonial history on islands economic performance, the paper concludes that the longer the Western colonial exposure was the greater benefit to the modern inhabitants of the islands in terms of GDP. However, "there is a discernable pecking order amongst the colonizers, years under US and Dutch colonial rule are significantly better than years under the Spanish and Portuguese" (*ibid.*). The authors believe that the good performance under the colonial rule owe largely to the efficient transfer of Western institutions or governance which have been pro-growth factors for the colonized.

(12) Pacific islands have developed enormously complex socio-cultural systems through the interactions of their traditional lifestyles with the Western legal system and cultures. Despite a rapid commercialization of their economic activities, the customary land ownership is still prevalent throughout the South Pacific. Like centrally planned economies, there are no or limited individual property rights to land, profit, and income and hence no or reduced incentive for people to pursue individual self-interest (ADB, 1999). The *Matai* (local chief) still plays very important economic, moral and political roles in village life.

(13) Finally, we have to touch on the environmental vulnerability of small island societies. Following the 1992 UN Conference on Environmental and Development which recognized special island issues for environment and development, the 1994 UN Global Conference held in Barbados adopted the program of actions for the sustainable development of small islands (see Briguglio 2004, for his painstaking efforts in constructing vulnerability indices). The latest report of the Intergovernmental Panel on Climate Change (IPCC), which was awarded the 2007 Nobel peace prize jointly with former US Vice-President Al Gore, stated the following on small islands:

Small islands, whether located in the Tropics or higher latitudes, have char-acteristics which make them especially vulnerable to the effects of climate change, sea level rise and extreme events. Deterioration in coastal conditions, for example through erosion of beaches and coral bleaching is expected to af-fect local resources, e.g., fisheries, and reduce the value of these destinations for tourism. Sea-level rise is expected to exacerbate inundation, storm surge, erosion and other coastal hazards, thus threatening vital infrastructure, settlements and facilities that support the livelihood of island communities. Climate change is projected by the mid-century to reduce water resources in many small islands, e.g., in the Caribbean and Pacific, to the point where they become insufficient to meet demand during low rainfall periods. With higher temperatures, increased invasion by non-native species is expected to occur, particularly on middle and high-latitude islands (IPCC, Summary for Policymaker, 2007).

The United Nations Division for Sustainable Development (SD) has devel-oped the Environmental Vulnerability Index (EVI) since the late 1990s for 235 countries and regions including thirty-six small island development states (SIDS). The EVI uses fifty key indicators of environmental vulnerability including climate change, biodiversity, water, agriculture and fisheries, human health aspects, deser-tification and exposure to natural disasters (see http:// www. vulnerabilityindex. net/EVIIndicators.htm for details). FIGURE 1-8 shows the results for 2004 with five ranks of vulnerability classification:

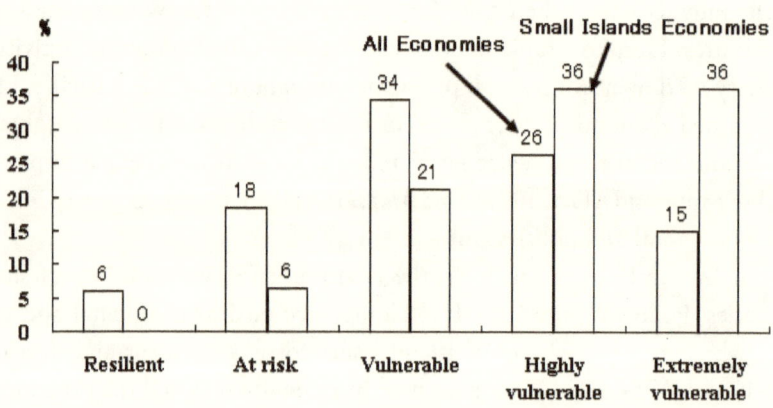

Source: UN Department of Economic and Social Affairs.

FIGURE 1-8. Vulnerability Index of Small Island Economies Compared with All Economies: 2004.

SIDS are estimated to be 34% economically as well as environmentally more vulnerable than other countries and regions largely because of their fragile environments, high exposure to natural disasters and high level of dependency on exports. Bertram (2004), however, is skeptical about constructing and interpreting the vulnerability index:

> I see little point in constructing measures of so-called "vulnerability" unless one starts from an explicit model that explains why future shocks to island economies might have consequences more severe than those which would appear in larger and/or landlocked economies. Small islands have, it seems to me, a myriad evolutionary responses to external forces that enable island peoples to seize opportunities that open up in the global economy, while ducking most of the big punches that the world economy throws.

These environmental disruptions are mostly man-made arising from increasing populations and rising material expectations which are placing considerable pressure on the extremely limited land resources and coastal marine ecosystems. It should be noted, however, that although proper environmental planning and conservation management are vital for the sustainable development of these small islands, a large part of global warming is attributable to industrial activities of much larger economies notably the United States, China and Japan.

Advantages of Small Islands

There are, however, a number of characteristics of small islands which can be considered to be economically advantageous over larger economies, such as the importance of being unimportant in external commercial policy, more unified national markets, greater flexibility, and perhaps greater potential social cohesion. Prasad (2004) vividly demonstrated that "the importance of being unimportant has allowed many small economies to pursue distinctively national policies seeking favorable deals which concede special advantages" such as sales of passports (Kiribati, Samoa, FSM), internet domain names (Tuvalu), shipping registries (Vanuatu), fishing rights (Pacific islands), postage stamps (Tuvalu) and military bases (Okinawa, Palau, Marshall islands). The South Pacific countries also "sell their "sovereignty" to other countries in order to finance their budget or to get foreign aid." (*Ibid.*)

The huge expanse of ocean surrounding these island masses may also provide rich marine resources and natural energy which can be tapped for future economic development. Okinawa, for example, is making full use of ocean resources including aquaculture, the utilization of deep-sea water for various healthy products and marine or "blue" tourism such as whale-watching and scuba diving.

As is fully discussed in Chapter 8 (Sustainable Island Tourism), the Pacific island countries have enormous potential to develop a tourism industry which is a future-oriented industry. The industry is becoming the most important source of foreign exchange earnings for small islands (TABLE 1-3). About one-half of the following island economies depend more on tourism income than their export earnings.

TABLE 1-3. Tourism in Selected Island Countries: 2003

	GDP ($million)	Trade balance ($million)	Tourism income ($million)	Exports/ GDP	Tourism income/ GDP	Tourism income > Exports
The South Pacific Islands						
Papua New Guinea	3,182	877	60	59.4%	1.9%	
Fiji	2,036	-464	431	31.5%	20.3%	
Vanuatu	283	-78	71	10.3%	26.8%	●
Samoa	268	-122	53	6.0%	18.1%	●
Solomon Islands	253	8	9	24.0%	3.6%	
Micronesia, Fed. Sts.	243	-65	17	6.6%	7.0%	●
Tonga	163	-75	15	7.8%	6.0%	
Palau	126	-129	59	11.7%	48.0%	●
Marshall Islands	106	-46	4	9.8%	3.9%	
Kiribati	55	-37	3	7.2%	5.8%	
The Caribbean Islands						
Dominican Republic	16,541	-2,444	3,110	27.2%	14.5%	
Jamaica	8,147	-2,435	1,621	14.8%	18.9%	●
Bahamas	5,260	-892	1,795	13.7%	35.6%	●
Haiti	2,921	-841	93	8.7%	3.1%	
Barbados	2,627	-923	767	9.2%	28.0%	●
Belize	989	-347	156	19.7%	14.6%	
Antigua and Barbuda	757	-275	301	5.1%	40.1%	●
Guyana	742	-60	39	68.7%	7.8%	
St. Lucia	693	-300	282	6.3%	37.4%	●
Grenada	439	-198	104	13.0%	22.4%	●
St. Vincent and the Grenadines	371	-162	85	11.6%	22.8%	●
St. Kitts and Nevis	346	-207	61	9.6%	17.2%	●
Dominica	259	-87	51	16.9%	18.3%	●

Note: ● indicate economies where tourism income is greater than exports.

Original Sources: World Bank (2005) *World Development Indicators*, WTO (2005) *Compendium of Tourism Statistics*, ADB (2005) *Key Indicators 2005*. Cited from Tetsuo Umemura, "An Empirical Analysis on International Tourism and Economic Growth in Small Island Developing States" *The Journal of Island Sciences*, No.1, December 2006, p.51.

As is explained in more detail in Chapter 8, the tourism industry, however, is in many ways beyond the control of these small islands because it depends not only on the economic conditions of industrialized countries but also on various imported inputs such as transportation, hotels, sales promotion, raw materials, souvenirs, and even foodstuffs, all of which consist of leakages from their economies. Even in Fiji, one of the largest Pacific island economies, more than 70% of tourist expenditures are leaked out of the country in the form of imports, profit expropriation and expatriate salaries (Kakazu, 2000).

Another future-oriented growth industry which is fitted to small islands is the information and communication technology (ICT) industry. The ICT industry is "footloose," and it does not require natural resources, transportation and heavy technology which are essential ingredients for agriculture and manufacturing. Okinawa has been emerging as a center of the ICT industry in recent years being supported by the incentive systems (mainly subsidies of wages and connection fees) of prefectural and Japanese governments (TABLE 1-4). As of December 2005, there are 105 ICT companies with new employment of about 20,000 which is a very large figure for a small island standard. Initially, NTT's telephone directory call centers were established in 2001 followed by more sophisticated call centers, software companies, Internet cafes and data centers. Some of them moved their operations from Singapore, Hong Kong, Taiwan, Shanghai and Dalian.

TABLE 1-4. Information and Communication Technology (ICT)
Companies in Okinawa: 2001-2005
(investments mainly from Mainland Japan)

	Unit	2001	2004	2005	Goals 2010
ICT Companies	number	54	90	103	
Employment	person	8,600	16,700	18,009	22,400
ICT Sales	¥100mil.	1,391	2,203	2,362	3,590

Source: Mid-term Review of Okinawa Promotion Plan (March 2007).

The ICT industry is also future-oriented because the next society will be a knowledge-based society. Knowledge will be its key resource, and knowledge workers will be the dominant group in its workforce. Its three main characteristics will be: 1)borderlessness, because knowledge travels even more effortlessly than money; 2) upward mobility, available to everyone through easily acquired formal education, and 3) the potential for failure as well as success. Anyone can acquire the "means of production," i.e., the knowledge required for the job, but not everyone can win. Together, those three characteristics will make the knowledge society a highly competitive one, for organizations and individuals alike. Manufacturing was the dominant social and political force in the 20th century, knowledge technologists are likely to become the dominant social and perhaps also political force over the next decades.

Small islands may also have comparative advantages in environmental economic activities such as recycling, reusing, and reducing the environmental hazards. Small islands can be a model case of a zero-emission society. Okinawa has been emerging as a model island of environmentally friendly products such as recycling used bottles, ethanol production from sugarcane and waste materials.

Notes

Kindleberger, C.P. (1968), p.82.
Marshall, A. (1927), p. 25.
Kanemitsu, H. (2005), p.174.
Feyrer, J. and Sacerdote, B. (2006), p.28.
Intergovernmental Panel on Climate Change (IPCC) (2007), p.2.
Bertram, G. (2004), p.7.

References

Armstrong, H. and Read, R. 2002. "Comparing the Economic Performance of Dependent Territories and Sovereign Micro-states." *Economic Development and Cultural Change*, vol.48, pp.285-306.

Asian Development Bank (ADB). 1999. *Pursuing Economic Reform in the Pacific*. Pacific Studies Series. Manila.

Baldacchino, G. (ed.). 2007. *A World of Islands*. Malta: Published by the Institute of Island Studies of Prince Edward Island. This book gives the latest rich information on island studies.

Bertram, G. 2004. "The MIRAB Model in the 21st Century." A paper presented at Islands of the World Vlll, Jinmen, Taiwan, November 2007, pp.1-37.

Briguglio, L. 2004. *Economic Vulnerability and Resilience: Concepts and Measurements*. Malta: Commonwealth Secretariat and the University of Malta.

Commonwealth Secretariat. 2007. *A Future for Small States: Overcoming Vulnerability*. London: Commonwealth Secretariat.

Dahl, A. 2007. "Island Locations and Classifications." In: Godfrey Baldacchino, G. (ed.), *A World of Islands.* Canada: University of Prince Edward Island, pp. 57-105.

Feyrer, J. and Sacerdote, B. 2006. *NBER Working Paper,* no.12546, October, pp.1-47.

Intergovernmental Panel on Climate Change (IPCC). 2007. "Summary for Policy-maker." In: *Climate Change,* Cambridge: Cambridge University Press.

Kakazu, H. 2000. *The Challenge for Okinawa: Thriving Locally in a Globalized Economy.* Naha: Okinawa Development Finance Corporation.

_____. 1994. *Sustainable Development of Small Island Economies.* Boulder: West-view Press.

Kanemitsu, H. 2005. "An Approach to the Small Islands Problems: Introduction." Nissology. Annual Report of the Japan Society of Island Studies, no.7, pp.168-175.

Kindleberger, C.P. 1968. *International Economics.* Illinois: Richard D. Irwin.

Kuznets, S. 1960. "Economic Growth of Small Nations." In: E.A.G. Robinson (ed.), *Economic Consequences of the Size of Nations.* London: Macmillan, pp.14-32.

Marshall, A. 1927. *Industry and Trade.* London: Macmillan.

Prasad, N. 2004. "Escaping Regulation, Escaping Convention: Development strat-egies in small economies." *World Economics,* vol.5, No.1, pp.41-65.

Rappaport, J., E. Muteba and J. J. Therattil. 1971. *Small States and Territories: Status and Problems.* New York: Arno Press for the United Nations Institute of Training and Research (UNITAR).

Royle, S.A. 2007. "Definitions & Typologies." In: Godfrey Baldacchino (ed.), *A World of Islands.* Canada: University of Prince Edward Island, pp. 33-56.

Shand R.T. 1979. *"Island Smallness: Some Definitions and Implications."* A paper presented to the Development Studies Centre Conference of the Australian National University. Canberra.

Umemura, T. 2006. "Kokusai Kanko to Toshogoku no Keizaiseicho ni Kansuru Jissho Bunseki "(An Empirical Analysis on International Tourism and Eco-nomic Growth in Small Island Developing States)." *Tosho Kagaku* (The Jour-nal of Island Sciences), no.1, December, pp.47-64.

United Nations Economic and Social Council (UNESC). 1975. *Economic Prob-lems and Development Needs of Geographically More Disadvantaged Developing Island Countries:* Note by the Secretary −General. New York.

Walsh, A.C. 1975. "Subsistence Agriculture and the Communication of Innova-tions: Some Niuean Examples." In: Hardaker, J.B. (ed.), *The Subsistence Sector in the South Pacific.* Suva: University of the South Pacific.

Chapter 2

Globalization and Regional Economy: A Growth Triangle (GT) Approach for Island Development

What is Globalization?

Globalization can be defined as a phenomenon of socio-economic integration on a global scale resulting from trans-border human activities. Economic globalization (thereafter globalization) is neatly expressed by such buzzwords as global standards, American standards, borderless, global capitalism, tyranny of market forces, interdependence, Big Bang, structural adjustment, privatization, market fundamentalism, and competitive liberalization.

According to Sawa (2000), one of the critics of globalization, the term globalization appeared after the collapse of the Soviet Union in 1990. Before that the term "internationalization" had been used in Japan to describe international socio-economic exchanges. Internationalization had been favorably accepted by ordinary citizens and participants in international activities because the term contained cross-cultural communications and socio-economic activities initiated by and beneficial to all participants.

Globalization, however, has been largely initiated by international organizations such as the IMF and WTO, and also by the most powerful capitalist nations, the United States and its allies. Naturally, the process of globalization through market forces has generated various domestic as well as international problems such as a widening income gap between the rich and poor, worsening global environmental disruptions and cultural uniformity.

Numerous papers and books appeared in recent years on the pros and cons of globalization. Some important ones are: Stiglitz (2002), Schirms (2002), Solos (2002), James (2001), Craft (2000) O'Rourke *et al* (1999), Collier and Gunning (1999) and Sen (1999). Particularly Stiglitz book on "Dissents on Globalization" has stirred up controversy not only because of his reputation as a Nobel Award winning economist, but also because he was responsible for promoting globalization in the past as Chairman of the U.S. Council of Economic Advisers and Chief Economist at the World Bank.

Globalization could be considered as a vehicle for disseminating American values through the unstoppable information technology (IT) revolution. But if we look at the latest behavior of the United States in the international arena, it is apparent that globalization and "Americanization" are not necessarily identical contents. U.S. withdrawal from the Kyoto Protocol on Global Warming in 2002, the institution of safeguard against imports of steel products, enactment of new protective farm bill, and the spate of scandals of world-class corporations such as a financial scandal of Enron in late 2001 are all convincing evidences that the U.S. lays behind the high ethical standards it promotes for the rest of the world. "Americanization" is a U.S.-centered globalization, or American "unilateralism" in international politics.

The Economist (11-17 May 2002) branded U.S. President Bush as "anti-globalist" in spite of the fact that his own Council of Economic Advisers assessed that "the U.S. economy is more integrated with the world economy than at any other period of U.S. history" (CEA, 2001). It is a common perception that the U.S. nation state has been strengthened through the expansion of free trade through such agreements as NAFTA and other thriving bilateral Free Trade Areas (FTAs).

Although globalization has been accelerated by the collapse of socialism and the IT revolution, its origin can be traced back to the IMF and GATT (=WTO) both of which emerged after World War II. Today's globalization should be distinguished from free trade under 19th century imperialism.

The most discussed dark side of globalization is the widening income gaps within a country as well as between countries. The latest study indicates that as a result of globalization of the Chinese economy, "provincial income inequality had emerged by 1992, and that the present level of provincial income disparity is unprecedented since the founding of the new China in 1949" (Sachs, 2001).

Global environmental issues have also been discussed intensively in relation to globalization. Although there are many empirical studies that argue economic expansion through global trade has improved welfare and reduced environmental disruptions for individual countries, environmental deterioration on a global scale has definitely accelerated in recent years as indicated by global warming and desertification (see ADB, 2001; Hayami, 2001). As far as the environmental impact of globalization is concerned, economists are more optimistic as well as myopic than natural scientists.

Globalization has been increasingly discussed in relation to global security and stability after the Asian financial crisis in 1997-98 and more crucially after the September 11 2001 terrorism attack which targeted the heart of world capitalism. George Solos, a global hedge-fund guru and the main target of Mr. Mahathier, Malaysian Prime Minister, for creating the Asian financial crisis, has written a book warning of unbridled global capitalism. It is quite ironic that the IT revolution, which accelerated globalization, has also threatened the integration of the world economic system by destabilizing global security on which global market activities are critically based. We can easily see that the above three global issues are intricately related to each other, and therefore need to be resolved simultaneously.

GLOBALIZATION OF ISLAND SOCIETIES

For small island societies, globalization has provoked strong reactions, both positive and negative. Despite the new opportunities it brings, globalization is feared because it exposes local agriculture, workers and small enterprises to global competition. As we have seen in Chapter 1, open trade has been the engine of growth for many small island economies. Wacziarg *et al.* (2002) demonstrate that in a free trade regime small island economies, whose domestic markets are extremely limited, can enjoy more prosperity than larger economies by creating export opportunities as well as importing cheaper goods. Many empirical studies support this argument (see Armstrong and Reed, 2002a). Girvan (2004), however, argues that Globalization, under the absence of labor mobility, global income redistribution and development finance, throws these small island economies into stark relief. Prasad (2004) convincingly demonstrates that most successful stories and strategies pursued by small island states are based on the bending of global trade rules, defying the principle of free trade such as Special Economic Zones, preferential trading agreements (PTAs), unconventional development strategies including selling sovereignty, passports, fishing rights, military bases and offshore businesses.

Despite pros and cons of globalization for small island economies, we have to admit that open trade is an inevitable process of the globalizing world. Indiscriminate protectionism is therefore likely to severely damage long-run growth performance of island economies. Given this process and at the same time recognizing a trade-off between greater risk and uncertainty and the growth effects of their increasing participation in the international economy, island economies need to seize growth opportunities brought about by globalization through what Armstrong calls "endogenous policies" by making use of islands' strategic location, natural, cultural, human and diplomatic resources (Armstrong and Reed, 2002b). I fully agree with the following assessment:

"Small islands have, it seems to me, a myriad evolutionary responses to external forces that enable island peoples to seize opportunities that open up in the global economy, while ducking most of the big punches that the world economy throws. Absence of market power means that island communities generally ride the waves more than they create them" (Bertram, 2004).

INDEX OF GLOBALIZATION

To see how the world economy has been globalized, we need to present some empirical evidence. Kearney (2002) constructed unique index for measuring globalization. The main components of his globalization index are (1) price differentials between international and domestic goods and services, (2) cross-border capital movements, (3) prevalence of the internet, (4) international exchange of peoples, and (5) participation in international political forums. TABLE 2-1 shows his ranking of globalization for forty countries out of sixty-two surveyed. The most globalized country in 1999 was Ireland followed by Switzerland, Singapore, Netherlands, Sweden, Finland, Canada, and so forth. The U.S., a flagship of globalization, was ranked 12th. Japan ranked 38th, which oddly was below Tunisia and Saudi Arabia.

TABLE 2-1. Globalization Index Rankings: 2000

Rank	Country	Rank	Country
1	Ireland	21	Australia
2	Switzerland	22	Slovak Republic
3	Singapore	23	Hungary
4	Netherlands	24	Italy
5	Sweden	25	Croatia
6	Finland	26	Greece
7	Canada	27	Poland
8	Denmark	28	Panama
9	Austria	29	Botswana
10	United Kingdom	30	Slovenia
11	Norway	31	Korea, Rep.
12	United States	32	Taiwan
13	France	33	Nigeria
14	Germany	34	Chile
15	Portugal	35	Uganda
16	Czech Republic	36	Tunisia
17	Spain	37	Saudi Arabia
18	Israel	**38**	**Japan**
19	New Zealand	39	Russian Federation
20	Malaysia	40	Senegal

Source: *Foreign Policy* (January/February 2002), pp.56-65.

TABLE 2-1 seems to indicate that the scale of an economy has little to do with the ranking of globalization. The level of per capita income, however, is positively related to the ranking, namely, the higher per capita income, the higher ranking or more globalized. We re-examined globalization by region utilizing the ranking in TABLE 2-1. Globalization in trade can be measured in terms of total trade (exports + imports) over GDP. Reductions in trade barriers, ceteris paribus, would promote globalization. The trade/GDP ratio, increased steadily from 20% in the 1960s to 40% in 2005 (FIGURE 2-1).

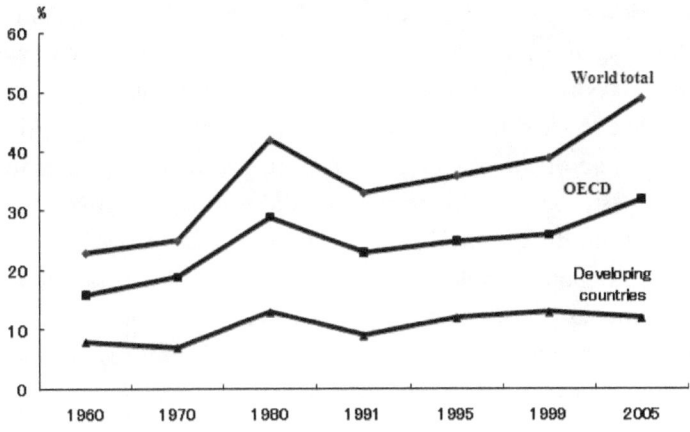

Note: Trade index is total trade (exports + imports)/World GDP.

Source: Asian Development Bank and UNCTAD Data Bases.

FIGURE 2-1. Globalization Index: Comoddity Trade.

It is worthwhile to note that, particularly in the 1970s, trade among the OECD countries increased much faster pace than the developing countries due mainly to a surge in intra-industry trade among the developed countries. Foreign direct investment (FDI), a proxy of globalization of capital flows, has also sharply increased particularly after the 1990s (FIGURE 2-2). Reflecting vibrant activities of multinational corporations in the fields of M & As and intra-industry trade, FDI among advanced countries far exceeded that of between developing countries.

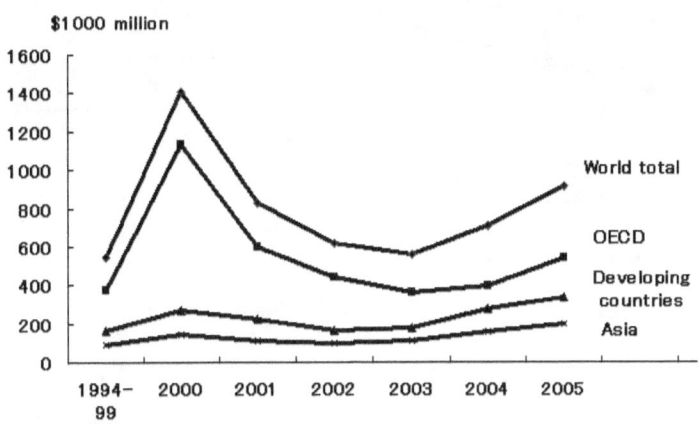

Note: Trade index is total trade (exports + imports)/World GDP.

Source: Asian Development Bank and UNCTAD Data Bases.

FIGURE 2-2. Globalization Index: Flows of Foreign Direct Investment.

Globalization of international exchange, measured in terms of international tourist traffic, has also recorded a fast rising trend supported by growing information and transportation technologies. The number of international visitors increased by about ten-fold in the past four decades (FIGURE 2-3). Although the EU and the U.S. absorbed larger numbers of international visitors than the other regions in the past, the Asia-Pacific region will be a major tourism market in the future. As we fully discuss in Chapter 8, tourism is a 'peace industry.' Peoples from country or region are welcome tourists. As we have witnessed in recent years through incidents as the terrorists' attacks on NYC and Bali, tourists are most sensitive to their own security. Therefore the bottom line for sustainable tourism is to secure "peace and stability" in tourist destinations.

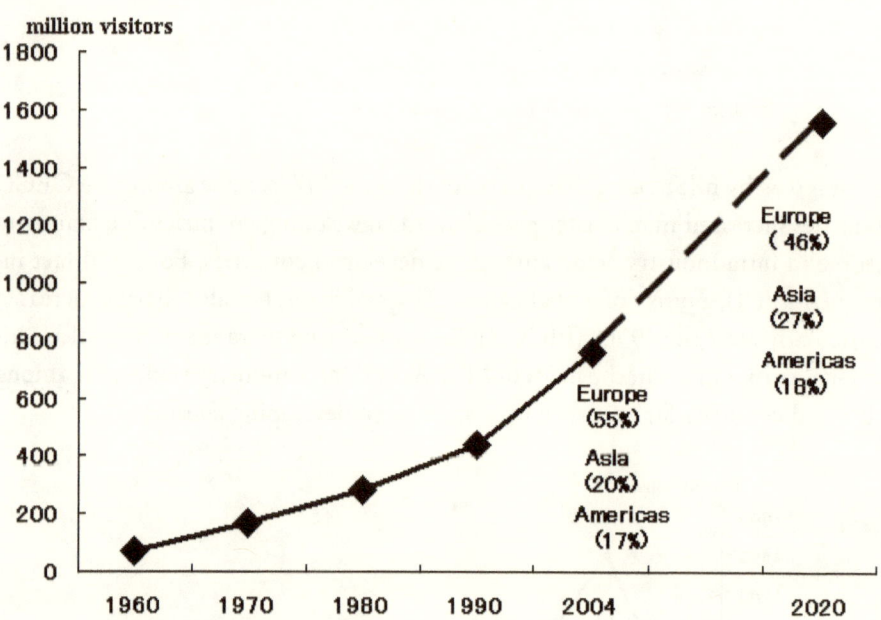

Note: Number of tourists' arrivals.

Source: World Tourism Organization

FIGURE 2-3. Globalization Index: Exchange of People.

Globalization has accelerated with internet communications which benefited from innovations as well as from ever-declining user fees resulting from keen competitions. As can be seen from FIGURE 2-4, the Internet penetration rate and per capita user fees are positively related.

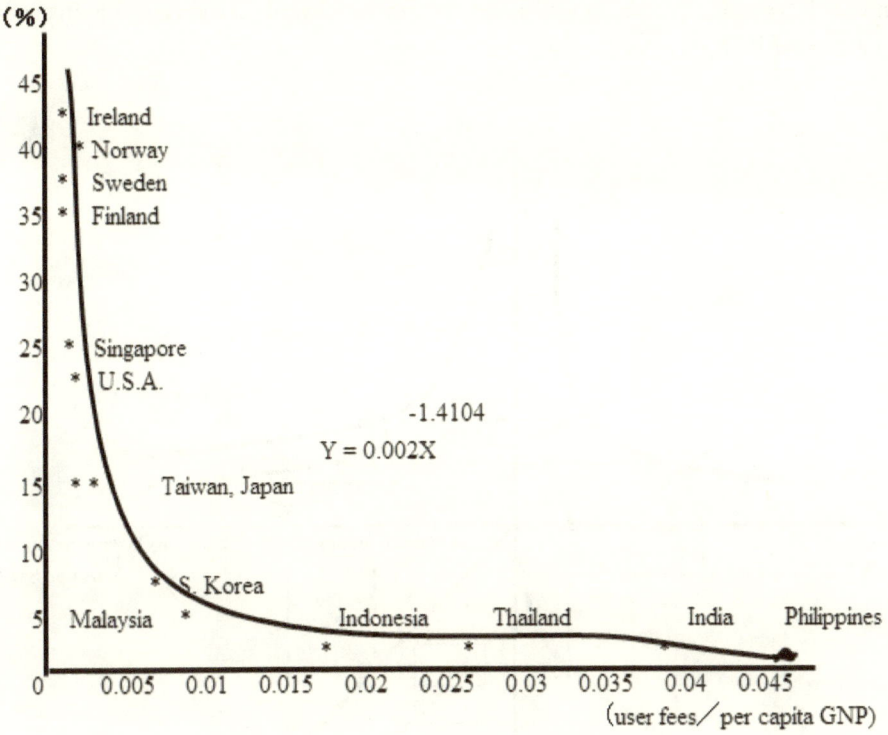

(%)

45
40
35
30
25
20
15
10
5
0

* Ireland
* Norway
* Sweden
* Finland

* Singapore
* U.S.A.

-1.4104
Y = 0.002X

* * Taiwan, Japan

* S. Korea

Malaysia * Indonesia Thailand India Philippines

0.005 0.01 0.015 0.02 0.025 0.03 0.035 0.04 0.045
(user fees / per capita GNP)

Notes: User fees are monthly basic charges of major providers.

Source: JETRO/IDE, *Asian Economy 2000*, p.87.

FIGURE 2-4. Globalization Index: Prevalence of the Internet: 1988.

The overall globalization rankings in TABLE 2-1 correspond more or less to the ranking of the Internet penetration rates; Ireland, Singapore, Sweden and Finland are spearheading global information technology as well as overall globalization.

A MECHANISM OF GLOBALIZATION FOR ISLANDS NETWORKING

Market and Scale Economy

A mechanism of expansion and evolution of globalization can be shown in the following simple diagram (FIGURE 2-5). Globalization is synonymous with an expansion of economic activities beyond national boundaries. Therefore given product quality, international price competition, which can be determined by unit production cost, plays a crucial role in the process of globalization. This is reflected in the "Silverstone Curve," a well-known empirical law observed typically in automobile and IC industries.

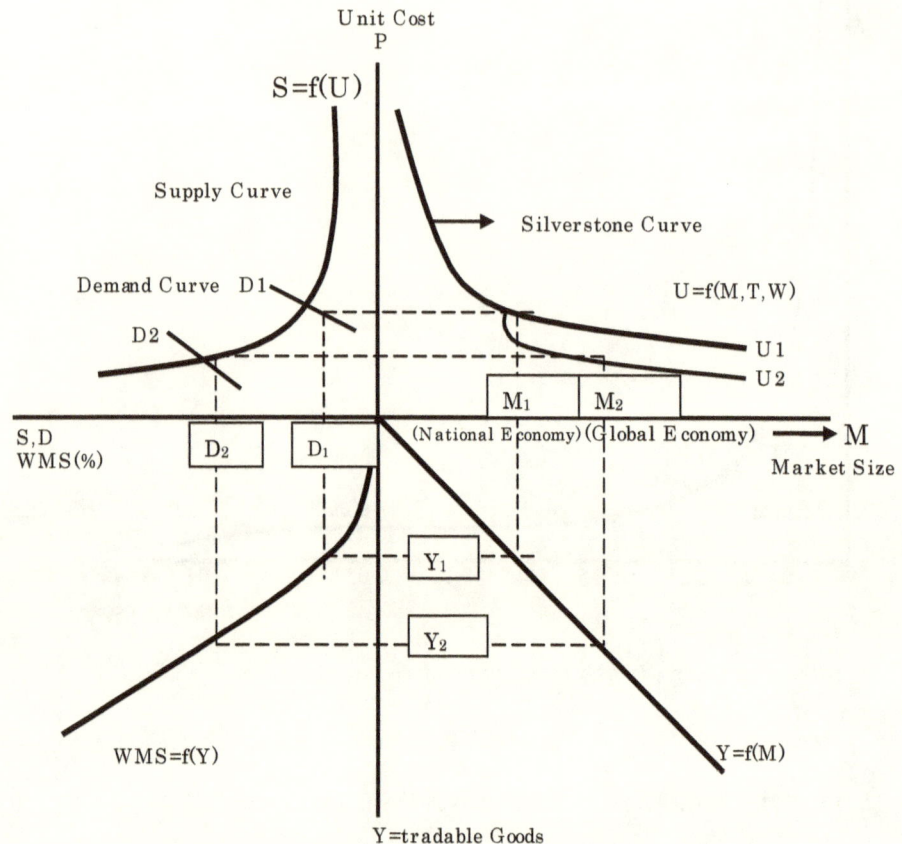

Notes: U1=Scale Economy, U2=Scale Economy
+ Innovation.
WMS=World Market Share (%).

FIGURE 2-5. A Scale Economy and Globalization.

Unit production cost declines as a result of expansion of production scale. The decreasing unit cost, or "increasing returns" on scale and innovation an economists' buzzword, is becoming a focal topic in recent economic literature due largely to Krugman's (1991) challenge to conventional development models. FIGURE 2-5 indicates that reduction of unit cost as a result of scale expansion would generates higher returns on capital under oligopolistic competition which will in turn accelerate innovation and thereby further capture world market shares (WMS).

Institutions

It is a well-known fact that the initiators of economic globalization since WW II have been the IMF and GATT=WTO regimes with the US dollar serving as the key international currency. IMF is mainly responsible for liberalization of capital and stability of foreign exchange, while GATT is concerned with trade liberalization and reductions of non-trade barriers (NTBs). TABLE 2-2 shows average nominal tariff rates of both developing and OECD countries have been substantially reduced in the postwar era, particularly after the late 1970s when trade liberalization accelerated. Despite regional variations, this is a clear indication that the world economy has been heading toward integration rather than isolation.

TABLE 2-2. Average Tariff Rates and NTBs by Region

A: Average Unweighted Tariff Rates (%)

	1978-80	1986-90	1996-2000
Africa	38.2	26.9	17.8
East Asia	23.5	20.7	10.4
Latin America	28.1	24.1	11.1
MENA (ex-OPEC)	29.6	24.1	19.3
South Asia	NA	69.8	30.7
Europe/Central Asia	12	14.9	10.1
OECD Economies	11.9	8.2	6.1

B: Non-tariff Barriers of Developing Countries (%)

	1989-94	1995-2000
East Asia	30.1	16.3
Latin America	18.3	8.0
Africa/Middle East	43.8	16.6
South Asia	57.0	58.3

Note: NTBs converted into tariff rates. NA = not available.

Of course we remember that the 1999 WTO Seattle meeting was disrupted by flag-waving anti-globalization forces organized mainly by international NGOs themselves a product of globalization. There is no doubt, however, that WTO's founding principles of "free, non-discriminatory and multilateral trade" have been strengthened by the admission of China in the 2001 WTO Doha meeting. China's admission to WTO is particularly significant because of its sheer size and another dynamism in this century. As of April 2002, 115 countries or about 80% of WTO's total members are developing countries. Stiglitz, however, severely criticized one of the pro-globalization institutions:

> *Globalization today is not working for many of the world's poor, it is not working for much of the environment. It is working for the stability of the global economy. The transition from communism to a market economy has been so badly managed that, with exception of China, Vietnam, and a few Eastern European countries, poverty has soared as incomes have plummeted. To some, there is an easy answer: Abandon globalization. That is neither feasible nor desirable. As I noted, globalization has also brought huge benefits—East Asia's success was based on globalization, especially on the opportunities for trade, and increased access to markets and technology. Globalization has brought better health, as well as active global civil society fighting for more democracy and greater social justice. The problem is not with globalization, but with how it has been managed. Part of the problem lies with the international economic institutions, with IMF, World Bank and WTO, which help set the rules of the game. They have done so in ways that, all too often, have served the interests of the more advanced industrialized countries—rather than those of the developing world. But it is not just that they have served those interests; too often, they have approached globalization from particular narrow mind-sets, shaped by a particular vision of the economy and society. (Stiglitz, 2002).*

Rodrick also argues that "national borders continue to act as serious impediments to economic exchange, even though formal trade barriers have all but disappeared" (Rodrick, 2002) because of socio-political institutions embedded in national markets. He contends that economic globalization or "deep" economic integration, the nation-state system, and democracy are mutually incompatible.

There are also various emerging regional institutions aimed at regional economic integrations such as FTAs, customs unions and economic unions as depicted in FIGURE 2-6 according to Balassa's (1961) stage of integration. It is particularly noteworthy that bilateral FTAs and economic partnership agreements (EPAs) are flourishing in recent years (see *2001 White Paper on International Trade*, Section

3). These FTAs and EPAs are based on "open regionalism" and approved under the GATT 24. Economic integration depicted in FIGURE 2-6 deals only among sovereign states. But our concern here is sub-regional economic integration which has been intensively discussed in recent years including a work of this author. Chapter 7 proposes an EPA among Taiwan-Okinawa-Kyushu.

Growth Triangle (GT) is also an emerging concept of regional as well as sub-regional economic integration and cooperation which will be fully discussed in the following sections.

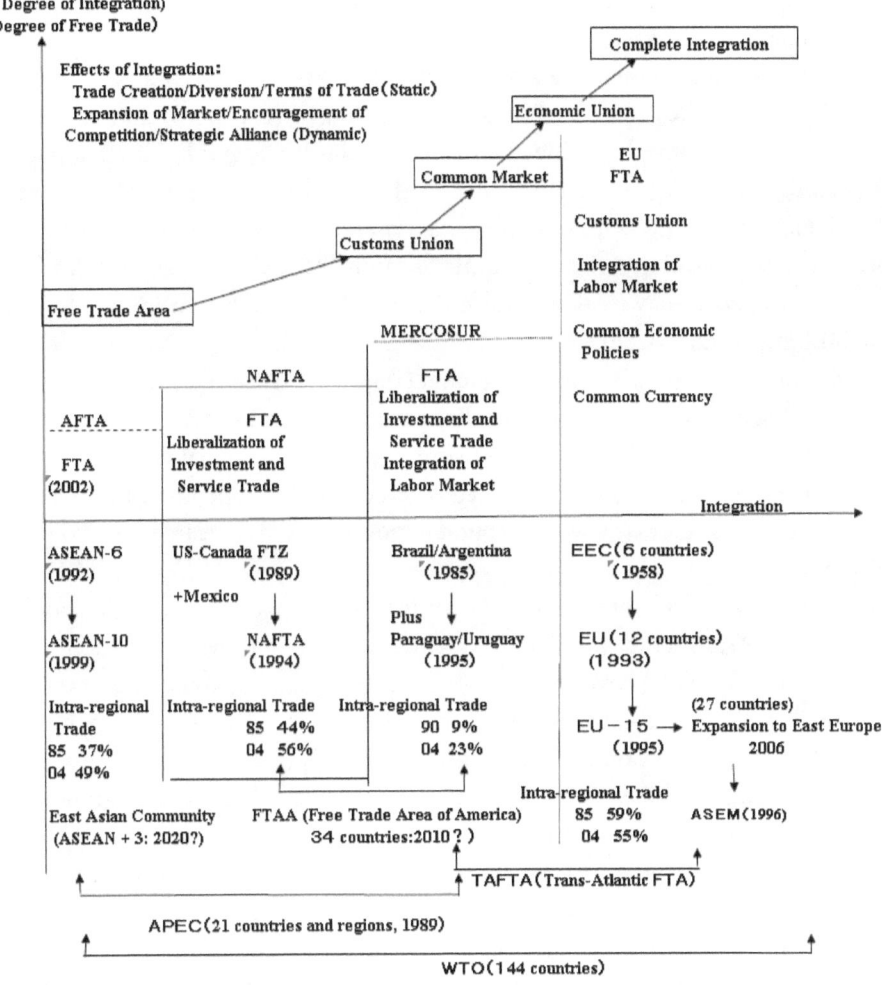

Source: Constructed by Hiroshi Kakazu based on Balassa (1961)

FIGURE 2-6. Recent Trends of Economic Integration.

Growth Triangles (GT) Approach for Islands Networking

GTs in Asia

Global economic expansion induced by trade, investment and the internet, coupled with the collapse of centrally planned economies and a rapid progress of the European Union (EU), has accelerated regional cooperation and economic integration in the Asia-Pacific in recent years.

The Asia-Pacific Economic Cooperation (APEC) discussed concrete action programs submitted by each member country on trade liberalization, facilitation and regional economic cooperation.

The expanded members of ASEAN Free Trade Area (AFTA) agreed to complete its targeted free trade area by 2008 based on its ASEAN Vision 2020. The ASEAN has also moved to bridge between the Asia-Pacific and EU by creating the Asia-Europe Meeting (ASEM) in 1996. Although the AFTA process has slowed down due to the 1997-1998 Asian financial crises, the political momentum has not been lost. The first East Asian Economic Summit (ASEAN + Japan, South Korea, China, Australia, New Zealand and India) was held in 2005 to initiate towards establishing an East Asian Community (see Chapter 7).

Stimulated by such a wave of regional cooperation, the South Asian Association for Regional Cooperation (SAARC) agreed to start the SAARC Preferential Trade Agreement (SAPTA) in 1995. Despite the Asian financial crises and subsequent recession, underlying zeal for regional economic cooperation has not been watered downed. China, a world economic power, has also an intention to play a pivotal role in regional economic integration.

Against the above broader context of increasing regional economic cooperation in the Asia-Pacific, localized economic cooperation and integration called growth triangles (GTs) have rapidly emerged in Asia. Among some important GTs are listed in TABLE 2-4, the South China GT, consisting of Hong Kong, Guangdong, Fujian and Taiwan, and the SIJORI GT, comprising Singapore, Malaysia's Johore State and Indonesia's Riau Province, have already become true growth legends. Meanwhile, the Tumen River Delta GT, the Mekong River Basin GT and the IMT GT in northern ASEAN have moved beyond the conceptual stage to the stage of working out concrete development plans. Furthermore, the East ASEAN GT (or BIMP-EAGA), the East Asian GT involving Iran and Turkey as well, and an Indian Ocean GT, with an eye to Africa, have also surfaced (ADB, 1993; Kakazu, 1999).

Growth Triangle (GT) can be defined as "transnational economic zones spread over well-defined, geographically proximate areas covering three or more countries where differences in factor endowments are exploited to promote external trade and investment" (Kakazu, 1995). Depending on the approaches, GTs are also referred to as subregional economic zones (Yamazawa, 1992), natural economic territories (Scalapino, 1992), or extended metropolitan regions (McGee and Greenberg, 1994). The term GT became popular after Goh Chok Tong of former Singapore Prime Minister used it in reference to SIJORI GT. The key words of GT are proximity, complementarities, network, and political consensus as shown in FIGURE 2-7.

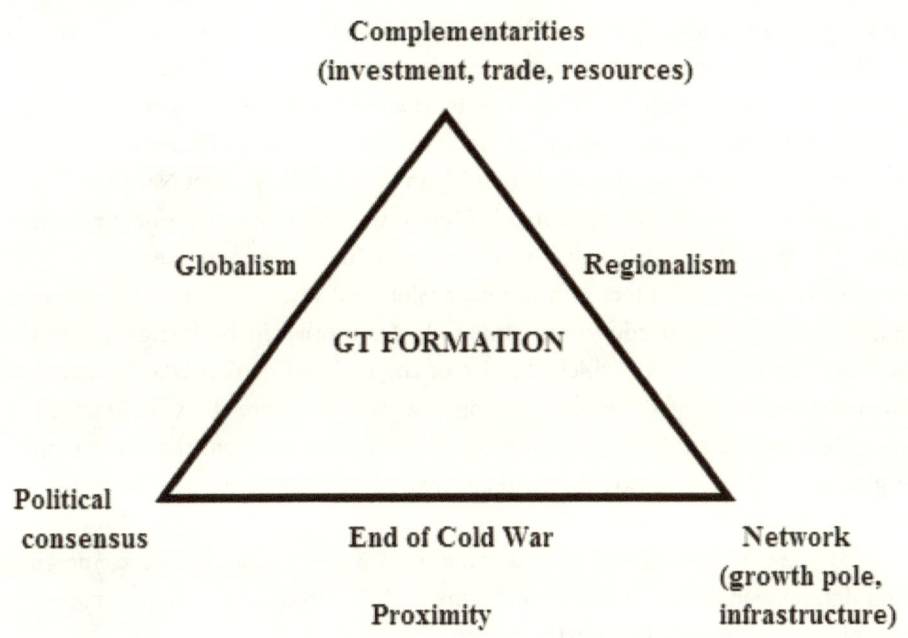

Source: H. Kakazu (1995).

FIGURE 2-7. GT Formation.

Merits of Growth Triangles

Compared to other on-going regional cooperation such as the EU and the NAFTA, the GT has the following merits:

(1) Unlike the trading bloc, which requires sweeping, nationwide institutional and administrative changes, the growth triangle approach involves only contiguous parts of countries. Therefore, politico-economic risks associated with regional integration will be localized or minimized when it fails. On the other hand, if it succeeds, its benefits will be easily expanded to the contiguous island regions such as SIJORI, BIMP-EAGA and Southern China growth triangles.

(2) Compared to establishing a formal trading block, which usually requires tedious, time-consuming intergovernmental negotiations and procedures, growth triangles can be established at a much lower cost and in a shorter period of time. This is one of the important reasons why countries such as Indonesia and Malaysia are establishing several growth triangles at the same time. The role of governments should be limited to that of shortening the period over which the GT process or natural process of economic integration takes place (Thant & Tang, 1996).

(3) The approach of GTs will be useful to initiate the trade liberalization of a country as can be seen in the SIJORI GT where in the Batam Island of Indonesia has been given a status of free trade area. The area is a model of the AFTA which aims at an ASIAN-wide free trade area by the year 2008. By the same token, the GT approach will also be useful to facilitate the transition of centrally planned economies to market economies such as Myanmar, Lao PDR, Viet Nam and Cambodia in the Mekong River Basin GT. One of the major objectives of the Tumen River GT is to open the North Korean economy to the world market.

(4) Trading blocks focus on the expansion and liberalization of the internal market of its member countries, while GTs are motivated by foreign direct investment and exports for which the size of the regional market is less important than the openness of the global trading systems. Therefore the GT approach is consistent with the GATT (WTO) principles of non-exclusional character of open regionalism. That is to say, the markets created by growth triangles are open to everybody.

(5) The GT method and process can also be useful to cope with the emerging and deteriorating environmental problems in Asia through cross border cooperative efforts and sub-regional participation.

(6) Lastly, the concept of GT can be effectively applied to develop remote, peripheral, island areas where economic complementarities and an adequate infrastructure with the neighboring national borders exist. It is interesting to note that almost all GTs in Asia are located in nations' peripheral and cross-border areas where informal border trade and crossborder labor mobility have been actively taking place.

GT is usually set up within a crossborder free trade zone which can be administered jointly by contiguous governments or by a jointly created development authority as can be seen in SIJORI GT. The Tumen River GT has also established a joint administrative authority. In this sense, GT is a crossborder, multinational free trade and investment area which is very much different from the conventional concepts of free ports, special economic zones, export processing zones and foreign access zones (FAZ) which are established within a country.

Factors for a Successful GT

One important factor for a successful GT is that the areas or regions participating in forming a growth triangle must be contiguous with each other, and the national boundaries must be easily accessible to each other if not completely open. In this regard, the Tumen River GT still has a long way to go to accomplish its objectives because the political boundaries among the three littoral areas have not changed significantly despite the end of Cold War.

Secondly, there must be at least one metropolitan center such as Hong Kong and Singapore which is capable of emanating dynamic spillover effects of trade and investment on adjoining areas. For the Tumen River GT and East ASEAN GT, Hunchun and Brunei respectively are expected to play the similar role.

A third factor is, as seen already in the case of SIJORI GT, complementary relationships in resource endowments, labor, technology and location among the participants of growth triangle must exist. The East ASEAN GT is probably the least justifiable area for a GT formation in terms of complementary relationships among the participating areas. Although some economists argue that Brunei together with Labuan islands can play an important role in providing air links, shipping services and finance, while Mindanao, Sulawesi and Sabah are suppliers of natural and tourism resources, labor and agro-industrial products, each area has more or less similar, competitive industrial structure (Pernia, 1997; Lim, 1996 and 1994).

Fourthly, the private sector is to become the engine of development for a successful GT. In order to vitalize the private sector, freer rein on trade, labor, and capital must be given than at present.

Fifthly, successful GT requires reasonably well-developed infrastructure, particularly in the transportation system. The lingering question is who and how these huge infrastructure requirements can be financed. The Tumen River Delta GT alone requires $30 billion over 20 years for infrastructure projects (UNDP, 1991). In order to finance these projects through debt security or equity issues by means of a now fashionable Build, Operate Transfer (BOT) or Build, Operate, Own (BOO) scheme, these projects must be justifiable on the basis of net financial internal rate of return (NFIRR) on capital. Our estimation of NFIRR for the Tumen River Delta GT is much lower than the projects in Southern China GT and Bohai Economic Zone projects (Kakazu, 1994c).

Sixthly, along with geographical proximity and complementarities among GT participants, strong cultural and social ties are the primary factors for establishing a successful GT. In this respect, the BIMP-EAGA has better advantage over the other ASEAN GTs because the EAGA has cultivated common ties through their long history of intra-regional migration and Islamic practices.

Lastly, one of the greatest challenges facing the successful development of GTs is a high degree of political commitment to the GT concept by participating regions and countries. This is particularly true for the Tumen and the BIMP-EAGA GTs where socio-politico-economic systems are complex and diversified. Strong political commitment is also absolutely necessary in order to ensure a functional institutional framework for cooperation among the central and local governments, the private sector, and the residents of GTs.

OKINAWA ISLANDS: DIAMOND PEACE TRADE ZONE (DPTZ) GT

Why Okinawa?

As we have discussed, the concept of GT can be usefully applied to develop a nation's remote, peripheral, cross-border island areas where socio-economic complementarities, common historical ties, and adequate infrastructure exist. There are three regions in Japan where the ideas of forming GTs are emerging. They are Okinawa, the Japan Sea Rim region encompassing Niigata, Ishikawa and Toyama (see Kakazu *et al*, 1994b), and the Yellow Sea Rim region centered on Fukuoka and Yamaguchi (see NIRA, 2001). Among these three possible GT regions, Okinawa seems to fit the GT concept best because of its geographical location and historical ties with her neighboring Asian regions.

Therefore, we focus our discussions on Okinawa's prospects and problems of GT formation. We will soon discover that Okinawa' problems in forming a GT are more or less common problems for Japan's other peripheral regions.

Okinawa has had a proud history engaging in maritime trade from the 12th to the 16th centuries in what may be described as a triangular trade between itself, Japan, and Asia. An inscription on a bell cast in 1458 for Shuri Castle, which was destroyed during WWII but reconstructed in 1992, tells the following story:

> *The Kingdom of Ryukyu is a place of beauty in the Southern Ocean. Gathered here are treasures of the three countries, Korea, the Great Ming, and Japan. It is a treasure island which emerged from the sea between China and Japan. Its ships ply between ten thousand countries. And it is filled with wondrous things which are to be seen everywhere.*

Okinawan merchants bought copper and iron products in Japan to exchange for sugar, silk, cotton textiles, spices, sappanwood and porcelain from Southeast Asia and China. Trade was initiated when the Chuzan Kingdom in central Okinawa accepted a tributary relationship with the Ming dynasty of China. This trade continued to produce surpluses for Okinawa until the Satsuma clan of southern Japan (current Kagoshima Prefecture) invaded the islands and took over the lucrative trade via the Ryukyus. Although commercial trade with various parts of Southeast Asia such as Siam, Palelmbang, Java, Malacca, Sumatra, Annam and Patani had ceased by the end of the 16th century, the tributary trade with China continued until the mid-19th Century. Historians refer to the period of the 15th and 16th centuries as Okinawa's trade-induced golden age (see Takara, 1998). This glorious period is still very much alive for many contemporary Okinawans. Whenever the future role of Okinawa is discussed, people nostalgically recall this self-generated, self-owned golden era.

Diamond Peace Trade Zone Growth Triangle

The Diamond Peace Trade Zone Growth Triangle (DPTZ GT), which would comprise Taiwan, Okinawa, Kyushu (Japan), and Shanghai, was proposed by this author in 1995 (see Kakazu, 1995 and 2000). The major purpose of the DPTZ GT are: (a) to create trade and investment opportunities through a subregional FTZ; (b) to enhance regional economic activities through decentralization of the decision making process; and (c) to reduce politico-military tension that had been building up in recent years, over the Taiwan issue and the territorial disputes on the Spratly Islands in the South China Sea, by intensifying mutual economic interests.

As can be seen in FIGURE 2-8, Okinawa is much closer to Taiwan (630km or 394 miles) and Shanghai (820km or 512 Miles) than to Kyushu (1,000km or 625 miles), and to Tokyo (1,600 km or 1,000miles) on which the Okinawan economy heavily depends upon today.

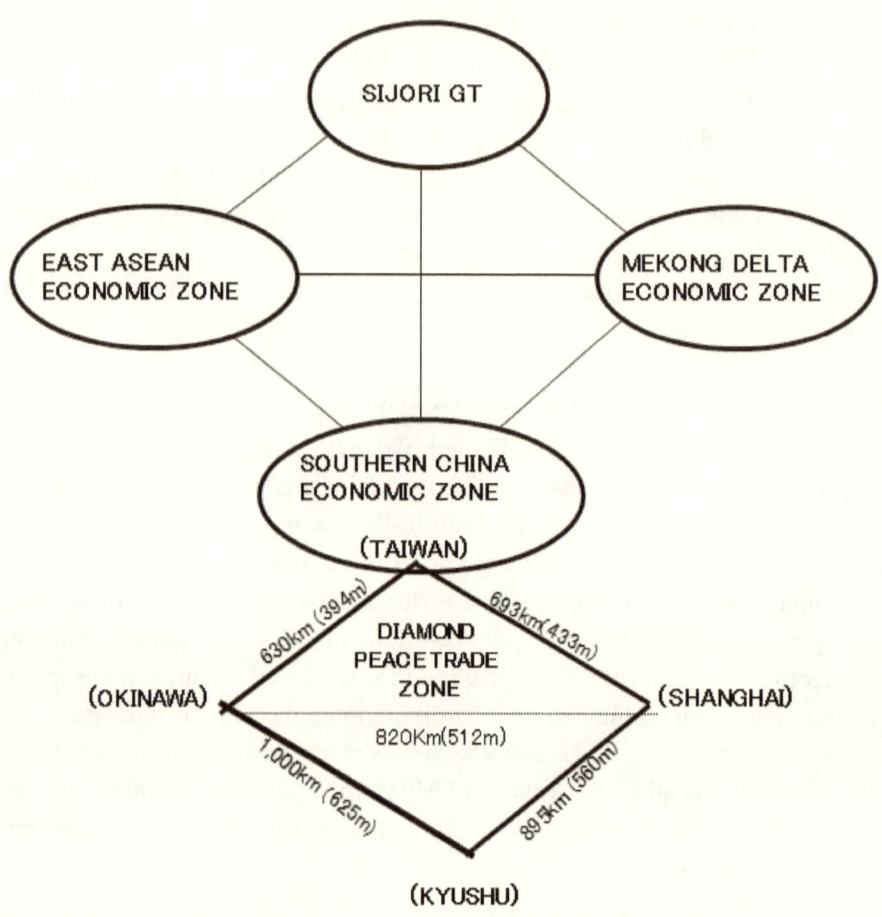

Notes: SIJORI GT: Singapore-Johore-Riau Growth Triangle.
EAST ASEAN ECONOMIC ZONE: Brunei, Indonesia, Malaysia and the Philippines.
MEKONG DELTA ECONOMIC ZONE: Cambodia, Lao,PDR, Myanmar, Thailand
Viet Nam and Yunan Province of PRC.
SOUTHERN CHINA ECONOMIC ZONE: Southern China, Hongkong and Taiwan.

Source: H. Kakazu, M. Thant, and M. Tang, ed., Growth Triangles in Asia: A New
Approach to Regional Economic Cooperation, Hong Kong: Oxford University
Press, 1998.

**FIGURE 2-8. Emergence of Subregional Economic Zones
and the Diamond Peace Trade Zone.**

If geographical proximity were a key factor for a successful regional economic
integration, since it implies lower transaction costs such as for travel, transportation, and communication, then it would be natural for Okinawa to have much
closer economic ties with Taiwan and Shanghai than Tokyo. The reality, however,
is the other way around.

A very strange practice has been pursued for many years whereby Taiwan products are first shipped to Yokohama or Kobe and then to Okinawa. This practice has been rationalized on the basis that there has been only one tanker trip per week between Okinawa and Taiwan, mainly because of the lack of cargo to and from Okinawa as we have seen already. If economic activities expand through DPTZ, more frequent trips among the participating regions would become economically feasible.

FACILITATORS OF DPTZ GT

The Special Free Trade Zone (SFTZ)

The Special Free Trade Zone (SFTZ), which was created in 1998, will be the most important facilitator creating DPTZ GT because GT will be successfully set up within cross-border free trade zones which can be administered jointly by contiguous administrative bodies like SIJORI GT.

SFTZ has the following functions: (a) It can be utilized as a center to process and assemble imported raw materials, semi-processed intermediate goods, and parts for domestic (mainly mainland Japan) and foreign exports; (b) It is a bonded area, thus it can be utilized as an international trading center, including entrepot and stock point; (c) It can be utilized as a testing and inspection ground for imported goods before those are delivered to consumers; (d) It can also be utilized as a world fair site which can provide facilities for the exhibition of products and actual transactions.

The SFTZ has the incentives for prospective investors (FIGURE 2-9). The most attractive one is tax exemptions. A corporate income tax of 35% will be deducted from taxable income for ten years for manufacturing, packaging and warehouse activities, provided the investor employs at least twenty local regular workers. This tax incentive is equivalent to 26% of corporate income tax, which can be favorably compared to the current tax rate of 40.9% for non-SFTZ investors. Furthermore, the SFTZ tax rate for small-and medium sized enterprises will be only 19% compared to 34% in the non-SFTZ enterprises. The other incentives are investment tax credit, special depreciation allowances for machinery and equipment, and wage subsidy for those investors who employ young regular workers through the Public Employment Office.

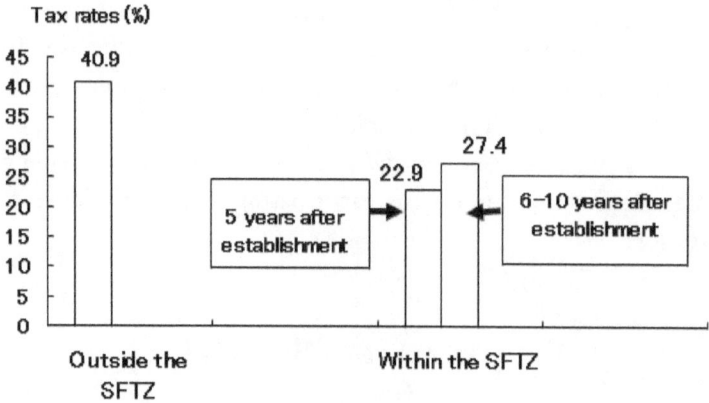

Tax rates (%)

Note: "Effective tax rate (ETR)" means actual tax burden of a corporation. ETR is lower than the nominal tax rate which is simple average of various taxes imposed on a corporate firm.

Source: Okinawa Prefecture.

FIGURE 2-9. Comparison of Effective Corporate Tax Rates Within and Outside of Okinawa Special Free Trade Zone (SFTZ).

High Technology Industries

Many possible entries to the SFTZ can be considered. One case is high technology industries such as manufacturing and assembling semiconductors, precision machinery, medical equipment, automotive and aircraft parts. A Tokyo-based engine maker, Speed Industries established a bike assembly factory in the SFTZ in 2002. The company imports engine parts from China and Taiwan, assemble them in the SFTZ for exports to Southeast Asia. Acrorado, a 100% subsidiary of Tokyo-based Crest Electronics started manufacturing special purpose semiconductors in the SFTZ in 2000. Although the company was particularly attracted to the zone's tax incentives, its activities, importing semi-processed parts and materials mainly from North America and exporting semiconductors to foreign countries, are designed to take the maximum advantage of the SFTZ system.

Food Processing

Food processing can also be profitably conducted in the zone by striking the huge tariff differentials between imported raw materials and processed products as illustrated by meat processing in the following (FIGURE 2-10). Duty for fresh beef, for example, will be 44.3%, while processed meat products will be taxed only 25% at the border. The difference is 19.3%. An investor in the Okinawa SFTZ, therefore, has a definite cost advantage over a mainland competitor who has to pay a 44.3%

tariff before selling meat products made with imported beef in the domestic market. Transportation and other additional costs between the Okinawa SFTZ and mainland markets, however, must be carefully considered.

Case 1: Meat Processing

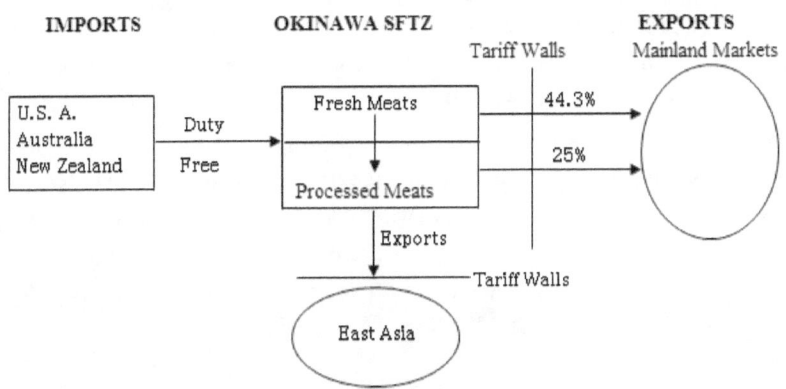

Case 2: Parts Operation Center

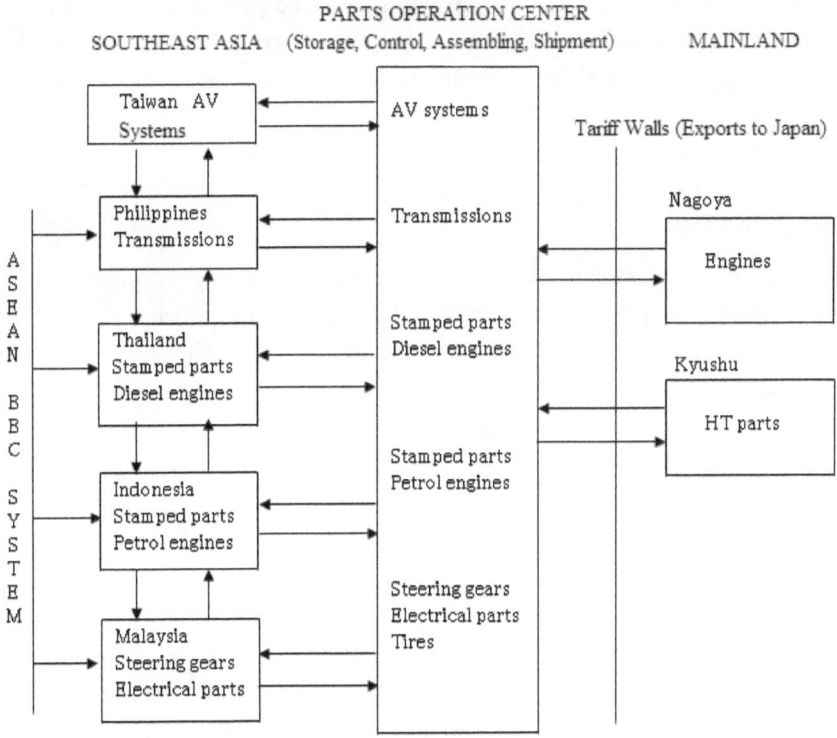

Source: Kakazu, H.(2007).

FIGURE 2-10. How can we make use of the Okinawa Special Free Trade Zone?

Another possible entry is a parts operation center (POC). The SFTZ may be an ideal site for storing, controlling, assembling and shipping a huge number of parts which are increasingly out-sourced within the Asia-Pacific region. A major operational problem is how quality-controlled parts can be delivered at the right time and at the right place. Toyota, for example, invented "just-in-time" system for its parts procurement operations. The Okinawa SFTZ can be utilized for a global just-in-time system. The system is worthy of further in-depth investigation. A similar scheme can also be applied to airplane inspections and repair operations in the Asia-Pacific region. The rapidly increasing demand for air transport in the region will soon justify such an aircraft repair and maintenance center.

A recent move of All Nippon Airways (ANA) to make Okinawa an Asian hub for its cargo operations by 2010 is an encouraging sign to strengthen Okinawa's comparative advantage as a Asian center for parts procurements (see *Japan Economic Journal*, July 6, 2007).

Stockpoint and Entrepot

The location of Okinawa provides comparative advantages in both stockpoint and entrepot operations. Although they are outside of the free trade zone, oil terminal facilities have been in operations, in the central part of Okinawa, since the oil shocks hit in the early 1970s. An international food-storage facility can also be viably established in the SFTZ. The facility will be useful as an emergency buffer stock for a potential future food crisis in the Asia-Pacific region.

Triangular Trade

It is a well-known fact that Taiwan has been trading heavily with mainland China indirectly through third countries, although it cannot engage in direct trade for political reasons. Okinawa's Ishigaki ports, only 100 miles from Taipei, have been used for indirect trade via the so-called "clearance shipping" between the two regions. Typically a Taiwan cargo ship visits Ishigaki port where the shipping documents are rewritten so as to list Japan as the origin of the shipment, thereby allowing clearance through Chinese customs.

As can be seen in more detail in Chapter 7, the so-called "clearance shipping" between Taiwan and mainland China has surged in recent years. Cargoes are shipped both ways between Taiwan and mainland China. Okinawa's SFTZ can be utilized not only for clearance purposes, but also for actual processing, packing, re-packing, re-labeling, storing, exhibiting, and shipping clearance cargoes. Furthermore, the increasing number of clearance ships will generate conditions favorable for the Naha port to be designated as one of Asia's base, or hub, ports. The designation as a base port means improved port facilities and lower transportation costs, which will serve to make Okinawa far more competitive in global trading. It is particularly important to improve nearly one-way cargo traffic between Okinawa and the mainland.

Despite geographical proximity, Okinawa's total trade with the three Chinas accounted for only 11% of its total foreign trade in 2005 (TABLE 2-3). It is, however, interesting to note that Okinawa, like the golden age, generated sizable trade surpluses from her Chinese trading partners despite her overall trade balance recorded chronic deficits.

TABLE 2-3. Okinawa's Economic Ties with Three Chinas: 2005
($million, 1000 visitors)

	Okinawa's Exports to	Okinawa's Imports from	Trade Balance	No. of Visitors from
Taiwan	440	151	289	67
China	19	270	-251	2
Hong Kong	38	3	35	1
Total	497	424	73	70

Sources: Ministry of Finance & Okinawa Visitors & Convention Bureau.

Okinawa's major export items to the three Chinas are petroleum products (re-export), scraps, used machinery and used papers, while major imports items are food products, furniture, construction materials such as sand and marbles. You may be surprised to know that Okinawa imports $36 million worth of fresh vegetables and fruits from mainland China.

Since completion of the 12-story Okinawa-Fuzhou Friendship Hall in 1998, more than ten Okinawan firms invested in mainland China in business ventures such as Awamori (rice brandy) manufacturing, shrimp aquaculture, marble carving, printing and tatami mat manufacturing. Trading businesses with China are also flourishing.

Taiwan accounted for more than 90% of Okianwa's total foreign visitors. Visitors from mainland China, particularly from Shanghai, are expected to increase in the near future stimulated by the recent opening of a regular commercial flight between Naha and Shanghai along with the abolishment of tourist's visa by the Beijing government. Shanghai in particular will become a large potential market for Okinawa's tourism industry considering its rapidly growing population and per capita income. Of course, Okinawa has to make painstaking efforts in reaping this potential market.

There is an encouraging move from mainland China. The Chinese trade mission visited Okinawa to disclose an ambitious plan to invest in the areas of tourism, restaurant and trade businesses (Ryukyu Shimpo, July 12, 2007).

Complementarities

The success of DPTZ GT depends on complementary relationships among the participating regions. Particularly how Okinawa plays the economic role in the region is crucial. Okinawa's strategic location in the region alone does not guarantee prosperous business opportunities for DPTZ-GT participants. As we have spelled out, Okinawa is identifying itself as the region's "healthy resort" with accompanying regional "hubs" of information network and entrepot. It is clear from our analysis that Okinawa is not well suited for intra-industry division of labor for a large-scale, labor-intensive manufacturing because of its high cost structure coupled with limited domestic and isolated market.

China (Shanghai) and Taiwan, on the other hand, possess comparative advantages in all range of manufacturing products. Kyushu will be an Asian gateway to mainland Japan as well as a provider of highly specialized technology products.

Okinawa Initiatives

Although Okinawa has a golden opportunity in the age of locally based global economy to take advantage of its strategic location in the Asia-Pacific region as well as its historical legacy in promoting DPTZ GT, there are obviously many hurdles and problems to overcome. These issues are examined in the following section. One of most important issues in realizing the idea is local politico-economic initiatives. Despite enhanced local autonomy in recent legislation, Okinawa and Kyushu are not in a position to negotiate with Taiwan and China in concluding trade related agreements. These are mandates of the central government in Tokyo. The Japanese government is reluctant to encourage the local initiatives to better relations with Taiwan as long as the Beijing government regards it as a "renegade province." There are, however, encouraging signs that Taiwan businessmen in particular have shown keen interest in investing in Okinawa in response to Okinawa's private sector initiative. As we have seen, Okinawa's healthy food industry is also looking for joint venture partners in Taiwan and in mainland China.

TRADING COSTS

Border Trading Costs

Obstfeld and Rogoff (2000) explained six enduring puzzles in macroeconomics by incorporating an overlooked factor---trading costs---into the theoretical model. Their study is based on McCallum's (1995) estimations of border trade between the U.S. and Canada. Using a gravity model, McCallum found that, despite close geographical proximity and existence of NAFTA, trade within Canada was twenty-two times greater than the trade between the U.S. and Canada in 1998. This seemingly illogical finding is due largely to border costs that are not accounted for by tariffs and NTBs in McCallum's model. The border costs include advertisements, commercial customs, various regulations and trade policies. Anderson and Wincoop (2000; 2001) made two empirical studies linking a gravity model with a CGE model, and found that U.S.-Canada trade would be increased by 44% if there were no border costs at all, or if the two economies were fully integrated.

Taking U.S.-Canada border trade as an example, we can reasonably assume that border costs between GTs would be much higher than the border costs between countries because GT economies are much smaller than their national economies. Home bias in trade and consumption would be much stronger in GTs than the national economies because GTs are more vertically integrated with their metropolitan centers.

In order to see home bias in Japanese import trade, we have calculated import (excluding oil)/GDP ratios for three metropolitan regions and the Southern prefectures (FIGURE 2-11). As is expected, the Tokyo metropolitan area accounts for 56% of Japan's total imports despite a 34% share of its GDP. On the other hand, the ratios are reversed for the Southern rural prefectures. The smaller the GDP, the greater the gaps between import shares and GDP shares. For example, Okinawa, one of the small economies, accounts for 0.2% of Japan's total imports although its GDP share is 0.7%. What is the reasons behind this home bias?

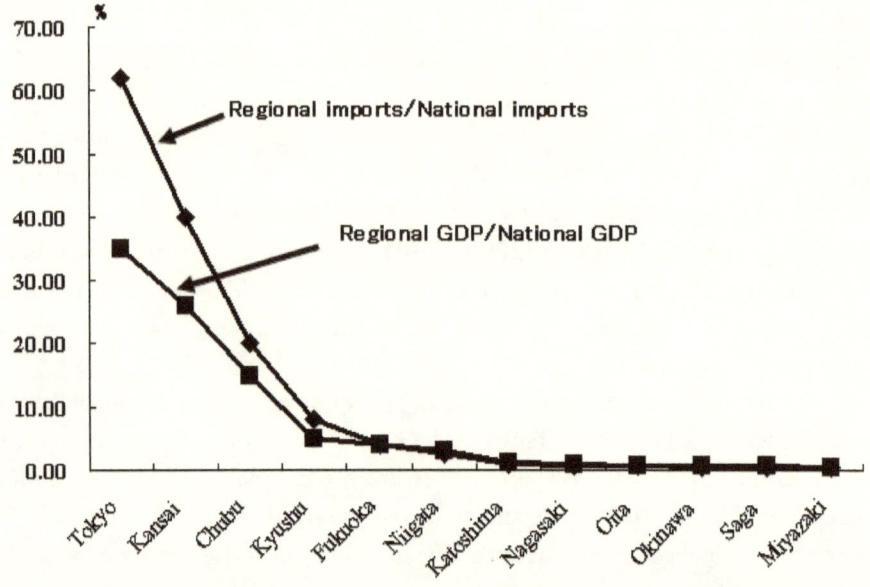

Notes: Tokyo includes Tokyo, Kanagawa, Chiba, Saitama and Shizuoka; Kansai includes Ssaka
Hyogo, Kyoto and Wakayama; Chubu includes Aichi and Mie.
Oil imports are excluded.

Sources: Prefectural Income Statistics and Trade Statistics, GOJ

FIGURE 2-11. Regional Shares of Imports and GDP: 2004.

Okinawa was an independent economy of Japan before 1972 because it used the U.S. dollar under the U.S. administration. As can be seen in FIGURE 2-12, Okinawa's imports from the U.S. declined sharply after Okinawa' reversion to Japan in 1972. The structural changes in trade pattern can be regarded as a consequence of institutional changes.

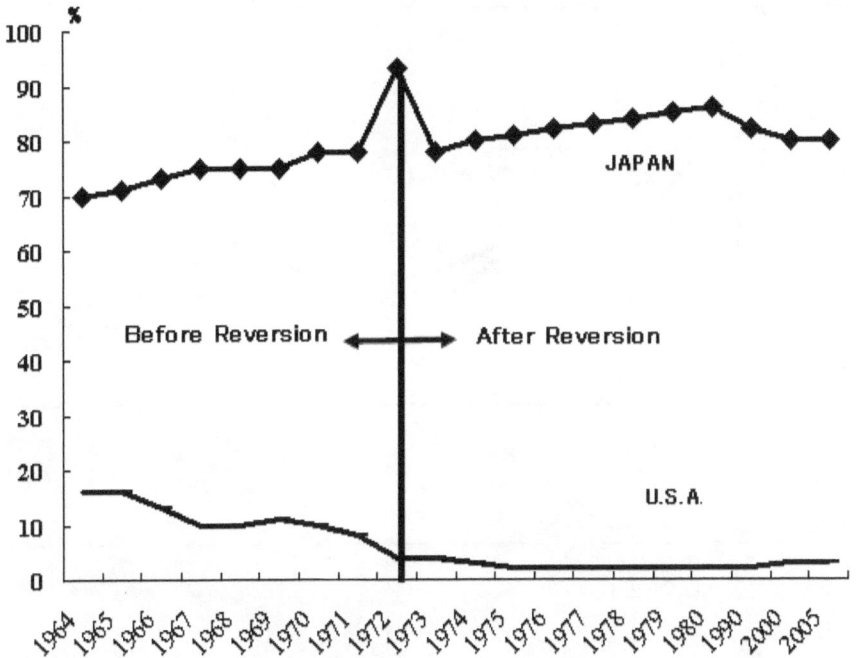

Note: Oil imports are excluded.

Sources: Okinawa Customs Office and Okinawa Prefectural Government.

**FIGURE 2-12. Okinawa's Import Shares from the U.S.A. and Japan.
Before and After Okinawa's Reversion.**

We use a very simple gravity model to estimate Okinawa's "trade bias" arising from institutional bindings such as distribution systems, personal connections, business practices, and various policy measures such as subsidies, preferential treatments for domestic products. Trade bias is defined as a difference between "theoretical" amount of imports and "actual" amount of imports. A generalized formula of gravity model is expressed as follows:

$$\text{Log}M_{ij} = \alpha_1 + \alpha_2 \text{Log}Y_i + \alpha_3 \text{Log}Y_j + \alpha_4 \text{Log}D_{ij} + E_{ij}.$$

Imports of i region from j region (Mij) are positively related to the size of GDP of both regions (YiYj), but they are negatively related to the distance of the two regions (Dij). Eij is an error term.

Therefore, signs of the parameters are:

$$\alpha_2, \alpha_3 > 0, \alpha_4 < 0.$$

The estimated results are shown in FIGURE 2-13.

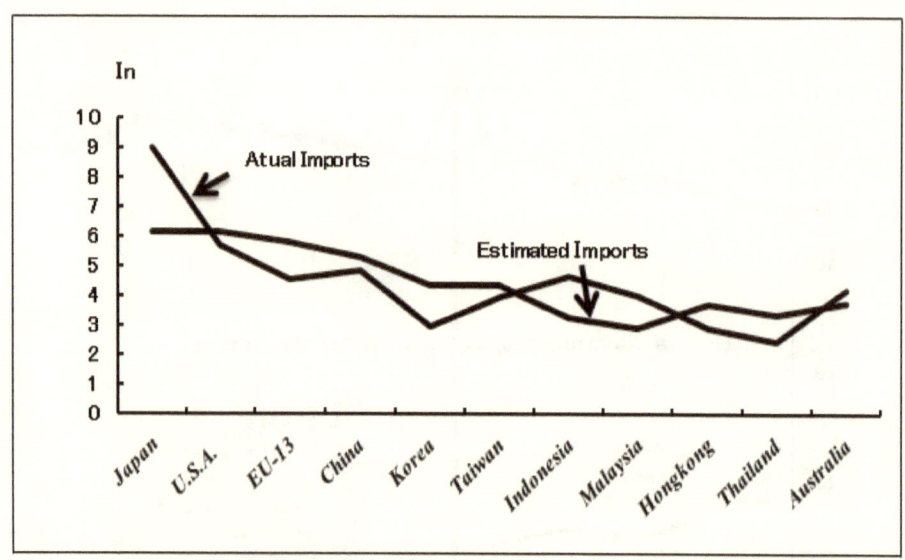

$$\ln M_{ij} = 0.2137794 - 0.392735 \ln D_{ij} + 0.7571303 \ln Y_i Y_j.$$
$$\phantom{\ln M_{ij} = }(0.046) \quad\quad (-0.688) \quad\quad\quad (2.626)$$

$R^2 = 0.680.$

$S = 1.461.$

M_{ij} = Imports of Okinawa (i) from the other areas (j).

D_{ij} = Distance between Okinawa (i)and the other areas (j).

$Y_i Y_j$ = GDP of Okinawa (i) and the other areas (j).

Using the dummy variable (α_{ij}):

$$\ln M_{ij} = 3.7467 - 0.292735 \ln D_{ij} + 0.7571303 \ln Y_i Y_j - 3.1883 \alpha_{ij}.$$
$$\phantom{\ln M_{ij} = }(1.092) \quad\quad (-0.2602) \quad\quad\quad (2.022) \quad\quad\quad (0.879)$$

$R^2 = 0.7659.$

$S = 0.8627.$

α_{ij} = dummy variable with Okinawa-Japan 1, Okinawa -the other areas 0.

Parentheses are t values.

FIGURE 2-13. Okinawa's Actual and Estimated Imports from Major Areas: 2000.

All estimated parameters satisfy our assumptions, but the explanatory power of distance is so weak that it is not significant at 5% cut off value. The results, however, show a clear home bias of Okinawa's import trade. Imports between the U.S. and Okinawa are actually conducted along with the model predicts, but there is a huge gap between Japan and Okinawa. Okinawa's imports are heavily biased towards Japan. Actual imports from China and Taiwan, regions under DPTZ GT, are lower than the model predicts. We also estimated a model which contains a dummy variable (δ_{ij}) assigning 1 for Japan and 0 for the rest of regions as McCallum used to measure trade bias between the U.S. and Canada. Here again signs of parameters satisfy our assumed values, but parameter for distance is not significantly estimated.

It should be noted that the dummy variable (δij) is not border cost as the case of McCallum's case, but it represents import bias from Japan. This bias represents about 40% of Okinawa's total imports in 2000. The preceding analysis demonstrates that there are two types of home biases for a local international trade. One is a bias between home country and international trading partners. The other one is a bias within country arising from small scale economy and various institutional trade barriers already discussed. The first type of bias has been intensively discussed in academia, but the second type of bias has not been well-analyzed so far (see Kakazu, 2001).

IMPEDIMENTS TO DPTZ GT FORMATION

Cabotage Regulation

One of notorious trade barriers for the local economy is the "Cabotage regulation" which is synonymous with the "use one's own carrier policy." The Cabotage regulation in Japan is stipulated in the 1899 "Vessel Act." The Act, in principle, prohibits foreign vessels to carry passengers and cargoes between domestic ports. The Cabotage became well-known when a mega earthquake hit the Hansin-Awaji areas in 1995. International carriers such as Sealand and Marsk had to use local feeder vessels to transship between Kobe and Yokohama because the Kobe port was unserviceable by the earthquake. This incident revealed that transportation costs between San Francisco and Kobe are less expensive than the costs between Kobe and Yokohama.

In addition to the Cabotage regulation, the Japanese vessel owners have to pay much higher wages for crew because they are prohibited to hire foreign crew under the "Act of Crew." These are national regulations governing all Japanese commercial vessels. There is another practice called the "use of local carrier policy." There are two major shipping companies in Okinawa catering passengers and cargos between Okinawa and mainland Japan. The rationale of this customary practice is to ensure stable supply of necessities and secure local employment.

The Cabptage regulation is also applied to sky. The foreign aircrafts, for example, are not permitted to carry passengers or cargos between Narita and Okinawa. Okinawa's transportation costs will be substantially reduced if these regulations and policies are removed.

Base Port Regulation

The base port regulation also makes local ports less competitive in the international market. This regulation is unique because the base port is designated by the Japan Shippers' Union, a private organization, based on the volume of cargo traffic. FIGURE 2-14 shows how the regulation affects Okinawa' cargo transportation cost. In order to carry a 40 feet container from the U.S. West Coast to Naha Port, Okinawa has to pay for $2,769 compared to Yokohama ($1,461) and Taiwan ($1,226). The major differences in cost components are a special fee imposed on the local ports in order to compensate for the loss arising from small lot. The other additional costs accrue to high weather risk, taxes and port user fees which are almost exempted in Taiwan. If we think that the transportation costs account, in average, for roughly 20% of the total value of cargos, Okinawa's comparative cost disadvantages are enormous in this age of mega-competition.

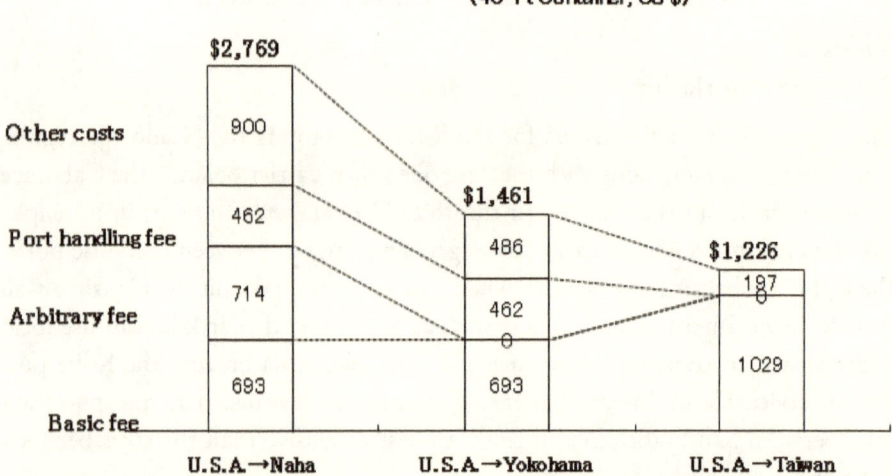

(40-Ft Container, US $)

Notes : Arbitrary fee is imposed on local ports such as Naha which are operated at a loss. "Other costs" include currency adjustment factor, which is the foreign exchange premium (or discount rate) to adjust for exchange rate fluctuations; Japan 58% and Taiwan 11%, and bunker adjustment factor which is the additional fee arising from an increase in fuel price (it can be negative when the fuel price declines).

Source : Okinawa Customs, Ministry of Treasury

FIGURE 2-14. Comparison of Cargo Transportation Costs: 2002.

Air routes are much less developed than sea routes, except for Naha and Taipei. A major problem is the high cost of transportation arising from Okinawa's small, isolated market together with the inward-oriented economic structure. Okinawa's exports account for only over 10 % of its GDP compared to more than 150% for

Hong Kong and Singapore in recent years. Besides, more than 90% of Okinawa's exports are destined for mainland Japan.

Distribution System and Commercial Practices

Although we cannot present in quantitative terms, the most important impediments to the globalization of the local economy is the obstinate domestic distribution system combined with time-honored commercial practices. Despite, a recent sea change in international trading practices, Japan's local distribution system is still tightly chained, or centralized from big domestic makers or importers in the metropolitan areas down to the local markets. The smaller the local markets, the greater the dependency on domestic suppliers. This is particularly so where transactions are "embedded in traditional social networks, which allow incentives to be aligned properly by providing sanctions against opportunistic behavior. One of the things that keep businessmen honest is fear of social ostracism" (Rodrik, 2002).

As deflation deepens and safety consciousness heightens, "resistance" toward imported goods may be enhanced particularly in small local markets.

We cannot also neglect "social resistance" particularly in fresh meat markets in Japan. The Okinawa Free Trade Zone, for example, allows lower import duty to be exported to mainland Japan after processing in the zone. The system, however, does not work because certain meat processors are said to be controlled by some highly sensitive people such as the *"Burakumin"* or *"eta,"* the outcast society of Japan.

Small-scale Diseconomy

As we have already noted, as far as cargo transportation is concerned small is not necessarily beautiful, but rather quite costly. Okinawa's GDP and international trade accounts for only 0.7% and 0.2% respectively of Japan. It is often cited with some element of sarcasm that fresh fruits from Taiwan are imported to Okinawa through Tokyo which is twice as far away from Taiwan as Okinawa is. But if we think of transportation and handling costs arising from "small lot" as well as frequency of marine transports between Okinawa and Taiwan, the practice is quite rationalized economically. The practice clearly demonstrates the difference between "physical distance" and "economic distance." Thus, physical proximity is not a sufficient condition for successful formation of GT.

Stumbling Block of One-Country-Two-System

Japan has been notorious for its centralized socio-economic system which worked well to accelerate the catch-up process with advanced Western systems after World War II. After the completion of the catching-up phase in the 1980s, however, the system seems to have worked as a brake or a stumbling block for further advancement.

Despite emerging voices of regionalism and new laws of decentralization, administrative power and cost sharing schemes between the central and local governments have not been effectively instituted. One good reason behind this lies in an inertia on the part of local governments themselves. Transfer of administrative power from the central to the local governments means more local initiatives as well as responsibility. Most local governments, including Okinawa, are heavily dependent on subsidies from the central government, and they are reluctant to commit to more self-reliant development.

Article 14 of the Japanese constitution that stipulates "Equality under the Law" is probably the most important stumbling block for regional initiatives to form a GT. An example is the aforementioned Okinawa's SFTZ. The Okinawa prefectural government strongly demanded the Japanese government to allow "one-country-two-system" for effective use of the zone. But the Japanese government stubbornly turned down the demand based on its interpretation of Article 14, that Okinawa should not be treated differently from any other national regions. Tokyo argued that if Okinawa enjoys one-country-two-system, the other national regions should also be granted the same privileges. The Governor of Okinawa was not convinced by the interpretation saying that Okinawa has been under "one-country two-systems" because the island has been burdened with about 75% of U.S. military facilities in Japan. The Japanese government's response to this assertion is "Okinawa is not the only place to have U.S. bases in Japan."

A full-fledged GT formation like DPTZ is not possible unless the local governments are allowed to institute independent globalization policies such as determining level of tariffs, local taxes and contracting cooperative agreements with local partner as well as those selected by the central governments.

Diplomatic Relations

In any country, diplomacy is exclusively left to the central government based on the idea of "integrated diplomatic policy." It is understandable because plural policies would lead to confusions and conflicts among negotiating partners particularly in highly sensitive fields such as security and national defense. Given overall national guidelines, however, there are many diplomatic negotiations to be left for the initiatives of each local government. The Japanese local governments are already conducting various "regional diplomatic policies" such as concluding friendship agreements, personal and cultural exchanges and establishing joint ventures. Economic affairs should be left the local private and public initiatives if they do not conflict with overall national guidelines.

Local diplomatic initiatives are crucial for successful formation of GTs. Regrettably, however, the Governor of Okinawa has so far hesitated to visit Taiwan because he is afraid of offending the Beijing government. Even on private business, the past governor Mr. Keiichi Inamine secretly visited Taiwan only once in his eight-year term (1998-2006) while the governor of Tokyo visited openly. It is rumored that the Okinawa Ambassador, who was first appointed by the Japanese Government in 1996 to smooth out military base issues on Okinawa, is a Tokyo "watchdog" discouraging the Okinawa governor from visiting Taiwan.

CONCLUSIONS

The term "enlightenment optimism" (Emmot, 1999) suggests that all problems are solvable by reason. In this spirit, we would like to argue that a growth Triangle (GT) approach as discussed in this paper might provide some rational solutions to the problems of Asia's peripheral regions in the age of global socio-economic activities. The GT approach in particular will be effectively applied to Japan's remotest, economically most backward prefecture, Okinawa, where achieving economic self-reliance has been its eternal dream.

In the past, the terms globalization and localization have provoked strong reactions, both positive and negative in Okinawa. Despite the new opportunities it brings, globalization has been feared because it exposes local workers and small enterprises to global competition. Localization is usually praised for raising levels of participation in decision-making and for giving local people more of a chance to shape the context of their own lives. We argue, however, that globalization and localization are not trade-offs. Instead they are essential, complementary tidal wave factors for the future development of Okinawa. Without full, efficient, value-added use of location factors such as labor, niche technologies, culture and natural resources, the local economy would not be ready for the sea change brought about by globalization.

NOTES

Sachs, J.D. (2001), p.4.
Council of Economic Advisors (2001), p.199.
Bertram, G. (2004), p.7.
Stiglitz, J.E. (2002), pp.214-215.
Rodrik, D. (July 2002), p.10.
Thant, M. and M. Tang, M. (1996), p.32.
Rodrik (July 2002), p.12.

REFERENCES

Armstrong, H.W. and Read, R. 2002a. "The Phantom of Liberty?: Economic Growth and the Vulnerability of Small States." *Journal of International Development,* vol.14, pp.435-458.

———. 2002b. "The Importance of Being Unimportant: The Political Economy of Trade and Growth in Small States." In: Murshed S.M. (ed.). *Issues in Positive Political Economy.* London: Rutledge, pp.71-88.

Anderson, J. and M. Wincoop. 2001. "Gravity with Gravitas: A Solution to the Border Puzzle." *NBER Working Paper,* no. 8079.

———. 2001. "Borders, Trade and Welfare," *NBER Working Paper,* no.8515.

Asian Development Bank. 2001. "Asia's Globalization Challenge," *Asian Development Outlook 200.* Hong Kong: Oxford University Press, pp.161-197.

———. 1993. *Economic Cooperation in the Greater Mekong Subregion.* Manila: ADB Publication.

Balassa, B.1961. *The Theory of Economic Integration.* Illinois: Richard D. Irwin, Inc.

Bertram, G. 2004. "The MIRAB Model in the 21st Century." A paper presented at Islands of the World II, Jinmen, Taiwan, November 1-5, pp.1-37.

Collier, P. and Gunning J.W. 1999. "Why Has Africa Grown Slowly?" *Journal of Economic Perspectives.* Vol.13, No.3 (summer), pp.3-22.

Crafts, N. 2000. "Globalization and Growth in The Twentieth Century," *IMF Working Paper.* WP/00/44.

Council of Economic Advisors (CEA). 2001. *Economic Report of the President.* Chapter 6 on "Opportunity and Challenge in the Global Economy."

Emmot, Bill.1999. "Survey: The 20th Century." *The Economist.* Sept. 11th-17th1999, pp.1-62.

Girvan, N. 2004. "Do Small Islands have a Future in a Globalised World?" A Keynote Address at Islands of the World II, Jinmen, Taiwan, November 1-5, pp.1-12.

James, H. 2001. *The End of Globalization: Lessons from the Great Depression.* Cambridge: Harvard University Press.

Hayami, U. 2001. *Development Economic From the Poverty to the Wealth of Nations,* 2nd edition. New York: Oxford University Press.

Japan Economic Journal, July 6, 2007, p.7.

Kakazu, H. 2001. "Economic Globalization and Regional Economies." A Paper Presented at the Kanto Branch of the Japan Society of International Economics. Tokyo: pp.1-15.

———. 2000. *The Challenge for Okinawa: Thriving Locally in a Globalized Econo-*

my. Naha: Okinawa Development Finance Corp.

————. 1998." Growth Triangles in ASEAN." UNCRD, *Regional Development Studies*, vol.4, pp. 1-36.

————. 1999. "Trade and Economic Cooperation of the Regions along the New Eurasian Continental Bridge." A paper presented at the International Symposium on Economic Development of the Regions Along the New Eurasian Continental Bridge. Beijing: May 7-9, pp.1-16.

————. 1995. *Cross border Growth Triangles in Asia*. Tokyo: Oriental Economist.

————. 1994-a. *Sustainable Development of Small Island Economies*. Boulder: Westview Press.

————. M. Thant and M. Tang, M. (eds.). 1994-b. *Growth Triangles in Asia: A New Approach to Regional Economic Cooperation*. Hong Kong: Oxford University Press.

————. B. O. Campbell and S. Sekiguchi. 1994-c. *A Northeast Asian Development Bank?: An Introductory Analysis*. Honolulu: East-West Center.

Kearney, A.T. Jan./Feb. 2001. "Measuring Globalization." *Foreign Policy*, pp.56-53.

Krugman, P. 1991. *Geography and Trade*. Cambridge: The MIT Press.

Lim, I. (ed.). 1996. *Growth Triangles in Southeast Asia: Strategy for Development*. Kuala Lumpur: ISIS.

————. 1994. *Growth Triangles in Southeast Asia*. Malaysia: ISIS.

McCallum, John.1995. "National Borders Canada-US Regional Trade Patterns." *American Economic Review*, 85 (3), pp.615-623.

McGee, T.G., and Greenberg, C. 1999. "The Emergence of Extended Metropolitan Regions in ASEANTowards the Year 2000." *ASEAN Economic Bulletin*, vol.9, no.1.

Ministry of Economy and Industry. 2002. 2001 *White Paper on International Trade*. Tokyo: Gyosei, pp.74-88.

NIRA. 2002. *A Strategy of Networking the Yellow Sea Rim Cities after the Asian Financial Crisis*. Tokyo.

Obstfeld. M. and Taylor, A.M. 2002. "Globalization and Capital Markets." *NBER Working Paper*, March, no.8846.

Obstfeld, M. and K. Rogoff. 2000. "The Six Major Puzzles in International Macroeconomics: Is There a Common Cause?" *NBER Working Paper*, no. 7777.

O'Rourke, K.H., and Williamson J.G. 1999. *Globalization and History: The Evolution of a Nineteenth-Century Atlantic Economy*. Cambridge: MIT Press.

Prasad, N. (2004). "Escaping Regulation, Escaping Convention: Development Strategies in Small Economies." *World Economics*, vol.5, no.1, January-March, pp.41-65.

Pernia, E.M. 1997. "A Study of Brunei-Darussalam-Indonesia Malaysia Philippines: East ASEAN Growth AREA." A paper presented at International Business Seminar, 8-9 January, Kota Kinabalu.

Rodrik, D. 2002. "Feasible Globalization." *NBER Draft Paper,* no.w9129.

Ryukyu Shimpo. July 12, 2007. "China has a plan to invest in Okinawa," p.8.

Sachs, J.D. 2001. "Geography, Economic Policy and Regional Development in China." *Asian Economic Papers,* vol.1, no.1.

Sasakibara, E. 2001. "Be Prepare for a Wartime Economy." *Bungei Shunju,* November, pp.174-180.

Sawa, T. 2000. *The End of Marketism.* Tokyo: Iwanami Shinsho.

Scalapino, R. 1992. "The United States and Asia: Future Prospects." *Foreign Affairs,* Winter, pp.19-40.

Schirm, S.A. 2002. *Globalization and the New Regionalism: Global Markets, Domestic Politics and Regional Co-Operation.* New York: Blackwell.

Sen, A.K. 1999. *Development as Freedom.* New York: Anchor Books.

Solos, G. 1998. *The Crisis of Global Capitalism.* New York: Little, Brown Book Group.

Stiglitz, J.E. 2002. *Globalization and its Discontents.* New York: W.W. Norton, pp.214-215.

Takara, Kurayoshi. 1998. *Ajia no Naka no Ryukyu Ogoku* (The Kingdom of Ryukyu in Asia), Tokyo: Yoshikawa Kobunkan.

Thant, M. and Tang, M. 1996. I*ndonesia-Malaysia-Thailand Growth Triangle: Theory to Practice.* Manila: Asian Development Bank.

The Economist. September 29, 2001. "A Survey of Globalisation," pp.3-24.

UNDP.1991. "Tumen River Area Development," mission report by M. Miller, A. Holm, and T. Kelleher presented at the Pyongyang International Conference. Pyongyang: 16-18 October.

Wacziarg, R.T., Spolaore, E. and Alesian, A.F. 2002. *Trade, Growth and the Size of Countries.* Institute Research Working Paper, no. 1995, Institute of Economic Research, Boston: Harvard University.

Yamazawa, 1992. "On Pacific Economic Integration." *Economic Journal,* November, 102, pp.1488-1490.

Chapter 3

NETWORKING ISLAND SOCIETIES UNDER GLOBALIZATION

WHAT IS NETWORKING?

Networks can be defined as physical linkages to carry humans, commodities, energy and information. Formally networks are composed of links that connect nodes. FIGURE 3-1 illustrates a simple network model comprising of a "star network'" and "long distance network" (see Economides, 1996). A phone call from A1 to A2, for instance, is facilitated by switching services at Sa (A1SaA2). A long distance exchange between A1 and B1 necessarily involves two switching service points (A1SaSbB1).

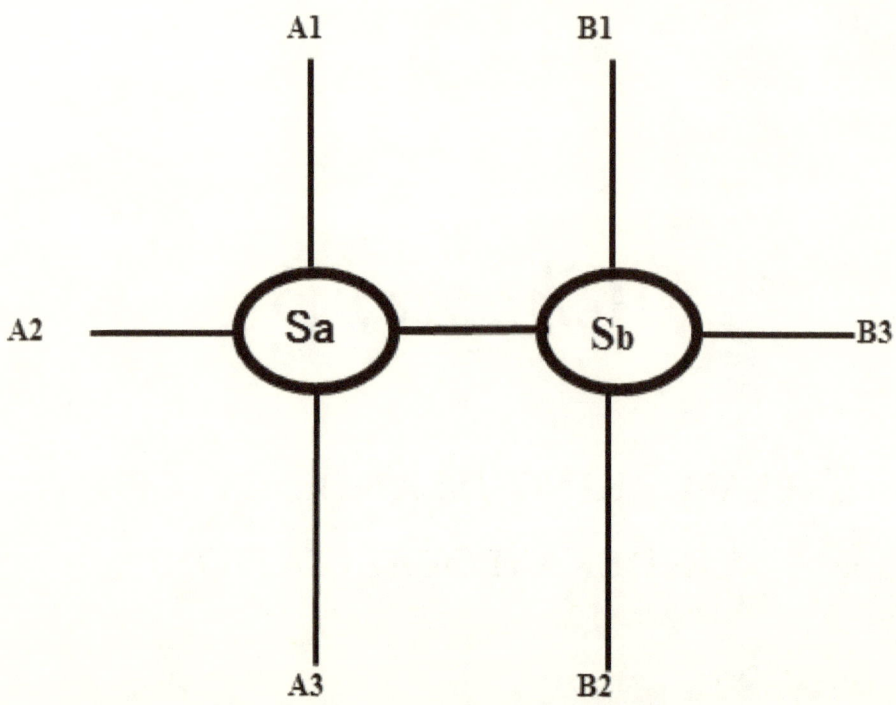

FIGURE 3-1. A Simple Star and Distance Nework Model.

Any mode of information network such as telephone, fax, TV, printed matter or the Internet conforms to the basic structure illustrated in FIGURE 3-1. Network activities exhibit positive externalities, commonly known as "network externalities" which are well illustrated by FIGURE 3-1. If a third person (A3) is connected to a telephone or by e-mail, then the first (A1) and second (A2) persons who are already in the network will benefit from A3's connection without there being extra cost. "The network externality is the reason why many colleges provide universal e-mail for all their students and faculty—the value of e-mail is much higher when everyone participates." (Samuelson & Nordhaus, 2001).

The property of network externalities is particularly important in small island societies because the benefits from externalities will be greater as the size or scale of economy increases. Thus the unit cost of networking will be reduced as the number of network participants increases. This fact gives rise to the existence of a critical mass point, that is, a minimum sustainable network size. For a small, isolated society, networking benefits are severely limited and costly compared to bigger ones.

INTENSITY OF NETWORKING

Geographical and Cultural Factors

The intensity of networking among island societies depend on several factors as illustrated in FIGURE 3-2. Geographical proximity is probably the most important factor in areas bonding together, because of the greater ease and lower costs of interaction. As such, islands within Okinawa Prefecture are intensively linked.

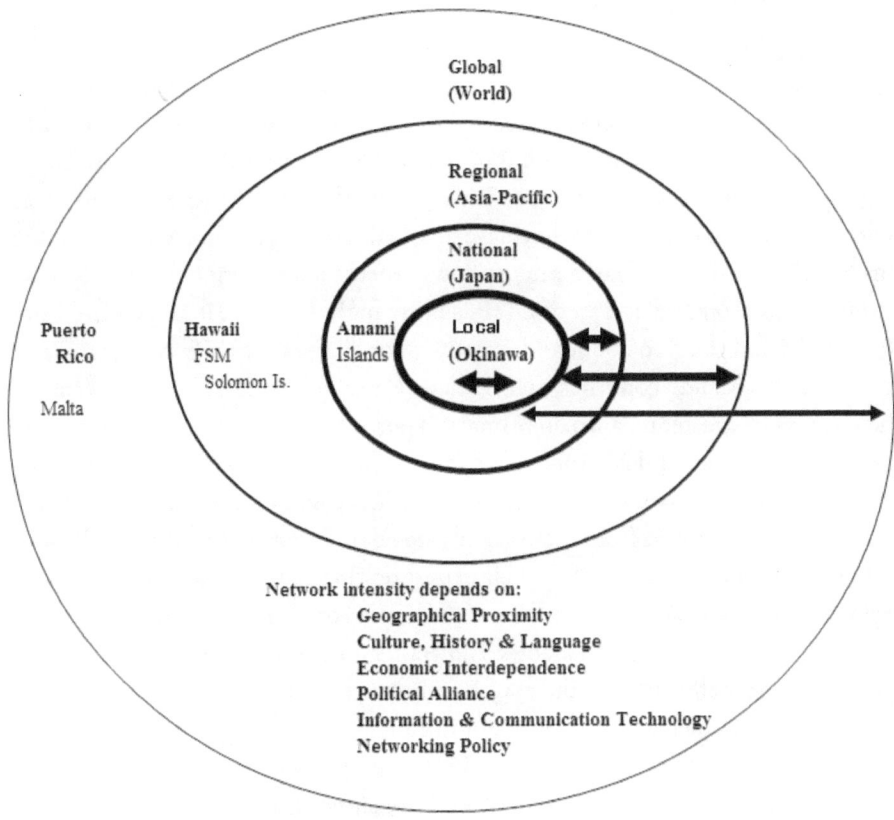

Source: Hiroshi Kakakzu (2004).

FIGURE 3-2. The Intensity of Internet Networking Among Island Societies.

The intensity of networking is also greatly affected by culture, history and language as well as the heritage or, if you will, "blood" factor. The Amami islands, which belong administratively to Kagoshima Prefecture, have kept a strong network with the islands of Okinawa because of the similarity of the culture and history of both areas. Hawaii is the most strongly networked overseas region with Okinawa because of the large number of *Uchinanchu* or emigrated Okinawans possessing a common cultural and historical background. *Uchinanchu* will be discussed in more detail later in this chapter. Crocombe points out that similarities in culture and language are the basic property for networking in the South Pacific islands societies. "*Wantok* (from English one talk) is extensively used as a broad classification in Melanesia. It refers to someone of the same language community and safe networking implying fellow feeling among Polynesians and Miconesians abroad." (Crocombe, 2001).

Economic Factor (Trade and ODA)

Networking in trade (exports and imports of goods and services) is increasingly becoming an important factor for island societies as economic globalization advances galvanizing entire island societies. Because of the small domestic market and limited resource base, international trade has been a matter of survival as well as an engine of growth for small, open island economies. The SPF countries are basically open economies. This is not because they have low trade barriers but because they cannot survive without relatively large import flows. Their total commodity trade (exports and imports) expressed as a % of GNP is fairly high. In 2000, it ranged from over 80% in Fiji and PNG to about and over 50% for all the other SPF countries.

For these islands countries, which have a negligible manufacturing capacity, there is a much greater reliance on primary exports. More than 60% of exports from the Marshall Islands and Micronesia are in fish. Copra accounts for more than 40% of Kiribati and Vanuatu's total exports. Squash accounts for in excess of 40% of Tonga's exports. Exports from these islands are not only concentrated around a small number of primary products, but their export destinations are also limited to a few regional large markets or to their former or current sovereign countries.

As we have discussed in Chapter 1, intra-regional trade among the SPF countries has been small among island countries because their economies are more competitive than complementary. The major intra-regional trading partners among the Forum island countries are Fiji and PNG because of their significant manufacturing base. Fiji has been exporting processed consumer goods, such as wheat flour, cooking oil and biscuits, in fairly large volumes to other SPF countries, particularly Tuvalu and Cook Islands where inter-regional trade is relatively high. Fiji's imports from the other SPF island countries are confined to a very small volume of agricultural commodities. PNG and Fiji's trade is more diversified because of their relatively large size.

Since 1993 the preferential trading arrangements under the Melanesian Spearhead Group (MSG) Agreement among Fiji, PNG, Solomon Islands and Vanuatu have encouraged intra-regional trade in specific commodities such as coffee, kava, and beef. Because of a large increase in imports from the other two MSG countries relative to their exports, however, both the Solomon Islands and Vanuatu have accumulated sizeable trade deficits with Fiji and PNG. As a result, the deficit countries have sought temporary withdrawal from MSG trade arrangements (see Jayaraman, 2003).

These islands' high economic dependency of these islands on external trade does not necessarily mean high economic interdependence or networking with the rest of the world. Instead, they depend crucially on a few large economies for trade and capital inflows including ODA. Evidence of this is the Asian financial crisis of the late 1990's which devastated larger and more networked Asian societies while having only a negligible impact on the region's smaller island economies. For those island economies, volatility in dependency is more important than volatility in interdependence or networking. As such, volatility in ODA and remittances will be a more crucial matter than volatility in financial and export markets for aid-dependent small states.

Political Alliances and Socio-Economic Policies

For small islands, socio-economic interdependence or dependency is quite often a direct consequence of political alliances or socio-economic policies created by colonial governments or by emigration policies. The Australian and New Zealand governments, for example, allow the free entry of migrants from Niue, the Cook Islands and Tokelau because of their past political relationships. People tend to move from a poor region to a rich region given free access. "92% of all Niueans now live in New Zealand and Australia and 83% of Cook Islanders live in New Zealand, Australia and elsewhere." (Crocombe, 2001).

Another example is the case of *Nikkeijin* (foreign nationals of Japanese descent). The Japanese government revised its Immigration Control Law in 1990 allowing Nikkeijin up to the third generation to reside in Japan without legal or employment restrictions. "This law has led to a significant increase in the employment of people of Japanese descent from South America, in particular from Brazil, where many Japanese had emigrated during the first half of the twentieth century" (Carvalho, 2003). In this case, blood relations are more important than proximity and economic ties. *Nikkeijin* networking policy may look strange to non-Japanese because having the same "blood" does not necessarily mean having or understanding the same culture and language. In actuality, third generation Nikkeijin from Brazil often face great difficulties adjusting to Japanese culture.

There has long been debate in the South Pacific over whether or not networking through migration is beneficial to the countries of origin where quite often out-migration means a "brain drain" of the most highly skilled, young labor. Hugo has, however, pointed out that the following beneficial effects for the origin country:

(1) Where there is insufficient capacity in the origin economy to productively absorb and use the migrants' skill.

(2) Where the inflow or remittances outweighs what the migrant would have contributed.

(3) Where there is significant return migration of the migrants with enhanced skills and capacities.

(4) Where the migrants forge productive economic linkages with the home country such as directing investment, providing beachheads for production from the home country. (Hugo, 2004).

Information Networking

In today's rapidly globalizing and knowledge economy "know-how replaces land and capital as the basic building blocks for growth" (Norris, 2001). Businesses in particular are faced with the maxim collaborate (internet) or die. Our island institutions must also find creative means of surviving in this digital economy where students have the freedom to receive educational opportunities over the Internet or by other means of distance delivery. It is even argued that imaginary territorial boundaries are truly imaginary in cyberspace.

Moreover, information and communication technology (ICT), particularly the Internet, is said to have a particular beneficial networking effect on small, isolated island societies because it destroys the "tyranny of distance." Of course there is always a danger that ICT might create a digital divide between the rich and the poor islands. In fact, FIGURE 3-3 indicates clearly that Internet prevalence rates are closely correlated with levels of per capita GDP. Small island developing countries are far behind richer countries not only because of lower incomes but also because of higher Internet connection costs than the richer countries.

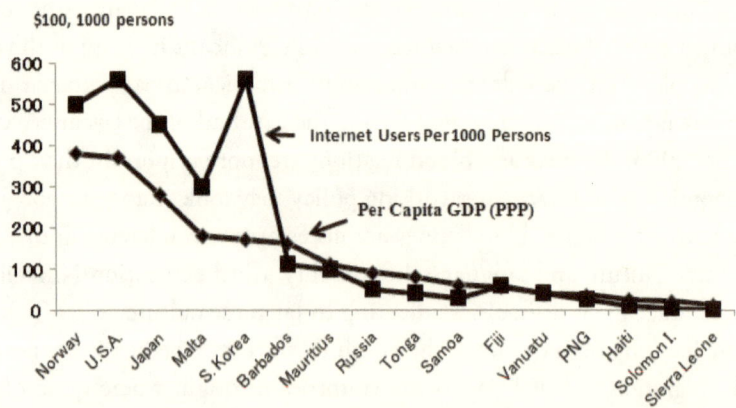

Source: Constructed from UNDP, *Human Development Report, 2004*.

FIGURE 3-3. Per Capita GDP and Internet Users by Selected Countries: 2002.

Within island nations themselves, smaller, remote islands are suffering a serious digital divide. A typical case is the State of Chuuk (also known as Truck) of the Federated States of Micronesia (FSM) where there are 105 schools of which 95 are located in outlaying islands and have no infrastructure—no power, phones, communication (90% of the schools are without such facilities). In these outer islands, the costs for travel to obtain training is very expensive relative to average salaries and wages (see Orita, 2004).

The current status of internet access in the SPF island countries, as shown in TABLE 3-1 constitutes more or less a mirror model for other small islands. All SPF countries have access to ICT in some form, be it telephone, facsimile and internet. Access to the internet is generally limited to the workplace, educational institutions, in the home, and through public means such as internet cafes. Although internet use among the SPF countries is on the rise, there are large gaps between and among countries reflecting the number of providers, market, regulatory and cost structures.

The SPF countries face various constraints in their ability to access internet services, including the high cost of telecommunication equipment and services, inadequate budgetary allocations, limited number of providers and trained personnel, not to mention the need to educate the internet users themselves. Retention of trained personnel is always a big problem in small island countries because they tend to emigrate overseas for better pay.

TABLE 3-1. Internet Access in the South Pacific Island Countries: 2000

	Homes	Primary Schools	Secondary Schools	Work Place	Public Acess Areas
Cook Islands	*	*	*	*	*
FSM	*	na	*	***	*
Fiji	*	na	*	**	*
Kiribati	*	nil	*	*	*
Marshall Islands	*	na	*	*	*
Nauru	na	na	na	na	na
Niue	na	****	****		****
Palau	**	na	*		*
PNG	*	na	*	*	*
Samoa	*	na	*	**	*
Solomon Islands	*	na	*	*	*
Tonga	*	na	*	**	*
Tuvalu	*	na	nil		*
Vanuatu	**	na	*	***	***

Notes: *less than 25%; **between 25-50%; ***between 50-70%;***more than 75% of population. na=not available.

Source: Pacific Islands Forum Secretariat.

The Pacific Islands Digital Opportunities (PIDO) Research Committee of the Sasakawa Pacific Island Nations Fund has recommended the following action plans to enhance networking among SPF island countries:

(1) Information sharing and joint content development for human capacity building;
(2) Develop and promote e-Health and Tele-center projects;
(3) Utilize wireless LAN technology to reduce costs of networking;
(4) Promote "one island, one product" projects;
(5) Strategic approach utilizing ICT for tourism industry development;
(6) Group study and collaboration among school teachers;
(7) Utilize existing network interconnection for education, training, and conferences. (see Chapter 1, Sasakawa PIDO Report, 2004).

NETWORKING PACIFIC ISLAND SOCIETIES

Okinawa, or the Ryukyu Islands, has a long history of networking domestically as well as internationally. This experience may be usefully applied to other island societies (see Kakazu, 2003). Okinawa is unique among Pacific island societies because of its rich culture, high living standards, having the world's highest longevity and diversity in ecosystems. Amid the rapid depopulation of most of Japan's outlying islands, Okinawa has kept its dynamic growth even after reversion to mainland Japan in 1972 as is fully discussed in Chapter 10.

During the past three decades, the population has increased by 28% from less than one million to over 1.3 million. Okinawa's per capita GDP is higher than the average of the OECD countries, and its life expectancy, particularly for women, is the highest (eighty-six years) in the world. The secrets of Okinawa's longevity have recently been revealed (see The New York Times' bestseller book on *The Okinawa Program: Learn the Secrets to Healthy Longevity* by Willcox, Willcox and Suzuki, 2001).

Networking Uchinanchu (Overseas Okinawans)

In the past, Okinawa quite skillfully balanced her limited land resources, particularly in terms of food production, with population growth. Out-migration became the primary mechanism for keeping the population of Okinawa at a sustainable level. The population remained almost constant prior to the Pacific war due in large part to net migration. Out-migration all but ceased after the war.

Okinawans, or *Uchinanchu* in the local language, migrated to Hawaii, North and South America, Southeast Asia, the South Pacific and other areas. It is estimated that these overseas migrants and their descendants, excluding mainland

Japanese, numbered about 300,000 (FIGURE 3-4). They were prosperous in their settled lands, and continued to remit money to their motherland until just after World War ll. At one point, these remittances covered Okinawa's trade deficits entirely. It was only quite recently, however, that they actively organized or networked themselves to enhance their *Uchinanchu* identity beyond national boundaries.

One active organization is the Worldwide *Uchinanchu* Business Association (WUB) which was inaugurated in Hawaii in 1997 with the support and sponsorship of the Okinawa Prefectural Government and business groups for the purpose of creating businesses through a worldwide network of Okinawans. As is shown in FIGURE 3-5, WUB has been organized across the five continents and in the Pacific. WUB is considering plans for a global company that will trade Okinawan products such as *Awamori* (rice wine) and various health foods.

It is ironic that during the early years of migration, around the turn of the last century, people were driven out of Okinawa by conditions of abject poverty and were regarded as *kimin*, or deserters, whereas today they have become valued catalysts in the networking of Okinawa with the rest of the world.

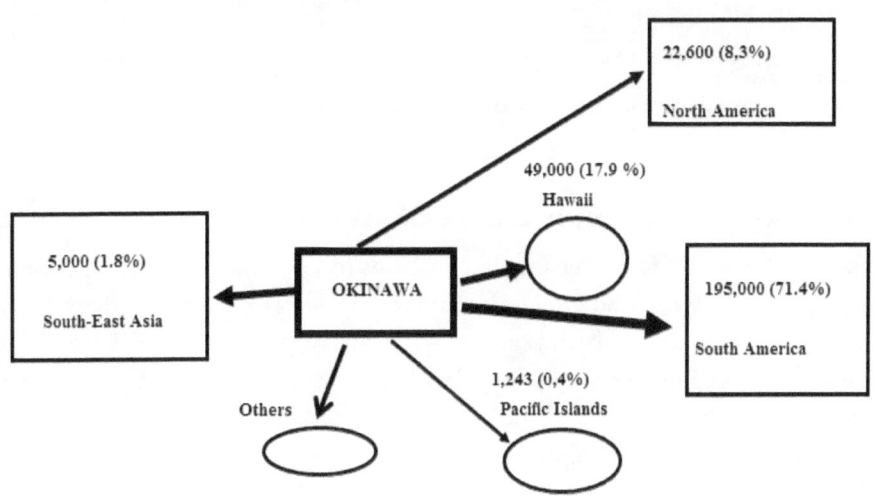

Source: Constructed from the data of Okinawa Prefectural Government

FIGURE 3-4. Network of Okinawa's Overseas Emigrants: 1899-1993.

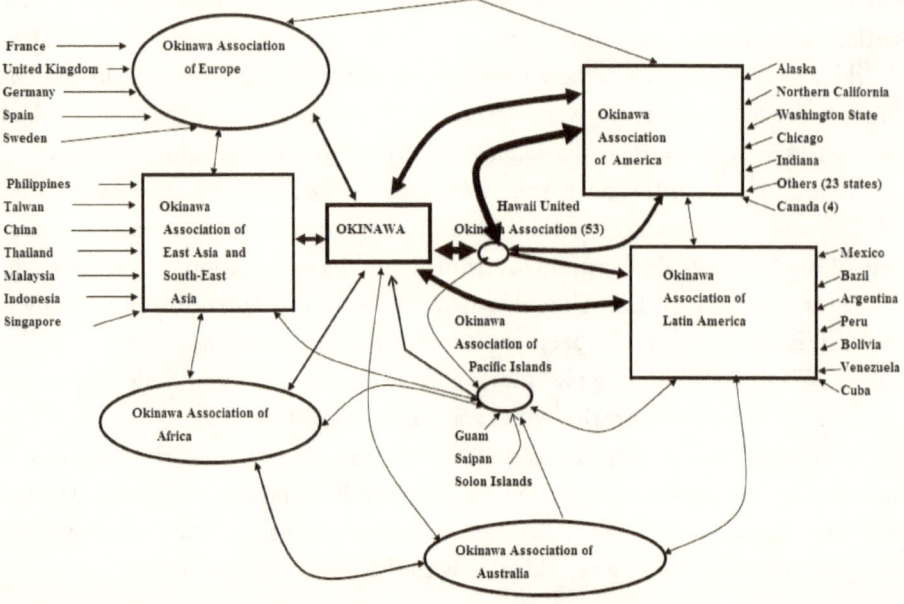

Note: ( ) figures are number of organizations.

Source: Constructed from the data of Okinawa Prefectural Government.

FIGURE 3-5. Current Networks Through Worldwide Uchinanchu Associations.

Networking Within the Islands of Okinawa

There are currently forty-one inhabited islands in Okinawa, comprising Okinawa Island, the Miyako Island group, the Yaeyama Island group, the Northern Islands group and the Southern Islands group (see major islands in TABLE 3-2 and FIGURE 3-6). The number of inhabited lands changes slightly every survey year due to emigration, migration and the construction of landbridges or reclaimed land roads which connect two separate islands.

Okinawa Island, the main island of Okinawa Prefecture, accounted for 91% of Okinawa's total population in 2005, whereas the share was 83% in 1960. All the island groups experienced depopulation from 1960-80, but in recent years the Yaeyama Island group recorded positive population growth and the continuous depopulation of the Miyako Island group has stopped. A close examination of TABLE 3-2 indicates that outlying islands such as Iriomote, Zamami and Aka have turned from negative to positive population growth in recent years. The common contributory factor for such positive growth is growing tourism activities particularly eco- and blue-tourism.

Okinawa experienced from net out-migration to mainland from the period of 1970-2000 to net in-migration in recent years. It is interesting to note that both the Yaeyama and Miyako Island groups recorded net in-migration from mainland Japan while simultaneously recording net out-migration to Okinawa Island. This relatively recent phenomenon is serving to halt depopulation of these areas.

The indigenous population of Okinawa's outlying small islands has long emigrated to neighboring larger islands, particularly Okinawa itself. An increasing number of Japanese mainlanders, in contrast, and particularly elder people, have been attracted to the healthy, relatively inexpensive, and leisurely island lifestyle. If this trend in population dynamics continues, the entire population of these islands may be replaced by outsiders, or non-islanders in the future. Nobody can predict what the socio-economic impact of these cultural dynamics might be. If migrants are environmentally conscious and skilled, they can be welcomed in to help resolve an island's skilled labor shortages and promote ecotourism. It should be pointed out, however, that we do not have solid empirical data on whether these migrants are temporary or circular migrants or permanent ones. It should also be noted that an increasing number of elderly Japanese prefer to live temporarily in low cost countries such as Thailand and Malaysia where there is reasonable security and where good communication and transportation systems are readily available.

TABLE 3-2. Population Changes of Okinawa's Islands: 1960-2005

	(Population, 1000 persons)				(% change during the Periods)	
	1960	1980	2000	2005	1960-80	1980-2005
Okinawa Total	883.1	1,107	1,318	1,361	25.3	23.0
Okinawa Island	730.3	988	1,199	1,220	35.3	23.5
Miyako Islands	72.3	60.5	55.6	58.1	-16.3	-4.0
Miyako	55.4	48.1	46.4	49.0	-13.2	1.9
Irabu	10.8	9.2	6.8	6.6	-14.8	-28.3
Tarama	2.7	1.7	1.3	1.5	-37.0	-11.8
Ikema	2.5	1.2	0.7	0.8	-52.0	-33.3
Kurima	0.5	0.2	0.2	0.2	-60.0	0.0
Oogami	0.2	0.1	0.0	0.0	-50.0	-100.0
Minna	0.2	0.0	0.0	0.0	-100.0	0.0
Yaeyama Islands	51.4	44.3	48.7	57.9	-13.8	30.7
Ishigaki	38.5	38.9	43.2	45.1	1.0	15.9
Yonaguni	4.7	2.1	1.9	1.8	-55.3	-14.3
Iriomote	3.5	1.5	2.0	5.5	-57.1	266.7
Hateruma	1.4	0.8	0.6	0.6	-42.9	-25.0
Kuroshima	1.1	0.2	0.2	0.2	-81.8	0.0
Kohama	0.9	0.5	0.4	0.5	-44.4	0.0
Taketomi	0.8	0.4	0.3	4.2	-50.0	950.0
Hatoma	0.4	0.4	0.0	0.0	0.0	-100.0
Shinjo	0.1	0.0	0.0	0.0	-100.0	0.0
Northern Islands	17.1	9.1	8.9	8.7	-46.8	-4.4
Iejima	7.5	5.0	5.1	5.1	-33.3	2.0
Izena	5.0	2.1	1.9	1.6	-58.0	-23.8
Iheya	3.2	1.4	1.4	1.5	-56.3	7.1
Kori	0.8	0.4	0.3	0.3	-50.0	-25.0
Noho	0.4	0.1	0.1	0.1	-75.0	0.0
Minna	0.1	0.1	0.1	0.1	0.0	0.0
Southern Isalnds	28.9	17.0	15.5	15.5	-41.2	-8.8
Kumejima	15.1	10.2	9.3	9.1	-32.5	-10.8
Minami Daito	3.4	1.6	1.4	1.4	-52.9	-12.5
Aguni	2.1	1.1	1.0	0.9	-47.6	-18.2
Tsuken	1.7	0.9	0.5	0.6	-47.1	-33.3
Tokashiki	1.5	0.8	0.5	0.7	-46.7	-12.5
Tonaki	1.5	0.6	0.5	0.5	-60.0	-16.7
Kita Daito	1.0	0.7	0.7	0.5	-30.0	-28.6
Zamami	0.9	0.5	0.6	1.1	-44.4	120.0
Aka	0.6	0.2	0.3	0.3	-66.7	50.0
Kudaka	0.6	0.3	0.2	0.3	-50.0	0.0
Keruma	0.2	0.1	0.1	0.1	-50.0	0.0
Oha	0.1	0.0	0.0	0.0	-100.0	0.0
Oojima	0.1	0.0	0.0	0.0	-100.0	0.0

Source: Compiled from Statistics Division, Okinawa Prefectural Government.

What Can a Simple Model Tell Us?

The most frequently used tool to predict the flow of people, goods, or communication between any two places is probably the gravity model which is based on Newton's Law of Gravitation as follow:

(Population of region 1 x Population of region 2)/ (Distance between them) ^{2}
or (GDP of region 1 x GDP of region 2)/ (Distance between them) ^{2}.

The above model shows that the relative strength of the bond between two regions is determined by multiplying the population (or GDP) of region 1 by the population (or GDP) of region 2 and then dividing the product by the distance between the two regions squared. Since the larger region attracts more people and goods than the smaller region, and with all other things being equal, the closer region has a greater attraction. This model has been particularly useful in explaining flows of trade and migration between two regions where the relatively free movement of goods and services including labor are guaranteed.

Actual estimations of migration flows between the regions (or islands) of Okinawa are made based on a logarithmic form as follow:

$$LogM_{ij} = \alpha1 + \alpha2 LogY_iY_j + \alpha3 LogD_{ij} + E_{ij}.$$

Migration from i region (or island) to j region (or island) is positively related to the size of GDP of both regions (Y_iY_j), but negatively related to the distance between the two regions (D_{ij}). E_{ij} is an error term. Therefore, the expected signs of the parameters are:

$$\alpha1, \alpha2 > 0, \alpha3 < 0.$$

The estimated results for the period of 1995-2000 based on a cross section of data are shown in TABLE 3-3. The parameters on migration from Okinawa to mainland Japan satisfy our assumptions and are significant at a 5% cut off value. It is noteworthy, however, that distance (D_{ij}) plays a positive role when it comes to migration from Yaeyama to Okinawa Island. That is to say, people from the distant islands of the Yaeyama region tend to migrate more to Okinawa Island. This can be explained by the 'push' and 'pull' factors between the two regions.

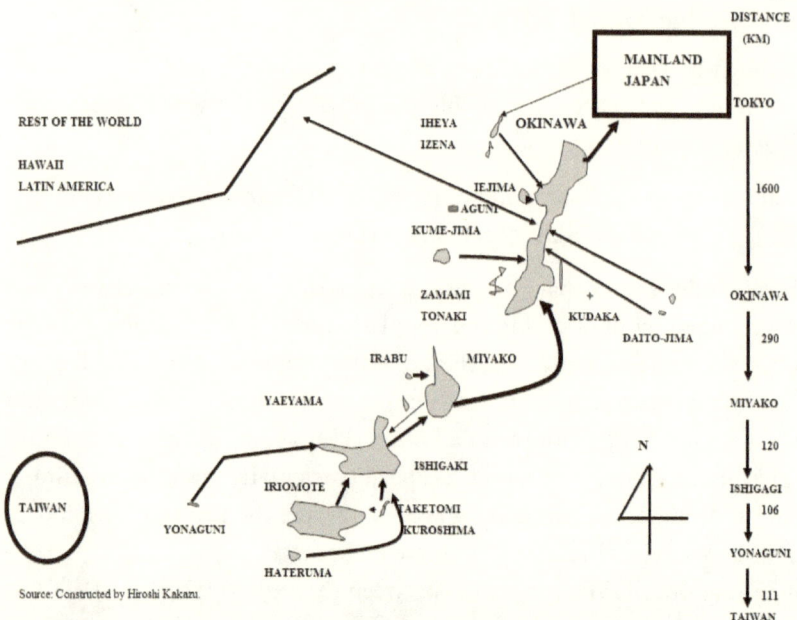

Source: Constructed by Hiroshi Kakazu.

FIGURE 3-6. Patterns of Migratory Networks of Okinawa's Islands.

TABLE 3-3. Net Migration among Major Island Groups in Okinawa: 1995-2000

	Mainland Japan	Overseas	Total	Gravity Model (see Text) $LogM_{ij} = \alpha1 + \alpha2LogY_iY_j + \alpha3LogD_{ij} + E_{ij}$
Okinawa				
in-migration	52,738	3,694	56,432	Migration from Okinawa to Mainland Japan
out-migration	58,657	0	58,627	$LogM_{ij} = 0.23 + 0.76LogY_iY_j - 0.39LogD_{ij}$
net change	-5,919	3,694	-2,195	(0.046) (2.61) (-0.690)

	Okinawa Island	Mainland Japan	Overseas	Total	
Miyako					Migration from Yaeyama Islands to Okinawa Island
in-migration	2,844	1,650	73	4,567	$LogM_{ij} = 0.12 + 0.56LogY_iY_j + 0.46LogD_{ij}$
out-migration	3,204	1,537	0	4,741	(0.023) (0.52) (0.223)
net change	-360	113	73	-174	
					Migration from Okinawa Island to Yaeyama Islands
Yaeyama					$LogM_{ij} = 0.54 + 0.89LogY_iY_j - 0.41LogD_{ij}$
in-migration	2,647	2,758	111	5,516	(0.045) (2.86) (-0.78)
out-migration	3,301	2,115	0	5,416	
net change	-654	643	111	100	

Source: Constructed from the Population Census, 2000.

Persons from smaller, distant islands tend to migrate to more prosperous, larger islands where social and economic opportunities are greater than in neighboring small islands (FIGURE 3-6). Of course, ease of transportation between these islands is also an important factor. The model confirms a frequently observed theory of "circular migration" among islands societies, though we certainly need to base it on more reliable data (see Hugo, 2005; Kakazu, 2003 and 1994).

CONCLUSIONS:

TOWARDS NETWORKING ISLANDS' LEARNING INSTITUTIONS IN THE PACIFIC

Based on the preceding discussion, it is extremely important to establish global learning networks for small island societies which, left to the mercy of market forces, would experience a widening of the information gap with larger economies rather than a narrowing. We should start by better connecting existing networks and focus on creating a competitive advantage for islands by providing unique and quality contents.

A simple networking scheme among the Pacific islands is illustrated in FIG-URE 3-7. Using UH Net (PEACESAT), the Micronesian Distance Learning Consortium has been established. The purpose of the Consortium is to eliminate geographic isolation, and to expand technical infrastructure, human resource development, local decision-making, and bring all Micronesians into the global village while preserving the positive aspects of local culture. All credits from the College of Micronesia are now transferable to the University of Guam. The goal is for students to be able to obtain their prerequisite coursework from an educational institution in their home location, with transferable credits to earn a bachelors degree from the U. of Guam or other universities in the region.

USPNet covers twelve USP member countries and territories. The USP-owned satellite communications network, using VSAT (Very Small Aperture Terminal) earth stations, is located at USP headquarters in Fiji and connects USP centers in eleven other members. When completed, the network will be able to provide satellite tutorials to all USP centers, and in the future, video capability for live lecture delivery and interactive video conferences (see University of Hawaii, 2000). Similar networking arrangements can be made between these islands and Australian nets (UNSW and ANU Nets).

International Small Islands Studies Association (ISISA)
www.ins.net

International Scientific Council for Island Development (INSULA)
www.insula.org

Global Islands Network (GIN)
www.globalislands.net

Small Island Developing States Network
www.sidsnet.org

The Island Gateway (UNU,1997)
www.geic.or.jp

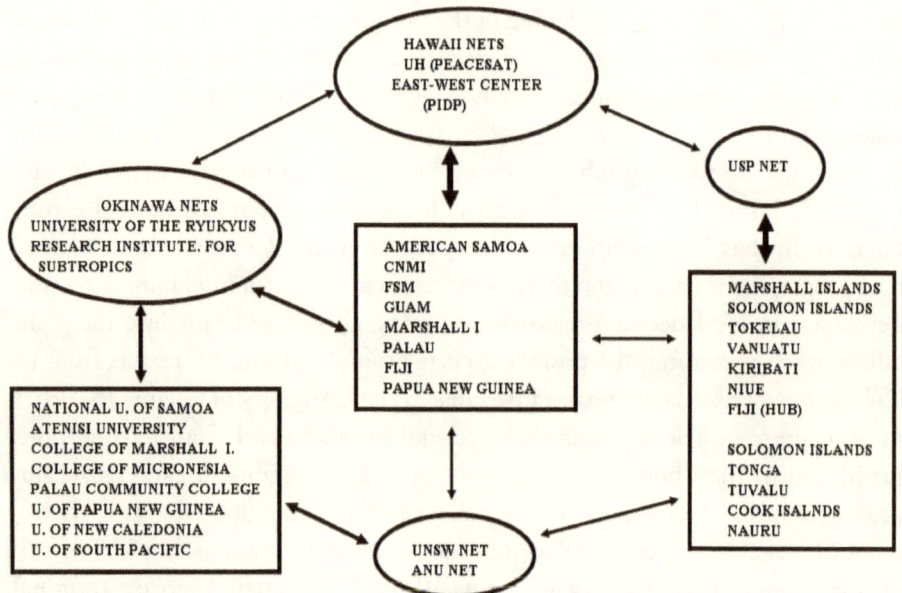

<table>
</table>

HAWAII NETS
UH (PEACESAT)
EAST-WEST CENTER
(PIDP)

USP NET

OKINAWA NETS
UNIVERSITY OF THE RYUKYUS
RESEARCH INSTITUTE. FOR
SUBTROPICS

AMERICAN SAMOA
CNMI
FSM
GUAM
MARSHALL I
PALAU
FIJI
PAPUA NEW GUINEA

MARSHALL ISLANDS
SOLOMON ISLANDS
TOKELAU
VANUATU
KIRIBATI
NIUE
FIJI (HUB)

SOLOMON ISLANDS
TONGA
TUVALU
COOK ISALNDS
NAURU

NATIONAL U. OF SAMOA
ATENISI UNIVERSITY
COLLEGE OF MARSHALL I.
COLLEGE OF MICRONESIA
PALAU COMMUNITY COLLEGE
U. OF PAPUA NEW GUINEA
U. OF NEW CALEDONIA
U. OF SOUTH PACIFIC

UNSW NET
ANU NET

Small Islands Information Network
www.upei.ca

Small Island Developing States
www.un.org/esa/sustdev/sids.htm

Research Institute for Subtropics (Okinawa)
www.subtropics.or.jp

Research Center for Pacific Islands (Kagoshima U., Japan)
cpi.kagoshima-u.ac.jp

Pacific Islands Development Program (East-West Center)
www.eastwestcenter.org

Center for South Pacific Studies (U. of NSW)
www.unsw.edu.au

Centre for Pacific and Asian Studies (U. of Nijmegen)
www.kun.nl

Japan Society of Island Studies (JSIS)
www.gakusen.ac.jp/jsis

Island Resources Foundation (Virgin Islands)
www.irf.org

Islands and Small States Institute (U. of Malta)
www.comnet.mt

MacMillan Brown Centre for Pacific Studies (U. of Canterbury)
www.pacs.cantgerbury.ac.nz

Institute of Island Studies (U. of Prince Edward Island)
www.upei.ca

Center for Pacific Island Studies (U. of Hawaii)
www.hawaii.edu

Research School of Pacific and Asian Studies (ANU)
http://rspas.anu.edu.au/

Center for Asia-Pacific Studies (Ryukyu U., Japan)
www.cc.u-ryukyu.ac.jp

University of the South Pacific (USP)
www.usp.ac.fj

Source: Constructed by H. Kakazu.

FIGURE 3-7. Information Neworking of Pacific Island Universities and Societies: 2005.

To promote such Pacific islands networks we need to work on strategic human resource development, capacity building programs and opportunities. We also need to encourage resource sharing in the region and support activities that will further the development of sustainable infrastructure. A review of the best practices for network utilization and maximization should be undertaken.

The Center for Asia-Pacific Island Studies of the University of the Ryukyus, an institution that this speaker is responsible for, has Memoranda of Understanding with several universities and colleges in the Pacific islands. It seeks to promote international collaboration and academic exchange focusing on interdisciplinary approaches to problems associated with islands, and aims at contributing directly to the advancement of measures for island development with a focus on issues such as environment, culture, human resources and limited island resources.

Major global, regional and local networking sites are also listed in FIGURE 3-7. The most extensive collection of island links and contacts is the Global Islands Network (GIN) which was officially launched after the Islands of the World VI conference on Prince Edward Island.

NOTES

Samuelson, P.A. and Nordhaus W. D. (2001), p.115.
Crocombe, R.(2001), p.119.
Ibid., p.661.
Carvalho, A. (2003), P.195.
Noris, P. (2001), p.6.

REFERENCES

Carvalho, A. 2003. "Nikkei Communities in Japan." In: Goodman, Peach, Takenaka, C. and White, P. (ed.). *Global Japan*. London: Routledge Curzon.
Crocombe, R.2001. *The South Pacific*. Suva: University of the South Pacific.
Economides, N.1994. "The Economics of Network." *International Journal of Industrial Organization*, no. 14, pp.651-662.
Higa, C. 2002. *The SCS/PEACESAT Integration Project: Bridging Satellite Networks and Evaluating Shared Program Areas Between Japan and the Pacific Island*. Chiba: National Institute of Multimedia Education.
Hugo, G. 2005. "Circular Migration: Keeping Development Rolling?" Washington, DC: Migration Policy Institute, pp.1-5.
Jayaraman, T.K. 2003. "Is There a Case for a Single Currency for the South Pacific

Islands?" *Pacific Economic Bulletin,* vol. 18, No.1, pp. 41-53.

Kakazu, H. 1994. *Sustainable Development of Small Island Economies.* Boulder: Westview Press,

_____. 2003. "Networking Pacific Island Societies." A Keynote Speech at the World Summit on Information Society (WSIS) Side Event. Tokyo: United Nations University, pp.1-12.

_____. 2003. "Globalization and Regional Economy." Economic Research Center, School of Economics, Nagoya University, *Monograph,* no. 127, pp.1-33.

Noris, P. 2001. *Digital Divide: Civic Engagement, Information Poverty, and the Internet Worldwide.* Cambridge: Cambridge University Press.

Orita, Tomonori. 2004. "Proposal for the Development of Distance Education and E-Health of Micronesia 3 Regions." *Report of Pacific Islands Digital Opportunities (PIDO) Research Committee: Towards Paradigm Shift of Pacific Islands.* Tokyo: Sasakawa Pacific Island Nations Fund.

Samuelson, P.A. and Nordhaus W. D. 2001. *Economics.* 7th edition. New York: McGraw-Hill.

Sasakawa Pacific Islands Nations Fund. August 2004. Pacific Island Digital Opportunity (PIDO) Research Committee, *A Report of Pacific Island Digital Opportunity: Towards Paradigm Sift of Pacific Islands.* Tokyo.

University of Hawaii (PEACESAT). 2001. Pacific Newsbytes Project. Tokyo: Sasakawa Pacific Island Nations Fund.

Willcox, B.J., D.C. Willcox and M. Suzuki. 2000. *The Okinawa Program: Learn the Secrets to Healthy Longevity.* New York: New York Times.

Chapter 4

Japan's Small and Remote Islands: Development Policy and Performance

Introduction

According to the Ministry of National Land, Infrastructure and Transport (MN-LIT), which is responsible for Japan's land development plan including small and remote islands (SRIs), "island" is defined as land area with the total coastal line of 0.1km and over. There are 6,852 SRIs extending 2,500 miles (4,000 km) from Northern tip of Hokkaido to Southern tip of the Ryukyu archipelago. Of which about 315 SRIs are inhabited at the end of 2000 (TABLE 4-1). These islands account for 2% and 0.6% of Japan's total land area and population respectively. They contribute to Japan's 4,470 thousands km2 of Exclusive Economic Zone (EEZ) which is twelve times larger than Japan's total land area.

The largest inhabited SRI is Sado Island with land area of 855 km2 and 72,173 resident population, while the smallest one is Shinjo Island of Okinawa Prefecture with land area of 1.58 km2 and 1 resident population.

Table 4-1. Outline of Japan's Islands: 2000

	Number of islands	Area km2	Population 1,000
All islands	6,852	377,873	737
Uninhabited	6,415	370,135	0
Inhabited	315	7,738	737
Under RIDA	263	5,267	473
Okinawa	40	1,015	129
Amami	8	1,239	132
Ogasawara	4	67	3
Major islands by land size and population			
Sado		855	72
Amamioshima		720	72
Tsushima		697	41
Yakushima		505	14
Tanegashima		446	36
Fukueshima		321	43
Iriomote		289	2
Tokunoshima		248	28
Shimajiri		243	18
Ishigakijima		223	43

Notes: RIDA = Remote Island Development Act
Okinawa Island is not included.

Source: Statistical Yearbook on Remote Islands, 2002

Japanese SRIs are so diversified geographically, culturally, historically and economically, four different national development laws and plans have been enforced. They are the Remote Island Development Act (RIDA) which covers 263 SRIs located in the vicinity of the Japanese mainland, Hokkaido, Shikoku and Kyushu. The Okinawa Development & Promotion Special Measures Act covers forty SRIs of Okinawa Prefecture; Amami Development & Promotion Special Measures Act covers eight SRIs; and Ogasawara Development & Promotion Special Measures Act covers four SRIs in 2002. The island areas covered by the Special Measures

Acts were administered by the United States military forces after the Second World War. This chapter focuses on the inhabited SRIs under the RIDA, Amami islands and Okinawa islands which cover 98% of Japan's SRIs designated by the above laws for policy measures.

Five years after the defeat of the Pacific War, the Japanese government implemented socio-economic reconstruction programs under the National Land Comprehensive Development Law which was enacted in 1950. The Law primarily aimed at reconstructing its war-devastated socio-economic structure and standards of living to that of the prewar levels. The major focus was to increase food production. The Law mandated to institute long-term as well as mid-term development plans and programs. In the process of implementing these national development plans, the regional imbalances in terms of social infrastructure and living standards became evident. Local governments, remote island governments in particular, pushed strenuously for development policies that focused on small and remote island areas. As a result, the RIDA was enacted in 1953 and revised in 2002 (see Suzuki, 2006).

THE REMOTE ISLAND DEVELOPMENT ACT (RIDA)

According to the RIDA, inhabited SRIs are classified into the following five categories:
   (1) outer ocean islands with an easy daily access to mainland city centers;
   (2) inland ocean islands with an easy daily access to mainland city centers;
   (3) cluster of very small islands with a difficult daily access to mainland city centers;
   (4)large, isolated islands with a difficult daily access to mainland city centers; and
   (5)very small isolated islands with a difficult daily access to mainland city centers.

The following major criteria must be satisfied to be designated by the Act as an outer ocean island:
   (1)it must be surrounded by ocean with a population of a 100 or over;
   (2)it is 5km or 3.1 miles from mainland;
   (3)islanders' daily life depends heavily on mainland;
   (4)transportation system is not reliable;
   (5)SRI authorities' "request principle" is adopted to be included in the RIDA.

A major objective of the 1953 RIDA was to improve relative underdevelopment of the SRIs through implementing socio-economic projects as to improve islanders' livelihoods as well as promoting the welfare of the people (see Japan Association of Remote Island Development, 1989). These development measures would at the same time contribute to the growth of the national economy. In order to achieve these objectives:

(1) The Remote Island Development Plan, programs and projects are prepared;

(2) The national government gives high priority to such programs and projects, and appropriates an annual budget for their the implementation;

(3) A Remote Island Development Council (RIDC) is established for the purpose of studying and identifying key development issues and proposals.

The RIDA has been revised every ten years to incorporate socio-economic changes surrounding the SRIs. Major revisions were made for the 2002 RIDA which clearly stated the three national roles of the SRIs: (a) national land conservation, (b) utilization of marine resources and (c) environmental conservation. The most important objective of the 1953 RIDA, namely improvement of underdevelopment was deleted. It is highly unusual to state clear national roles in regional development acts such as the RIDA. This can be understood from recent incidents and disputes surrounding Japanese uninhabited islands located on international borders such as the Senkaku/Diaoyutai islands bordering China and Takeshima (Bamboo) Island or Tokdo (Lonesome Island) bordering with Korea. These uninhabited rock islands have become a matter of hot socio-economic as well as security issues in recent years as we have already discussed in Chapter 7. Senkaku Island is a typical case of territorial dispute over resources (oil and natural gas), while Takeshima Island is a dispute over the Exclusive Economic Zone (EEZ) and security. Particularly security has become an imminent issue because of recent discoveries that these islands have become key bases for smugglings and reconnaissance activities.

Under the new RIDA, ten regions were initially designated as remote island development regions for actual implementation of the development plans. Initially, all SRI projects were implemented under separate and individual government agencies. After the enactment of the RIDA, the Division of Islands Affairs, City and Regional Development Bureau of the Ministry of Land, Infrastructure and Transport (MLIT) shoulders the sole responsibility in administrating the island affairs including planning and budgeting for the SRIs. The consolidation of SRI affairs into one agency was a remarkable breakthrough in Japan's remote island development policies considering the notorious administrative red tape and cumbersome interagency negotiations and coordination.

THE REMOTE ISLAND DEVELOPMENT PLANS AND PERFORMANCES

The Plan serves as basis for such island development and is revised approximately every ten years. These plans are devised by the local authorities, which are then presented to the MLIT which in turn presents it to the Diet. The Plan and programs must include projects with priority. After careful deliberation and assessments, the MLIT will determine the projects which should be subsidized and the projects which should be implemented directly by the national agencies. It should also be noted that each prefectural government implements its own SRI projects such as subsidizing transportation costs and sponsoring various island events.

Following the First Ten-Year Plan (1953-1962) which focused on basic human needs, the Second Plan (1963-1972) emphasized the improvement of basic socio-economic conditions to close the existing socio-economic gaps between the remote islands and the mainland. The Third Plan (1973-1982) focused on improving facilities for basic living environments such as roads, electricity and water supply, and production activities while the Fourth Plan (1983-1992) was concerned with improving social infrastructures to improve the living conditions. Under the Fifth Plan (1993-2002), both hardware (improvements of infrastructure) and software (management of facilities and organizations) approaches have been adopted so that a more comprehensive approach to development may be taken.

The Sixth Plan (2003-2012) has been implemented under the new RIDA which emphasized island ownership and initiatives in improving all aspects of island life. Thus, the concepts of the Plans have changed over time in response to national development needs as well as specific needs of the SRIs.

Development Projects and Incentives

Currently the MLIT implements various projects including (a) community islands development projects, (b) study on fiscal and monetary incentive systems to stimulate SRIs' economic activities, (c) projects to facilitate exchange between SRIs and the rest of the world and (d) infrastructure development.

These projects are implemented with fiscal as well as monetary incentives such as (a) higher rate of subsidy for infrastructure development, (b) special depreciation for machinery and equipment for manufacturing and hotel businesses, (c) exemption of special land holding tax for manufacturing and hotel related businesses, (d) national subsidies for exempted local business and property taxes, and (e) special low lending rate of the government-affiliated financial institutions.

Performances

More than forty years after the implementation of the RIDA and the Plans, the performance is mixed. As can be seen from FIGURE 4-1, the total population of the SRIs has continuously declined from over one million, or 1% of the national total in 1960 to about half million, or 0.4% of the total in 2000. The depopulation in the SRIs was particularly accelerated during the period of Japan's high economic growth in the 1960s and early 1970s. Japan needed to mobilize its human and non-human resources to catch up with the Western industrialized economies in a short period of time. Resources including human, technology, capital, and infrastructure were shifted to metropolitan industrial belts such as Tokyo, Osaka and Nagoya areas. As a result, massive labor force migration from remote areas began to fill the labor demand gap caused by high economic growth in the metropolitan areas.

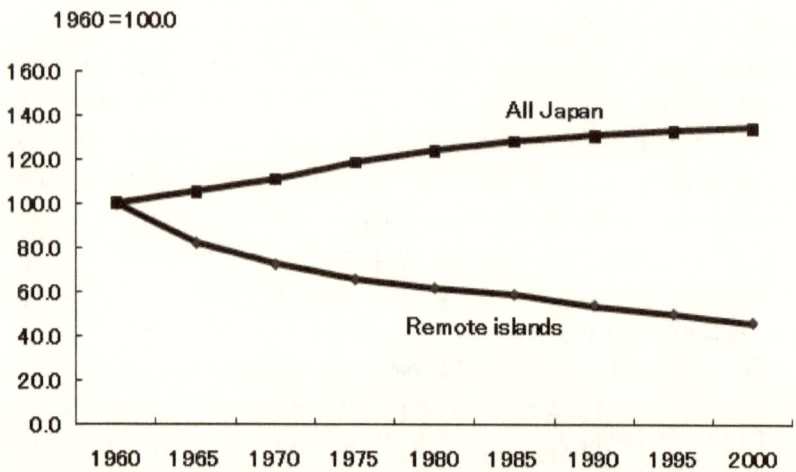

1960＝100.0

Source: Same as TABLE 4-1.

FIGURE 4-1. Population Trends of Japan's Remote Islands: 1960-2000.

In many cases, entire populations of small islands out-migrated by the early 1970s. Japanese style of large-scale development inevitably accompanied a massive relocation of human resources from remote underdeveloped areas to metropolitan high growth centers. Although the out-migration from the SRIs has slowed down in recent years as a consequence of Japan's stagnated economic growth rate coupled with the changes in lifestyle, the population is still declining due mainly to reduced birth rate or negative natural rate of increase (birth rate – death rate). Japan's total population declined in 2005. If current depopulation continues, those very small SRIs with populations of less than 500 each, which account for nearly 60% of the total SRIs, may become unpopulated islands within the foreseeable future unless effective policy measures are implemented (TABLE 4-2).

The population decline due to the low birth rate and high rate of out-migration naturally accelerated the aging of SRIs population (TABLE 4-3). The people sixty-four years old and above accounted for 29.4% of the population in 2000, much higher than the national average of 20%. An aging population not only reduces economic activities, but also creates additional burden to households and local municipalities in the forms of health care and social welfare expenditures.

TABLE 4-2. Japan's Remote Islands
by Size of Population: 1997

Population Size (person)	Number of Islands	Percent Composition
1~99	97	29.8
100~500	98	30.2
500~999	46	14.2
1000~1999	25	7.7
2000~2999	14	4.3
3000~3999	10	3.1
4000~4999	8	2.5
5000~9999	13	4.0
10000~29999	6	1.8
30000~49999	6	1.8
50000 and over	2	0.6
Total	325	100.0

Source: See TABLE 4-1.

TABLE 4-3. Japan's Remote Island Population by Age and Sex: 2000

	Percent Composition	Male	Female
Young population age under 14	14.2	15.0	13.4
Productive population age 15-64	56.4	59.7	53.0
Elder population age over 64	29.4	24.8	33.2
Total	100.0	100.0	100.0

Source: See TABLE 4-1.

Under the plans, the national government spent about four trillion yen for the period of 1953-1998 in various infrastructure projects such as industrial development (45%), transportation (37%), land conservation (14%) and social and environmental improvements (4%). The amount of public expenditures increased from \741 million in 1953 to \167,948 million in 1998, or an increase of more than 200 times. SRIs' share of public expenditure in Japan's total public expenditure increased from 0.73% to 1.8% during the period. The share is more striking considering the fact that SRIs' population accounts for only 0.4% of the national total.

These public expenditures have not only improved various infrastructures of the SRIs, but also they have contributed to sustain island life providing jobs in public works. Public works, which are included in the secondary industry together with manufacturing in TABLE 4-4, have expanded more rapidly than the national average. The primary industrial activities, which account for more than 26% in terms of employment compared to less than 10% of the national average, have been largely supported by public work activities in the past decades.

TABLE 4-4. Employed Persons by Industry: 1985-2000
(percent composition)

	Remote Islands			All Japan		
	Construction Industry	Manufacturing Industry	Tertiary Industry	Construction Industry	Manufacturing Industry	Tertiary Industry
1985	34.7	21.8	43.5	9.3	33.2	57.5
1990	31.2	21.1	47.7	7.2	33.5	59.3
1995	27.5	21.2	51.3	6.0	31.8	62.2
2000	26.0	21.0	53.0	5.0	30.0	65.0

Source: See TABLE 4-1.

Per capita income of the SRIs increased about three times in the past decades narrowing the income gap with the national average from 68% in 1980 to 73.3% in 1997 (FIGURE 4-2). Although this is a remarkable achievement, a large portion of improvement in the standards of living was attributable to the depopulation of the SRIs. We should note, however, that some SRIs experienced population increase along with the expansion of tourism and agricultural activities.

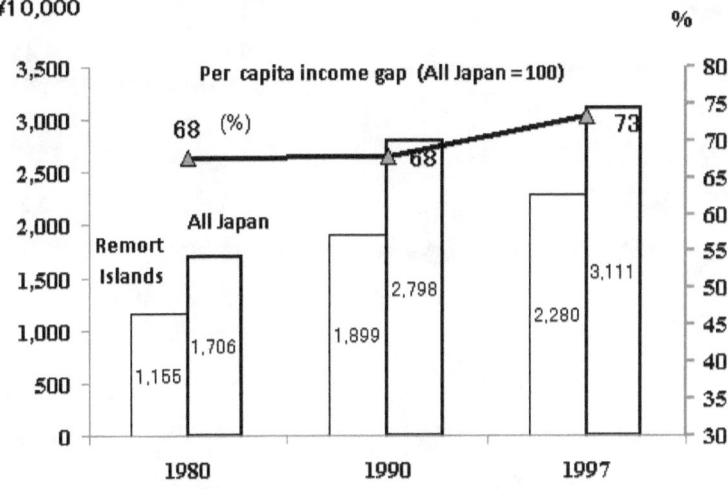

Source: See Table 4-1.

FIGURE 4-2. Per Capita Income Gap between Japan Proper
and Remote Islands: 1980-1997.

SRIs have increasingly depended on fiscal transfers from national as well as prefectural governments to finance their growing fiscal needs. As a result, the municipal governments of the SRIs could meet only about 20% of their fiscal needs from their own revenue sources compared to the national average of about 40% (FIGURE 4-3). Almost all SRI municipal governments face serious financial shortfalls.

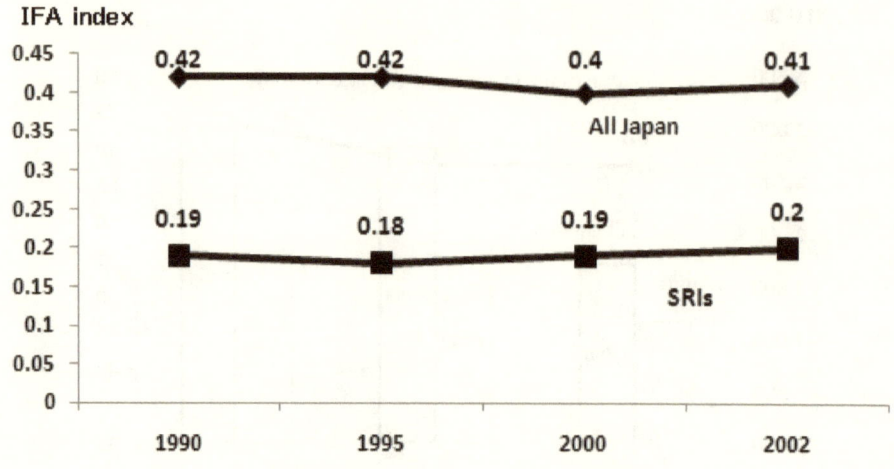

Notes: IFA (%)= Normal Fiscal Revenues/Normal Fiscal Needs
IFA less than 1% means fiscal supports from the central government.
Only those "island municipalities."

Source: See Table 4-1.

**FIGURE 4-3. Index of Financial Affordability (IFA)
Japan Proper and Islands Compared: 1990-2002.**

Except for a few islands of Okinawa, almost all SRIs have experienced net out-migration. Particularly younger generation and young women tend to migrate more than the elderly and men because of limited opportunities for job and higher education on island communities. Only 11.6% of all high school graduates of the SRIs remain on the islands after graduation in 2003 (FIGURE 4-4). Continuous out-migration of the younger generation has been a serious issue for many years from the standpoints of sustainable development of island communities. This trend will accelerate in the coming years because of declining public investment and job opportunities on the islands unless drastic policy changes along with islanders' efforts are made.

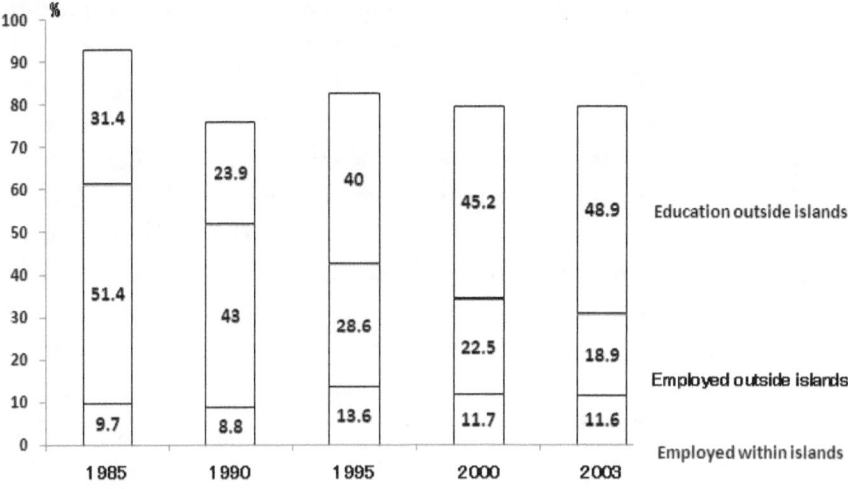

Notes: It does not add up to 100% due to "unknown responses."
Source: See FIGURE 4-1.

FIGURE 4-4. High School Graduates and Their Career Paths.

Other indicators such as per household medical service, broad band and sanitation facilities all lag behind of the mainland. As we have seen in Chapter 1, information and communication technology (ICT) is an effective tool to overcome the tyranny of distance and to reduce the cost of communication for the SRIs, the actual performance indicate the widening digital divide between the island communities and the mainland. Only 25% of SRIs' households benefited from the broadband facilities (ADSL, cable internet and optical fiber) compared to 62.8% of the national average in 2004.

AMAMI DEVELOPMENT & PROMOTION SPECIAL MEASURES ACT

This section briefly introduces the Amami Development & Promotion Special Measures Act and its performances (for detail discussions, see Minamura, 2003, Development Bank of Japan, 2003 and Oshiro, 2007). Amami islands are geographically, historically and culturally deeply linked with Okinawa islands as an integral part of the Ryukyu archipelagos. The Unites States Civil Administration of the Ryukyu Islands (USCAR) ruled Amami and Okinawa after the Pacific war. Amami islands, however, were returned to the Japanese administration in 1953, and became a part of Kagoshima Prefecture. The main reason for the early return to Japan was that Amami islands did not house any U.S. military bases. Thus Amami's development started after 1953 under the Amami Development & Promotion Special Measures Act which was implemented in 1954. It is interesting to note that Kagoshima Prefecture was already implementing Japan's Remote Island Development Act (RIDA) for its nineteen islands.

The reason for a separate special development law was that Amami islands struggled to recover from their war-torn economy and social infrastructures. Amami's per capita income in 1953 was only 50% of Kagoshima Prefecture whose per capita income was one of the lowest in Japan. In contrast to Okinawa, where recovery from the war-devastated economy progressed rapidly owing mainly to massive military base construction activities, Amami's development was totally left to islanders' self-efforts without any significant impetus from the national government. Thus under the U.S. administration, socio-economic development occurred unevenly among the islands.

Under the Amami special development law, eight islands including Amami-Oshima, Tokunoshima, Okinoerabujima, Yoron, Kikaijima, Kakeromajima, Yorojima, Ukejima are covered. The first ten-year development plan (1954-63) aimed to recover islands' standards of living to their pre-war levels through public investments in infrastructures and promoting local industry. Amami is now implementing its fifth development plan (2003-2021).

The accumulated total public expenditures to finance Amami's development plans amounted to nearly two trillion yen in the past fifty two years (FIGURE 4-5). Of which, 63% are met by national government and the rest by Kagoshima Prefectural Government. The public expenditures, however, declined in the first part of the fifth plan reflecting tight financial conditions at both the national and prefectural levels. This trend will, no doubt, continue in the foreseeable future.

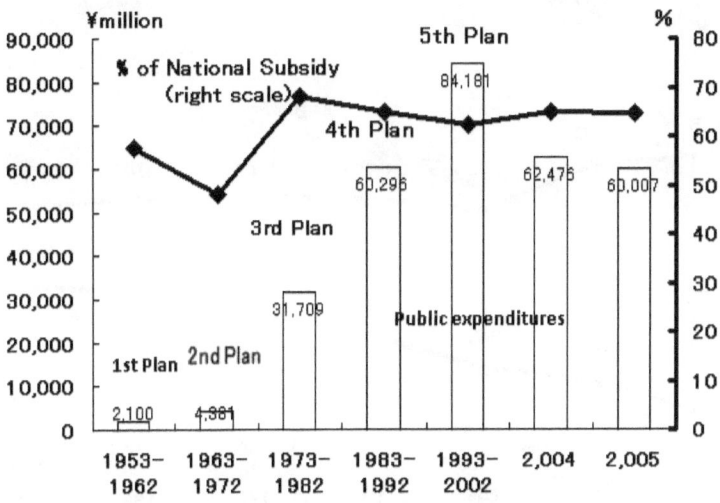

Notes: Plans are implemented for five-year periods.
Public finance or expenditures are yearly averages.

Source: Kagoshima Prefecture Amami Office, *Outline of Amami Gunto*, various issues.

FIGURE 4-5. Public Finance for Amami's Development Plans: 1953-2005.

Overall evaluations of the plans are mixed. The islands' basic needs such as food security, housing, water, electricity, sanitation and infrastructures are successfully being met, but the plans have failed to create self-reliant, sustainable economic growth process (see Minamura, 2003). As a result, Amami's population declined continuously from about 200,000 when the first plan was implemented to 126,000 in 2005, a decrease of 39%. This decline is in stark contrast to Okinawa where population nearly doubled during the period (FIGURE 4-6). All major islands of Amami experienced continuous depopulation, particularly during the first and second development plans (FIGURE 4-7). Amami islands' depopulation was due to net out-migration to Amami City (former Naze City) areas and the mainland where job and educational opportunities are greater than on these small, rural islands.

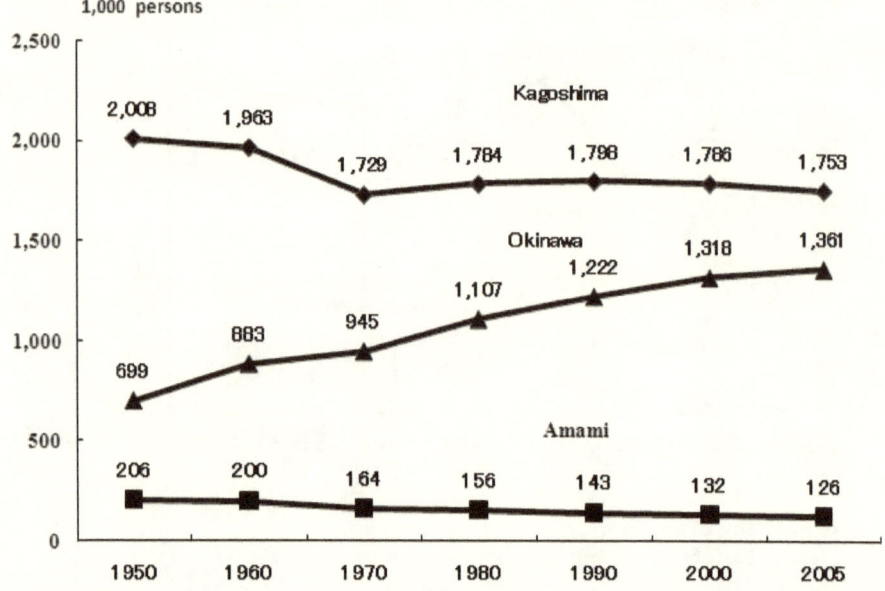

Source: National Census.

FIGURE 4-6: Population Trends of Kagoshima, Okinawa and Amami: 1950-2005.

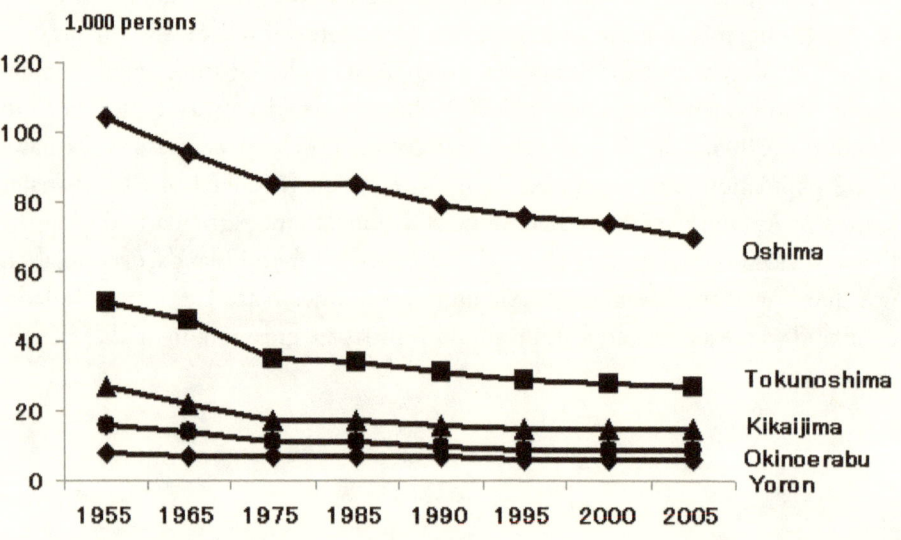

Source: Population Census.

FIGURE 4-7. Population Trends of Amami Gunto by Island: 1950-2005.

Amami's gross island product (GIP) was about 10% of Okinawa. But Amami's per capita income was higher than Okinawa in 2004 (FIGURE 4-8). This is due to its continuous depopulation because per capita income is calculated through dividing GIP by total population.

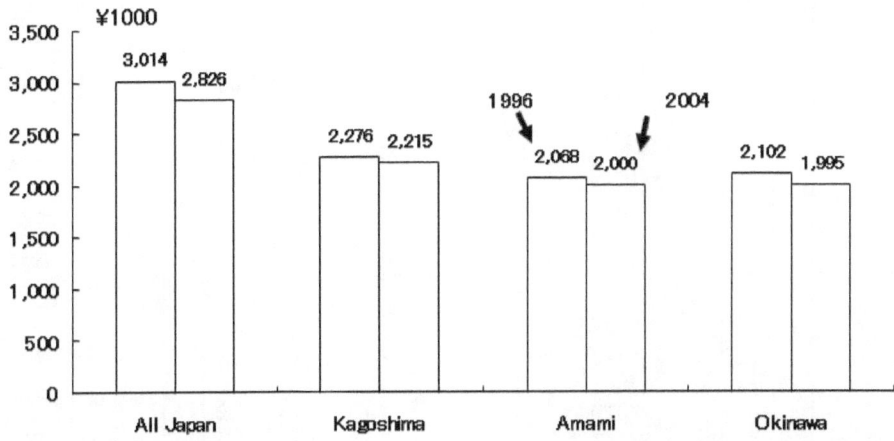

Source: See FIGURE 4-6.

FIGURE 4-8. Per Capita Incomes of All Japan, Kagoshima, Amami and Okinawa: 1996 & 2004.

Like any other island economies, Amami followed industrial transformation from goods producing activities such as agriculture and manufacturing to tertiary activities such as services, trade, utilities and communications (FIGURE 4-9). Particularly Amami's share of manufacturing income declined to one-fourth in the past decade due mainly to declining trends of Amami's major manufacturing products such as sugar processing and Oshima *tsumugi* (silk weaving).

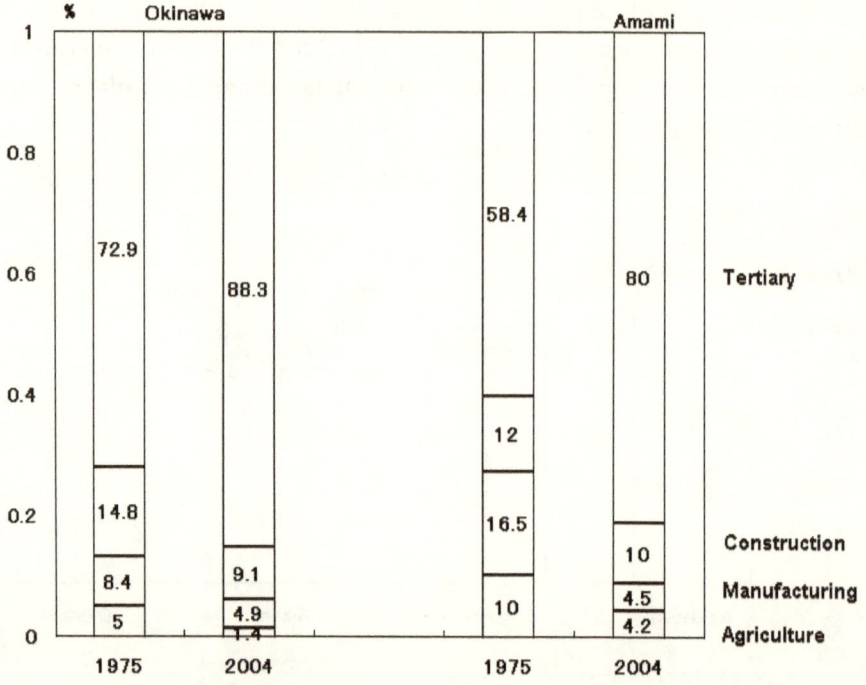

Source: Kagoshima Prefecture *Amami Office Outline of Amami Gunto*, various issues.

FIGURE 4-9. Changes in Industrial Structure Compared: Okinawa and Amam: 1975 & 2004.

Sugar processing depends on Amami's main agricultural crop, namely sug-arcane, which has rapidly lost its international competition. Despite protection policies for domestic sugar producers, Japan's sugar is still about five times higher than its international price. The construction activities, which play an important role in supporting the agriculture of islands and rural communities, have also de-clined in recent years due largely to fiscal constraints of central as well as local governments.

For many decades, sugar and Oshima *tsumugi* were pillar export products of Amami, so much so that Amami islanders proudly call these two most important products as two black diamonds, namely brown (black) sugar from the locally grown sugar canes and the brilliant black color of Oshima *tsumugi* derive from the traditional method of *dorozome* (dyed by muddy clays).

Unlike the typical Japanese kasuri, Oshima tsumugi is distinctive in its shiny black-brown color, symbolic design, and the complexity of the process of creating. Oshima tsumugi represents all the qualities of Japanese high-grade silk fabric with symbolic patterns and textures. It is dyed with special mud and wood from the native tree Teichigi/Sharinbai which exists only in Amami-Oshima. The process is so complex that to make a bolt of cloth takes up to a year (http://www. csuchico. edu/-mtoku/ vc/ Exhibitions/oshima/ voices html).

The *tsumugi* industry employed about 20,000 persons with ¥300 million sales in 1980. The sale of the best-known Amami product, however, plummeted to less than ¥50 million in just two decades in 2005 owing mainly to keen international competition particularly from Korea and lack of innovation and successors (FIGURE 4-10).

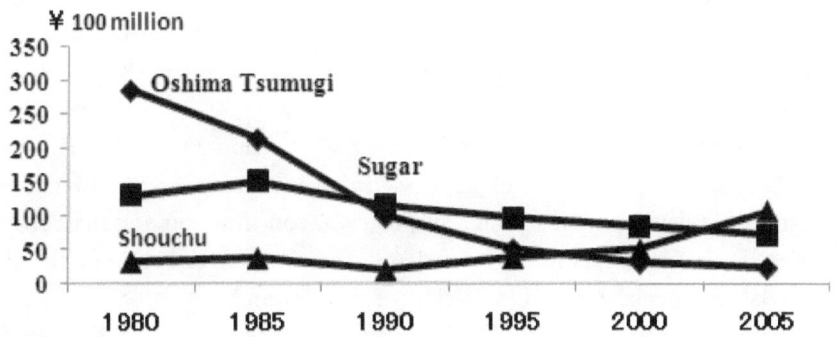

Note: Sugar = sales of sugarcane.

Source: See FIGURE 4-5.

FIGURE 4-10. Sales of Amami's Main Local Products.

Sales of sugar also suffered the same plight as *tsumugi* declining from ¥300 million in 1990 to ¥200 million in the past decade. *Kokuto Shochu*, liquor made from black-brown sugar molasses, however, pushed up its sales along with nationwide "*Shouchu* boom."

Although Amami islands are facing serious development issues, they are blessed with rich natural and cultural heritages for sustainable tourism development. Amami islanders are also well-known for their healthy lifestyles which result in envious longevity. The current fourth development plan aims to capitalize on Amami's comparative advantages. Amami's ambitious so-called "*Thalassotherapie*" or *thalasso* therapy (water in Greek) projects and sustainable natural park concept which is aimed at registering as a natural world heritage such as Japan's Yakushima and Shirokami Sanchi, are progressing well.

Amami should also make use of its well-known longevity and high fertility rate. Amami's number of centenarians per ten thousands population was sixty-six persons in 2003 compared with Okinawa (forty-two persons) and national average (sixteen persons). Also Amami's fertility rate, number of birth per woman, was 2.22 compared with the national average 1.44. This is an important "sales point" for Amami in view of Japan's rapid aging population and projected continuous depopulation.

In spite of their high fertility rate, Amami islands are facing enormous challenges ahead mainly because of their shrinking population and industrial bases. The islands, however, are blessed with rich natural endowments including fertile soil, unspoiled beaches, natural bays and rich forests. Despite continuous depopulation, islanders maintain their strong identity as Amamians through their traditional cultures and mutual help systems called *yuimaru*. Amami's future sustainable development depends largely on how the islanders can make use of these endowments.

A concept of "islands-to- islands network" is proposed (FIGURE 4-11). The main idea is to have divisions of labor or "linkages" among Amami islands toward a sustainable development through production, consumption and networking activities. Each island has its comparative island advantage. For example, Okino-erabu Island specializes in production of flowers and vegetables, Tokunoshima in livestock, Yoron in fishery, Oshima in Oshima-*tusumugi* and *Kokuto Shochu,* and eco- and green tourism in all islands. Despite a great potential of tourism development, particularly eco- and green tourism, Amami's tourism industry has stagnated for many years with about 400,000 visitors (see Kagoshima Prefecture, 2006).

Goods produced within the chain of islands should be consumed within the islands to "displace imports" which will be discussed in more detail in the next chapter. Locally produced goods must be able to compete with imports in terms of quality and price to give fair choice to the consumers. At least islands should have comparative advantage in transporting these goods. Therefore in order to realize this development model, the most efficient intra-island transportation systems must be established.

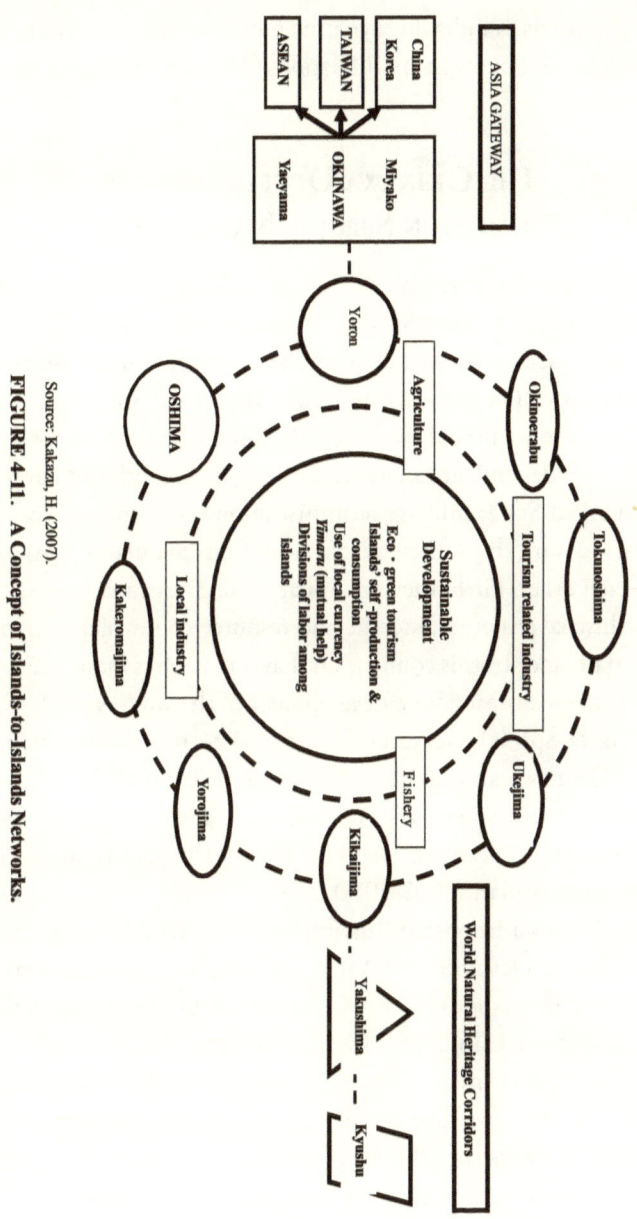

Source: Kakazu, H. (2007).

FIGURE 4-11. A Concept of Islands-to-Islands Networks.

Creating markets within islands may not be enough to sustain islands' growing productive capacity. At the same time, Amami islands need to network with other islands such as Okinawa, Miyako, Yaeyama Yakushima which are also linked with large metropolitan markets. In view of Amami's abundant flora and fauna, including the world famous "Amami rabbit" (Amami *no Kuro Usagi*), a primitive dark-furred rabbit which is found only in Amami Oshima and Tokunoshima), have been appealing to create corridors of world islands natural heritage covering the entire Ryukyu archipelago. Amami also needs to link with dynamic East Asia such as Taiwan, China, Korea and the Association of Southeast Asian Nations (ASEAN) through Okinawa islands.

THE OKINAWA DEVELOPMENT & PROMOTION SPECIAL MEASURES ACT

Okinawa or Ryukyu Islands are covered by the Okinawa Development & Promotion Special Measures Act (Okinawa Special Measures Act) because of special historical, geographical and socio-economic characteristics of these small islands (Okinawa's development issues will be fully discussed in Chapter 10). Okinawa islands differ in many ways from those covered by Japan's Remote Island Development Act. First, Okinawa was an independent kingdom until 1878. Second, Okinawa islands were under direct United States military administration for twenty-seven years after the end of the Pacific war. Third, they are far away from mainland Japan. Fourth, they are far from each other. Fifth, they are much more diversified in terms of size, flora and fauna, industrial structure, income and resource endowments than islands near the Japanese mainland. In this context, Okinawa may offer many interesting aspects and lessons for the socio-economic development of the world's small islands.

The Okinawa Special Measures Act are: (a) to fill socio-economic gaps that exist between Okinawa and mainland Japan, and (b) to achieve, in the long run, a self-sustainable development. The Act mandated the drafting of a ten-year development plan which has been renewed four times. The plan is now in its mid-stage of the fourth ten-year plan (2002-2011). In order to implement the Okinawa Special Measures Act, two important institutions were established at the same time. One is the Okinawa Development Agency (ODA) which is a central government organization directly responsible for Okinawa's overall development. The ODA was integrated into the Cabinet Office in 2002 as a part of the administrative reform of the central government. Despite the reform, the basic functions and implementations of the Okinawa development plan, however, has remained almost unchanged. The other one is the Okinawa Development Finance Corporation (ODF) which is a government -affiliated, long-term development bank.

The Okinawa Special Measures Act is based on three incentive programs. The most important program is direct government investment in infrastructures such as roads, ports, dams and human resources development. The second incentive program is government subsidies to prefectural and local governments which range from 70% to as high as 90% of project costs. The third one is indirect incentives program such as tax credits, subsidized interest rates, wages, preferential import quota and duties and reduced administrative procedures. These incentive systems are summarized in TABLE 4-5.

TABLE 4-5. Incentive Systems of Okinawa Development & Promotion Measures Act

Okinawa Development Measures Act (Revised in 2002) →

Okinawa Development Plan (Fourth Plan, 2002-2011) ←

	Corporate tax credit	Special Measures (Incentive)		Tax credit on real estate	Import duties	Finance	Special subsidies
		Investment credit tax Special depreciation					
Tourism plan	X	Machinery '(15%)	Building '(8%)	●	X	●	
ICT plan	35%	Machinery 35%				●	80% of connection fees
Primary industry plan	X	Machinery (15%)	Building '(34%)	●	X	●	Infrastructures
Employment plan	X				X	●	Wage subsidy
Special measures for industrial development							
High technology promotion area	X	Machinery (15%)	Bldg. (34%)		X	●	
Special free trade zone	35%	Machinery (15%)	Bldg. (34%)	●	Duty free	●	
Special finance & IT area	35%	Machinery (15%)	Bldg. (34%)	●	X	●	
Small business promotion	X	Machinery (15%)	Bldg. (34%)	X	X	●	
Culture/technology/int'l cooperation							National project
OIST						●●	National project
Industry-government-university collaboration							
R&D							
		Human Resources Development					
						●	Compensation for 3-5 yr. 95%

OIST = Okinawa Institute of Science and Technology

Source: Compiled by Kakazu from the data of the Cabinet Office.

Conversion of returned U.S. military bases: subsidies under the Special Measures Law by 2014
Subsidies for infrastructures (roads, airports, dams, sanitation, etc.)

Government's public investment in infrastructures such as roads, sewage, harbor, rural development, human resources, water and housing amounted to about eight trillion yen since the Okinawa Special Measures Act was implemented in 1972 (FIGURE 4-12). Investments in roads accounted for one-third of the total accumulated investment followed by sewage & sanitation, rural development, harbor & ports, human resource development, water conservation and housing.

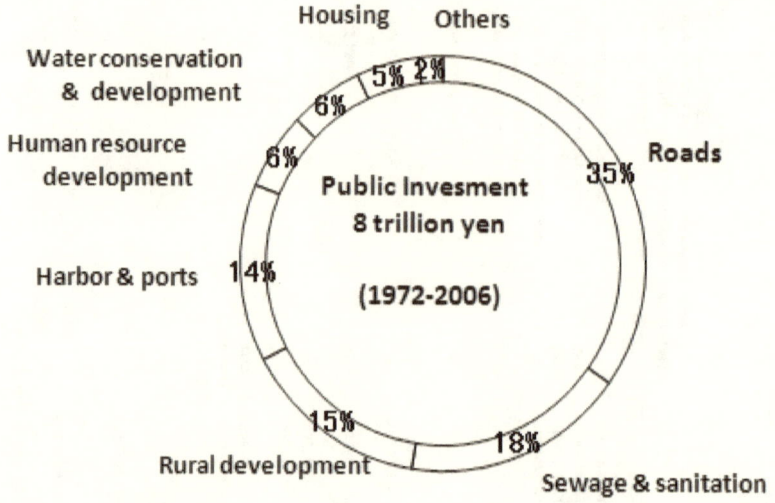

Source: Cabinet Office, *Outline of Okinawa's Economy*, various issues.

FIGURE 4-12. Accumulated Public Investment by Infrastructures Under Okinawa's Development Plans: FY1972-2006.

The levels of these infrastructures have rapidly caught up with the levels of Japan proper. Public investments have gradually shifted from "hard infrastructures" such as roads and ports to "soft infrastructures" such as human resource development, research and development (R&D) and information and communication technology (ICT).

On an annual basis, these public expenditures accounted for more than 30% of Okinawa's GDP in any given year. The massive inflows of public expenditures together with United States military expenditures and rising tourists' spending were the three main engines for Okinawa's higher growth rate than that of mainland Japan. The amount of annual investment, however, declined sharply in the fourth development plan due largely to fiscal constraints of the central government coupled with growing criticism against environmentally unfriendly public works (FIGURE 4-13). The economic impact of public expenditures was also questioned because they did not improve Okinawa's chronic high unemployment rate which will be fully discussed in Chapter 10.

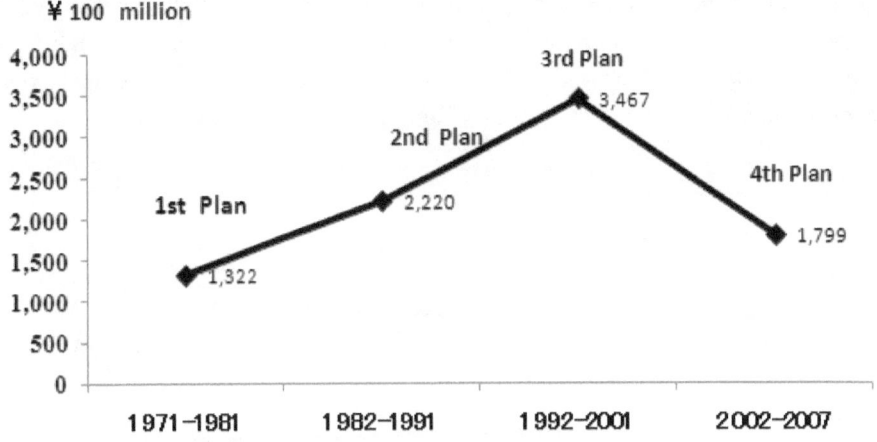

¥ 100 million

Note: Figures are annual averages.

Source: Cabinet Office, *Outline of Okinawa's Economy.*

FIGURE 4-13. Public Investment for Okinawa's Development Plans.

The first objective of the Okinawa Special Measures Act, namely bridging socio-economic gaps between Okinawa and Japanese mainland, has been achieved near satisfaction of Okinawans through four ten-year development plans. However, the economy's capacity and capabilities to transform from a dependency structure to a self-reliance, that is to say, financing its mounting trade deficits through internally generated incomes, has not been achieved successfully like many other island economies. General problems and characteristics of the economy such as rising pressure on the limited land resources, rising unemployment, heavy reliance on government and U.S. base expenditures as major sources of income and employment, reliance on a limited number of primary products and tourism for export earnings, chronic trade balance deficits, diseconomies of scale and high transportation costs still remain unsolved. Particularly creating job opportunities for the young has been the most pressing task for the governing authorities. These development issues and future prospects will be fully discussed in Chapter 10. Here I will focus on Okinawa's outlying very small islands.

Okinawa is the only "island prefecture" in Japan. Within Okinawa Prefecture there are forty small, inhabited, outlying islands. Under the Okinawa Special Measures Act, the Prefectural government is responsible for drafting and implementing Okinawa's remote island development plans. These islands are diversified in population and socio-economic structure. Unlike Japan's remote islands, many islands have experienced an increase of population in recent years being supported by islands tourism boom and new settlements from mainland Japan (FIGURE 4-14). Iriomote, Taketomi, Kohama and Hateruma islands in Yaeyama archipelago are favorite tourist spots for their natural beauty and rich cultures.

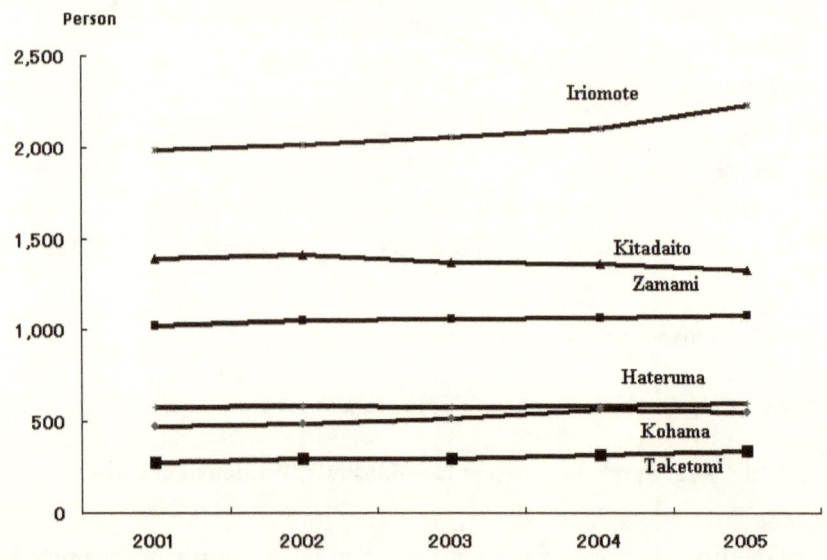

Source: See TABLE 4-5.

FIGURE 4-14. Recent Population Trends of Okinawa's Typical Remote Islands: 2001-2005.

Taketomi Island with a population of less than five hundred is particularly unique because of its following "Sustainable Island's Constitution" adopted in 1987:

The Constitution of Taketomi Island (1987)

1. No Sale! Lands and Houses should not be sold unruly.
2. No Contamination! Beaches, coastal zones and villages should not be contaminated.
3. No Damage! Villages, roads, beaches should be kept unspoiled.
4. No Destruction! Traditional houses, village landscape, natural beauty should not be destroyed.
5. Cultivation! Traditional festivals, ceremonies should be sustained as spiritual symbols, and should be further cultivated for the folk arts and local industry.

[Taketomi Island] Coastal line 9.2km, Elevation 21m, Population 342
Ten minutes from the Ishigakai port.

Zamami Island located nearby Okinawa Island is also a world-famous diving spot because of its well-known pristine beaches, clean, sparkling water and above all colorful tropical fishes and coral reefs. Whale-watching is also a well-publicized tourist attraction of the island. Zamami's population declined to a mere 761 in 1980 from its peak size of 2,074 in 1930 due mainly to net out-migration of the islanders to mainland Okinawa and Japan for better job and educational opportunities. The island population, however, picked up gradually in commensurate with its booming tourism industry recording more than 1,000 residents in 2005.

The number of tourists to Zamami Island reached over 80,000, about eight times more than its total population. The growing number of tourists and increase in the islands' population in recent years have had a major impact on its environment and living conditions. The most important and eminent issue of Zamami's sustainable tourism is its limited water supply. Zamami Island's tourism season overlaps with the dry season from July to February. It is reported that per capita tourists' water consumption is three times higher than the island residents' water consumption (Kamiya, 2007). Its limited water reservoir (dam) will depletes rapidly when tourists flock to the island. As a matter of fact, Zamami suffered severe water shortage in 2004, and consequently water had to be transported from Okinawa Island. The Zamami authorities are considering a tax for visitors in order to support the basic resources to sustain its tourism.

Zamami's tax scheme is shown in FIGURE 4-15. Two tax rates (5% and 10%) are considered as is indicated on the vertical axis, while the number of visitors (NV) are shown on the horizontal axis. Given tourism demand curve (D1), at the 5% of tax level, the number of visitors to the island will be 0NV2. If this level of visitors still exceed island's social carrying capacity, then the tax rate can be raised to 10% (0T2) which will bring the number of visitors to 0NV1. There is no instant, magic solution to the problem. The Zamami authorities need to experiment with the tax rate to provide for the island's sustainable development, that is to say, balancing between incomes generated from the tourism industry and its environmental conservation.

The tax revenues raised in this scheme can be used to improve island's carrying capacity. It is quite possible that Zamami has been selling its tourism resource way below its true market value. Then the tax rate at 10% may have no affect on the number of tourists as indicated by a shift in the tourist demand curve (BD). In this case, the island authority can reap tax revenues without reducing the number of visitors. There are, of course, other means to reduce the number of visitors including direct control of air or boat passengers destined to the island and limiting the number of facilities to accommodate visitors. But these methods are costly and cumbersome for actual implementations compared to the tax scheme.

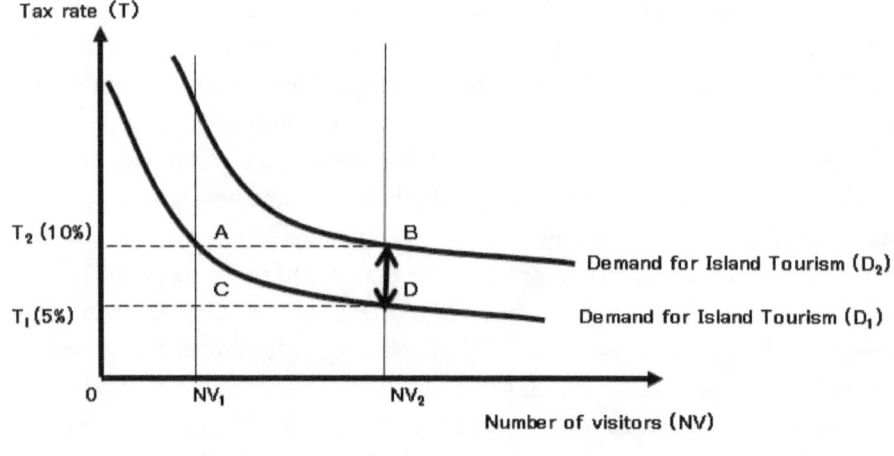

Source: Kakazu, H.

FIGURE 4-15: A Scheme of Sustainable Island Tax.

Kitadaito and Minamidaito islands with combined population less than fifteen hundred, is boast the highest per capita income in Okinawa, supported by large-scale sugarcane cultivation. Minamidaito island is Okinawa's only producer of rum. Rum is an alcoholic beverage made from sugarcane byproducts such as molasses and sugarcane juice by a process of fermentation and distillation. The rum production started just a few years ago by a young female entrepreneur who discovered the high-quality sugar from Minamidaito island.

There are many other unique islands in Okinawa which deserve a separate coverage elsewhere. Yonaguni island, Japan's westernmost and closest island to Taiwan, is one of them. The island produces age-old rice wine called *donan* which contains the highest alcohol content produced in the Asia-Pacific region. Yonaguni island is also famous for its socio-economic exchanges with neighboring Taiwan, and also its mysterious and archeologically controversial underwater rocks which is claimed to be a lost continent such as Plato's Atlantis (see Kimura, 2002).

As we have already discussed, Okinawa's remote islands depend largely on three sources of income namely agriculture, construction and tourism (TABLE 4-6). Some agro-industries such as brown-sugar processing, rice wine and health foods are constantly produced in many islands using indigenous technologies. Except Iejima island located close to the mainland of Okinawa, no remote islands are housing U.S. bases which are major sources of income for many Okinawan municipalities.

Agriculture and fisheries are the mainstays for many small islands. Iejima is well-known for its cut flowers, tobacco and peanuts; Kumejima is blessed with rich marine resources including aquaculture of shrimp and seaweeds; Miyako islands are now a major producer of sugarcane and tobacco as well as high-valued tropical fruits such as mangos. As we have seen, Yaeyama islands including Ishigaki, Taketomi have been rapidly developing in tourism and tourism-related service industries.

Public expenditures for construction projects and public services have been major sources of income accounting for more than 50% of gross island incomes for many very small islands. Public expenditures, however, have steadily declined in recent years due largely to the growing fiscal deficits of all public organizations. Particularly municipalities of very small islands are facing serious financial issues. A new island business opportunities such as environment, tourism and health-related fields must be developed to avert financial disaster in the future (Oshiro, 2007).

TABLE 4-6. Employment Shares of Okinawa's Outer Islands: 2000

	Employed Persons	Primary Industry	Construction Industry	Manufacturing Industry	Tertiary Industry	Services
All Okinawa	555,562	6.1	13.4	5.3	74.2	33.4
Ishigagi	19,805	12.2	13.7	5.5	66.8	30.2
Miyako	21,791	21.3	14.1	4.1	60.0	27.5
Kume Jima	4,041	26.8	13.6	6.2	52.8	22.5
Iejima	2,554	39.2	15.0	3.5	42.3	19.5
Taketomi	142	12.0	4.9	2.1	81.0	50.0
Yonaguni	983	14.1	18.1	9.2	57.9	26.9
Minami Daito	913	23.7	25.6	7.4	42.8	15.3
Iheya	650	14.9	30.8	3.1	51.2	25.1
Aguni	366	4.1	26.2	4.9	64.8	31.4
Tokashiki	387	6.7	6.2	2.6	84.5	58.4

Notes: Ishigaki and Miyako islands are city areas only.
Tertiary Industry includes "Services."

Source: Statistics Division, Okinawa Prefecture.

We briefly discussed the relationship between per capita income and the size of islands in Chapter 1, and concluded that the size of population or GDP is not directly related to the level of per capita income. FIGURE 4-16 shows that this hypothesis holds true for Okinawa's remote islands. Kitadaito with a population of only 700 has the highest per capita income in all of Okinawa's municipal governments, followed by Tokashiki, Minamidaito, Tonaki, Taketomi, and Ishigaki which is the largest island in Okinawa's outlying islands. Both Kitadaito and Minamidaito have recorded top per capita incomes for many years because of their large-scale sugarcane production. It is interesting to note that the per capita incomes for these five remote islands are higher than the average per capita income of Okinawa Prefecture and Naha City, the largest municipality in Okinawa by any measures. Unlike Amami islands, where per capita incomes increased due largely to continuous depopulation, some of Okinawa's remote islands such as Taketomi and Tonaki recorded both increases in population and per capita incomes. The main underlying reason is the expansion of tourism and tourism-related industries which promoted islands' industrial structure from low income primary industry to high income tertiary industry centered on tourism. This suggests that the tourism industry is the main engine to sustain both population and the standards of living in small, remote islands.

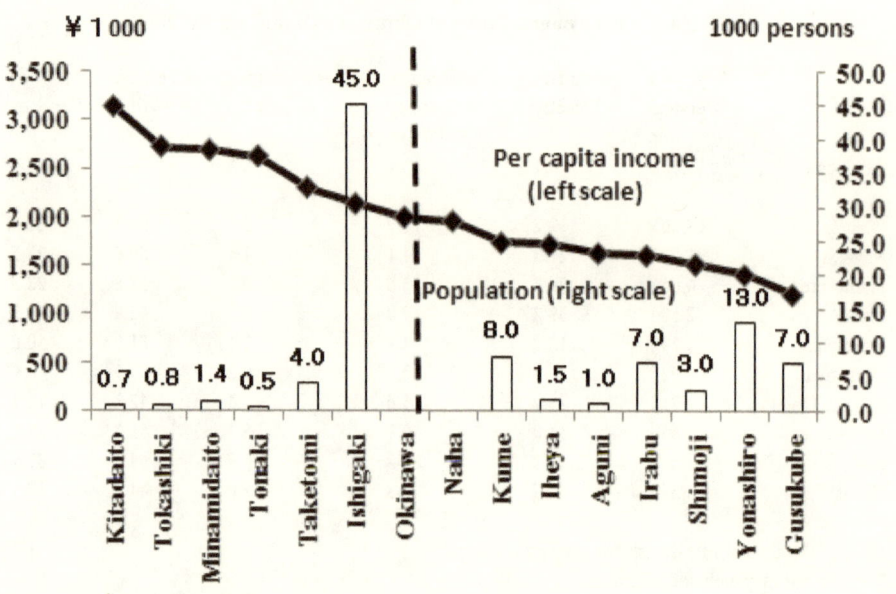

Source: See FIGURE.4-15.

FIGURE 4-16. Population and Per Capita Income of Okinawa's Outlying Islands: 2004.

CONCLUSIONS: LOOKING TOWARDS THE 21ST CENTURY

Japan's SRIs are facing many socio-economic challenges which must be taken up in the immediate future. These challenges are categorized into the following five components:

(1)"Think globally, act locally" has been a Japanese catch word in recent years. The Japanese island communities which have heavily depended on government subsidies and special measures are also facing the consequences of globalization and deregulation of the Japanese economy. SRIs' future plans and programs must shift its emphasis from a domestic orientation to a global perspective.

(2) Sustainable development is another key word for SRIs' future development path. The SRIs are particularly vulnerable to environmental disruptions and natural hazards. How to balance between economic development and environmental protection is probably the most difficult tasks for all island communities.

(3) As discussed, except for several islands in Okinawa, the SRIs are experiencing more rapid depopulation than any other regions in Japan. Depopulation together with a rapidly aging population has become a source of much pessimism, since it may eventually deprive SRIs' socio-economic dynamism, while leaving heavy welfare cost burdens to future generations. Of course, the negative consequences of depopulation can be avoided if SRIs' human resources, particularly women's labor force, are utilized more efficiently with the higher fertility rate.

(4) Another important current tidal wave is a revolution in Information and Communication Technology (ICT) which may free the SRIs from the "tyranny of distance." The information revolution is particularly important to the SRIs because it may solve a seemingly eternal problem of the SRIs, namely the high socio-economic costs arising from its smallness and isolation. On the other hand, the IT revolution may bring the so-called digital divide between the mainland and the SRIs if it is left to unbridled market forces.

(5) The role of and relationships between the SRI authorities and the national government must be carefully reviewed in revising development policies and programs of the SRIs. The recent promulgation of "Decentralization Act" encourages positive roles and initiatives in conducting socio-economic development of the SRIs. It is obvious now that the winner of the 21st century will be those SRIs which can seize development opportunities offered by globalization, tourism, eco-business, ICT revolution, "niche" resources of biodiversity and decentralization.

(6) As is seen in Okinawa's remote islands, tourism and related activities are probably the most important future-oriented industry for particularly very small islands for sustainable development. The development of tourism, however, must be within islands' social carrying capacity.

(7) Japan's SRIs, particularly islands in Amami and Okinawa, are net absorbers of Japan's CO_2 emissions through their huge ocean areas and forestry. Their roles in Japan will be vastly different from the present marginal status if the central government include these island territories in CO_2 emissions reduction scheme.

(8) Finally, some SRIs are located on the international borders establishing

Japan's extended EEZs which can be utilized not only for fishing and marine resources but also for protecting Japan's economic lifeline, namely sea-lane and border security.

REFERENCES

Development Bank of Japan. 2003. *Amami:Korekara no Gojunen* (Amami: Fifty Years from Now). A Report of the Kyushu Branch of the Development Bank of Japan, vol.6, pp.1-12.

Japan Association of Remote Island Development (ed.). 1989. *Thirty Years of Remote Island Development.* Tokyo: Japan Association of Remote Island Development.

Kamiya, D. 2007. *A Study on Okinawa's Water Use and Risks associated with Water Shortage.* Faculty of Engineering, University of the Ryukyus, pp.1-2.

Kimura M. 2006. *Shinsetu Mu Tairiku Chinbotsu: Okinawa Kaitei Iseki wa Mu Bunmei Iseki ka?* (Okinawa's Underwater Rock Remain: Is it the Submerged Mu Continent?). Tokyo: Jitsugyo no Nihonsha.

Hanai, T. 2007. "Amami's Nature, Culture, Economy and *Ugaminshora.*" In: The Asia-Pacific Island Study Center of the University of the Ryukyus (ed.). *Interim Activity Report on Amami Study Team.* Okinawa: pp.1-7.

Kagoshima Prefecture. 2006. *Amami Gunto no Gaikyo* (Outline of Amami Gunto).

Minamura, T. 2003. *Sengo Amami Keizai Shakai Ron: Kaihatsu to Jiritsu no Jirenma* (A Study of Postwar Socio-Economic Development of Amami: Dilemmas of Development and Sustainability). Tokyo: Nihon Hyoron Sha.

Oshiro, H. 2007. "Tosho Chiiki to shiteno Okinawa" (Okinawa as an Island Area). In: Oshiro, I. (ed.). *Zusetsu Okinawa Keizai* (Okinawa's Economy Explained by Charts). Okinawa: Toyo Kikaku, Chapter 1, pp.10-23.

Oshiro, I. 2005. "The Policy to Underdeveloped Area in Japan at the Postwar Recovery Decade: A Case Study of Amami Islands." *Ryukyu University Economic Review,* no.70, pp.17-43.

Suzuki, Y 2006. "Rito Shinko Ho no Genten to sono Mokuhyo" (Original Idea and Aims of the Remote Island Development Act). *Bulletin of the Research Institute of Regional Area Study.* Nagasaki Wesleyan University, vol.4, no.1, pp.245-252.

Chapter 5

Changing Agricultural Environments in the Pacific Islands

Introduction

Agriculture plays crucial roles in economic development. As the theory for "vent-for-surplus" (Myint, 1958) suggests, agricultural surplus (production over domestic consumption) is a kind of savings which will be used for investments in the manufacturing sector in the early stage of development. Increase in agricultural productivity is not only important for supporting increasing rural population, but also it is an essential condition for an economy to pursue industrialization. Therefore, in the early stage of economic development, agriculture is usually taxed for industrial development as an important source of industrial capital formation. In the later stage of development, however, agriculture is subsidized because of its declining productivity coupled with national food security.

The mechanism of agricultural development for small island economies, however, is quite different from that of industrialized economies where industrial structure has transformed successfully from agriculture to manufacturing, then to service-oriented activities as per capita incomes have increased.

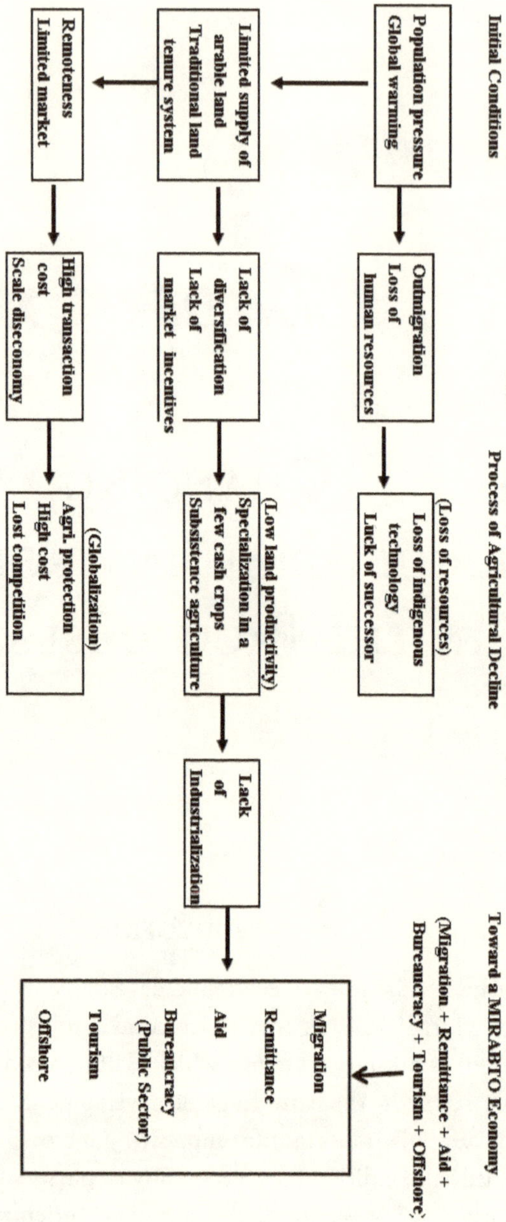

Initial Conditions

| Population pressure |
| Global warming |

| Limited supply of arable land |
| Traditional land tenure system |

| Remoteness |
| Limited market |

Process of Agricultural Decline

(Loss of resources)

| Outmigration |
| Loss of human resources |

| Loss of indigenous technology |
| Lack of successor |

| Lack of diversification |
| Lack of market incentives |

(Low land productivity)

| Specialization in a few cash crops |
| Subsistence agriculture |

| Lack of Industrialization |

| High transaction cost |
| Scale diseconomy |

(Globalization)

| Agrl. protection |
| High cost |
| Lost competition |

Toward a MIRABTO Economy

(Migration + Remittance + Aid + Bureaucracy + Tourism + Offshore)

| Migration |
| Remittance |
| Aid |
| Bureaucracy (Public Sector) |
| Tourism |
| Offshore |

Source: Kakazu, H.

FIGURE 5-1. A Mechanism of Islands' Agricultural Development.

As is shown in FIGURE 5-1, initial conditions of island economies are characterized by constant population pressure, limited supply of economic resources, notably arable land supply, traditional land-use systems and extremely limited market with high transportation and transaction costs. Diseconomy of small scale, which is directly related to agricultural productivity, may be the most important discouraging factor for successful agricultural development. Increasing out-migration, especially young adults, from island societies has resulted in a loss of human resources and indigenous technology. Low agricultural unit cost coupled with global competition led these islands to specialize in service-oriented activities such as tourism, offshore banking, information and communication technology (ICT) back offices in addition to remittances and external assistance. These economies may be expressed as MIRABTO, namely Migration, Remittance, Aid, Bureaucracy, Tourism and Offshore business to modify Bertram and Watters' (1985) well-cited MIRAB economy characterization.

Food security is particularly important for a small, isolated island economy where a stable supply of food is often interrupted by natural disasters such as drought, typhoons, tsunami and unexpected environmental changes. Quite often, for these small islands, domestic food supply is the last resort for survival when natural disasters occur. This is particularly true for small Pacific islands where islands are fragmented and located far from their major markets. Ironically, however, domestic food supply in these small islands has been neglected for a long time. As is fully discussed later, subsistence agriculture, which has provided the basic food necessities to indigenous islanders has been rapidly disappearing in all Pacific islands (Crocombe, 2001). Increasing cheap and subsidized food imports at the expense of traditional food supply have been major issues in terms of food security and the nutrition of the peoples (Kakazu, 1994).

STATE OF AGRICULTURE IN THE PACIFIC ISLANDS

Agriculture, which was the dominant industry in all the Pacific islands during the 1950s, now accounts for 28% (Tonga) to 1.9% (Taiwan) of islands' Gross Domestic Products (TABLE 5-1). The importance of agriculture tends to diminish as per capita income rises. This is because the agricultural sector tends to generate low incomes in part because of the low income elasticities of its products as a whole compared to those of other sectors—as the cost of producing farm products fall with technological progress, prices tend to fall (See Watanabe, 1986). Moreover, the skills required for traditional agricultural production are less highly developed and do not demand extensive education. These island economies follow this pattern more than larger market economies.

TABLE 5-1. Land and Agricultural Shares in Selected Pacific Island Economies: 2000-2002

| | Total Land Area (1000 sq km) | Cropped Land Per Capita (sq m) | Population (1000 persons) | Annual Population Growth Rate (%) | Trade:GDP (%) | Per Capita GDP (U.S.$) | Shares of Gross Domestic Products (%) | | | | | |
| | | | | | | | Agriculture | | Manufacturing | | Services | |
	2000	2000	2002	1995-2000	2002	2001	1990	2002	1990	2002	1990	2002
Okinawa	2,274	317	1,308	0.7	47.7	20,000	10.8	5.8	5.9	5.8	69.0	75.0
Taiwan	36.2	382	22,500	0.8	81.9	12,630	4.2	1.9	33.3	25.7	54.6	67.1
Cook Islands	0.2	3,911	18	1.1	69.0	4,270	21.1	12.4	3.9	2.9	73.8	83.0
Marshall Islands	0.2	590	57	3.8	65.0	2,190	12.4	13.8	1.2	1.6	71.8	69.0
Fiji	18.3	3,519	819	0.7	82.0	2,150	22.2	NA	12.7	NA	53.7	NA
Tonga	0.7	4,786	101	0.3	50.0	1,530	34.7	28.6	6.0	5.6	51.7	56.4
Samoa	2.8	7,147	178	0.5	60.0	1,490	23.0	14.3	19.6	14.8	48.7	63.1
Tuvalu	0.03	NA	11	2.0	46.0	1,260	25.6	16.8	6.0	5.6	59.9	56.4
Vanuatu	12.2	6,260	202	2.7	46.2	1,050	20.7	17.4	5.5	3.9	67.0	73.4
Kiribati	0.7	4,379	87	1.7	56.0	830	18.6	14.2	1.2	0.8	73.8	75.0
Papua New Guinea	452.9	1,647	5,500	3.2	89.0	580	29.0	26.9	9.0	8.5	40.6	31.5

Notes: 2002 Figures for Okinawa, Cook Islands, Marshall Islands are refer to 2001, and Tuvalu to 1998.
Trade:GDP = (Imports + Exports)/ GDP (%).

Sources: Asian Development Bank, Key Indicators of Developing Asian and Pacific Countries, Okinawa Prefectural Government.

Agricultural activities have been rapidly replaced by manufacturing, construction and service activities such as public works and tourism—all of which bring in higher incomes for workers. In the case of small island economies, agricultural and manufacturing activities are severely constrained by their size and remoteness which deprive them of any comparative cost advantage in the rapidly globalizing world (Kakazu, 2004).

Despite the general recognition that agriculture is more important in small island economies than in larger ones, they are facing formidable tasks to sustain their domestic sources of food supply. First, increasing population pressure on extremely limited land forces islanders to cultivate smaller plots of land in marginal land areas for food production which contributes to declining agricultural productivity. Marshall Islands, for example, has now only 590 square meters cropped land per capita which has rapidly declined from 750 square meters a decade ago while its population has 3% annual increases (TABLE 5-1).

Second, most of these islands are suffering from an accelerated rise in the sealevel which is thought to be linked mainly with the El Nino weather phenomenon caused by global warming. Some of the islands in Kiribati, Tuvalu and Nauru are about to disappear beneath the ocean. "Pacific island countries have contributed just 0.06 per cent to global greenhouse gas emissions. But now, the changing climate and sea levels linked to global warming are affecting their water supply, food production, fisheries and coastlines" (Tutangata, 2000).

Third, these islands specialize in a few export crops such as copra, sugar, palm oil, cocoa, banana, taro and squash which are highly vulnerable to the weather and external market conditions. Almost all Pacific island economies were severely hit by devastating droughts in 1998. Owing to the droughts, Fiji's sugar, which accounted for about 40% of its export earnings, fell by two-third. Tonga's squash crop, about half of its export earnings, was cut in half. Export prices of these products have also been depressed for many years. Because of these unforeseen external shocks, economic growth rates of these small island economies subjected to a wide range of fluctuations preventing any type of macroeconomic planning and management (FIGURE 5-2).

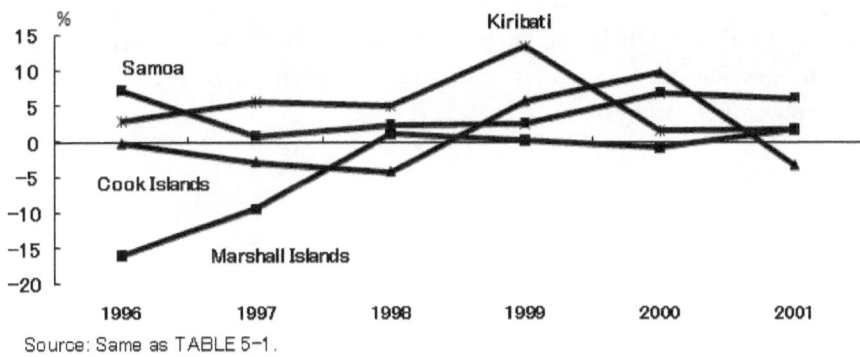

Source: Same as TABLE 5-1.

FIGURE 5-2. Economic Growth Rates of Selected South Pacific Economies: 1996-2001.

Fourth, almost all Pacific island economies are facing the age-old problem of efficient use of agricultural land due largely to complex land tenure systems. The most common pattern in the Pacific islands' land tenure regimes is that land proprietary rights are held by an extended family or clan with restricted but complex rights for the individual cultivator. Restrictions on access to property rights will always restrict the full realization of the potential productivity of the land (ADB, 1998). Fiji's sugarcane production, for instance, has suffered from a complex land leasing contracts between Indian sugar growers and indigenous Fijian land owners. Although it is clearly understood that both parties would get benefits from stable, secure and productive use of cane land under the long-term lease contract, Fijians have been reluctant to do so owing to socio-political reasons. Because of uncertain renewal guarantees of the lease land, "Indian farmers engaged in farming do not make much efforts to increase productivity" (Sharman, 2005).

AGRICULTURAL SUCCESS STORIES IN THE PACIFIC ISLANDS

Despite increasingly adverse agricultural environments in these Pacific islands, some success stories are reported. One well-documented story is Tonga's squash (small pumpkins). In the late 1970s, Tonga started diversifying its cash products from traditional products such as desiccated coconut, coconut oil, taro, yams, sweet potatoes and bananas to vanilla beans and squash. Vanilla beans gradually replaced coconut products and became the most important export crop by 1988 accounting for more than 30% of total agricultural exports. After a long gestation period, squash emerged as an important cash crop in 1989. Squash exports amounted to $T13 million in 1993 accounting for 70% of its agricultural exports (FIGURE 5-3). The success is due largely to easy market access to Japan as well as Tonga's October-March squash production season which fits neatly into the off seasons for other competitive suppliers. As is reflected in fluctuating export trend, squash production has been suffering from risks arising from uncertain market prices and weather conditions.

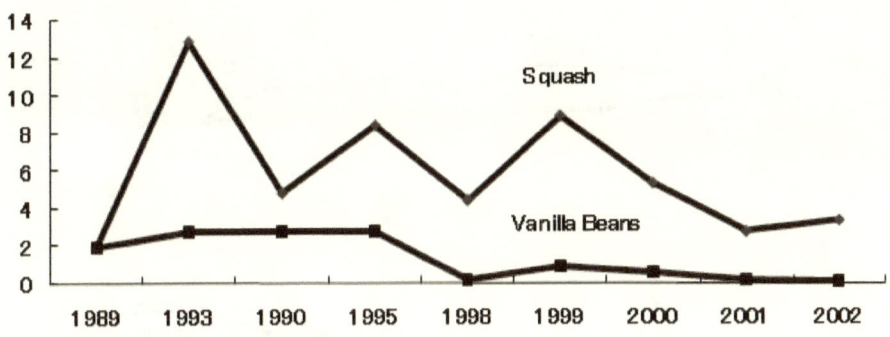

Source: Same as TABLE 5-1.

FIGURE 5-3. Exports of Tonga's Squash and Vanila Beans: 1989-2002.

Another success story is Okinawa's rising exports of diversified agricultural products such as flowers, bitter melon, mango, tobacco, string bean, green pepper, and various "health foods." Traditionally sugarcane and pineapple have been the most important cash crops, accounting for more than 20% of all farm incomes and 50% of cultivated land. Incomes from sugarcane production, however, have declined significantly in recent years as a result of stagnant prices and productivity as well as increased international competition (FIGURE 5-4). Although pineapple production declined sharply in the past, it has gradually picked up in recent years because of the rising demand for fresh pineapple from tourists. Okinawa's sugar industry would not survive without the government's price support programs. Only fresh pineapple and pineapple wine are holding their own, and this is due primarily to tourists' consumption. It has been an urgent task for the local government and farmers to move from sugarcane-centered monocultural agriculture to diversified cash crops.

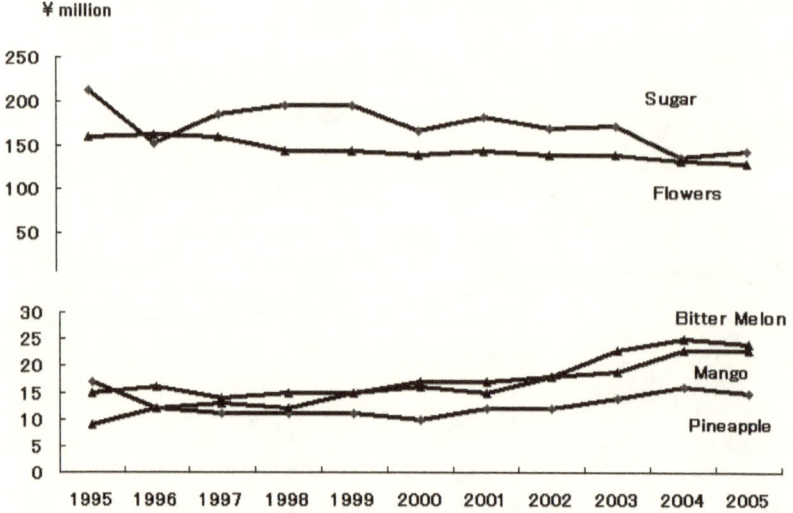

¥ million

Source: Okinawa General Bureau, the Cabinet Office.

FIGURE–5–4: Value of Traditional and Diversified Agricultural Producrts of Okinawa: 1995–2005.

Okinawa's promising agricultural products are in the area of high value-added health foods. Okinawa is fast becoming a brand name for "health and longevity" because of its world-renowned longevity image. Okinawa's life expectancy, in the past two decades, has increased from 72 to 79 years for men, and 79 to 87 years for women, making Okinawa the healthiest place in the world. Okinawa's longevity is the product of a complex combination of climate, culture, closely-knit social organizations, foods and lifestyles. Foods are considered the most important factor for long life (see a best-selling book on this subject; Willcox, Willcox and Makoto Suzuki, 2000). Okinawans are accustomed to consuming less salty, mineral rich foods than mainlanders. As is discussed in Chapter 8, changes in food consumption patterns from traditional healthy foods to the Western style of high fat foods may derail Okinawans' famed longevity.

Various healthy foods have been developed and marketed nationwide, including *ukon* (turmeric), bitter melon (well-known as *goya*) products, naturally processed salt, sea vegetable products (*mozuku*), dietary ostrich meat, and various deep-sea water products, just to name a few well-known examples. Bitter melon especially became popular and the best selling healthy vegetable. Although production scales of these niche products are still small, they possess comparative advantages in uniqueness of resource use and technology. Furthermore, these products usually require more local inputs, including raw materials and labor, than conventional trading products.

As is fully discussed in Chapter 6, a breakthrough towards high value-added, diversified agriculture came after the complete eradication of the melon fly from all the Okinawa islands in 1993. The melon flies affected more than forty important vegetables and fruits including highly-priced mangos and bitter melon, thereby preventing these infested products from exporting to fly-free areas in mainland Japan. Mangos and bitter melon became Okinawa's star cash crops after the melon fly eradication. The technological know-how and strategies for the success will be transferred successfully to infested areas worldwide, particularly island areas such as Hawaii and the South Pacific.

DIVERSIFICATION OF ISLANDS' AGRICULTURAL PRODUCTS

The development of high value-added agri-products based on local resources is one of the positive directions for island's sustainable efforts. Okinawa's development of various healthy foods and medicinal products and *kariyushi*-wear, or "cool business-wear" are additional examples. Okinawa's traditional, declining sugarcane has been revalued in recent years because of its high-valued alternative use. As is shown in FIGURE 5-5, sugar-related inputs such as molasses and bagasse, which in turn can be transformed into urethane resins, particle boards, rum, wax, paper products and recently ethanol, have been pursued at local research institutes.

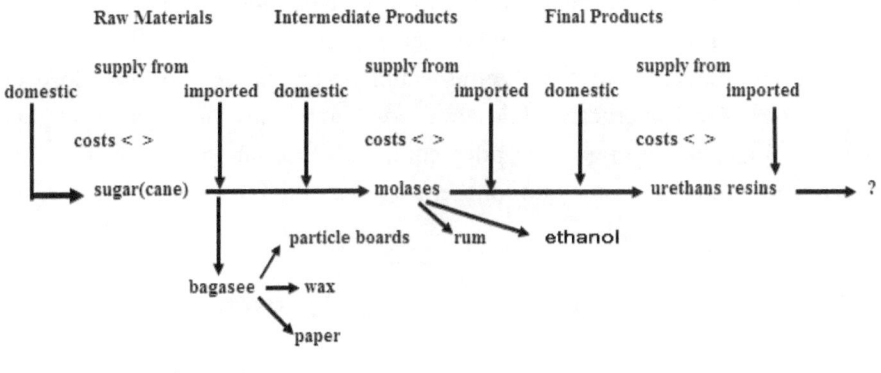

Source: Kakazu, H.(2007).

FIGURE 5-5. Diversification of Sugar(cane) Products.

The urethane products, which were developed by the Tropical Technology Center (TTC) in Okinawa, have an enormous potential for a wide-range of products from pet bottles to home and industrial appliances. These products are decomposable (biodegradable) and therefore can be substituted for environmentally hazardous plastic products if quality and prices are reasonably acceptable to users and consumers. Miyako Island, which is a major producer of sugarcane, has been designated by the national government to produce ethanol for fuel. Islanders are hoping to substitute this renewable and environmentally friendly fuel for gasoline in the future.

For the successful development of these islands' resource-based products, several problems must be resolved. One important factor is the size of the market, which in turn, determines the cost of production. As can be typically seen in the case of integrated circuits, the initial unit cost of production is very high. But as the market expands, the cost is reduced approximately to one-half within a decade. Products such as urethane resins require a large segment of the market in order to compete with plastic products.

The second important consideration is cost escalation, which will quite often accompany when local resources are used as raw materials or intermediate inputs, as in the above illustration. The price of Okinawan sugar, for example, is about four times higher than the international price because of government protection. The high cost results in high costs for molasses and consequently for the production of urethane resins. Here the producers of urethane resins face a dilemma because they are obliged to import molasses in order to compete in the international market.

It is important to realize that in order to diversify local products toward more value-added products, domestically produced raw materials must be available at international prices. Unless there are incentives such as subsidies and taxes which will compensate for the cost disadvantage during the initial stages of production, an Okinawan producer of urethane resins would always choose imported molasses over the costly local alternative. Okinawa's low-quality discarded molasses (by-product of sugar processing) have price competitiveness at the moment simply because there is not much demand for them.

SUBSISTENCE AGRICULTURE REVISITED

The Role of Subsistence Sector in the Pacific Islands

There is no doubt that most of the people in the small Pacific islands lived on autarchic subsistence, or probably what Fisk (1982) has termed "primitive affluence" long before the European navigator-traders introduced various cash crops into these islands, along with new goods such as tobacco, cloth, iron goods, and Western foodstuffs which could be exchanged for cash. Long before the arrival of Europeans, Pacific islanders were already engaged in sophisticated trading systems through feasts and gift-giving. The reciprocal transfer of goods "often evolved on the basis of resource complimentarity, so that a dry island might trade yams for the taro of a wet island, or an island people might trade fish for the sago and vegetables of the mainlanders on larger land bodies." (Couper, 1973).

It is interesting to note that the dependency on trade, which has often been considered by modern development economists to be a major source of economic instability, was considered to be a practical wisdom of the ancient islanders not only to complement each other's scarce resources, but also to keep peace and cohesion in social intercourse among different islanders as stated by Couper:

> *When a community was called upon to trade with another it could not readily refuse, so that islanders were able to exchange their craft products for foodstuffs in distant islands in times of natural catastrophe, such as hurricanes and drought. In this way, the quasi-oligopolistic nature of production in particular goods was transformed through the social pressure to conduct trade into a system of natural support (ibid).*

Furnas (1937) cited the following amusing conversation from the writing of the Rev. James Chalmers who visited New Guinea in the 19th century:

> *Have you coconuts in your country?*
> *No.*
> *Have you yams?*
> *No.*
> *Have you breadfruits? "No."*
> *Have you sago?*
> *No.*
> *Have you plenty of hoop iron and tomahawks?*
> *Yes in great abundance.*
> *We understand now why you have come. To have nothing to eat in Beritani; but you have plenty of tomahawks and hoop iron with which you can buy food.*

We define the subsistence sector as a portion of production activities which are directed solely towards the producers' own consumption, since there is ample evidence that a pure form of subsistence economy vanished long before the arrival of the European traders. Today, most developing island economies are more or less under the mixed cash-subsistence system of production.

The main role of the subsistence sector is to reduce the increasing heavy dependency on imported foods which has aggravated the balance of payments positions and the nutritional standards of many Pacific islanders. Subsistence activities, however, are not limited to food production. They can be classified into broad categories: foodstuffs as well as their processing; building activity; capital works; furniture; and traditional crafts. They also include village councils, the local government rule of village elders and chiefs, indigenous medicine, the entrepreneurial role of family heads, the maintenance and upkeep of village facilities and utilities, and family funerals and religious services (see Fairbairn, 1975).

A range of specific subsistence-based activities with employment potential are: handicrafts, dressmaking, carpentry, and producing a range of agricultural products such as cassava, taro, coconut, breadfruit, fish, pork and poultry. Other possibilities are capital items such as the traditional building of houses, canoes, bridges, and control measures. Processing and household manufacturing activities are also important in many countries; some examples are the processing of cassava flour, rice, tapioca powder, homegrown tobacco, and coconut oil; home brewing; and food preservation (e.g., breadfruit in Samoa and *babai* in Kiribati and Tuvalu).

Contributions of these subsistence activities to the social and economic life of island countries are summarized as follows (see more details in Kakazu and Fairbairn, 1985).

(a) They provide many categories of goods and services that form a basic and highly valued ingredient of contemporary village life: these often have no direct substitute in the modern trade sector.

(b) They provide a source of livelihood for those unable to find secure employment in the wage sector.

(c) They constitute a familiar base from which innovations in commercial agriculture and other areas can be carried out by villagers should they desire such changes;

(d) Many subsistence foodstuffs are highly nutritious (and cheap), compared with imported substitutes.

(e) Subsistence activities are valued as integral elements of what many Pacific Islanders conceive of as the sort of life-style they wish to maintain and encourage.

Most Pacific island economies are hybrids, or dual systems, where the monetary sector co-exists with a substantial subsistence sector. Subsistence activities have remained strong despite long contact with the modern trade economy. Walsh (1975) suggests that "semi subsistence involvement should be regarded as at least a *semi-permanent* feature of Pacific island society, and policy makers should operate within this term of reference."

We attempted to estimate the subsistence component of national income for selected Pacific island countries (see Chapter 2, Kakazu, 1994). The subsistence sector accounted for as high as 35% for Papua New Guinea (PNG) and Samoa, 20% for Solomon Islands and Tonga, and less than 6% for Fiji, American Samoa and Micronesian islands in the 1980s. Although recent figures are not available, the shares of the subsistence activities of these economies will likely be lower than the 1980s because of the rapid globalization and urbanization of these economies.

The continuing importance of subsistence productions in the Melanesian economies is due to such factors as limited contact with the cash economy for a large section of the population, the often unusually productive nature of the traditional rural sector, and continually strong preferences for traditional foods and other goods. Subsistence productions are relatively low in Fiji and most Micronesian islands due to high levels of cash incomes made possible by a fast growing monetary sector and strong preferences for trade goods built up over time (one also suspects significant underestimation of subsistence production).

Caution, however, needs to be exercised in the interpretation of these estimates because of differences in how the estimates are calculated and the areas and activities covered. A common deficiency is a failure to cover the range of major subsistence activities (e.g. construction of village houses, canoes and capital tools and handicrafts). The estimate for Western Samoa, for example, applies only to agricultural production. In many cases, therefore, subsistence production is probably significantly underestimated (see Kakazu, 1994).

With regard to sustainable development of these island economies, Hald, a United Nations economic advisor, questioned whether "the peoples of the southern part of this vast ocean might be better off if left alone to live their lives in traditional ways" (Hald, 1975). Such a viewpoint, however, could adversely influence official policy. It could, for example, divert attention away from tackling urgent social and economic problems that are sometimes present in the rural-subsistence sector, e.g., high infant mortality rates, short life expectancy, malnutrition and lack of adequate protection against the danger of periodic droughts and storms (Fairbairn, 1975).

Since it is too late for Pacific islanders to go back to their villages and, at the same time, the capitalist aspects are in direct conflict with their traditional lifestyle, we should attempt to find a balance between subsistence and cash production systems for small island economies because most islanders want neither a return to a primitive life-style nor a move toward a high-technology society that is beyond their means to sustain, but rather, they want to go forward in ways that improve their well-being without destroying their self-reliance and culture.

Trade and the Subsistence Sector: A Possible Collapse Case

Under the initial stage of economic development, there would be no incentive for the peasant farmers to produce more than they consume because the value of surplus products (output - consumption) is zero, unless these products are stored for a feast or anticipated gifts. Initially, as often documented, it was the external demand for the peasants' products which gave farmers the incentive to produce the surplus products for exports. With these foreign exchange earnings, they then imported new products and served to foster new wants among the peoples.

The expansion of imports was a major dynamic force facilitating the further expansion of exportable goods which could be exchanged more favorably in the international market than the domestic market. This is what we call improvement of terms of trade or real exchange rate. Although the overall terms of trade for developing countries have worsened from the 1950s through the 1960s, the unit prices for export commodities from Pacific islands, such as sugar, copra, and coffee, have fluctuated considerably (see Kakazu 1994).

When discussing the terms of trade for Pacific islands, where trade specialization is limited to a few agricultural products such as sugar and copra, and where a wide variety of other agricultural products such as rice and wheat are imported, we should pay attention to the relative productivity of sugar or copra in a country compared with rice or wheat. Even though the terms of trade deteriorate vis-à-vis manufactured goods, it may still be better off for Fiji to export sugar or for Tonga to export coconut products as long as they possess comparative advantages over rice and other products in producing these products. This is particularly so if the islanders continuously prefer to consume imported foodstuffs to sweet potatoes, taro, or yams, despite the convincing warning from Thaman (1982) and many others about the deteriorating nutritional standards.

An important thing to emphasize in the trade-based growth path is that both the exportable goods and the subsistence goods have expanded together. This type of development is possible only under the conditions of surplus arable land and labor, as has been documented by Myint (1958) in his celebrated "vent-for-surplus" theory of international trade. Under this type of development path, it is not difficult to see that further expansion in both cash and subsistence crops is possible only up to the point where all arable land is cultivated. The essential lubricant which pushed the peasants so smoothly and rapidly into export production and the money economy was the existence of a considerable margin of surplus productive capacity in the form of both surplus land and surplus labor over and above their minimum subsistence requirements.

Aided by foreign traders and the improved transportation system, peasant farmers ventured into producing rather risky export crops on a part-time basis because they could fully secure their minimum subsistence food. In the early phase of export expansion, therefore, the farmers could obtain extra cash income simply by putting more unused land and surplus labor into cultivation for export crops, without endangering the subsistence affluence.

The basic problem with this type of island development is that expansion in production has been made possible through extending cropland without changing the traditional mode of production. Therefore, the productivity of land has remained unchanged or has decreased due to the cultivation of marginal land over a long period of time. In-depth study of the Fiji sugar industry and recent statistical data on selected crops, though fragmentary, support the relevancy of the vent-for-surplus theory to the export-led growth path of the South Pacific island economies (see Moynagh, 1981 and Kakazu, 1994).

Even under the technological innovation of modern times, the land productivity in cash crops, such as sugar and cocoa, and subsistence foods, such as sweet potatoes and yams, has essentially remained unchanged. This lag in technological innovation in the primary export industry was a major reason why the expansion in exports in many developing countries did not bring about the spread effects, that is, the positive impact of export activity on the diversification of the domestic economy as had been explained by the staple theory of export-led growth (see Buckley 1958 and Watkins 1963).

From the forgoing discussions, we have to fully recognize the importance of identifying where an island economy is located on the expected growth path when we map possible development options and strategies open to small island economies. It is particularly important to identify the role of subsistence agriculture quantitatively as well as qualitatively in order to provide a more complete picture for national planning purposes, including the formulation of a soundly conceived development policy and strategy.

Exhaustion of Natural Resources

For the Pacific island economies, where the diversification of economic base is severely limited mainly because of small domestic markets, external trade was not only the vehicle of peaceful coexistence among the islanders, but it was also the powerful engine of growth. A steady rise in real per capita incomes for these island economies was largely made possible through exporting a few comparatively advantageous agricultural and mining products. Some of the island countries rely heavily on one or two export products, for example, American Samoa relies on processed tuna, Kiribati on copra, Nauru on phosphate, and New Caledonia on nickel products; while in Fiji and Papua New Guinea, sugar and copper concentrates, dominate export earnings. Okinawa and Hawaii used to heavily depend on sugar exports.

Specialization in a few primary export products in small Pacific islands has been intensified both by colonial economic policies and new demands created through imported goods. In the process of export-led growth, resources have been transferred from the subsistence sector to the monetized sector. Although there are great variations in the degree of monetization, island economies such as Hawaii, Okinawa, Micronesia, Nauru, New Caledonia, French Polynesia and Tuvalu are now highly monetized. The key question raised by Fairbairn and Tisdell (1984) was whether or not such export-led growth is sustainable. There are two possible ways that a small export-oriented economy with relatively high per capita income might collapse into subsistence poverty. One is the exhaustion of natural resources. This was the case with the phosphate of Nauru which was almost entirely depleted in the past decade. The possible collapse case of very small island economies such as Nauru and Kiribati is illustrated in FIGURE 5-6 using the conventional production possibility curve (PP) with two commodities: E=exportable good and C=consumption good (imports + subsistence goods) under the usual assumptions (see more details in Chapter 2, Kakazu, 1994).

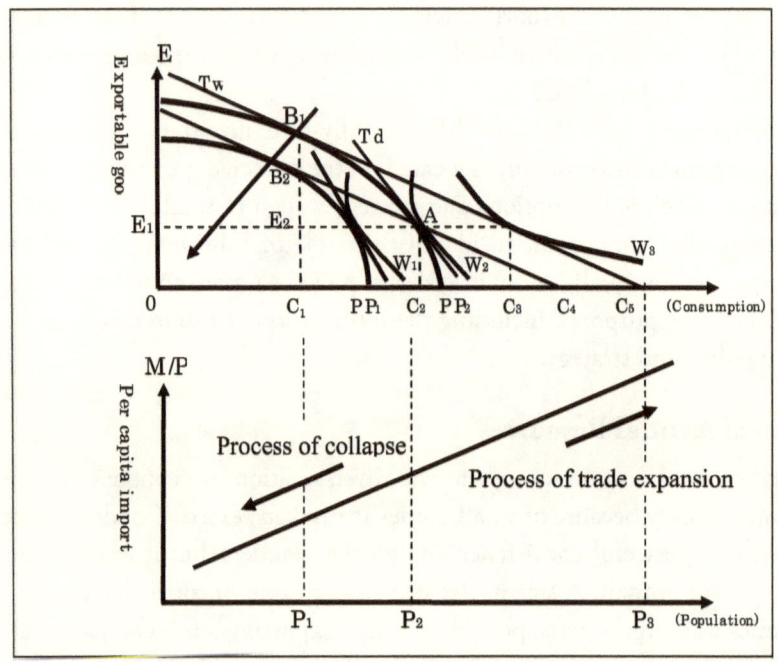

Source: Kakazu.

FIGURE 5-6. The Case of Possible Collapse as a Result of Natural Resources Exhaustion.

Let us start from point A on the transformation curve where, given the pre-trade domestic terms of trade (Td), the economy will produce both OE1 quantity of exportable goods and OC2 quantity of consumption goods. Since there is no trade, all produced goods are consumed domestically. But if the economy finds that the international terms of trade (Tw) is more favorable for the exportable good than the consumption good, it will respond to the difference in the price ratio by moving from A to B1 on the curve, that is to say, producing more exportable good (E) at the expense of subsistence consumption good (C). In addition to the favorable terms of trade, there is no doubt that the movement from A to B1 has been accelerated through new tastes and "demonstration effect" induced by imports.

At the production point B1, B1E1 quantity of exportable good can be exported in exchange for C1C3 quantity of consumption good. The welfare level of the economy represented by indifference welfare curve (W3) is much higher than that of the pre-trade level (W2). If we convert all exportable goods into consumption goods (subsistence goods + imported goods), international trade brings OC5 level of consumption which is a higher level than the pre-trade level (OC4).

Given the state of technology, the gradual exhaustion of the exportable (phosphate) resource will push the transformation curve downward, say from PP2 to PP1. With the terms of trade remaining unchanged, the possible welfare level in terms of consumption is the same as the pre-trade level (W2). If we further assume that the deterioration of the terms of trade, which happened in the past, to the pre-trade (Td), the welfare level will be further reduced to W1.

This process of collapse of the transformation or production curve may come gradually depending upon the rate of exhaustion of the phosphate resource as is suggested in the lower part of FIGURE 5-6 which shows in contrast to the process of trade expansion. In addition to the exhaustion of the exportable resource, the loss of the arable land due to the rising sea level as a result of global warming and loss of indigenous technology will accelerate the process of collapse.

This simple model indicates a danger of specializing in one resource specific non-renewable export good. According to the theory of comparative cost advantage, the gradual exhaustion of an exportable resource means gradual increase in the relative cost of exploiting the resource. Before the resource is completely exhausted, exports will be halted through market mechanism, that is to say, whenever the unit production cost of the exportable good exceeds the world price. We have witnessed a number of resource specific export goods which had disappeared or nearly so from some Pacific island countries such as the phosphate of Kiribati, Nauru and Makatea, gold of Fiji and bananas of (Western) Samoa because of relative disadvantage in the international markets.

The theory of comparative advantage is better served for large economies where alternative resources for exports can more easily be developed. For very small economies of the South Pacific such as Nauru and Kiribati, the exhaustion of non-renewable exportable resource means the complete collapse of external trade and return to a subsistence economy. Can these export-oriented small island economies be rescued from collapsing? I have suggested two possible approaches.

Balance of Payments Approach

In order to prevent a small island economy from collapsing into subsistence poverty, we have to find some operational criteria which assure a stable mix between export and subsistence production. One such simple yet manageable criterion is a balance of payments approach.

These small island economies have tended to expand their exports beyond the limit permitted by the market mechanism in order to finance the ever-growing import demands. Excessive outward export-biased policies may be more damaging to these small resource-poor island economies than excessive inward-looking policies which have been denounced by many development economists such as Myint and Little, Scitovsky and Scott (see Kakazu, 1994).

A development path, which prevents an island economy from collapsing, can be expressed in the following simple macro model. If we assume that investment is zero for convenience,

$$C = Y + (M—X)$$
$$= Y + F$$

Development path A: $X > M$ or $Y > C$

Development path B: $X = M$ or $Y = C$

Development path C: $X < M$ or $Y < C$

where, C = consumption, Y = gross national product, M = imports, X = exports, F = net foreign capital inflows. Currently almost all small Pacific island economies are in the positions of $(X − M) < 0$, or $C > Y$. That is to say, they are spending beyond their means and the differences are financed largely through inflows of foreign aid.

The balance of payments approach suggests that consumption should be kept within the limit of domestic productive capacity (Y) or that subsistence production should expand to assure $C = Y$ or $M = X$. This approach will be more easily implemented for relatively resource-rich and subsistence-oriented economies such as the Solomon Islands, Papua New Guinea, Fiji and Western Samoa than those smaller highly export-oriented economies such as Nauru and Kiribati. We will discuss specific feasible policy to achieve this development path in the later part of this chapter.

The Safe Minimum Standard (SMS) Approach

Another approach to prevent these small island economies from collapsing is the SMS approach, which was originally conceived by Ciracy-Wantrup (1952) and highlighted by Yamauchi and Onoe (1983). SMS suggests to us another possible criterion for finding a socially optimum balance between export and subsistence production. The concept, which was developed in the field of conservation economics, rests upon the idea that for certain classes of renewable resources in ecosystems where production is an important consideration, there are potential critical zones in their use which might lead to irreversible losses.

Critical zones are those bio-physical conditions brought about by human actions, which would make it uneconomical to halt or reverse depletion. If we use a resource beyond the critical zone, not only will this result in the depletion of the resource but also result in economic and social uncertainties which might threaten the continuity of a social group. The SMS approach to the production system of the Pacific island economies provides policy makers with a simple yet potentially powerful tool to achieve a balanced development between the export-oriented cash sector and the subsistence food sector.

The quantification of such a standard is not an easy task and must depend upon the specifics of each situation. Institutional rules which define performance standards, in terms of practices and results, are typically involved. The conceptual framework can be adapted to economic development and food security strategies. For example, to obtain a numerical standard, let's begin with a safe minimum self-sufficiency rate of foodstuffs for an island economy. Such a rate might be derived from a minimum caloric requirement for survival of the population on the island. An effort along this line is currently being developed by Okinawa. The essence of the procedure is illustrated by the following example for Okinawa:

minimum caloric intake for survival 2,000cal/day;
current average caloric intake 2,500cal/day.

Thus, the Okinawan people currently consume 2,500/2,000, or 1.25 times as many calories as necessary for theoretical minimum level of calorie intake. Since the overall food self-sufficiency rate of Okinawa is currently 40%, this is 1,000 calories or 50% short of insuring human survival in case of emergency.

i.e. $\dfrac{2,000 - 0.4\ (2,500)}{2,000} = 50\%$.

There are many technical problems involved in translating such a figure into rules governing production for domestic consumption vs. exports, and a major interdisciplinary effort is necessary.

The above procedure cannot currently be applied by many Pacific island economies owing, among other things, to lack of data. Food import statistics are generally good but reliable quantitative indicators of local food production, consumption and nutrition are absent. Evidence on average dietary intake is available in a few cases, but these are invariably too aggregated to be of practical value. Taylor *et al* (1983) cite figures of adult dietary intake for the Cook Islands as 3,350 calories in the early 1980s. These figures may no longer be valid. The operational application of the minimum caloric requirement approach among Pacific island countries therefore awaits refinement of food consumption and dietary data, and such a hiatus may be remedied by current research efforts in this field.

This concept of food security has much more practical meaning for the very small Pacific islands than large ones because of their isolation, unstable export incomes, and frequent occurrences of natural hazards such as tropical cyclones, droughts, earthquakes, tsunamis and the consequences of global warming. This approach can also be defended from the standpoint of improving the nutritional standards of the Pacific islands where malnutrition, due mainly to the increasing consumption of imported foodstuffs at the expense of subsistence foods, has emerged as the major developmental issue.

Import-replacement and Import-displacement Approaches

Although there are great variations in degree, the subsistence sector of the Pacific islands has gradually eroded due mainly to the foreign-trade-induced monetization of economies, high population growth and the loss of traditional production skills in the sector. It will become more difficult for these economies to redirect their resources from export-oriented production to domestic consumption-oriented production as the subsistence activities become less important. Fisk (1978) argues that subsistence affluence should be seized as early as possible because the greater the degree of subsistence sector, the more unused resources of land and labor concealed in the sector may be mobilized in order to diversify the economic base without reducing the level of subsistence consumption.

For most Pacific islands, there are two qualitatively different ways to produce domestic goods at the expense of exportable goods. One direction suggested by Demas (1975) is "import replacement," namely substituting domestic production for what they are now importing such as rice, canned fish and soft drinks which require new technologies, investments and large markets. This is the equivalent version of "import-substitution" which has been intensively discussed in modern development literatures (see Kakazu, 1994). The Newly Industrialized Economies (NICs) such as, Taiwan, South Korea, Singapore and Hong Kong successfully adopted this approach. Taiwan, for example, initially imported personal computers (PC) from Japan and the United States, but in the later stage, she developed its own PC industry to become world's major exporter

The other approach is "import-displacement" which seeks to substitute traditional food products such as taro, yams, sweet potatoes, tapioca (cassava), paw paw, coconut juice, kava (piper methysticum) and fish for imported rice, flour, beer, coke and canned fish. The former direction may be more realistic than the latter if it is true that the island people may become so accustomed to the taste and convenience of imported foodstuffs that they do not want to return to a diet of traditional root crops.

Judging from the experiences of other developing countries, however, there is a good probability that the import replacement approach will not only bring higher food prices, which may be resisted particularly by urban dwellers, but it also may worsen the trade deficits through reduced export earnings and increased import requirements such as fertilizer inputs and capital goods for domestic production. On the other hand, the problems of traditional foodstuffs, to which import-displacement is directed, are not only a matter of distaste, inconvenience and non-marketability, but some of them are more expensive than imported foods in terms of calories and protein as is revealed by Harris (1982). It is clear, however, that given available resources, the import-displacement approach is generally more effective than import-replacement in reducing the heavy burden of trade imbalances and improving the nutritional standards of the Pacific islands.

Though the dependency on imported foodstuffs has been generally high for all Pacific economies, there has been a great deal of variation in the degrees of dependency from country to country. For example, the per capita food imports of French Polynesia, American Samoa, and New Caledonia were more than eleven times higher than those of Papua New Guinea and the Solomon Islands (see Chapter 2, Kakazu, 1994,). Since the production and marketing conditions are also significantly different from country to country, there must be different approaches for reducing the dependency on food imports.

For relatively resource-rich and subsistence-oriented countries such as Papua New Guinea, the Solomon Islands and Samoa, the import-displacement approach may be more successful than for much smaller and resource-poor countries. Ward (1979) has concluded that, under the present environmental conditions of Kiribati, import-displacement through local production of starchy root is virtually impossible. The same conclusion can also be drawn for Nauru, the Cook Islands and Tuvalu.

In order to succeed in import-displacement strategy, other interrelated questions must be answered. Contrary to the general belief that arable land is extremely scarce and labor is underemployed in the subsistence sector of many Pacific islands, Desai and Ponter (1975) reveal some convincing evidence that the chief scarcity factor is not land but labor. Young male laborers, who are most needed in subsistence food production, are the most likely members of the population to migrate to the urban centers. Despite the serious unemployment problems in the urban centers, these migrated workers are most likely to stay there or migrate further to the overseas urban centers.

It should also be noted that foreign aid, particularly United States surplus food aid, has discouraged subsistence food production from both supply and demand sides; aid made these countries able to spend far beyond their means on imported foodstuffs which inevitably depressed the domestic food supply through adverse terms of trade. Although foreign aid in the Pacific islands is, to a large extent, considered to be the payoffs of political and strategic interests of donor countries, there has been a legitimate fear among concerned economists about the cumulative effects of foreign aid on the rising urban and consumption levels which might destroy the entire socio-economic fabric of these small island nations.

Further development of tourism is an important alternative to earn foreign exchange for a number of Pacific island countries. Success, however, depends on improving transportation and local support services, undertaking promotional work overseas and promoting local tourism-related industries.

CONCLUSIONS

This chapter has analyzed two possible ways in which the highly export-oriented small island economies in the Pacific might collapse into subsistence poverty. One way of collapse may be brought about by the exhaustion of non-renewable natural resources such as the phosphates of Nauru and Kiribati and nickel of New Caledonia. The other way may be brought about by the deterioration of terms of trade, or the disappearance of demand for exportable goods. The speed of collapse will be accelerated by deliberate specialization in exportable goods, population growth, global warming, and the loss of traditional production skills.

There are two clear-cut approaches for diversification which may prevent these economies from collapsing into subsistence poverty or severe deprivation. One approach is to conduct the development policies so as to maintain the balance of payments equilibrium. This approach will particularly be effective in the South Pacific where the growing trade deficits have been a source of alarming concern for policy-makers. The other approach is based upon the concept of the SMS which is designed to secure a minimum caloric requirement for survival of the island people through domestic food production. Although this approach is particularly relevant for small island economies, we need to refine this concept as well as to acquire more reliable data base for a successful application of the concept to the South Pacific.

Policy implications of the two approaches are mutually reinforcing; they require a resource shift from the export sector to the subsistence sector which is a mainstay of many South Pacific island economies and has a great potential for development. We have suggested that in order to diversify the economic base through revitalizing the subsistence sector, an import-displacement approach may be much more effective than an import replacement or import substitution approach.

It should be noted, however, that policy prescriptions derived from the present analysis may differ according to the stage of socio-economic development, natural resource endowments and the importance of the subsistence sector. The best available policy mix for each island economy cannot be found without answering the interrelated issues such as possible changes in technology, demographics and decision making process at all levels.

Island economies, particularly small Pacific economies, are facing the compound problems of development; in addition to the general problems of developing countries, they have economic and political disadvantages stemming from their insular nature, e.g., smallness, isolation from the major markets, and fragmentation within their own markets.

A rapid rise in the real per capital income in these economies was largely made possible by exporting advantageous primary products, including mineral and agricultural products. In the process of export-led growth, the resources were rapidly transferred from the subsistence sector to the monetized sector. Though there are great variations in the degree of monetization that has occurred, island economies such as Nauru, New Caledonia, French Polynesia, Tuvalu and some Micronesian economies are now almost totally monetized. The monetization of island economies and the attainment of political independence inevitably brought about the "revolution of rising expectations" to the island people.

The deeper specialization in primary export goods, which were susceptible to the vagaries of price fluctuations in the international market, meant greater dependency on import which, in turn, generated new wants through the demonstration effect. The result has been the growing trade deficits which have largely been financed through foreign aid. Every conscientious planner now recognizes that this process of economic development is not only unsustainable in the long run, but is also inconsistent with the strategy of self-reliant economic development which has been incorporated into all development plans in the Pacific islands including Okinawa.

Sustainable development or self-reliant development is easy to talk about, but difficult to pursue. We can find sustainable or self-reliant development plans in virtually all development strategies proposed in the various international forums, such as import-substituting industrialization, trade-oriented development, collective self-reliance through regionalism, zero growth strategies based on a mixed subsistence-plantation mode, and basic human needs strategies. Planners should seriously think of how to prevent some of the resource-poor island economies from falling back into what Fisk (1982) calls "subsistence poverty."

The simple model discussed in this Chapter indicates a danger of specializing in one resource specific non-renewable export good. The theory of comparative advantage may work for large economies where there are alternative resources for exports, but it is not suited for very small island economies. For very small island economies, the exhaustion of non-renewable exportable resource means the complete collapse of external trade and a return to a subsistence economy with a real possibility of falling below the level of pre-trade due to the loss of traditional subsistence skills and the consequences of global warming.

NOTES

Sharma, K.L. (2005), p.12.
Couper, A. (1973), p.231.
Ibid.
Furnas, J.C. (1937), p.7.
Hald, E.C. (1975), p.4.
Fairbairn, I.J. (1975), p.192.
Harris, G.T. (1982), p.5.
Ibid.
Tutangata, T. S. (2000), p.1.
Ward, R.E. (1979), p.16.

REFERENCES

Asian Development Bank. 1998. *Improving Growth Prospects in the Pacific*. Manila: ADB Pacific Studies Series, pp.1-130.

Bertram, I.G. and Ray Watters. 1985. "The MIRAB Economy in South Pacific Microstates." *Pacific Viewpoint*, 26 (3), pp.497-519.

Buckley, K. May 1958. "The Role of Staple Industries in Canada's Economic Development." *Journal of Economic History, pp.*439-50

Couper, A. 1973. "Islanders at Sea, Change and the Maritime Economies of the Pacific." In: H.C. Brookfield (ed.). *The Pacific in Transition: Geographical Perspectives on Adaptations and Change*. London: Edward Arnold, pp.229-248.

Crocombe, R. 2001. *The South Pacific*. Suva: University of the South Pacific.

Ciriacy-Wantrup, S.V. 1952. *Resource Conservation Economics and Policies*. Berkeley: University of California Press.

Demas W.G. 1975. "Economic Independence." In: Selwyn P. (ed.). *Development Policy in Small Countries*. Sussex: Institute of Development Studies.

Desai, A.B. 1975. "Commercialization of Subsistence Agriculture." In: J. B. Hardaker (ed.). *The Subsistence Sector in the South Pacific*. Suva: University of the South Pacific.

Fairbairn, I.J. 1975. "The Subsistence Sector and National Income in Western Samoa." in Hardaker (ed.). *op.cit.*

_____ and Tisdell, C. 1984. "Subsistence Economies and Unsustainable Development and Trade: Some Simple Theory." *The Journal of Development Studies,* vol. 20, No. 2, pp.227-241.

Fisk, E.K.1982. "Subsistence Affluence and Development Policy." In: Benjamin Higgins (ed.). *Regional Development in Small Island Nations.* A Special Issue in the United Nations Centre for Regional Development, Regional Development Dialogue, Nagoya.

_____. 1978. *The Island of Niue: Development or Dependency for a Very Small Nation.* Occasional Paper, No.9. The Development Studies Centre of the Australian National University.

Furnas, J.C. 1937. *Anatomy of Paradise: Hawaii and the Islands of the South Seas.* New York: William Sloane Associates.

Hald, E.C. 1975. "Development Policy and the Subsistence Sector." In: J. B. Hardaker (ed.). *The Subsistence Sector in the South Pacific.* Suva: University of the South Pacific.

Hardaker J.B.(ed.). 1975. *The Subsistence Sector in the South Pacific.* Suva: University of the South Pacific.

Harris, G.T. 1982. *Food Imports and Macroeconomic Policy in the South Pacific.* Unpublished Paper. Economics Department of the University of New England.

Kakazu, H. 2004. "Changing Agricultural Environments in Small Islands: Cases of the South Pacific and Okinawa *"INSULA: International Journal of Island Affairs,* Paris, year 13, no.2, pp. 85-88.

_____, H. 1994. *Sustainable Development of Small Island Economies.* Boulder: Westview Press.

_____. and Fairbairn T. 1985. "Trade and Diversification in Small Island Economies with Particular Emphasis on the South Pacific." *Singapore Economic Review,* vol. 30, no. 2, October, pp.46-76.

Moynagh, M. 1981. *Brown or White? A History of the Fiji Sugar Industry, 1873-1973.* Pacific Research Monograph, no. 5. Canberra: Australian National University.

Myint, H. 1958. "The Classical Theory of International Trade and the Underdeveloped Countries." *Economic Journal,* June, pp.313-337.

Sharma, K.L. 2005. *Food Security in the South Pacific Island Countries with Special References to Fiji Islands.* A paper presented for the Workshop of UNU-WIDER Project: Hunger and Food Security: New Challenges and Opportunities, Helsinki, Finland, 12-14 October 2005, pp.1-23.

Taylor, R., G. Koteka, and Mokoputua, K. 1983. *Prevention and Control of Non-Communicable Diseases: Present Situation in the Cook Islands.* Noumea: South Pacific Commission.

Thaman, R.R. 1982. "Deterioration of Traditional Food Systems, Increasing Malnutrition, and Food Dependency in the Pacific Islands." *Journal of Food and*

Nutrition, 39, pp.109-120.

Tutangata, T. S. 2000. "Sinking Islands, Vanishing Worlds." *Earth Island Journal*, vol.15, no.2

Walsh, A.C. 1975. "Subsistence Agriculture and the Communication of Innovations: Some Niuean Examples." In: J. B. Hardaker (ed.), *op.cit.*

Ward, R.E. 1979. *Agricultural Options for the Pacific Islands. A* paper presented for the 1979 Development Studies Centre Conference of the Australian National University.

Watanabe, T. 1986. *Economics and Contemporary Asia*. Tokyo: Nihon Hyoron Sha.

Watkins M.H. 1963. "A Staple Theory of Economic growth." *Canadian Journal of Economics and Political Science*, 29, May, pp.143-158.

Willcox B., C. Willcox and M. Suzuki 2000. *The Okinawa Program: Learn the Secrets to Healthy Longevity*. New York: New York Times.

Yamauchi H and H. Onoe. 1983. "Analytical Concepts and Framework for Environmental Conservation." *International Review of Economics and Business,* vol. XXX, no. 8, May, pp.759-778.

Chapter 6

A New Frontier of Okinawa's Agriculture: Economic Evaluation of the Melon Fly Eradication Project

Introduction

There are four species of fruit: the Mediterranean fruit fly or med-fly, the oriental fruit fly, the Solanaceous fruit fly, and the melon fly. Complete eradication of the melon fly from all the Okinawa islands has become one of Japan's success stories (Ito 1980). The Nihon Hoso Kyokai (NHK), a well-established nation-wide public broadcasting corporation, selected up the eradication project for the topic of one of its popular TV programs called *"Project X."*

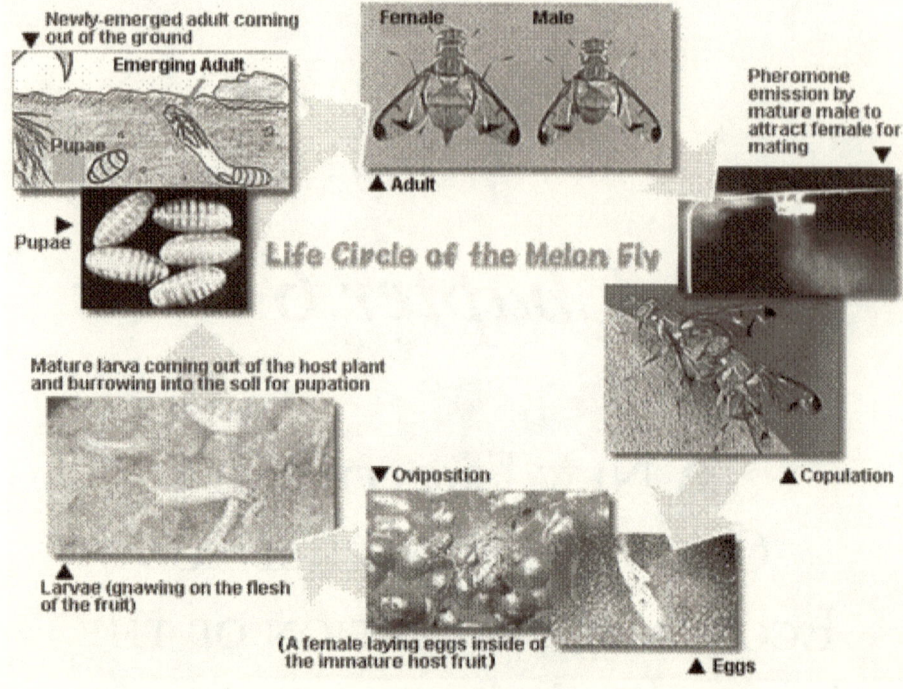

Source: Okinawa Prefectural Government (1999).

FIGURE 6-1. Life Circle of the Melon Fly.

This chapter attempts to post-evaluate the melon fly eradication project in Okinawa by the sterile insect technique (SIT) method. The eradication was successfully completed in Kume Island in 1978, followed by the Miyako Islands in 1987, the Okinawa Islands in 1990, and the Yaeyama Islands in 1993. The total project costs during the eradication period amounted to ¥17billion (about $US850 million), utilizing 320,000 man-hours. Although the costs of the project are easily identified, possible benefits arising from the project are difficult to estimate without some important assumptions, particularly the social benefits arising from pesticide-free and pest-free environments and preventing the insect pests from spreading into mainland Japan. Although we briefly compare the merits and demerits of the alternative eradication strategies, we assume that the SIT eradication method was chosen as the best melon fly control strategy in Okinawa. As is demonstrated later in this chapter, the SIT eradication method is not only the best strategy in Okinawa, where islands are relatively small and isolated, but also the method that maximizes the project benefits in the long run, say after eight years, despite the high initial costs.

The International Atomic Energy Agency (IAEA 1995, 2001) and the Food and Agriculture Organization (FAO 2001) have published extensive fruit fly cost-benefit studies including a manual on which this chapter draws heavily. Before we go into an evaluation of melon fly eradication, we do need to grasp overall roles and changes of Okinawa's agriculture, particularly vegetable and fruit products which are affected by the melon fly.

THE ROLES AND PERFORMANCE OF AGRICULTURE IN OKINAWA

The structure of the Okinawan economy is very similar to that of the Hawaii Islands where the service industry dominates economic activities (see Kakazu 2006; Oshiro 2007 for the latest development). Agriculture (primary industry), which was the dominant industry during the 1950s, now accounts for only 4.5% in terms of the labor force and 1.6% in terms of income (TABLE 6-1). The agricultural positions are slightly better than Japan's 4.1% and 1.5% respectively. However, it should be noted here that manufacturing and service (tourism) industries include agricultural products as inputs or raw materials such as sugar, various healthy foods and souvenirs.

TABLE 6-1. Changes in Okinawa's Industrial Structure: 1972-2006
(% of Total Employment)

	OKINAWA					JAPAN	
	1972	1982	1992	2006	(2005)	2006	(2005)
Primary industry	18.1	13.2	9.6	4.2	(1.8)	3.9	(1.4)
Secondary industry	20.9	20.2	20.2	17.3	(12.1)	27.0	(26.4)
Manufacturing	9.1	6.7	6.7	5.4	(4.7)	18.2	(20.2)
Construction	11.8	13.2	13.5	11.9	(7.6)	8.8	(6.1)
Tertiary industry	61.0	66.6	69.8	77.6	(89.7)	68.7	(72.2)
Trade	25.0	28.7	28.2	20.8	(28.4)	21.1	(31.7)
Services	24.5	23.1	28.8	34.8	(48.7)	29.3	(31.7)
Others	11.5	14.8	12.8	22.0	(12.6)	18.3	(8.8)

Notes: "Trade" includes wholesale and retail trade, finance, insurance and real estate. Data in parentheses are nominal GDP shares.

Source: Statistics Bureau, Management and Coordination Agency (2007).

Empirical law, as discovered by Kuzunets (1965) and others, suggests that the agricultural sector tends to generate low incomes in part because of the low income elasticities of its products as a whole compared to those of other sectors—as the cost of producing farm products fall with technological progress, prices tend to fall. Moreover, the skills required for traditional agricultural production are less highly developed and do not demand extensive education. Okinawa has followed this pattern more than any of Japan's other prefectures (Kakazu, 2000).

Agricultural activities have been rapidly replaced by more productive secondary (manufacturing and construction) and services activities such as public works and tourism. In the past decades, the growth of agricultural income per worker lagged behind incomes of manufacturing and services.

The values of total agricultural production peaked in the mid 1980s, then absolutely declined thereafter. Vegetables and fruits, particularly, which are subjects of this study, declined sharply in past decades. A number of factors contributing to the decline have been pointed out by agricultural economists including increasing international competition, scale demerits, high costs, transportation disadvantage especially, an aging farming population and small, isolated communities remote from Japan's major consumer markets (Hayami and Ruttan, 1985).

Although Okinawa's agriculture has been moving away from traditional sugarcane and pineapple cultivation, to flowers, such as orchids and chrysanthemums, and tropical fruits such as mangoes and citrus fruits, their relative importance in the economy may continue to decline in the future as a result of increasing international competition, stagnated productivity gains, and aging farm workers (TABLE 6-2). As a result, the self-sufficiency rate of Okinawa's food supply has declined to a mere 28% which is much lower than the national average of 40% in 2005 (see Oshiro, 2007).

Table 6-2. Trends of Okinawa's Major Agricultural Production: 1975-2005
(¥ 100 million)

	Sugarcane	Vegetable	Pineapple	Tobacco	Flowers	Rice	Sugarcane Yield/ha
1975	205	131	20	17	10	10	6.5
1980	271	217	31	25	23	7	6.2
1985	374	225	22	34	89	7	7.5
1990	250	204	18	26	149	7	6.0
1995	212	158	16	47	159	12	6.9
2000	166	120	10	49	139	9	5.9
2005	143	116	15	35	129	8	5.5

Source: See TABLE 6-1.

Of Okinawa's agri-resources, sugarcane has been the most important cash crop, accounting for about 16% of all farm incomes and 55% of cultivated land. Incomes from sugarcane production, however, have declined significantly in the past decades (1975-2005) as a result of stagnant prices and productivity as well as increased international competition. The farmgate price of sugarcane was about 20,000 yen ($170) per ton, on average, for the 2005 crop year, which was about ten times higher than the price per ton in Thailand. Moreover, the land productivity of sugarcane per hectare planted declined from 7.5 tons in 1985 to 5.5 tons in 2005 (TABLE 6-2). Okinawa's sugar industry has only been surviving through the government's heavy price support programs. The Okinawa Prefectural Government has estimated that Okinawa's sugarcane and related industries will be totally wiped out if economic partnership agreements (EPAs) with ASEAN and Australia are concluded in the near future (*Okinawa Times*, June 16, 2007). Okinawa's sugar industry, however, has shown a sign of recovery in recent years due largely to increased world demand for ethanol products derived from sugarcane.

Pineapple production, another important traditional cash crop in Okinawa, has also declined rapidly for similar reasons. Only fresh pineapple and pineapple wine are holding their own and sales have picked up in recent years, and this as a result of increased tourists' consumption. Rice is now marginally produced in certain areas of Okinawa.

These traditional crops have been gradually replaced by new crops such as flowers, tobacco and tropical fruits. Okinawa's mangoes particularly are perceived to have a high value in the mainland market. Flowers, which grew most rapidly in the past decades, have faced stiff competition with other parts of Japan as well as with China.

The other promising agricultural products are in the area of healthy foods such as turmeric (ukon) and bitter melon (well-known as goya or *nigauri*) products. These products have been developed and marketed nationwide supported by Okinawa's image of healthy islands which has been fading as islanders' health indicators deteriorated. Bitter melon especially became popular and the best selling healthy vegetable, fueled by a long-running NHK television drama called *Churasan* ("Beauty" in the Okinawa dialect) set in Okinawa. Although production scales of these niche products are still small, they possess comparative advantages in uniqueness of resource use and technology. Furthermore, these products usually require more local inputs, including raw materials and labor, than conventional trading products.

A COST-BENEFIT ANALYSIS OF FRUIT FLY ERADICATION PROJECT

Economic evaluation or cost-benefit analysis (CBA), of the project has been extensively used to determine whether the project, in this case the melon fly eradication project, is consistent with the overall national, regional and sectoral objectives, and whether the investment represents the best means of achieving the intended objectives. The eradication of the melon fly, which was first discovered in the Yaeyama Islands in 1919, was the most urgent and highly prioritized project at the local as well as national levels in the early 1970s because the fly rapidly spread to the main island of Okinawa and could spread into mainland Japan unless specific eradication measures were taken (Teruya, 1997). Therefore, the project was well supported by the people and fully justified from public as well as private standpoints. The potential loss to farmers nationally outweighed the costs of eradication if the pests were not eradicated at the waterfront of Okinawa islands.

The first step in the CBA is to identify the social and/or private need of, or demand for, the project. The second step in CBA is to identify which method of eradication is the most effective in terms of costs and benefits. This chapter briefly evaluates three eradication methods due to unavailability of information for the other alternative methods of eradication. Our data and analysis in this section are mainly based on a report by the IAEA (2001) and Enkerlin and Mumford (1997).

The three methods under discussion, which are all area-wide eradication methods, are: (a) Bait suppression, (b) SIT suppression, and (c) SIT eradication. The bait suppression method using bait sprays has been extensively used in many countries. "In the case of Israel, a national area-wide BAIT-SUPP program is at present being successfully operated in fruit orchards. The program consists basically of a very well established trapping network using Modified Steiner traps baited with trimedlure. Traps are serviced weekly and Medfly captures are used as an action threshold to start repeated aerial bait sprays of malathion mixed with hydrolyzed protein" (IAEA, 2001). This method does not eradicate the pest completely requiring costly post harvest treatment to eliminate any risk of pest introduction. Another important problem is "the substantial and permanent use of malathion which affects the levels of pesticide residues in fruits, induces secondary pest outbreaks by killing natural enemies, and limits the use of beneficial insects in area-wide integrated pest management (IPM) program for other pests"(IAEA, 2001).

The SIT suppression method, which is also widely used because of national boundaries, regional constraints, and cost effectiveness, is based mainly on weekly or fortnightly releases of sterile flies. Compared to the bait suppression method, this method uses up a much smaller amount of pesticide and does not require additional quarantine activities. The disadvantage, however, is that it involves a gradual process and access to fly-free export markets that can be achieved only by using post harvest treatments (IAEA, 2001).

The SIT eradication method is the most effective way of completely eradicating the pest, and within a relatively short time, although it requires the highest initial capital costs and best geographical locations for success. The method would "eliminate direct damage, no post harvest treatments would be required and access to high value export markets would be possibility. Residues of harmful malathion would be eliminated" (IAEA, 2001). "The primary benefit is that once fly free status is achieved no further management is required other than quarantine and monitoring so that accidental introductions can be eradicated quickly" (FAO/IAEA, 2001). The continuous release of sterile male flies is required in Okinawa to prevent the occurrence of an outbreak of melon fly in the already eradicated areas.

The total costs and net benefits of the three eradication options discussed above are summarized in TABLE 3. As can be gleaned, although the SIT eradication option involves the highest cost during the initial years, it offers the least-cost solution longer term. This is also reflected in the realized net benefits from the three options. The SIT eradication option realizes the greatest net benefits after nine years of project implementation. This would suggest that the longer the project life, the greater the net benefits.

In Okinawa, the SIT eradication method was chosen from the different alternative area-wide melon fly control strategies discussed above, although detailed comparative assessments of the strategies are not available to this author. According to an IAEA report, the SIT eradication method "has become even more cost-effective due to new technological breakthroughs such as better diets for mass rearing, development of male only strains, increased precision in sterile fly releases and more sensitive monitoring networks" (IAEA, 2001). The SIT eradication method has demonstrated itself to be the best strategy for Okinawa, partly because islands are relatively small and isolated. In addition, the methods adopted would maximize the project benefits in the long run, say after fourteen years, as shown by the IAEA study (2001).

PROJECT COSTS AND BENEFITS

We need to identify incremental costs and expected benefits of the project, and compare the net benefit (total project benefits – total project costs) "with" and "without" project implementation to determine whether the project is economically viable or not (see Kakazu and Yoshida, 1998). The "incremental" streams of costs and benefits are used to exclude past investments or sunk costs and benefits accrued only to these investments. We carefully need to identify not only costs and benefits of the project, but also the incremental outputs brought by the project implementation. The idea is illustrated in FIGURE 6-2.

Net Benefits

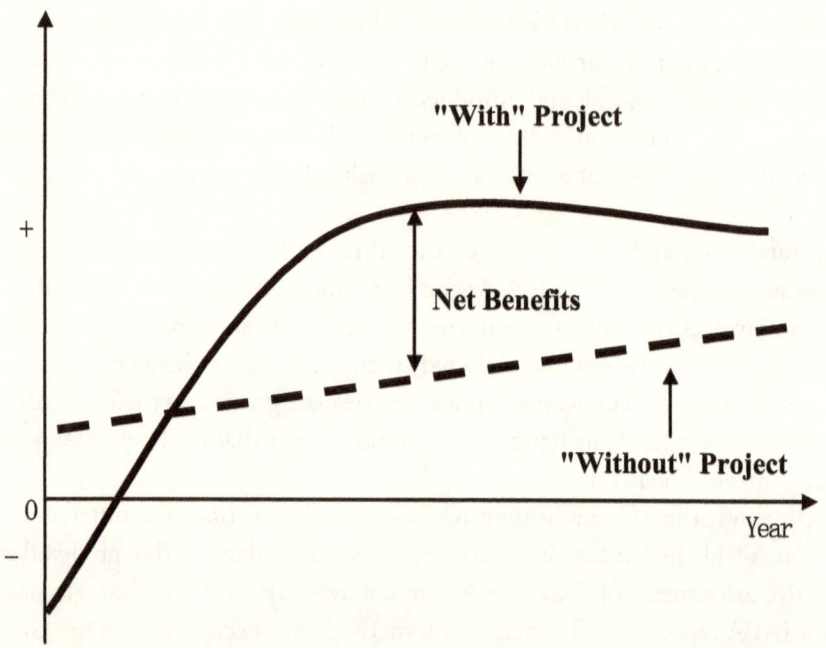

Source: H. Kakazu.

FIGURE 6-3. A Concept of Net Benefits With and Without Project.

We assume that even "without" the project, net benefits increase, although at a much slower pace than the "with" project scenario. Alternatively, we can assume, as it may be the case for Okinawa's farm products, that both "with" and "without" cases are projected to have declining trends. In this case, the "with" project scenario will have a slow pace of decline compared to the "without" project case. The net benefits of the "with" project case will be maximized at a certain point during the project life due to the discount factor.

Project Costs

Projects costs are broken down as follows:

(1)   Capital costs including depreciation allowances

(2)   Eradication costs including SIT males production and release, traps, bait sprays, fruit sampling, quarantine.

(3)   Administration costs including wages, research and training and maintenance.

The total costs of the melon fly eradication project in Okinawa amounted to ¥17billion (US $85 million) during the 1972-1993 period. This figure includes project preparations costs, capital costs, implementation costs, and prevention costs (TABLE 6-3). The annual prevention and maintenance costs after 1993 are estimated at ¥765million (US$38 million).

TABLE 6-3. Cost Profiles of Melon Fly Eradication Project in Okinawa

		Kume Island 1972-1977	Miyako Islands 1983-1987	Okinawa Islands 1986-1990	Yaeyama Islands 1989-1993	Total
Total cost	¥million	NA	NA	NA	NA	16,964
Construction cost	¥million	NA	NA	NA	NA	4,306
Project cost	¥million	309	1,558	4,562	2,774	9,203
Prevention cost	¥million	850	825	1,705	75	3,455
Total	¥million	NA	NA	NA	NA	317,932
Total staff employed	person	30,068	70,516	135,250	317,932	553,766
Area subject to eradication	ha	5,992	22,714	137,920	225,238	391,864
Number of sterile flies released	million	357	6,342	30,941	15,438	53,078

Notes: Construction costs are the costs of sterile insect mass-rearing facilities during the period of 1980-1993.
Prevention costs are for the period of 1978-1993.
Annual prevention and maintenance costs are estimated to amount ¥765 million.
NA = not available.

Project Benefits

We can distinguish between two types of project benefits:
(1)   Direct benefits reflected in increased production, sales, profits and quality; and
(2)   Indirect benefits arising mainly from preventing the spread of the insect pests and reducing substantially the use of environmentally hazardous chemicals such as pesticide. The natural enemies are also kept alive by the SIT eradication method, however these benefits are difficult to identify.

As for the indirect benefits, damages to human health (in terms of lives saved in by not using pesticide) can be calculated as follows:

Cost per treated person = $(C_a * N_a) + (C_h * N_h) + (C_w * N_w)$.
Where:

Ca=Cost of each atropine injection (¥)
Na=Average number of atropine injections per person
Ch=Hospital fee per day (¥)
Nh=Average number of days in hospital per person
Cw=Average daily wage of pesticide application personnel (¥)
Nw=Average number of productive days lost (spent in hospital and home).

Total costs can be obtained by multiplying the number of persons treated.

Although we do not attempt to estimate these benefits in this chapter due to insufficient data, it may be useful to suggest the estimating method here for future researchers on the subject.

Equalizing Discount Rate, Net Present Value, and Internal Rate of Return

In lieu of benefit quantification from the eradication strategies, due to insufficiency of data, it is possible to adopt the least-cost principle. This can be expressed in terms of the estimating the equalizing discount rate (EDR), i.e., equalizing the cost flows of the three different options that deliver the same benefits. The EDR (d*) is defined as the discount rate which equalizes the three cost streams:

$$\sum_{t=0}^{T} (X1xC1)/(1+d^*) = \sum (X2xC2)/(1+d^*) = \sum (X3xC3)/(1+d^*).$$

Where X1, X2 and X3 are inputs, and C1, C2 and C3 are unit costs of each input from years (t) 0 to T for the Bait suppression, the SIT suppression and the SIT eradication options, respectively. As already seen, although the SIT eradication potion requires the highest initial costs, in the long run, operation costs are the lowest among the three options. Therefore, assuming longer project implementation period and higher discount rate, or higher opportunity cost of capital, it is found that the SIT eradication method will present the least cost option. It should be noted, however, that the least-cost solution by itself does not give any indication of the economic merits of the project.

Since we can identify, though not completely, the project costs as well as project benefits, we can estimate the net present value (NPV), defined as the difference between the present values of the cost and benefit streams of a project which have been discounted at a rate equal to the opportunity cost of capital. The project is viable and acceptable if the NPV exceeds zero or is equal to zero, and is rejected if this value is negative. Assuming that the project life is from year 0 to T years, the NPV is given by

$$\sum_{t=0}^{T} Pt/(1-i) > 0$$

where, Pt is net profits (total sales – total costs) of the year t and i is the real market rate of interest or financial cost of capital investment. An alternative way of expressing project viability or profitability is by estimating the internal rate of return (IRR), which puts the NPV as zero, greater or equal the rate of real interest rate (i) as follows:

$$IRR \geq i.$$

The NPVs for the three eradication options are estimated by this author are shown (TABLE 6-4). As already noted, the SIT eradication option realizes the highest net benefits and the NPV at 5% discount rate after eight years of project implementation. This suggests that the longer the project life, the higher the IRR, the higher the net benefits.

TABLE 6-4. Comparison of Net Present Value of Three Options
($million)

Year	Bait-Suppression			SIT-Suppression			SIT-Eradication		
	Net Benefit	NPV 5%	NPV 10%	Net Benefit	NPV 5%	NPV 10%	Net Benefit	NPV 5%	NPV 10%
1	0	0	0	0	0	0	0	0	0
2	350	317	262	330	299	247	420	381	346
3	400	346	260	450	389	292	410	354	306
4	400	329	225	470	387	264	410	337	278
5	400	313	195	500	392	243	450	353	276
6	400	298	168	550	410	232	520	388	290
7	400	284	146	550	391	201	530	377	268
8	400	271	126	550	372	174	560	379	257
9	400	258	109	550	355	150	600	387	249
10	400	246	95	550	338	130	600	368	226
Sub-total	3,550	2,662	1,586	4,500	3,333	1,933	4,500	3,324	2,496
11	400	234	82	550	322	113	600	351	205
12	400	223	71	550	306	98	600	334	186
13	400	212	61	550	292	84	600	318	169
14	400	202	53	550	378	73	600	303	153
15	400	192	46	550	265	63	600	289	139
Total	5,550	3,725	1,899	6,700	4,896	2,364	7,500	4,919	3,348

Notes: Net benefits = Total benefits - Total costs, assuming 25% potential market gain.
Annual data for Mediterranean fruit fly control in the regions of Israel, Jordan, the Palestinian Territories and Syrian Arab Rep. Costs include program and environmental costs.

Source: IAEA (September 2001).

MAJOR HOST PRODUCTS

According to the Okinawa Prefectural government (1999), there are forty-one types of vegetables and fruits which are affected by the melon fly. The major important products, which accounted for more than 80% of the melon fly infested farm products, were selected in this study (TABLE 6-5). Although the overall trends of vegetables and fruits production have been decreasing due mainly to domestic as well as international competition and the island's high cost structure of agriculture, Okinawa's high-valued niche products such as bitter melon and mango have risen sharply particularly since 1990 when the melon fly was completely eradicated from the island.

TABLE 6-5. Production and Commercial Shipments of Major Host Products of the Fruit Fly: 1980-2000

	Production (ton)				
	1980	1985	1990	1995	2000
Bitter Melon	3,950	3,340	2,720	5,710	6,220
String Bean	3,650	4,110	4,500	3,360	2,830
Cucumber	5,220	4,290	3,890	3,910	2,610
Watermelon	6,620	2,980	4,650	5,760	5,570
Sponge Gourd	2,240	2,630	2,070	2,470	1,610
Squash (Pumpkin)	12,700	12,400	3,650	1,620	1,490
Green Pepper	2,560	2,450	2,090	1,610	2,300
Mango	6	48	278	635	1,290
Papaya (Fruits)	19	25	88	230	171
Wax Gourd	3,190	3,280	3,310	3,780	3,210
Tomato	1,330	2,480	2,520	2,160	2,340
Melon	52	190	727	754	572
Total	41,537	38,223	30,493	31,999	30,213

	Commercial Shipments (ton)				
Bitter Melon	2,727	2,223	1,820	4,480	4,990
String Bean	2,972	3,318	3,740	2,860	2,450
Cucumber	3,936	3,162	3,020	3,100	2,080
Watermelon	4,730	2,428	4,030	5,220	4,750
Sponge Gourd	1,752	1,968	1,500	1,860	1,270
Squash (Pumpkin)	10,290	9,445	2,870	1,240	1,200
Green Pepper	1,996	1,886	1,650	1,240	1,900
Mango	3	45	241	572	1,160
Papaya (Fruits)	13	20	63	190	147
Wax Gourd	2,385	2,489	2,550	2,970	2,730
Tomato	1,032	1,899	1,990	1,690	1,930
Melon	44	168	622	623	480
Total	31,880	29,051	24,096	26,045	25,087

Source: Same as TABLE 6-1.

About 80% of total production is commercially shipped for domestic and mainland markets. The remaining products are mostly either self-consumed or allowed to spoil in the farmyards.

The rates of damage to host products, which are crucial data in estimating the benefits or reduction in damages/losses as a result of complete eradication, were derived from a report of the Japan Atomic Energy Research Institute (JA-ERI, 2001). It should be noted that because of unavailability of damage data for mango, we used the damage rate for mandarin orange for mango (see APPENDIX data). The damage loss data, however, needs to be modified because these assumed 100% damage loss rate for exports. This assumption holds true only when the host products are allowed to be exported only after the complete eradication under the quarantine regulations.

In reality, however, except for mango and papaya, most host products were exported to mainland markets even prior to the eradication under fumigation treatments. Therefore the damage loss rates, weighted by exports and domestic markets, were used to derive the benefits.

NET BENEFITS (NB) AND THE NET PRESENT VALUE (NPV)

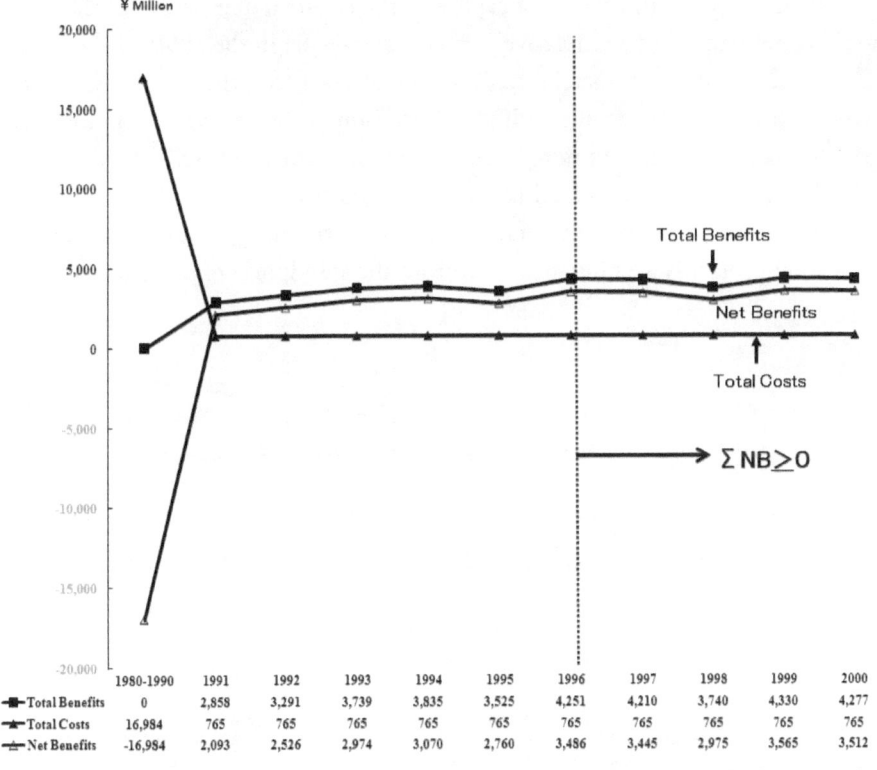

	1980-1990	1991	1992	1993	1994	1995	1996	1997	1998	1999	2000
Total Benefits	0	2,858	3,291	3,739	3,835	3,525	4,251	4,210	3,740	4,330	4,277
Total Costs	16,984	765	765	765	765	765	765	765	765	765	765
Net Benefits	-16,984	2,093	2,526	2,974	3,070	2,760	3,486	3,445	2,975	3,565	3,512

Note: Assuming zero discount rate, or zero opportunity cost of capital investment, the project produced net accumulated benefits after 6 years (1966) as indicated by the dotted vertical line.

Source: Computed from TABLE 6-5.

FIGURE 6-3. Net Benefits (NB) of the Melon Fly Eradication Project in Okinawa: 1980-2000.

As we have noted earlier, a large amount of host products, which are self-consumed by farmers or disposed by the growers' households, were excluded from the estimates. Furthermore, fumigation and quarantine costs as well as freshness of products for exports after the complete eradication, are not included in the benefit stream. Thus, we can say that the estimated benefits presented in FIGURE 6-3 are considered to be underestimated (see APPENDIX data for detailed estimates for each host product).

Assuming zero discount rate, or zero opportunity cost of capital investment, the project produced net accumulated benefits after six years of the eradication as indicated by the vertical line (FIGURE 6-3). This is a remarkable achievement amid the countless failures of and mounting criticism against public investment projects in Japan.

In calculating the net present value (NPV) of the melon fly eradication project, we used the real discount rate of 3.26% during the period. The rate is an average yield of a 10-year national bond during the 1990s. We are assuming that the relatively high opportunity cost of capital in the construction period of the 1980s should be refinanced by the relatively cheap capital cost in the 1990s if the project was carried out on a commercial basis. As a matter of fact, the project was totally financed through public funds with no expectation of cost recovery from increased agricultural production. As noted, the project pays for itself (self liquidating) in 1997 with ΣNPV roughly equal to the total project costs of $172 million (FIGURE 6-4). Therefore, we can conclude here that the decision to implement the eradication project is well justified even from the standpoint of commercial basis.

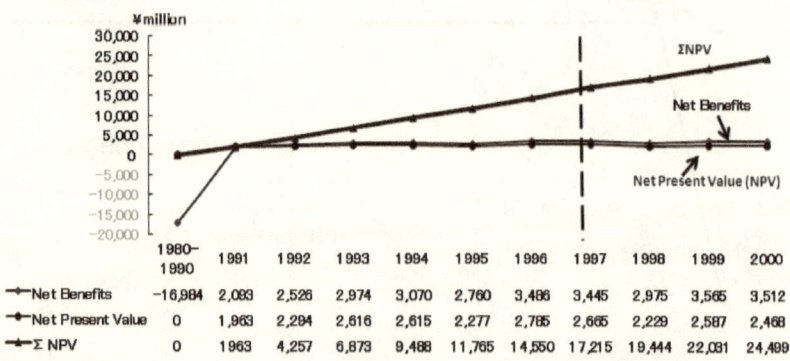

	1980–1990	1991	1992	1993	1994	1995	1996	1997	1998	1999	2000
Net Benefits	−16,984	2,093	2,526	2,974	3,070	2,760	3,486	3,445	2,975	3,565	3,512
Net Present Value	0	1,963	2,294	2,616	2,615	2,277	2,785	2,665	2,229	2,587	2,468
Σ NPV	0	1963	4,257	6,873	9,488	11,765	14,550	17,215	19,444	22,031	24,499

Notes: Discount rate (nominal interest rate - rate of inflation) is 3.26%, annual yield of 10-year government bond.
ΣNPV stands for annual accumulation of NPVs. The dotted line indicates that the eradication project pays itself in 1997
with ΣNPV roughly equals to the total project costs of $172 million.

Source: Computed from Table 6-6.

FIGURE 6-4. Net Present Value (NPV) of the Melon Fly Eradication Project in Okinawa: 1990-2000.

Conclusions

Okinawa's melon fly eradication project took more than fifteen years since it started actual planning. When the eradication was finally completed in 1993 in the beautiful Yaeyama Islands, the news was transmitted immediately to the concerned communities in the outside world. The reason for the publicity is that Okinawa recorded the first success story on eradicating the melon fly in island communities by using a biological area-wide SIT method. Okinawa's accomplishment was particularly significant because the other island areas, including Hawaii, attempted a similar eradication method but without the same success (Tan, 2000).

Even though the eradication project was totally financed through public funding, the project proved to be viable even on commercial basis. That is to say, the project recovered its total investment costs within eight years after project completion, while covering the opportunity cost of capital. We should be reminded again that the net benefits estimated in this study are those arising from the commercial shipments of melon fly host products. So that if we include environmental and preventive benefits such as pesticide-free farming, preservation of the natural enemies, and above all preventing the insect pests from further spreading into mainland Japan, the net private as well as social benefits far exceed the estimated commercial benefits. But because of time and data constraints, we could not estimate the indirect social benefits.

Any success story is accompanied by a great deal of painstaking effort, both in research and development as well as massive mobilization of human and capital resources. Most important, avid support of the local people and public organizations, including the prefectural and central governments, were an integral part of the success story. The story probably contains more than it has been told. Although continuous efforts to fight against potential intrusion of the insects are vital, the technological know-how and strategies for the success will be transferred successfully to infested areas worldwide.

APPENDIX TABLE 6-1 ESTIMATED BENEFITS OF MAJOR HOST PRODUCTS OF THE MELON FLY: 1991-2000

(×Million)

Product	Category	Rate of Damage (%)	1980-1990	1991	1992	1993	1994	1995	1996	1997	1998	1999	2000	Total 1980-2000
Bitter Melon	Total Shipments	45.0	7,074	528	603	668	741	602	1,114	1,019	1,052	982	1,047	15,431
	Exports	45.0	53	34	63	98	96	133	163	154	172	214	218	1,399
	Domestic Market	45.0	7,021	493	539	570	645	469	951	865	880	769	829	14,032
String Bean	Total Shipments	15.0	5,458	561	563	550	465	433	489	476	394	356	315	10,059
	Exports	15.0	4,065	474	429	320	310	304	301	271	191	172	167	7,003
	Domestic Market	45.0	1,393	87	133	230	155	129	188	204	203	183	148	3,055
Cucumber	Total Shipments	27.0	0	0	299	347	385	324	270	266	190	189	153	2,422
	Exports	100.0	0	5	19	27	40	19	13	20	15	15	13	217
	Domestic Market	25.2	0	294	320	320	345	293	251	253	170	173	106	2,205
Watermelon	Total Shipments	41.1	7,265	847	702	730	753	640	626	742	729	996	990	15,019
	Exports	41.1	3,575	419	365	285	259	248	237	259	173	175	208	6,204
	Domestic Market	41.1	3,689	428	337	444	494	392	389	483	556	820	781	8,815
Sponge Gourd	Total Shipments	45.0	2,313	348	347	486	488	489	462	469	430	384	471	6,687
	Exports	45.0	0	0	1	2	2	2	2	3	3	2	3	20
	Domestic Market	45.0	2,312	348	346	484	487	487	459	466	427	382	468	6,666
Squash (Pumpkin)	Total Shipments	22.8	5,419	132	117	102	80	80	99	73	74	66	68	6,310
	Exports	22.8	3,495	71	64	38	48	56	48	45	24	33	32	3,933
	Domestic Market	22.8	1,924	61	52	64	33	43	51	29	51	34	36	2,377
Green Pepper	Total Shipments	15.0	942	114	72	133	99	94	95	102	60	74	74	1,841
	Exports	15.0	0	0	0	0	0	0	0	0	0	0	0	1
	Domestic Market	15.0	942	114	72	133	99	94	95	102	60	54	74	1,840
Mango	Total Shipments	50.5	0	0	207	316	401	447	674	714	505	1,062	915	5,240
	Exports	100.0	0	0	122	180	300	274	395	505	403	732	630	3,541
	Domestic Market	25.0	0	0	85	136	100	173	279	208	102	330	285	1,699
Papaya (Fruits)	Total Shipments	56.1	0	0	39	22	61	62	53	76	24	33	29	400
	Exports	100.0	0	0	36	18	40	46	39	65	12	10	9	276
	Domestic Market	26.3	0	0	2	3	21	16	15	12	12	23	20	124
Wax Gourd	Total Shipments	22.0	1,389	112	115	140	129	149	164	157	157	112	113	2,683
	Exports	22.0	250	40	38	38	42	42	41	49	39	40	44	659
	Domestic Market	22.0	1,139	73	77	102	91	107	122	118	54	72	69	2,024
Tomato	Total Shipments	15.0	454	98	118	132	108	96	117	91	71	47	54	1,385
	Exports	15.0	4	2	5	5	8	6	5	5	12	11	12	74
	Domestic Market	15.0	450	96	112	126	100	90	112	86	59	36	42	1,311
Melon	Total Shipments	26.3	506	120	111	113	125	110	87	79	54	49	48	1,401
	Exports	25.3	25	16	10	5	6	4	12	20	15	11	8	133
	Domestic Market	26.3	481	103	101	108	118	105	75	58	38	37	40	1,263
Total			61,638	5,717	6,583	7,479	7,670	7,050	8,502	8,419	7,480	8,659	8,554	137,750

Notes: Rates of damage for cucumber, mango and papaya are weighted averages of exports and domestic market.
Benefit or Damage Saved = Value of Shipment * Rate of Damage.

Sources: Rates of damage are taken from a report of Japan Neucler Energy System Study Group (June 2001).

NOTES

International Atomic Energy Agency (IAEA) (2001), P.30.
Ibid., p.31.
Ibid., p.32.

Food and Agricultural Organization (FAO) (2001), P.5.
International Atomic Energy Agency (2001), p.5.
Ibid., p.58.
Okinawa Times (2007), p.8.

REFERENCES

Enkerlin, W. and J.M. Mumbord.1997. Economic Evaluation of Three Alternative Methods for Control of the Mediterranean Fruit Fly in Israel, Palestinian Territories, and Jordan. *Journal of Economic Entomology,* vol.90, no.5, pp.1066-1072.

Ito, Y. 1980. *Mushi o hanashite, Mushi o korosu* (Killing the Insect Pests by Releasing the Insects). Tokyo: Chukoshinsho.

Japan Atomic Energy Research Institute (JAERI) and the Japan Atomic Industrial Forum (JAIF). 2001. "Economic Scale of Nuclear Energy Utilization," *NSA/ Commentaries,* no.9.

Food and Agricultural Organization (FAO). 2001. *Fruit Fly Cost Benefit Analysis Program Manual.* Vienna.

International Atomic Energy Agency (IAEA). 2001. *Economic Evaluation of Three Alternative Methods for Control of the Mediterranean Fruit Fly (Diptera: Tephritidae) in Israel, Jordan, Lebanon, Palestinian Territories, and Syrian Arab Republic.* Vienna.

International Atomic Energy Agency (IAEA). 1995. *Economic Evaluation of Damage Caused by, and Methods of Control of the Mediterranean Fruit Fly in the Maghreb: An Analysis Covering Three Control Options, Including the Sterile Insect Technique.* Vienna.

Hayami, Y. and V.W. Ruttan. 1985. *Agricultural Development: An International Perspective.* Revised Edition. Baltimore: Johns Hopkins Press.

Kakazu. H. 1994. *Sustainable Development of Small Island Economies.* Boulder: Westview Press.

————.2003. "Economic Evaluation of the Melon Fly Eradication Project in Okinawa." *INSULA: International Journal of Island Affairs,* year 12, no.1, pp.41-50.

————. 2000. *The Challenge for Okinawa: Thriving Locally in a Globalized Economy.* Naha: Okinawa Development Finance Corporation.

————. and T. Yoshida (eds.). 1998. *Problems and Prospects of the Asiatic Patterns of Development.* Nagoya: Nagoya University Press.

Kuznets, S. 1965. *Modern Economic Growth and Structure.* New York: Norton.

Nakahara, L. M. 1977. *Re-Appraisal of the Importance of Fruit Flies to Hawaii's*

Agricultural Economy. Honolulu: Hawaii Department of Agriculture.

Okinawa Prefectural Government, Fruit Fly Eradication Project Office.1999. *Fruit Fly Eradication Project in Okinawa.* Naha.

Okinawa Times, June 16, 2007. "A Collapse of Okinawa's Agriculture by EPA."

Oshiro, K.2007. *Okinawa no Nogyo to Dojo* (Okinawa's Agriculture and Soil). Haebaru: Mitsuwa Fukushi Kai.

Tan, K.H. (ed.). 2000. *Area-Wide Control of Fruit Flies and Other Insect Pests.* Penang: Penerbit Universiti Sains Malyasia.

Teruya, T. 1997. Studies on the Sterilization of the Melon Fly, Bactrocera Cucurbitae Coquillett, by Gamma Radiation. *Bulletin of Okinawa Prefectural Fruit Fly Eradication Project Office.* Supplement, no. 2.

Chapter 7

Networking Okinawa and Taiwan

Introduction

Okinawa and Taiwan are so close physically as well as historically that the Chinese governments in both Beijing and Taipei used to regard Okinawa or the Ryukyu Islands as a part of their sovereign land. It is natural to assume a deeper socio-economic tie between two peripheral regions in the East China Sea. The reality, however, is far from what it should be. Particularly since Okinawa's administrative reversion to Japan in 1972, her socio-economic ties with mainland Japan have strengthened, while her ties with international societies including Taiwan have weakened. Despite Okinawa's struggle to pursue self-reliant economic development, her socio-economic life has been increasingly dependent on and integrated into the Japanese system. More than 90% of Okinawa's trade and tourism activities are conducted with mainland Japan. The Japanese government has also expended a huge sum of financial transfers into Okinawa's development partly to maintain the U.S. military bases which still account for 75% of all military base facilities in Japan.

The systematic deepening and widening of networks with mainland Japan after reversion made Okinawans more risk-averting and inward-looking, creating a dependency syndrome within the minds of Okinawans. Okinawans have, however, gradually come to realize that the islands' sustainable economic development and ownership cannot be realized without networking with the dynamic neighboring Asian region, particularly with Taiwan. Reflecting such a mood, Okinawa-Taiwan ties in terms of trade, investment and exchange of peoples have been growing. Okinawa's exports to Taiwan, for example, have tripled in recent years generating a sizable trade surplus for Okinawa. Taiwan's investment in Okinawa's tourism and information industries is also on rise. There are, however, many impending issues including security issue in the region, military bases in Okinawa, disputes over the Daioyu/Senkaku Islands, border regulations and regional governance and autonomy to be resolved in order to further strengthen ties between the two regions. The concept of a Taiwan-Okinawa-Kyushu Economic Zone has been proposed.

Geopolitical-economic configurations in the East Asian region, where Taiwan and Okinawa are located, have been changing rapidly, particularly since the collapse of the Soviet Union in the early 1990s. One striking change is the rising politico-economic power of China relative to Japan where the population has started to decline, coupled with a decade of economic stagnation without any clear prospective of sustainable economic growth. Another important change is an increasingly uncertain security balance in the region described as an "arc of instability" in the 2001 *U.S. Quadrennial Defense Review* (QDR, U.S. Department of Defense, 2001). The QDR placed particular emphasis on the possibility of a security vacuum in the vast Asia-Pacific region because of the unpredictable behavior of North Korea, the impending China-Taiwan issue and territorial disputes over small islands coupled with the declining influence of the United States.

There are, however, encouraging politico-economic movements in the region, as demonstrated by the second East-Asian Summit held in the Philippines in 2007 which aimed at creating an economic community similar to the EU in the future. After a brief review of current geopolitical-economic trends in East Asia, this chapter discusses the past performances and future prospects for the Okinawan economy, Okinawa-Taiwan networking and challenges to be resolved in creating a Taiwan-Okinawa economic partnership. Naturally, much emphasis will be placed on Okinawa's sustainable development through possible interactions with her most proximate cross-border neighbor which the local people used to call "Taiwan" or "Formosa."

Although Taiwan and Okinawa are isolated islands and located far from major international markets, they are very parts of the emerging East Asian economic community. Therefore, a brief discussion of recent move toward building an East Asian economic community is justified before focusing on an Okinawa and Taiwan economic partnership.

Emerging Economic Partnership

The East Asian Economic Caucus (EAEC), whose assumed members comprising ASEAN+3 (Japan, Korea and China) was initially proposed by Malaysian Prime Minister Dr. Mahathier Mohamad in 1990. The concept was totally forgotten during the early 1990's, however, due primarily to the rapid advance of globalization under the GATT/WTO regime. Fortunately, the concept of the EAEC has been revived recently, stimulated by a surge of open regionalism represented by Free Trade Agreements (FTAs) or Economic Partnership Agreements (EPAs). The ASEAN Foreign Ministers meeting, held in Brunei in 1995, endorsed the EAEC concept as a framework within which to pursue economic cooperation in the East Asian region. It is interesting to note that World Bank's Development Indicators classify the world economy by regional blocs including EAEC, NAFTA and EU. In this chapter we use EAFTA (East Asian Free Trade Area) instead of EAEC to represent the East Asian region though the EAFTA, which includes Taiwan and Okinawa, is still at a highly formative stage (see Kakazu, 2004-A).

It is useful to identify the changing status of the EAFTA in comparison with NAFTA and the EU (FIGURE 7-1). The EAFTA accounts for 29.5-30% of world's population compared with NAFTA (8%) and the EU (5.8%) in 2005. If we think of the size of population as an important basis for economic development in terms of market and production base, then the EAFTA has about five times more economic potential than the two blocs. This enormous potential has been exploited in recent years as can be seen in the expansion of its GDP which increased from mere 13.5% in 1980 to 22.7% in 2005. This is almost comparable with the EU and is rapidly catching up with NAFTA.

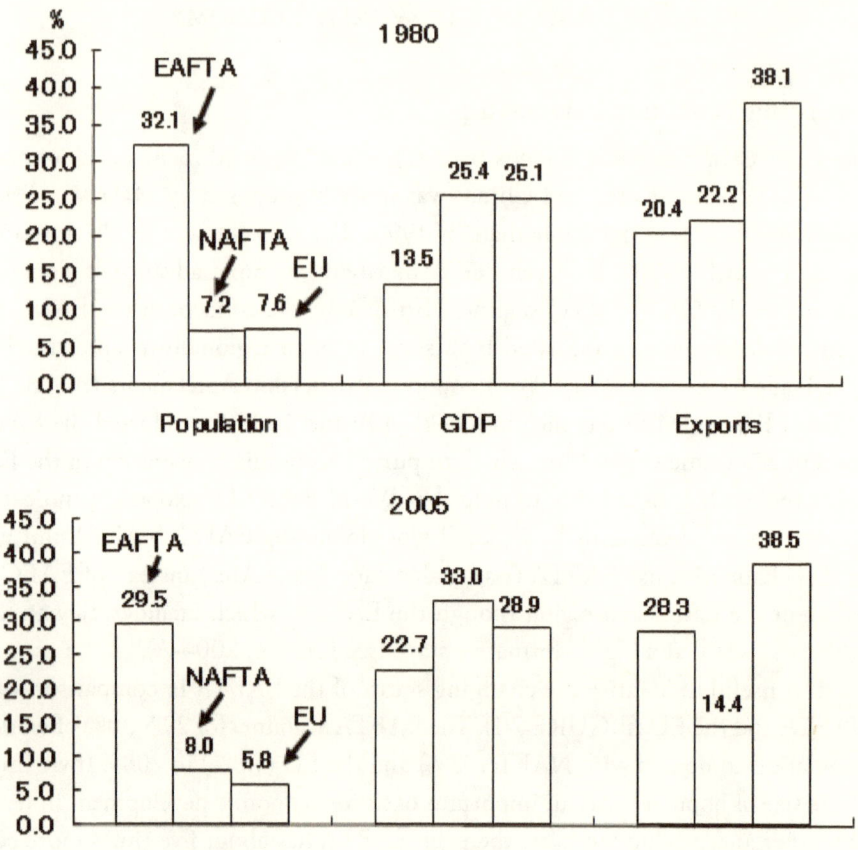

Notes: Figures indicate shares of world totals.
EAFTA=East Asian Free Trade Area includes Japan, ANIES and ASEAN5.
NAFTA=North American Free Trade Area includes U.S., Canada and Mexico.
EU=European Union (15 European nations).

Sources: Complied from World Bank, World Development Indicators
ADB, Key Indicators, various issues.

FIGURE 7-1. EAFTA'S Srengths in World Economy.

The economic dynamism of the EAFTA can be more adequately represented in terms of its exports, which increased from 20.4% in 1980 to 28.3% in 2005, catching up rapidly with those of the EU. These macro figures indicate that the economic power of the EAFTA is now almost equivalent to those of NAFTA and the EU. Furthermore, it is only a matter of time before EAFTA runs ahead of the other two most powerful blocs in the world. According to the latest estimates, China's GDP alone in terms of the purchasing power parity (PPP) will easily surpass that of the U.S. and EU by 2020 (*The Japan Economic Journal*, 17 January 2007). It should also be noted that Japan's GDP in 2020 is estimated as being no more than one quarter of China's.

Although the current per capita GDP of EAFTA is about 15% of NAFTA and the EU, due primarily to the China factor. China's population accounts for more than 70% of the EAFTA total, and it is rapidly caching up with the other two blocs. If we measure per capita income in terms of PPP, the gap will be substantially narrowed. Furthermore if we include only China's coastal areas, whose population alone accounts for a population the same size as NAFTA, the per capita gap will be further substantially narrowed. There is no doubt that the EAFTA is the most dynamic growth center in the world and the most important engine in promoting regional cooperation. This is demonstrated by a sharp increase of EAFTA's intra-regional trade which is almost comparable to EU and NAFTA (FIGURE 7-2).

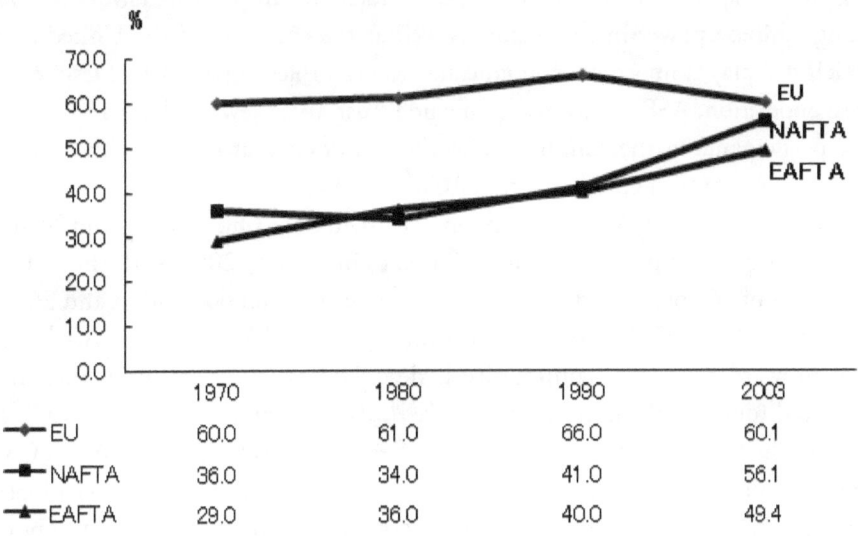

	1970	1980	1990	2003
EU	60.0	61.0	66.0	60.1
NAFTA	36.0	34.0	41.0	56.1
EAFTA	29.0	36.0	40.0	49.4

Source: Compiled from The World Bank, *World Development Indicators, 2005*.

FIGURE 7-2. Intra-regional Exports Trade: 1970-2003 (% of total regional trade).

The increasing interdependence among EAFTA countries can also be seen in their changing export markets. Although the U.S. is still the most important single market for all EAFTA countries, notably for China, regional shares have substantially increased for all countries in the past decade. The EAFTA now accounts for 40% of Japan's export market, a jump from 29% a decade ago. In view of anticipated dynamic economic growth, trade liberalization and complementarities in the EAFTA region, economic interdependence among the region will only accelerate in the future.

Towards an East Asian Community

Since the ASEAN+3 Summit was launched in 1997, various regional cooperation initiatives have emerged from this framework. Probably the most important initiative was the 2001 report entitled "Towards an East Asian Community (EAC): Region of Peace, Prosperity and Progress" which recommended the establishment of an East Asian Summit. The first East Asian Summit was held in Kuala Lumpur in 2005, where Japan proposed a two-tiered approach that includes core ASEAN-3 and important regional partners such as Australia, New Zealand and India. Japan, and notably Singapore and Indonesia, advocated that the community be built on a clear concept of open regionalism (open, inclusive, transparent and outward-looking) instead of fortress Asia which tends to be influenced by a rising regional hegemony. Japan and some major ASEAN members in particular worried about rising Chinese power in the region as well as the exclusion of the United States which still plays important economic and security roles in East Asia. Despite Chinese opposition, ASEAN agreed to include Australia, New Zealand and India as full participants in the summit under the condition that they sign the ASEAN Treaty of Amity and Cooperation (TAC).

The second East Asia Summit on the theme of "One Caring and Sharing Community" took place in Cebu, Philippines in January 2007, with the full participation of 16 countries that account for about 3 billion population and 20% of the world's GDP. Citing an editorial from *The Asahi Shimbun*, East Asia's latest move toward a regional community is described as "the start of an uncharted voyage through challenging waters." (*The Asahi Shimbun*, January 17, 2007). Although the Cebu Summit revealed two different visions for the East Asian Community building on proposals by China and Japan, the Cebu Declaration adopted, among other things, to address regional energy security including the development biofuel and energy-saving technology as well as the development of information and communication technology (ICT).

For Japan, the summit became an important forum to further ramify soured China-Japan, South Korea-Japan relations which have been improving since Prime Minister Shinzo Abe took office in autumn 2006. The summit clearly revealed that China has taken more positive initiatives than Japan even in trade and economic cooperation among ASEAN countries, pledging to open its market through more liberal FTA arrangements than Japan.

The new regional framework of the East Asian Community is also a welcome event to the peripheral regions such as Taiwan and Okinawa where hegemonic rivalries among regional big powers namely China, US and Japan have worked as negative factors for networking two regions. The East Asian Community framework and its development process can be expected to contain perceived Chinese military threats to Taiwan.

Economic integration, however, is not a linear process. It took Western Europe nearly half a century of tedious negotiations and painstaking efforts to realize the European Union, the highest form of economic integration we can think of at the present time. If we think of enormous diversity among the East Asian regions compared to Western Europe in terms of the stages of economic development, institution and capacity building, geopolitics, history, culture and geography, the EAFTA face a formidable task ahead in achieving an EU type of integration (Hara, 2005).

There are, for example, huge gaps in the stages of economic development among the EAFTA countries in terms of nominal as well as real (PPP) per capita income (FIGURE 7-3) The gaps between Vietnam, the lowest per capita income in the region and Japan, the highest, are 1/88th and 1/13th respectively. Diversity, however, means complementarities, which is a positive factor for regional economic integration as is demonstrated in increasing intra-regional trade between ASEAN and non-ASEAN EAFTA countries.

Japan has concluded FTAs and EPAs with countries including Singapore, Mexico, Thailand, Malaysia, Philippines, Chile, Indonesia and Brunei, and it is now negotiating an EPA with Australia which may work against the interest of Okinawa because of it's highly protected agricultural products. Sugar and beef production, in particular, may not be viable under the EPA trade liberalization program with Australia. The Okinawa Prefectural Government (OPG) has estimated the overall impact of the EPA on Okinawa's agriculture as much as 80 billion yen, or 9% of Okinawa's agricultural production in 2005. Sugarcane is grown mainly in Okinawa's relatively poor rural areas and outlying islands. There must be some kind of safety net to compensate for the lost income arising from the EPA implementation.

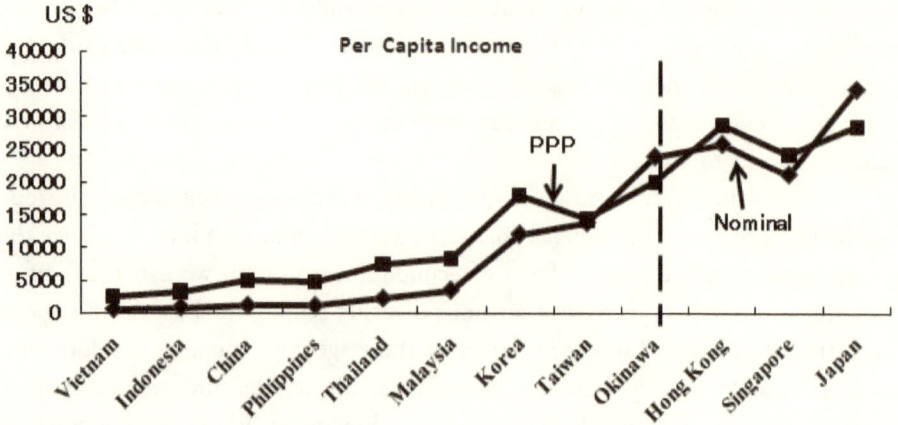

Sources: World Bank, *World Development Report 2003* and ADB, Key Indicators 2003.

FIGURE 7-3. EAFTA's Stagess of Development in Tterms of Per Capita Income: 2003.

ECONOMIC RELATIONS BETWEEN TAIWAN AND OKINAWA

Economic Network

Okinawa's main island is much closer to Taiwan (630km or 394 miles) than to Kyushu (1,000km or 625 miles), and to Tokyo (1,600 km or 1,000miles) on which the Okinawan economy heavily depends. It takes only about an hour to fly from Naha to Taipei. If geographical proximity were a key factor for a successful region-al economic integration---since it implies lower transaction costs such as for travel, transportation, and communication---then it would be natural for Okinawa to have much closer economic ties with Taiwan than Tokyo. The reality, however, is the reverse situation. For many years Taiwanese products are first shipped to Yokohama or Kobe and then to Okinawa. This practice has been rationalized on the basis that there has been only one tanker trip per week between Okinawa and Taiwan, mainly because of the lack of cargo to and from Okinawa (Kakazu, 2004-B).

Okinawa's trade depends heavily on mainland Japan. Foreign trade accounts for less than ten percent of Okinawa's total trade. Okinawa's exports to Taiwan have risen dramatically since 2000, accounting for about 70% of Okinawa's total foreign trade in 2006 (FIGURE 7-4). Okinawa's imports from Taiwan, however, account for less than 10% of Okinawa's total foreign trade. Okinawa has con-tinuously generated sizable trade surpluses with Taiwan despite her overall trade balance recording chronic deficits. Okinawa's major export items to Taiwan are petroleum products, scrap metal, used machinery and recycled paper, while major import items from Taiwan are food products, furniture and construction materials such as sand and marble.

Taiwan's investments in Okinawa particularly in the areas of hotel, IT and real estate are on the rise in recent years. On the other hand, there is a rising demand in Taiwan for Okinawan health foods and Okinawan restaurants.

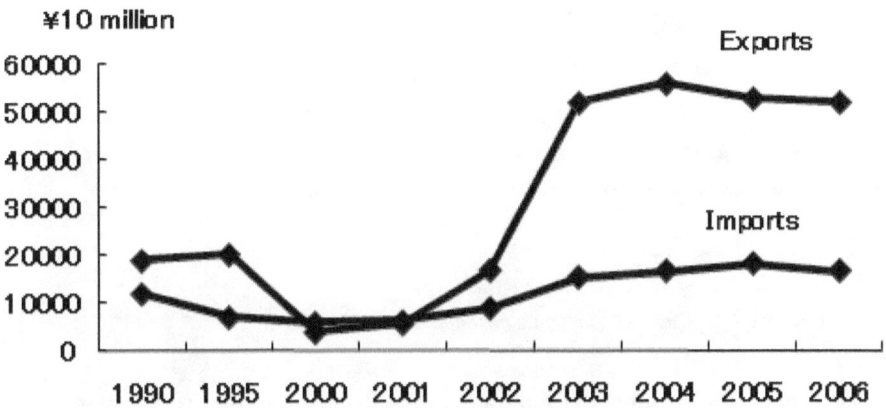

Source: Okinawa Customs Office, Ministry of Treasury.

FIGURE 7-4. Okinawa's Trade with Taiwan: 1990-2006.

On the other hand, Taiwan's trade with Okinawa accounts for only 0.1% of Taiwan's total trade. Taiwan's trade and investment have been rapidly shifting from its traditional trading partners such as the United States and Japan to mainland China in recent years. This trend is clearly seen in the amount of the so-called clearance shipping between Taiwan and mainland China as we have briefly discussed in Chapter 2. The number of clearance ships increased from 907 in 1994 to 3,217 in 2001 and to over 5,000 in recent years or from 36% of Okinawa's total foreign vessel visits in 1994 to over 80% in the 2000s. Ishigaki City benefited about \200 million in tonnage tax revenues yearly from customs clearance operations.

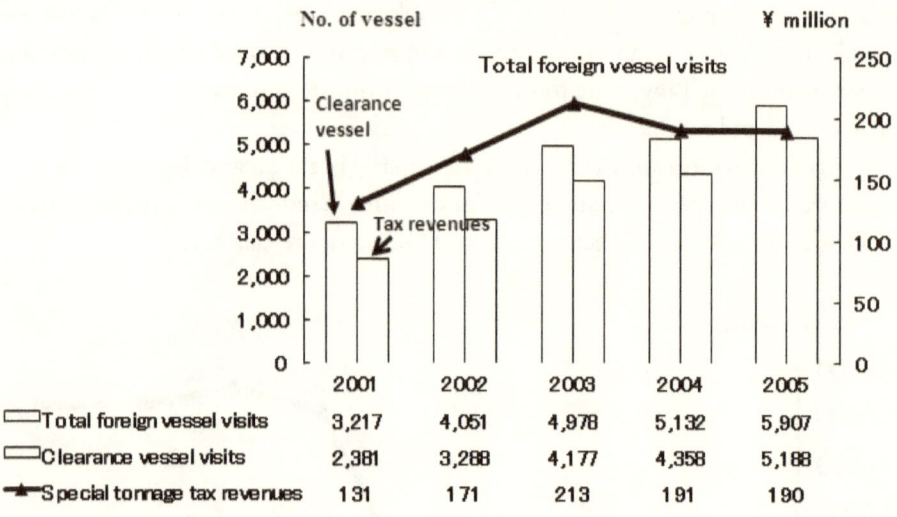

	2001	2002	2003	2004	2005
Total foreign vessel visits	3,217	4,051	4,978	5,132	5,907
Clearance vessel visits	2,381	3,288	4,177	4,358	5,188
Special tonnage tax revenues	131	171	213	191	190

Source:See FIGURE 7-4.

FIGURE 7-5. Clearance Shipping between Taiwan-Okinawa.

The increasing number of clearance ships will generate conditions favorable for Naha port to be designated as one of Asia's base, or hub ports, which will systemically reduce Okinawa's transport and insurance costs. The designation as a base port means improved port facilities and lower transportation costs, which will serve to make Okinawa far more competitive in global trading. There is, however, a possible turnaround for the clearance system if the Nationalist Party or Kuomintang (KMT) replaces incumbent President Chen Shui-bian of the Democratic Progressive Party (DPT) in next year's presidential election. The KMT is steering in the direction of direct trade with mainland China which is now Taiwan's most important trade and investment partner (*Economist*, January 15, 2005).

Networking of People

As we have already discussed, Okinawa's international interactions have declined since her reversion. This can be seen in the number of flights from Naha Airport. There are twenty-two daily flights from Okinawa to Tokyo, while international flights are reduced to four destinations (Seoul, Shanghai, Manila and Taipei) from six in the past (FIGURE 7-6). Japan Airline stopped its direct flights from Naha to Hong Kong in 2003. Asiana and China Eastern are having a difficult time maintaining even the current two flights a week. China Airlines operates two flights daily. The airline has been picking up its lost passengers in recent years. Taipei, however, is becoming an important regional hub airport for Okinawan travelers in recent years. A large portion of Okinawan travelers flying on China Airlines are using Taipei as a transit point to China, Southeast Asia and other destinations.

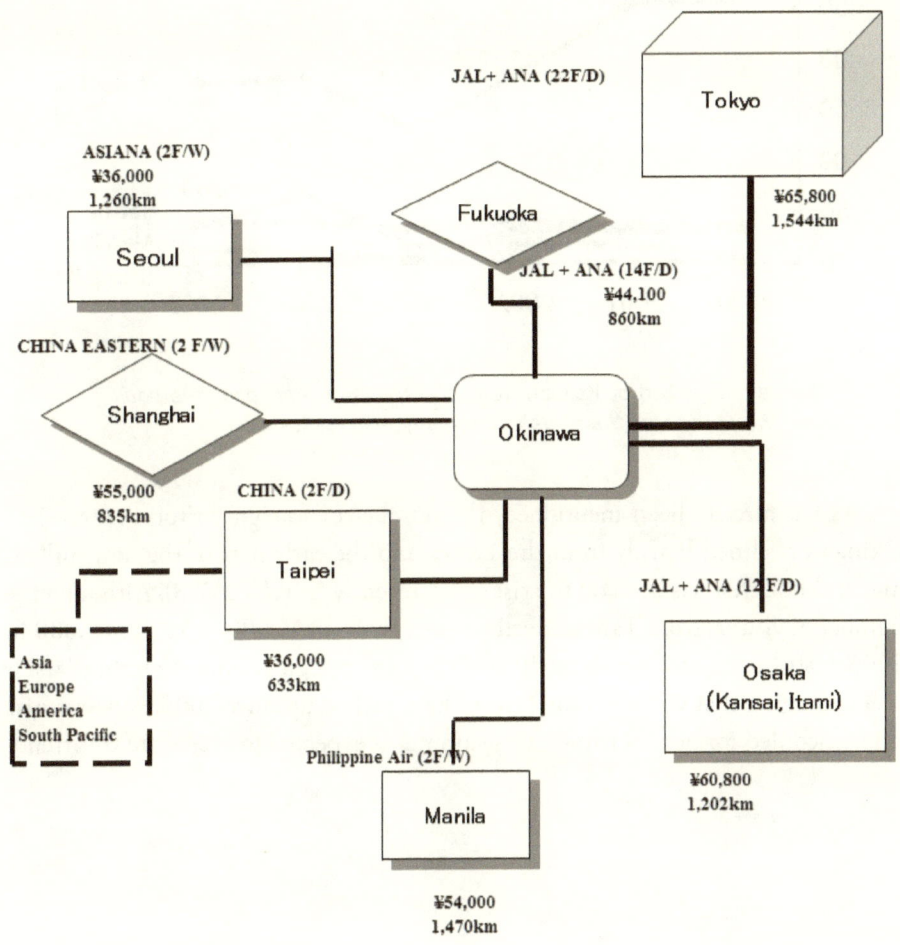

Roundtrip normal fees as of February 1, 2007.

Source: Okinawa Tourist.

FIGURE 7-6. Airline Netwoks from Okinawa.

The number of international flights from Okinawa reflects Okinawa's intensity of international interactions. Sixty percent of international travelers from Okinawa head to Taiwan, followed by China and South Korea (FIGURE 7-7).

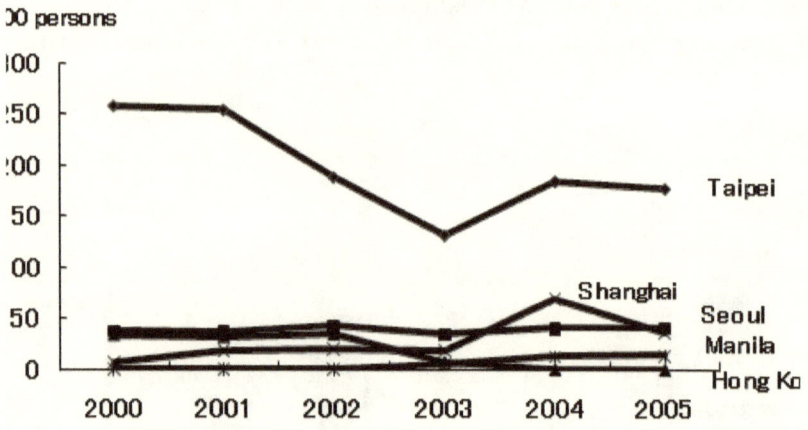

00 persons

100
:50
:00
50
00
50
0

Taipei

Shanghai

Seoul

Manila

Hong Ko

2000   2001   2002   2003   2004   2005

Sources: Compiled by Kakazu from *The Okinawa Statistical Yearbook* and *The Outline of the Kyushu Economy*, various issues.

As has already been mentioned, the number of foreign visitors (tourists) to Okinawa declined sharply from the 1990's into the early part of the new millennium, although it has been on the rise again recently (FIGURE 7-8). Although the number of visitors from Taiwan declined sharply from 15,000 in 1999 to 5,000 in 2006, it still accounted for about 70% of the total foreign visitors in recent years. It is encouraging that visitors from Taiwan have picked up since 2003. A new cruise ship scheduled for official launch this summer is expected to accelerate this trend.

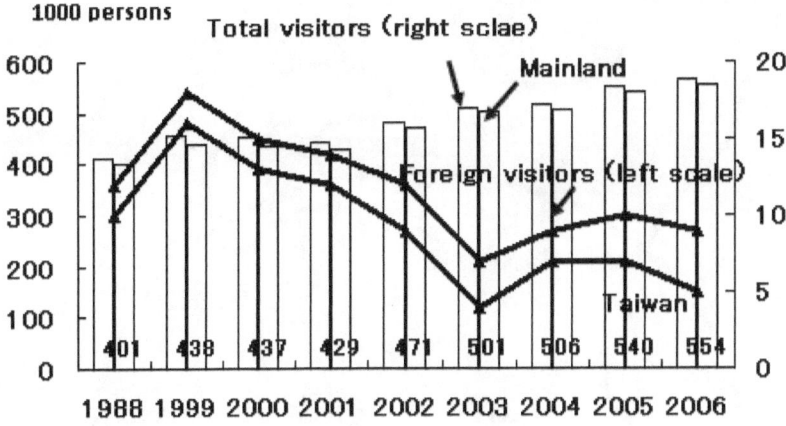

Source: Constructed from *Tourism Statistics of Okinawa*.

FIGURE 7-8. Okinawa's Inbound Visitors.

A TAIWAN-OKINAWA-KYUSHU ECONOMIC ZONE

Okinawa and Taiwan are close enough to be within "whistle" distance. It takes only an hour by airplane from Naha to Taipei, and on a clear day we can see Taiwan's highest mountain *Gyokuzan* from Yonaguni, the westernmost island of Japan. It is natural to consider that there should be deeper socio-economic ties between our two peripheral regions in the East China Sea. Although there has been a far greater degree of interaction between Okinawa and Taiwan in recent years in terms of trade and in the exchange of people, the strength of the network is far from what it could and should be. In order to strengthen networking activities between the two regions, we would like to propose the establishment of a Taiwan-Okinawa-Kyushu Economic Zone (TOKEZ) (FIGURE 7-9).

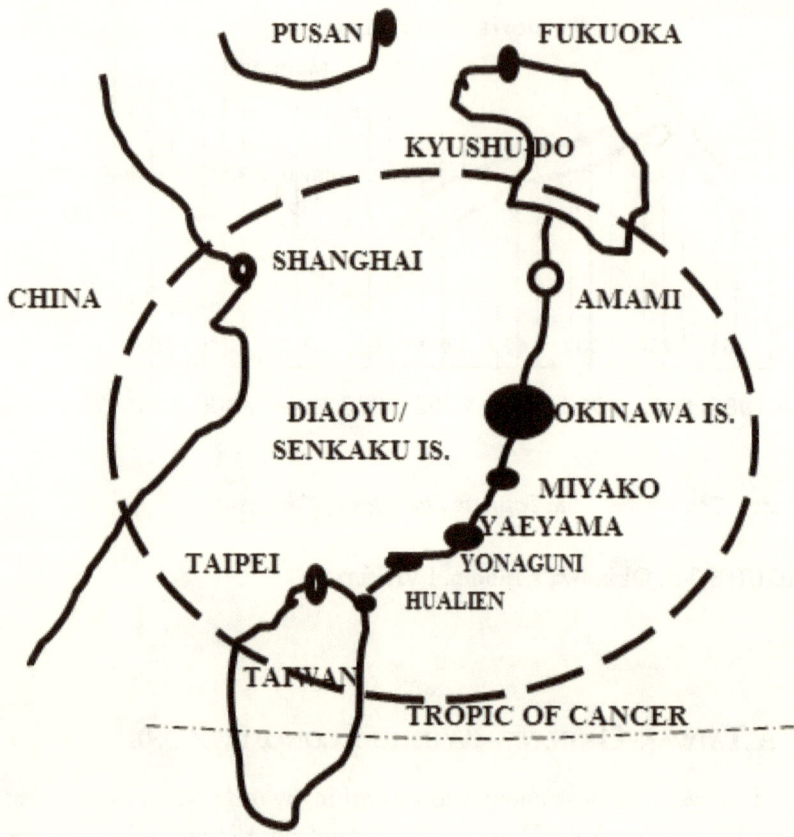

Source: Kakazu, H. (2007).

FIGURE 7-9. A Concept of Taiwan-Okinawa-Kyushu Economic Zone.

As an initial step to realize this scheme, we would propose establishing an Okinawa Taiwan Special Economic Zone (OTSEZ). Ideally the OTSEZ should be located in facilities within recently returned U.S. military bases such as the Naha Military Port or Camp Kinser in Urasoe City (FIGURE 7-10). The Taiwan Special Economic Zone in Subic Bay in the Philippines, which was successfully established on returned naval U.S. bases in the 1990's, stands as a model for OTSEZ.

176

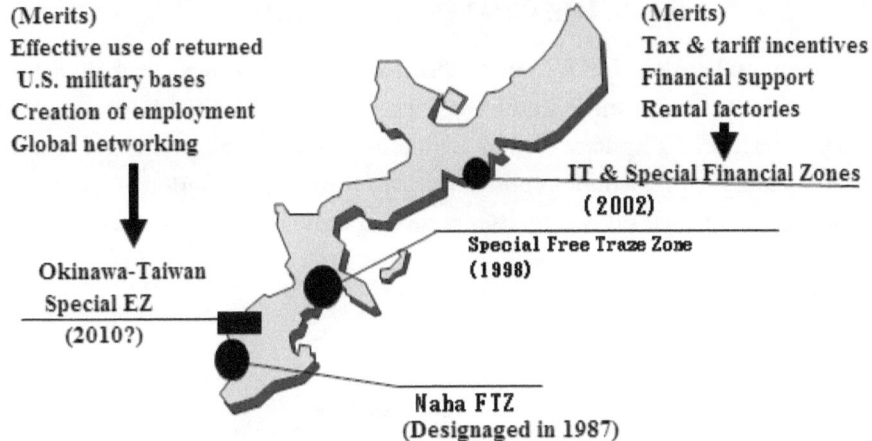

(Merits)
Effective use of returned
 U.S. military bases
Creation of employment
Global networking

(Merits)
Tax & tariff incentives
Financial support
Rental factories

IT & Special Financial Zones
(2002)

Special Free Traze Zone
(1998)

Okinawa-Taiwan
Special EZ
(2010?)

Naha FTZ
(Designaged in 1987)

Source: Industrial Policy Division, Okinawa prefecture.

FIGURE 7-10. Okinawa-Taiwan Special Economic Zones.

The OTSEZ will be used as a trade center, including a stockpoint for parts, exhibitions of new products, processing parts, data and information center (back-office), design center, R & D center and human resource development center. Just as the existing Okinawa Special Economic Zone, the OTSEZ should have a special tax credit system as well as duty-free imports for export purpose. In order to realize the OTSEZ, several complicated problems must be resolved as detailed in the following sections.

It should be noted here that Yonaguni Island, Japan's closest island to Taiwan and a sister city with Taiwan's Hualien, has proposed a "Yonaguni-Taiwan Cross-border Exchange Special Zone" to the Japanese Cabinet Minister (see Oshiro, H., 2007). The Special Zone aims at Yonaguni's sustainable development through direct socio-economic exchanges between Yonaguni and Taiwan, particularly through direct trade. Yonaguni prospered through direct trade with Taiwan until the early 1950s (Okuno's book, 2005 provides a fascinating account of this trade). Yonaguni Island has also attracted worldwide attention in recent years for its mysterious and archeologically controversial underwater rocks which may be a lost continent such as Plato's Atlantis or Mu (see Kimura 2002). The Yonaguni proposal, no doubt, will be beneficial to both Yonaguni and Taiwan, but the Cabinet office has not been receptive to the idea mainly because the Japanese government does not have formal diplomatic relation with the Taiwan government.

THE CHALLENGES AHEAD

In order to realize the TOKEZ and OTSEZ schemes there are a number of thorny issues to be considered and/or resolved. These include U.S. military bases, regional security, territorial disputes, various regulations, the liberalization of Okinawa's economy and the problems and possibilities for the decentralization and autonomy of local governments. I'd like to discuss each of these issue in more detail.

U.S. Base Issues

Source: Okinawa Prefectural Government.

FIGURE 7- 11. U.S. Military Bases in Okinawa.

U.S. bases have been the most controversial socio-political and economic issue since the inception of the U.S. occupation of the island. It is not too much to say that Okinawa's daily life has revolved around the U.S. bases. U.S. bases have been a main source of livelihood for Okinawans, particularly in the 1950's and 60's. At the same time, however, bases have always been associated with "The Battle of Okinawa" which devastated not only Islands' properties and priceless cultural assets that had been preserved for centuries and which implanted a key "cultural cord" into the minds of islanders, namely *nuchidotakara* (life is the most precious thing in the world). The anti-base movements have intensified as time has passed not only from the standpoint of anti-war sentiments, but also from the detrimental consequences of having bases in Okinawa such as base-related environmental pollution and as a result of heinous crimes committed mostly by the Marines which make up more than 60% of the troops stationed on Okinawa. Hawaii-born UC Davis Professor Darrell Hamamoto, describes the presence of US bases on Okinawa as "soft colonialism" which, unlike neo-colonialism or postcolonialism, functions culturally and physiologically to maintain an unequal, exploitative political relationship (Hamamoto, 2006).

The former pro-business governor of Okinawa, Mr. Keiichi Inamine, used to say that "the weight of the military bases was bubbling deep down like hot magma ready to explode." (*The Asahi Shimbun*, November 15, 2006). The magma actually burst in 1995, when a twelve-year old school girl was raped by U.S. servicemen. The incident triggered island-wide resentment against the U.S. military bases. Both the U.S. and Japanese governments took immediate action to calm down the consequences of the incident by establishing the Special Action Committee on Okinawa (SACO) which aimed at reducing military bases located close to residential areas. SACO's final report (MOFA, 1996), which was released on December 1996, stated that the number of US military facilities and areas would be reduced by approximately 25% and 18% respectively.

The symbol and currently hottest issue within the continuing base realignment debate is U.S. Marine Corps Futenma Air Station (FIGURE 7-11) which is planned to be relocated to the vicinity of Camp Schwab. Okinawa's burden for US military facilities in Japan increased from 59% in 1972, at the time of reversion, to 75% in recent years. It should be noted that even after the successful implementation of parts of the SACO program, Okinawa's burden still remains as high as 70% (FIGURE 7-12).

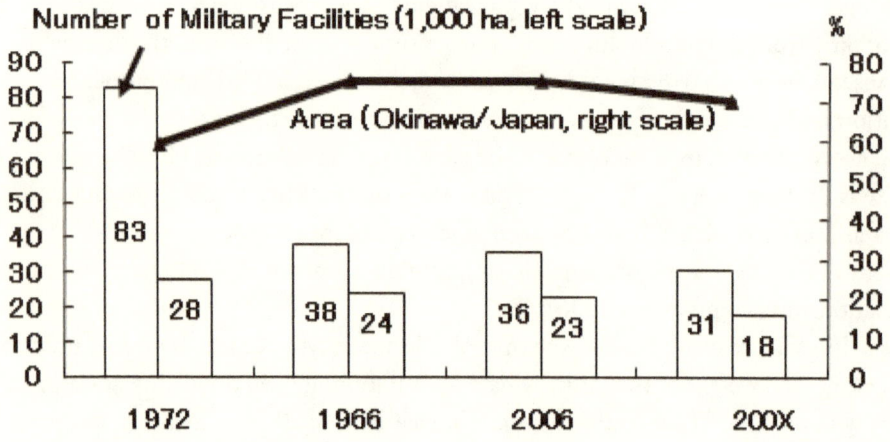

Number of Military Facilities (1,000 ha, left scale)

Area (Okinawa/Japan, right scale)

Source: See FIGURE 7-11.

FIGURE 7-12. Reduction of the U.S. Military Bases in Okinawa.

Following the SACO final report, the U.S.-Japan Security Consultative Committee (two-plus-two) approved a document on the realignment of U.S. military forces and bases in Okinawa in May 2006. According to the document, about 8,000 Marines and 9,000 of their dependents will relocate from Okinawa to Guam by 2014. The implementation of the realignment will accompany the return of six bases south of Kadena Air Base including the controversial Futenma Air Station, covering about 1,500 hectares. The base return program, however, is conditioned on the relocation of Futenma Air Station. If this realignment program is implemented as scheduled, Okinawa will face a daunting task in making commercial use of the returned base lands. Although the majority of islanders are against the presence of U.S. bases, they are fully aware of the economic consequences of base withdrawal. The planned closure of U.S. bases has revealed a wide range of complicated problems to be resolved.

Security of the Asia-Pacific Region: The Arc of Uncertainty

The collapse of the Soviet Union and particularly after the 9.11 terrorism attacks on the Continental United States in 2001, the United States global security strategy has drastically changed from the Cold-War legacy to new global geopolitical threats. The 2001 Quadrennial Defense Review (QDR), which reviewed U.S. global security strategy every four years, concisely described the areas from the Middle-east to the Korean Peninsula as an "arc of instability," vulnerable to terrorism attacks, but strategically important for regional security, stability and prosperity (Calder, 2001, 2006). The QDR particularly stressed a possible security vacuum in the Asia-Pacific region where China is rapidly emerging as an undemocratic world economic and military power house with the impending Taiwan issue and territorial disputes over surrounding islands and where the Korean Peninsula with imminent threat from North Korea.

Following the QDR, President George Bush unveiled one of the largest planned troop redeployments since the onset of the Cold War in 2004. The Bush initiative intends to reduce about 70,000 troops stationed in Asia and Europe over ten years.

> *The Pentagon confirmed plans to sharply cut forces stationed at large U.S. bases in Germany, South Korea and Okinawa, Japan, and to redeploy many troops to smaller, more widely dispersed facilities—sometimes called 'lily pads'—along an 'arc of crisis' stretching along a wide band from Southeast Asia to West Africa, as well as to bases at Guam in the Pacific Ocean and back home (Eli Clifton, 2007).*

Open Economic Systems

As we have discussed in Chapter 2, Okinawa's high cost of international as well as domestic transportation costs are largely attributable to cabotage regulations which prohibit a foreign shipping company (i.e. Taiwan) from operating within the domestic borders of another country (i.e. within Japan). The cabotage regulations and open sky policy air transportation are primarily designed to protect domestic transportation businesses from international competition. The regulations need to be abolished in order to promote trade between Okinawa and Taiwan.

Furthermore, Okinawa needs to restructure its economic policy in order to reap benefits from the TSEZ which should not be an enclave of the local economy. Uncompetitive sectors in particular, such as sugar and pineapple, must be gradually phased out. Since we can expect strong political resistance to the liberalization of these protected products, there must be a range of well-designed safety nets or support measures such as compensations of lost income and creating new businesses to help provide a soft-landing.

Senkaku (Japanese name)/Diaoyutai Islands (Chinese name) Dispute

The Senkaku/Diaoyutai islands are a group of eight uninhibited isalnds on the continental shelf, separated from the Ryukyu Islands (Okinawa) by a deep underwater trench. The largest island, Uotsuri (Japanese)/Diaoyu (Chinese) with 8 hectares, is located 170 km northeast of Taiwan and 410 km west of Okinawa. The islands, which were administered by the U.S. military government (USCAR) after

WWII and by Okinawa Prefecture under the Japanese government since 1972, has became a hot geopolitical issue among China, Taiwan and Japan since 1969 when a report by the UN Economic Commisson for Asia and the Far East (ECAFE) revealed a possibility of large underwater oil reserves in the vicinity.

Territorial issues over the islands gained new momentum since China started drilling for natural gas in the Chunxiao field which is located in the vicinity of the disputed islands. The UN convention on the Law of the Sea allows the Exclusive Economic Zone (EEZ) from the coastal lines of each territorial land. Obviously, the EEZ area is pivotal in terms of who will claim the Senkaku/Diaoyutai islands. Since the EEZ of both countries overlaps, Japan claims a division of the EEZ on the median line between the coastlines of both countries. According to well-documented research works (Suganuma, 2000; Taira 2007), the territorial issue surrounding the Senkaku/Diaoyutai islands goes back as far as the Ming Dynasty in the early 15th century when the Kingdom of Ryukyu (current Okinawa) enjoyed a trade-induced golden age through trading with China. Although Japan has claimed the islands by the Treaty of Shimonoseki concluded in 1895 after the first Sino-Japanese war, China and Taiwan used these islands as a fishing base for many centuries. China's Vice-Premier Deng Xiaoping once remarked that "Our generation is not wise enough to find common language on this question. The next generation will certainly be wiser. They will surely find a solution acceptable to all" (Cited in Taira, 2007). There has been progress in recent years since the Chinese government has offered to the Japanese government the idea of joint development of the oil field in the area. This issue will be discussed at meetings between China and Japan when Chinese President Hu Jintaro visit Japan in 2008.

Introduction of the Region System (Doshu-Sei)

Although Okinawa has a golden opportunity in the age of locally-based global economy in taking advantage of its strategic location in the Asia-Pacific region as well as its historical legacy in promoting the Taiwan-Okinawa Economic Partnership Agreement (TO-EPA), there are obviously many hurdles and problems to be overcome in the realization of this scheme. The thorniest issue is probably politico-diplomatic-security relationships within the regional context. Despite enhanced local autonomy in recent Japanese legislation, Okinawa and Kyushu are not in a position to negotiate with Taiwan and China in order to conclude trade related agreements. These are mandates of the Tokyo government.

The Japanese government is also not accommodative toward local initiatives in advancing on Taiwan which the Beijing government regards as a "renegade province." The success of TO-EPA depends on complementary relationships among the participating regions. The economic role Okinawa plays in the region is particularly crucial. Okinawa's strategic location in the region alone does not guarantee prosperous business opportunities for the TO-EPA participants. Okinawa is identifying itself as the region's health resort with accompanying regional hubs of information networks and entrepot. It is now abundantly clear that Okinawa is not suited for intra-industry division of labor for large manufacturing because of its limited domestic and isolated market. Taiwan, on the other hand, is a well-established manufacturing base in the Asia-Pacific along with the Kyushu-DO. Okinawa and Taiwan not only compliment each other in terms of industrial and trade structure, but they also compliment in terms of labor supply and demand. Okinawa's structural unemployment can be resolved by labor-intensive investment from Taiwan to Okinawa.

In order to resolve these issues, introduction of the Region System (Doshu-Sei) is an essential first step. The Region System has been intensively discussed at the Japanese Cabinet Office as well as within academia. Okinawa and Kyushu are natural candidates for autonomous regional governments with special administrative status (see Shimabukuro, *et al*, 2005). The Region System must go beyond current special regulatory measures which allow local governments to set up various special zones under the guidance of the Cabinet Office. The Region System must guarantee a "One State, Two systems" granting each local government the ability to conduct its own economic diplomacy and internal affairs at its own risk and responsibility. Although Okinawa's "independence advocates" have been weakening since reversion, the notion of Okinawan independence is deeply rooted in the minds of the local peoples, and it has been hotly debated in recent years. "With its population of 1.3 million, it could, if so chose, seek to become an independent state larger than more than forty of the current UN states" (McCormack, 2007).

It should be noted here that a recent reliable scholastic survey made by John C. Lim (2007) indicates that Okinawa's younger generation (18-24 years old) tends to oppose Okinawa's political independence (78% comparing to all respondents 65%) reflecting the weakening Okinawa identity as time passes. In contrast, Taiwan's younger generation tends to support political independence (70% comparing to all respondents 62%). The survey also shows that the most important factor for political independence is economic concerns.

APPENDIX TABLE 7-1. Main Socio-Economic Indicators, Taiwan and Okinawa: 2005

	Unit	OKINAWA	TAIWAN	OKINAWA TAIWAN EPA	KYUSHU-DO
Land area	km²	2,274	32,260	34,534	42,176
Population	million	1.36	22.77	24.1	13.40
65 years and over	%	16.1	9.8	10.1	19.5
Labor force	million	0.65	10.37	11.0	6.70
Employment	million	0.60	9.94	10.5	6.20
Unemployed	1000	51	428	479.0	453
Jobless rate	%	7.9	4.1	4.4	6.8
GDP (exchange rate)	$ billion	30.9	300.0	330.9	379.7
GDP shares by industry	%	100.00	100.0	100.0	100.0
Agriculture	%	1.8	1.7	1.7	2.5
Construction	%	8.4	1.6	2.3	6.2
Manufacturing	%	5.7	22.5	20.8	16.1
Tertiary	%	84.1	77.5	78.2	75.6
Per Capita GDP	$	19,815	13,274	13,730	24,226
GDP ann. growth rate (ave. in recent 5 years)	%	1.1	3.1	2.9	1.4
Exports	million	704	188,944	189,648	39,393
Imports	million	1,896	181,522	183,418	40,501
Trade balance	million	(1,192)	7,422	6,230	(1,108)
Life expectancy	year				
Women		86	80	80.3	85
Men		78	75	75.2	78

Sources: Compiled by Kakazu from *The Okinawa Statistical Yearbook, ADB Key Indicators* and *The Outline of the Kyushu Economy*, various issues.

NOTES

The Japan Economic Journal (17 January 2007), p.29.
Hamamoto, Darrell (2006), p.29.
McCormack, G. (2007), p.6.

REFERENCES

Asahi Shimbun (January 17, 2007), p.13.
Asahi Shimbun (November 15, 2006), p.12.
Calder, K. 2001. "The New Face of Northeast Asia." *Foreign Affairs*, January/February, pp. 106-109.

―――. 2006. China and Japan's Simmering Rivalry." *Foreign Affairs*, March/ April, pp.129-139.

Clifton, E. 2007. "U.S. Military to Extend Reach Into an 'Arc of Instability'." *Inter Press Service News Agency (IPS)*, January, 14.

The Economist. January 15th 2005. "A Survey of Taiwan." pp.3-12.

Emmot, B. (1999) "Survey: The 20th Century," *The Economist*, September 11th- 17th.

The Japan Economic Journal. 17 January 2007.

Hook, G.D. and Richard Siddle (eds.). 2003. *Japan and Okinawa: Structure and Subjectivity*. London: Routledge Curzon.

Hamamoto, Darrell. 2006. "'Soft Colonialism': A *Nikkei* Perspective on Contem- porary Okinawa." *The Okinawan Journal of American Studies*, no.3, pp.28- 34.

Hara, Y. 2005. *Higashi Ajia Keizai Senryaku (*Economic Strategy of East Asia). Tokyo: NTT Publication.

Kakazu, H. 2004-A. "Strategies and Issues of Establishing an East Asian FTA: A Japanese Perspective." *The Study of Business and Industry,* no.20, pp.39-58.

―――. (2004-B) "Changing Agricultural Environments in Small Islands: Cases of the South Pacific and Okinawa." *INSULA: International Journal of Island Affairs,* Paris Year 13, no.2, pp. 85-88.

Kimura, M. 2006. *Shinsetu Mu Tairiku Chinbotsu: Okinawa Kaitei Iseki wa Mu Bunmei Iseki ka?* (Okinawa's Underwater Rock Remain: Is it the Submerged Mu Continent?) Tokyo: Jitsugo no Nihonsha.

Lim, John C. 2007. "A Comparison of Identity in Okinawa and Taiwan: A Quan- titative Analysis from the 'Peripheral East Asia' Survey in 2005-2006. A pa- per presented at a workshop of "Japan-Taiwan Relationship," Naha, Okinawa, March 9, 2007. See also Lim John C. Lim (2005), *Identity Politics in "Periph- eral East Asia": Okinawa, Taiwan, Hong Kong,* Tokyo: Akashi Shoten.

McCormack, G. 2007. "Okinawa and the Revamped US-Japan Alliance." *Japan Focus,* November 27, pp.1-7.

Ministry of Foreign Affairs of Japan. 1996. *The SACO Final Report*. Tokyo: MOFA.

Okuno, S. 2005. *Natsuko: Okinawa Mitsuboueki no Joo* (Natsuko: The Queen of Okinawa's Smuggling Trade), Bungei Shunju Sha.

Oshiro, H. 2007. "The Idea of a Special Regional Border Exchange Zone in the Context of State Border Policy." *The Journal of Nissology,* no.1, the Center for Asia-Pacific Island Studies, University of the Ryukyus, *pp.65-72.*

Simabukuro, J., H. Hamazato, and S. Manabu. 2005. *Okinawa Jichishu: anatawa do kangaeru?* (Okinawa Region State: What do you think?). Okinawa Region State Study Group, Naha.

Smith, S.A. 2006. *Shifting Terrain: The Domestic Politics of the U.S. Military Presence in Asia*. East-West Center Special Reports, Honolulu.

Suganuma, U. 2000. *Sovereign Rights and Territorial Space in Sino-Japanese Relations: Irredentism and the Diaoyu/Senkaku Islands*. Honolulu: University of Hawaii Press.

Taira, K. 2004. "The China-Japan Clash Over the Diaoyu/Senkaku Islands." *The Ryukyuanist,* spring, pp.1-9.

U.S. Department of Defense. 2001. *Quadrennial Defense Review Report,* Washington DC, pp.1-71.

Yonaguni-cho. 2005. *A Proposal on Yonaguni Cross-border Special Exchange Zon,* Yonaguni.

Chapter 8

Sustainable Island Tourism

The Roles of Tourism for Small Island Economies

Tourism as an engine of growth

According to the World Tourism Organization (WTO, 1995, 2007), about 700 million people traveled abroad in 2000, generating an estimated tourists' expenditure of $400 billion in 2002. WTO's "Tourism 2020 Vision" forecasts that globally the number of tourists will rise to more than 1.56 billion by 2020. While Europe currently accounts for about 60% of all tourists, the East Asian region is expected to witness the most dynamic growth in the coming years (FIGURE 8-1 and also see Appendix A for more details).

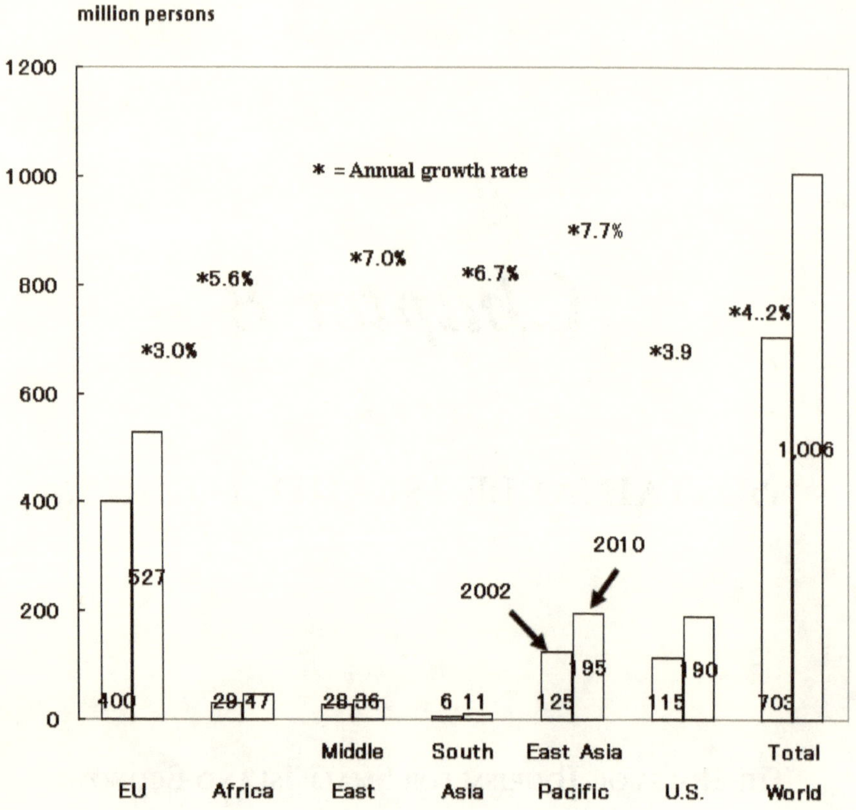
million persons
1200
1000
800
600
400
200
0
* = Annual growth rate
*3.0%
*5.6%
*7.0%
*6.7%
*7.7%
*3.9
*4..2%
400
527
29
47
28
36
6
11
125
195
115
190
703
1,006
2002
2010
EU
Africa
Middle East
South Asia
East Asia Pacific
U.S.
Total World

Source: World Tourism Organization (2005).

FIGURE 8-1. Number of Tourist Arrivals and Annual Growth Rates by Region: 2002-2010.

For small island economies, the tourism or visitors' industry has been the fastest growing and most important industry accounting for 20-70% of their current external receipts (see Chapter 1). Small islands, in particular, transformed rapidly into tourism dependent economies because (1) they lack natural resources to exploit for export earnings; (2) their market sizes are too small to develop a viable manufacturing industry, (3) tourism-related industries are usually small scale and labor intensive; (4) they are endowed with marine resources, particularly beautiful beaches; (5) these islands are part of or surrounded by richer countries such as the United States and Japan with well-organized transportation networks; (6) their tropical or semi-tropical climatic and cultural conditions are complementary with those rich countries; and (7) these island communities have maintained internal political stability and offer warm hospitality to visitors (see Kakazu, 1996; 2002).

Tourism as a composite industry

Tourism is usually classified as a service industry. As such tourists' expenditures are recorded as service receipts in the balance of payments statistics. Tourists' expenditures, however, are, quite different from other external service receipts such as sales of transportation, insurance, intellectual property rights and labor. Apart from lodging, a large portion of tourists' expenditures are in the form of local consumption and purchases of local or imported products and services such as souvenirs, meals, transportation and various entertainments. Therefore, sales to tourists are directly reflected in local production or imports of goods including agriculture and manufacturing.

TABLE 8-1. Okinawa's Tourists' Expenditures by Category: 2005

	(¥ 100 million)	(%)
Total Expenditure	3,984	100%
Lodging	1,347	33.8
Souvenirs	1,028	25.8
Meals	725	18.2
Transportation	446	11.2
Entertainment	335	8.4
Others	104	2.6

Impacts on		
Production	6,991	¥ 100million
Value-added	3,797	¥ 100million
Employment	7	10,000
Taxes	11	¥ 100million

Source: Okinawa Prefecture.

For small island economies in particular, tourism needs to be conceptualized as a composite industry, not merely a service industry. Such a re-conceptualization of the tourism industry in small island economies will provide a development framework to diversify and revitalize diminishing local agriculture and manufacturing as well as conserving tourism resources including marine and historical and cultural assets (see Kakazu, 1998). In Okinawa, for example, aside from conventional tourism industry such as hotels, travel agents, transportation, souvenirs and travel guides, the industry is deeply and extensively related to local cultures, production sectors, information and communication technology (ICT), various entertainments and sports, transportation, marketing and promotional activities, conventions and preservation of natural and cultural assets (FIGURE 8-2).

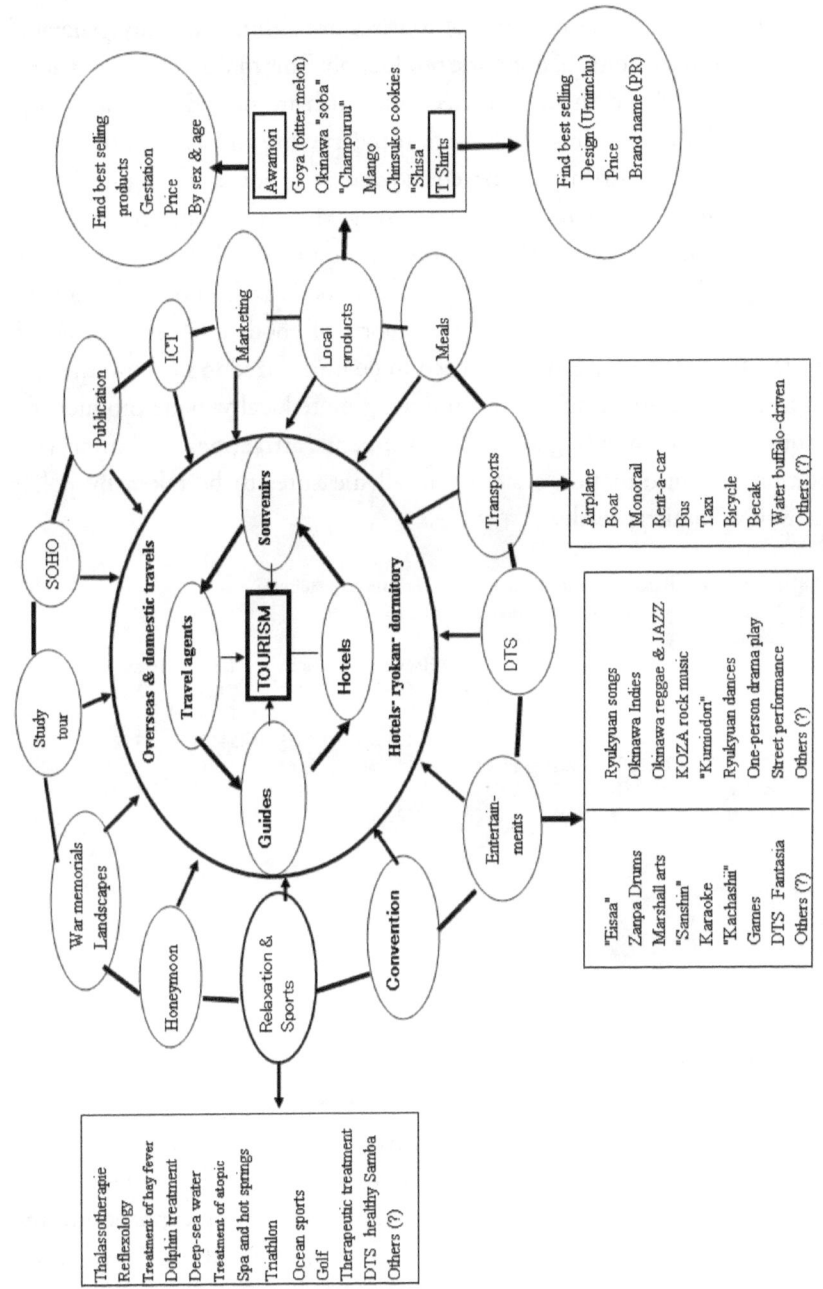

FIGURE 8-2. Main Tourism-related Industrial Activities.

In this sense, tourism and goods producing sectors (agriculture and manufacturing) are supposed to be complementary each other and not necessarily a trade-off as many economists have asserted in their development theories (see Kakazu, 1994). The case of Okinawa demonstrates that one unit of tourist's expenditure actually generated about 1.5 units of gross income of domestic production. This multiplier effect is actually higher than Aomori and Shizuoka prefectures which are located in the heartland of Japan (TABLE 8-2) (see Ministry of Land, Infrastructure and Transport, 2006).

This suggests that tourism can be considered as a powerful engine for industrial diversification for small island economies where the domestic market is extremely limited by their small size of population and small, fragmented markets. Tourists provide additional markets for local goods and services. Of course, leakages of tourists' expenditures through imports of goods and services, which accounted for 40% of the expenditures, need to be minimized to improve the economic impact of the tourism industry. Producing more locally-made products for tourists' consumption, providing local entertainments, attractions, and improving transportation and information systems are all measures to be taken by policy makers as well as industry leaders.

TABLE 8-2. Comparison of Economic Impacts of Tourism Expenditures for Selected Regional Economies

	Unit	Okinawa (2004)	Hokkaido (1999)	Aomori (2004)	Tokyo (2004)	Shizuoka (2002)	Kyoto (2004)
Tourists' expenditure	¥ 100 mil.	4,549	12,163	1,759	34,870	7,723	5,348
Gross income	¥ 100 mil.	6,903	18,773	2,342	75,750	9,673	10,103
Net income (value-added)	¥ 100 mil.	3,794	NA	1,331	NA	5,189	4,336
Gross regional product (GRP)	¥ 100 mil.	35,001	196,356	42,515	818,429	157,543	57,962
Net income/GRP	%	10.8	NA	3.1	NA	3.3	7.5

Note: NA = Not Available.

Source: OPG, *Outline on Okinawa's Tourism*.

Tourism as an export industry

As previously mentioned, tourists' expenditures are recorded as service receipts in the external balance of payment statistics. Tourism incomes, in effect, are equivalent to exports of not only services but also goods which are sold to non-resident tourists. Conceptually, the only difference between income from export trade and tourism incomes are where the goods and services are traded and consumed. Tourists' receipts imply precisely the same effect as exports of goods and services.

Factors to determine the comparative advantage of the tourism industry differs greatly from that of the goods producing industries such as agriculture and manufacturing. According to modern trade theory, comparative advantages in goods industries are determined by relative costs or productivity of trading partners. Comparative advantage in 'tourism products', however, is determined by both economic and non-economic factors such as geographical location, culture, history and even by 'hospitality spirits' which are difficult to capture in rational economic terms.

The tourism industry also faces more or less the same kind of competition, and displays similar characteristics to the goods producing industry. The CNMI (Saipan), Guam, and Okinawa, in particular, have been competing with each other for the growing Japanese tourism market. In the past, Okinawa suffered cost disadvantages in comparison with these tourist destinations because of the rapid appreciation of the yen. The CNMI also has a labor cost advantage over Okinawa because it has been able to import cheap labor primarily from the Philippines (Kakazu, 1994).

Tourists' income accounted for about 10% and 18% of Okinawa's gross prefectural income and total external receipts respectively in recent years (FIGURE 8-3). Unlike Japan proper, Okinawa has recorded a huge surplus in tourism balance of payments. Although external receipts from tourists jumped about twelve-fold since Okinawa's reversion climbing to $3.6 billion in 2006, the amount is only one-third of that of Hawaii. As we discuss in later part in this chapter, Okinawa's per capita tourist expenditure has declined in recent years.

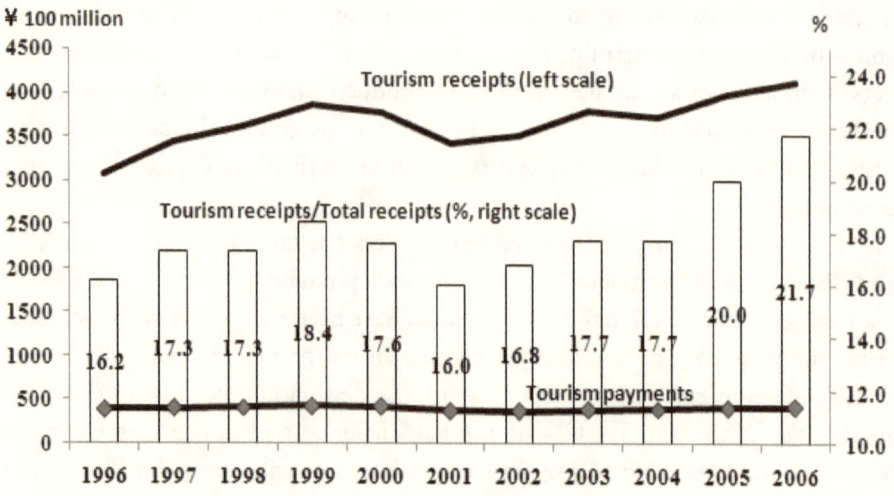

Notes: Except for tourism receipts, figures for 2005-2006 are estimated by this author.
All figures are in current prices.

Source: See Table 8-2.

FIGURE 8-3. Tourism in Okinawa's Balance of Payments: 1996-2006.

Although Okinawa has been struggling to diversify its tourism markets in order to reduce instability in the tourism industry as well as to capture the emerging East Asian market, it is not succeeding. One important bottleneck for the diversification is the lack of networks in terms of transportation, hotels and promotional activities between Okinawa and other Asian countries. The tourism industry in Okinawa is so meticulously tailored toward mainland Japan that it will require tremendous effort to make it appealing in other markets.

Tourism as a "cultural catalyst" and friction

An important difference between commodity exports and service exports through tourism activities is that the former are consumed or stocked in the imported region, while the latter are inseparable from the exporting region where the services are rendered. In this sense, tourism is considered to be a package of economic as well as non-economic factors. In any country, tourists are mostly welcomed not only because of the income and employment they generate, but also because they are regarded as "cultural catalysts" (Kakazu, 1997).

Despite a welcome attitude toward tourists, however, there are always deep-rooted fears among the island people that their fragile environments and rich culture might be eroded or degraded by a massive and continuous intrusion of outsiders. There are also constant complaints on the part of island economies that major tourism businesses, including hotel facilities and airline transportation, are dominated by mainlanders and that the majority of tourism-generated revenue is boomeranged back to the mainland. Similarly, many small islands' tourism industry over-expanded through imported foreign labor which has created various socio-economic problems and uncertainty for the life of islanders including water shortages, food insecurity, imported inflation and family problems (Kakazu, 1994). Therefore, it is an urgent task for tourism dependent island economies to determine the "carrying capacity" of tourists' absorption for sustainable development which will be discussed later.

Tourism as a Peace Industry

Tourism is well-recognized as a peace industry. No country or region has ever adopted a policy to reject genuine tourists unless they are hostile or detrimental to host countries. As we have witnessed in recent years, tourists are most sensitive to their own security. Recent terrorists' attacks on NYC (September 11, 2001) and Bali (October 2002), the outbreak of the SARS, avian flu and tsunami disaster all scared off potential visitors in America and the Asia-Pacific.

FIGURE 8-4 clearly demonstrates that the number of Japanese tourists to Bali noticeably declined after the terrorists' bomb attack on October 12, 2002 in the tourist resort of Kuta which killed 202 people, largely foreign tourists. The effects of the incident were immediate, arrivals for the year declined sharply from the previous year. Further bombings occurred on October 1, 2005.

Japanese tourists are considered to be particularly sensitive to such incidents. Therefore the bottom line for sustainable tourism is to secure peace and stability in tourist destinations. In this context, island tourism policy makers are requested to learn risk management, namely how to assess political as well as unexpected risks arising from travel. Although insurance is one of the means to reduce such risks, it usually does not cover unexpected socio-political risks. Tourism risk management is particularly important for small, remote islands where travel risks associated with both natural and man-made are more difficult to manage than larger areas.

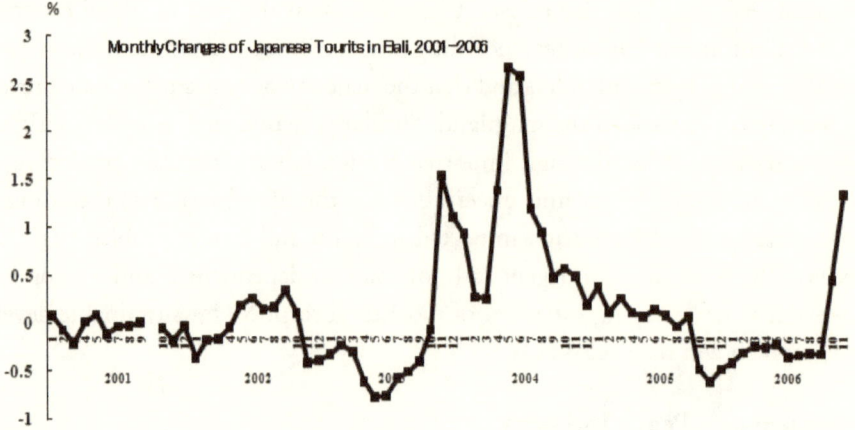

Source: Compiled from the Japan National Tourist Organization (JNTO) data on Japanese Overseas Travelers.

FIGURE 8-4. Risk of Island Tourism: The Case of Bali.

ISSUES AND PROSPECTS FOR OKINAWA'S TOURISM INDUSTRY

Issues of Tourism as a Key Industry

Tourism has been a main engine for Okinawa's economic growth since reversion (see Appendix B for recent statistics on tourism). The industry continues to be the most powerful engine for future development because it possesses the archipelago's potential comparative advantage. The tourism industry, however, faces challenging problems to be resolved. First, despite the rapid growth of tourists in the past decade, tourism expenditures have not grown in commensurate with the number of visitors. As a matter of fact, tourism incomes declined during 2000-2005 despite that the number of visitors increased by 630,000 persons (FIGURE 8-5A). The decline is also reflected in a sizable decrease in per capita tourism spending from \84,000 to \70,000 (FIGURE 8-5B).

(A) Disparities between Visitors and Incomes

1,0000 visitors; ¥ billion

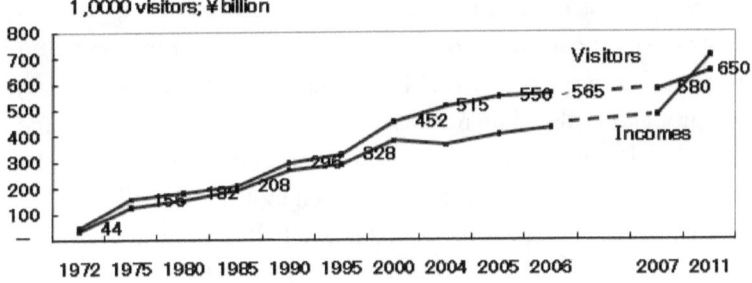

(B) Per Capita Tourist's Spending

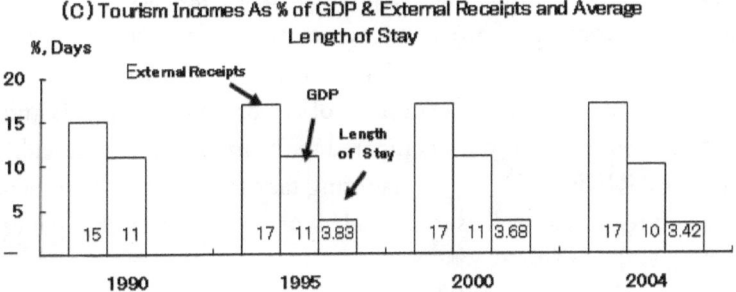

(C) Tourism Incomes As % of GDP & External Receipts and Average Length of Stay

(D) Tourist Arrivals by Major Islands

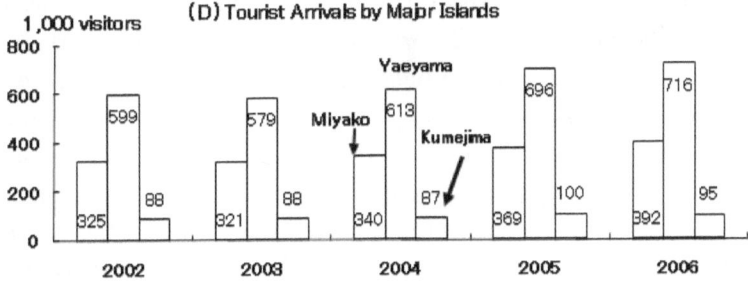

Notes: Figures for 1972-2005 are actual, figures for 2006-2011 are estimated or projected by the OPG.

Source: Compiled from the *Okinawa Statistical Yearbook*, various issues.

FIGURE 8-5. Okinawa's Tourism Industry and Issues: 1972-2011.

Alternatively, a ¥10,000 decrease in per capita spending means a loss of 450,000 visitors in terms of total tourism income. This clearly suggests that the tourism industry, which consumes local resources, should not be a mere number game. Okinawa is facing the problem of how to upgrade its tourism industry.

The same problem is also shown in terms of tourists' incomes as a percentage of GDP and external receipts which have been almost constant for more than the past decade despite the number of visitors have risen by 1.6 times (FIGURE 8-5C). Okinawa's per capita tourist spending is about one-half of Hawaii's reflecting the length of stay and quality of services (see APPENDIX FIGURE 1).

Deepening the structure of tourism is the most effective measure that can be taken to address the recent declining trend of per capita tourism consumption. "Cheap, Near, and Short" has been a recent slogan to attract mainland tourists to Okinawa. As a result, despite high hotel-room occupancy rates, per-room revenue has actually declined substantially. Such excessive competition by means of price-cutting may eventually damage tourism in Okinawa. Okinawa needs to shift its paradigm from a quantity-oriented tourism policy to a quality-oriented one.

Second, tourism is becoming more important in smaller islands where comparative advantage lies in the location of specific indigenous endowments including marine resources, local culture and hospitality. As we have seen, Ishigaki and Miyako islands are becoming Japan's prime resort islands. We should note, however, that economic benefits such as rising incomes and employment from tourism differ greatly from island to island. The number of visitors to Kumejima Island, for example, has stagnated in recent years compared to the more popular Ishigaki and Miyako islands (FIGURE 8-5D). It is a daunting task to spread tourism benefits among islands and regions as well as to upgrade tourism quality so that per capita tourism spending will increase.

Third, Okinawa's tourism heavily depends on mainland tourists. More than 95% of tourists are mainlanders. The Tokyo, Kansai and Fukuoka areas account for nearly 80% of the total tourists. Okinawa should learn a lesson from the bitter experience of Miyazaki where tourism boomed once and burst soon after. As we have noted already, although Okinawa may continue as one of the favorite resorts in Japan for the foreseeable future, this assessment depends largely on Okinawa's future comparative advantages in environmental quality, rich cultural heritage and hospitality which support the tourism industry. For Okinawa, this is a good time to realize and take necessary actions to diversify its customers. Fortunately, Okinawa is located between rich mainland Japan and emerging regions such as China, Korea and Southeast Asia. There is no reason why Okinawa should not take advantage of these prospective, dynamic customers. What we need are more promotional campaigns for Okinawa's niche tourism in these areas.

Fourth, the future growth of Okinawa's tourism industry will be constrained by its limited carrying capacity which will be fully discussed in the following section. In particular, the limited supply of quality water and environmental degradation are the most important constraints. Although the OPG has planned to achieve 6.5 million tourists by 2011 and ten million by 2017, there is no convincing data to support at all whether this target is consistent with Okinawa's carrying capacity or not.

Finally, what is crucial in enhancing tourism activities is the availability of a highly flexible, skilled labor force. As we have noted, Okinawa has been experiencing a growing mismatch in the labor market arising from a rapid transformation in economic structure and lagging human resource development. Despite the rising unemployment rate, which is not only an indicator of an underutilized labor force, but also an indicator of multiple deprivations such as social exclusion, loss of self-reliance, self-confidence and psychological and physical health, many resort hotels are having a difficult time finding qualified managers. This widening mismatch can be addressed by improved human resource development in targeted economic activities, namely tourism-centered and information-based activities. The University of the Ryukyus, nationally-incorporated institution established the Faculty of Tourism and Industrial Management (FTIM) in 2008 to meet the growing demand for professional human resources in the tourism industry.

Prospects

Despite these pressing issues, tourism remains Okinawa's most important leading industry in the future. TABLE 8-3 shows the latest (as of November 2005) experts' rankings of Japan's resort destinations in terms of "attractiveness" and "future prospects." The resort ranking survey was conducted by the *Japan Economic Journal* group based on assessments of resort experts (researchers, consultants and resort businessmen and women) who visited forty-nine pre-selected resort areas over the past five years. "Attractiveness" was measured with the scores of 1-7 points and "future prospects" for the coming decade was assessed within the range of minus two and plus two with the current status as the zero benchmark. In terms of "attractiveness," Karuizawa topped the list followed by Okinawa's Ishigaki and Kohama islands.

In terms of "future prospects," Okinawa captured the top two rankings which clearly demonstrate Okinawa's sustainable comparative advantage as a tourist destination. The survey has also pointed out that the enhanced hospitality to the elderly and Asian tourists is key to succeed in the future prospects.

| Rankings | | | | | Ranking Scores | |
Attractiveness	Future Prospects	Resorts	Prefectures		Attractiveness	Future Prospects
1	2	Karuizawa	Nagano		5.9	0.9
2	1	Ishigaki/Kohama Islands	Okinawa		5.7	1.4
3	2	Onna, Busena, Yomitan	Okinawa		5.6	0.9
4	4	Okuma, Motobu, Kanucha	Okinawa		5.5	0.8
5	4	Kusatsu	Gunma		5.4	0.8
5	4	Miyako Island	Okinawa		5.4	0.8
7	4	Niseko	Hokkaido		5.3	0.8
7	9	Hakone	Kanagawa		5.3	0.5
9	19	Urabandai, Bandai Heights	Fukushima		5.0	0.1
9	11	Nasu Heights	Tochigi		5.0	0.3
9	8	Yufuin	Oita		5.0	0.6
12	15	Furano	Hokkaido		4.8	0.2
12	11	Onuma	Hokkaido		4.8	0.3
12	27	North Karuizawa	Gunma		4.8	-0.2
12	9	Yatsugadake South Highland	Yamanashi		4.8	0.5
12	19	Tateshina, Shirakaba Lake	Nagano		4.8	0.1
17	46	Kiroro	Hokkaido		4.7	-0.7
17	24	Rusutsu	Hokkaido		4.7	-0.1
17	11	Izu Heights	Sizuoka		4.7	0.3
20	24	Nikko, Kirifuri Heights	Tochigi		4.6	-0.1
20	24	Shiga Heights	Nagano		4.6	-0.1

Notes: See text for the survey method.

Source: *Japan Economic Journal* (7 November 2005), P.12.

Another survey by JTB also indicates that Okinawa is the number one island destinations for the next five years (2005-2010) followed by Hawaii, Bali Guam/ Saipan, New Caledonia and others (FIGURE 8-6).

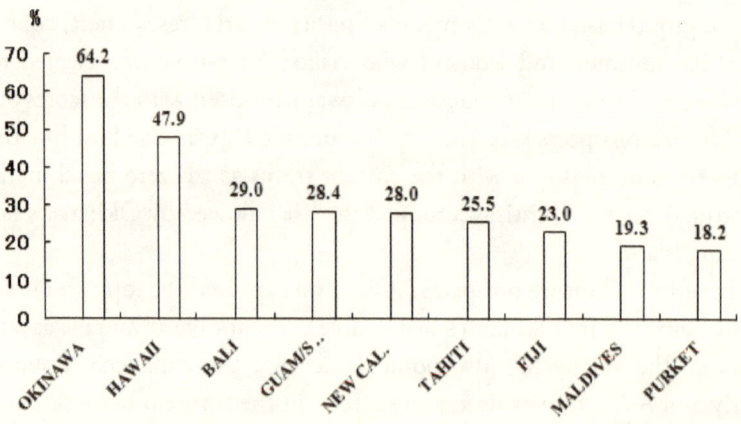

JTB's Travel Intention Survey (2005).

FIGURE 8-6. Most Favored Island Tourists' Destinations: 2005.

CONCEPT AND APPROACHES TO SUSTAINABLE TOURISM DEVELOPMENT

Concept of Sustainable Tourism

The concept of "sustainable development" was first used by the Brundtland Report in *Our Common Future* (1987) as follows: "...a process of change in which the exploitation of resources, the direction of investment, the orientation of technological development, and institutional change are all in harmony and enhance both current and future potential to meet human needs and aspiration."

The concept is illustrated in FIGURE 8-7 (see Kakazu, 2007 for an in-depth analysis).

Δx = rate of renewable resource utilization

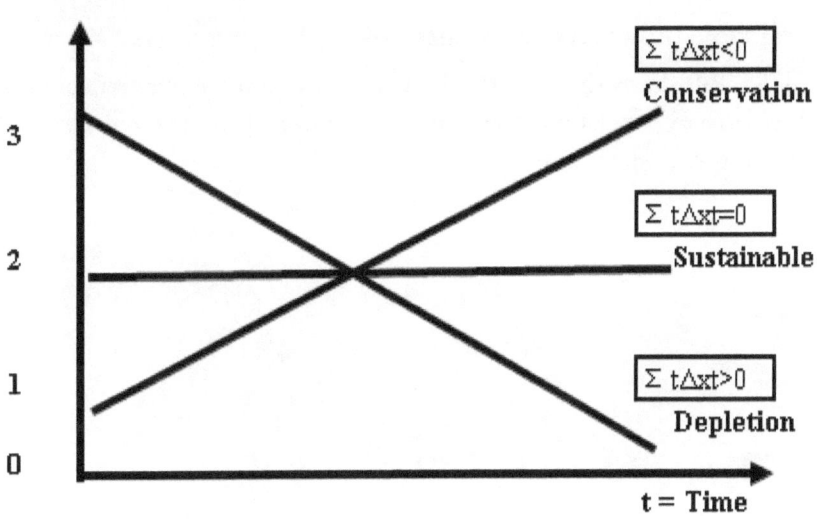

Source: Kakazu, H. (1994).

FIGURE 8-7. A Concept of Sustainable Tourism.

Assume (t) is the passage of time and (Δx) is the rate of tourism resource use. As such, then "sustainable tourism development (STD)" can be defined as $\Sigma t\Delta xt = 0$, while unsustainable resource use (depletion) and over-conservation can be defined as

$\Sigma t\Delta xt < 0$ and $\Sigma t\Delta xt > 0$, respectively.

According to the World Tourism Organization (WTO), STD meets the needs of present tourists and host regions while protecting and enhancing opportunity for the future. It is envisaged as leading to management of all resources in such a way that economic, social, and aesthetic needs can be fulfilled while maintaining cultural integrity, essential ecological processes, biological diversity, and life support systems. We must also add that STD should meet the needs and wants of the local host community in terms of improved living standards and quality of life (QOL). The concept should also satisfy the demands of tourists and the tourism industry, and continue to attract them in order to meet the first aim; and, safeguard the environmental resource base for tourism. Therefore, "sustainable tourism in its purest sense, is an industry which attempts to make a low impact on the environment and local culture, while helping to generate income, employment, and the conservation of local ecosystems. It is responsible tourism which is both ecologically and culturally sensitive." (Association for Tourism and Leisure Education, 2007).

Sustainable Indicators and Constraints

FIGURE 8-8 shows the trends of Okinawa's water and electricity consumption as the de facto population (including the number of tourists and U.S. military personal) rises in the future.

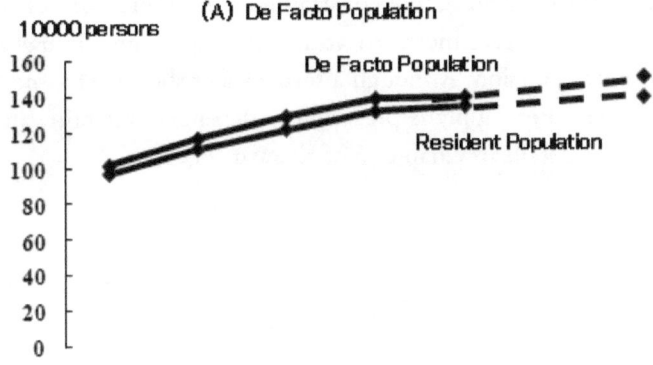

(A) De Facto Population

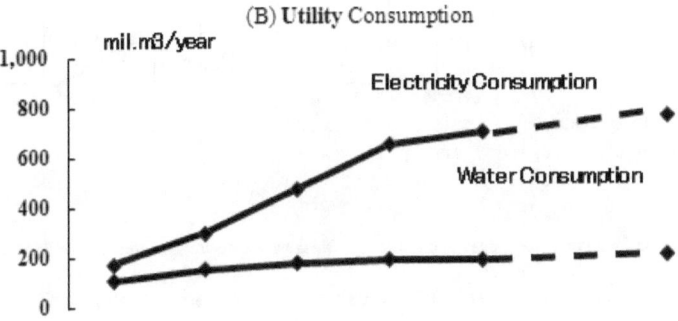

(B) Utility Consumption

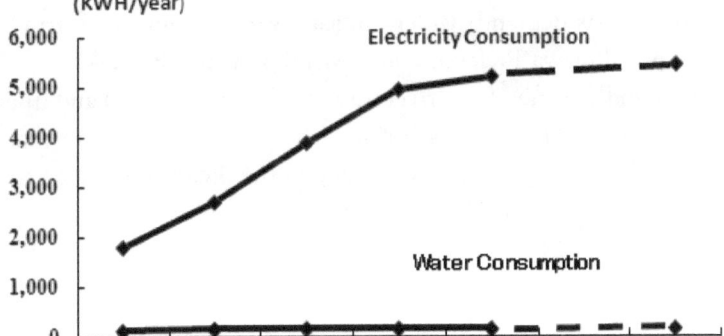

(C) Per Capita Utility Consumption

Notes: De Facto Population = Resident Population + Non-resident Population
Figures for 2020 were estimated by this author.
Water and electricity consumptions include all Okinawa islands.

Sources: Compiled from the *Okinawa Statistical Yearbook*, various issues.

FIGURE 8-8. Okinawa's Main Sustainble Indicators: 1972-2020.

There are also possible supply constraints with public utilities such as water and electricity which have increased at a faster pace than Okinawa's economic growth rate since reversion. Although a severe water shortage has not occurred in recent years, the water supply is precariously dependent on rainwater (FIGURE 8-9 and see more details in Chapter 5 of Kakazu, 1994).

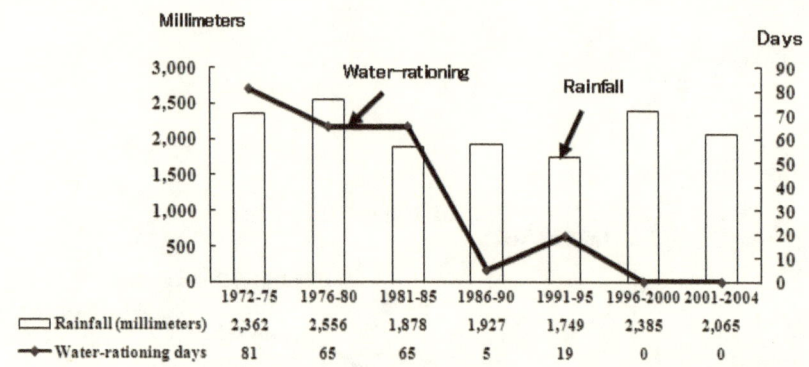

	1972-75	1976-80	1981-85	1986-90	1991-95	1996-2000	2001-2004
Rainfall (millimeters)	2,362	2,556	1,878	1,927	1,749	2,385	2,065
Water-rationing days	81	65	65	5	19	0	0

Source: Constructed from Water Resources Statistics of the Okinawa Prefecture Water Enterprise Bureau.

FIGURE 8-9. Okinawa's Average Yearly Rainfall and the Number of Water-rationing Days: 1972-2004.

Water supply in terms of quantity and quality has been a serious issue for Okinawa and particularly for small outlying islands. TABLE 8-4 shows water balances (supply minus demand) which indicate various sources of drinking water and its use for Okinawa Prefecture and Miyako Island. For Okinawa, water resources have rapidly shifted from river water (from 55% to 21%) and underground water (from 31% to 8%) to dams (15% to 68%) in the past thirty years to meet the increasing demand for water consumption. The site to construct a future dam, however, is extremely limited on the mainland of Okinawa.

TABLE 8-4. Water Balances of Okinawa and Miyako Islands: 2004

	Okinawa Island	Miyako Island
Total rainfall	2,065	36.4
Evaporation	516	9.1
Surface water	1,446	15.3
Surface runoff	332	15.3
Riverwater	1,113	0
Used water	33	0
Unused water	1,080	0
Groundwater	103	12.0
Used water	12	7.8
Unused water	91	4.2
Total withdrawal	158	7.8
Used riverwater	33	0
Used groundwater	12	7.8
Dams	113	0
Desalnization	4	0
Actual supply of water	142	7.0

Unit: 10^6 M^3/yr.

Notes: Total rainfall = Yearly rainfall (mm/yr) x total area (km^2).
Leakage rate = 10%.

Sources: See FIGURE 8-9.

Miyako Island has been a showcase for occasional water shortage and droughts because of its flat topographical conditions. The island has no river. Thus, groundwater has been a lifeline for nearly 50,000 islanders. The islanders, however, discovered that they could store rainfall water underground by constructing subsurface or underground dams. The first underground dam was completed in 1979 with 0.7 million m^3 storage capacity for irrigation (mainly sugarcane fields). The second and third dams were completed in the 1990s to the total storage capacity of 20 million m^3 which are enough to irrigate entire sugarcane fields.

The structure of the underground dam is shown in APPENDIX FIGURE 2. An underground dam is defined as "an artificial structure constructed in geologic strata containing groundwater flow that is blocked and stored for use" (Miwa, Yamauchi and Morita, 1988). Miyako Island is formed by the porous Ryukyu limestone which has high permeability rates. Rainfall percolates rapidly into the ground and is stored as groundwater in between limestone strata and siltstone strata (bed rock).

Despite the construction of expensive underground dams, Miyako Island's water balance has been deteriorating every year due largely to the influx of tourists (FIGURE 8-10). It is highly questionable whether or not the current water supply capacity can meet the future demand.

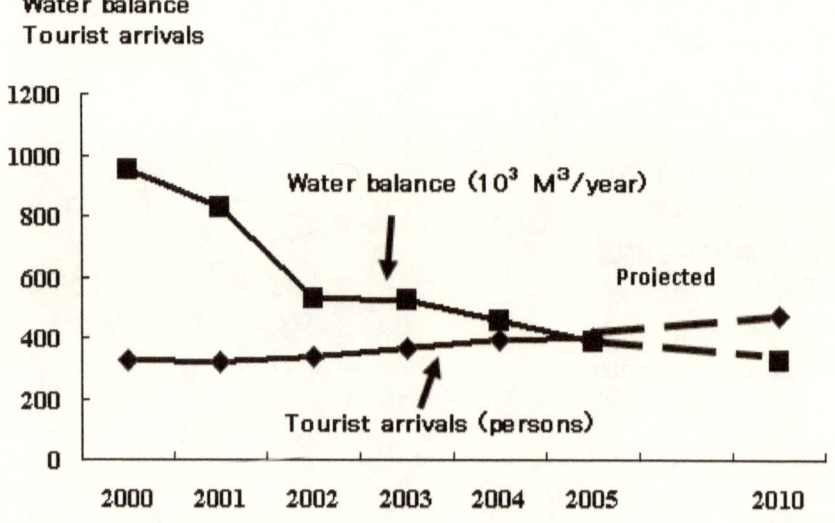

Water balance
Tourist arrivals

Source: See FIGURE 8-9.

FIGURE 8-10. Tourist Arrivals and Water Balance of Miyako Islands: 2000-2010.

In addition to the increasing demand for water and energy resources as the population and tourists increase, the economy's carrying capacity and environmental disruptions will become serious impediments to future development. It is particularly serious for Okinawa where tourism, which depends on clean, sunny beaches, is the most important engine of the economy. There is already sufficient evidence to suggest that Okinawa's world-renowned coral reefs are on the verge of extinction due largely to global warming, overfishing and various construction activities. We need to assess whether or not Okinawa's small, environmentally fragile islands can sustain their ever-increasing de facto population with their extremely limited capacity of renewable as well as non-renewable resources. Therefore, capacity as well as capability building towards sustainable island development are a crucial issues. In view of an importance of water supply in particular, this author organized an expert meeting on "Island Biodiversity and Sustainable Livelihoods," and adopted "The Miyako Declaration" (see APPENDIX 8-4).

With the increasing number of tourists and cars, air pollution and waste disposal are another serious obstacles for future sustainable tourism in Okinawa. As is shown in FIGURE 8-11, Okinawa's air pollution in terms of CO2 emission has increased by over 40% since 1990 along with a rapid increase of automobiles. Okinawa's per capita CO2 emission is twice as high as Japan proper. The increasing air pollution is not only a limiting factor for Okinawa's sustainable tourism, but it also damages the image of Okinawa's healthy lifestyle.

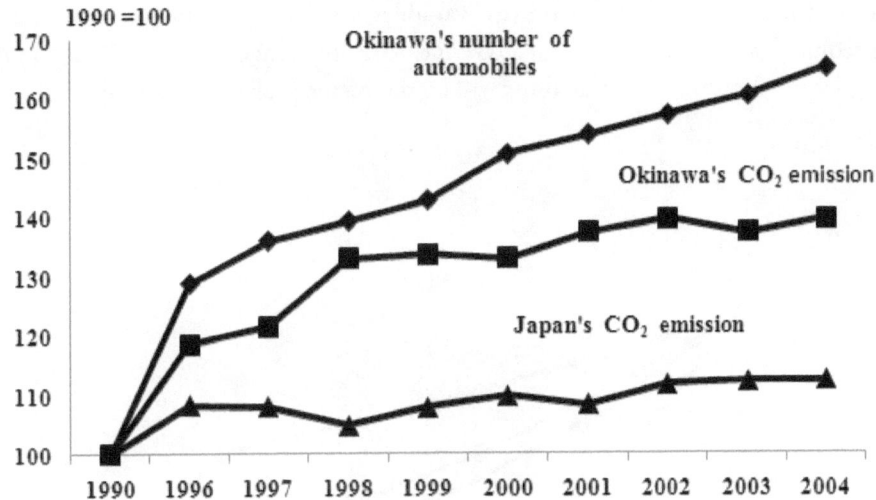

Sources: Okinawa Statistical Yearbook and the National Institute for Environmental Studies.

FIGURE 8-11. Automobile Ownership and CO₂ Emission: 1990-2004.

APPROACHES TO SUSTAINABLE TOURISM DEVELOPMENT

Net Present Value (NPV) Approach

I would like to suggest two popular methods to evaluate carrying capacity and environmental disruptions to Okinawa's infrastructure such as transportation, water and environmental resources and amenities which support sustainable tourism. One is the method of the "Net Present Value (NPV)" approach. Here I present just a skeleton of the method as follows:

R = Present Value of Tourism Resources (i.e. water, electricity, amenities, beaches, etc.)

DPV = Discounted Present Value of future tourism resources

i = discount rate

n = number of years a particular renewable and non-renewable resource can be used then, DPV can be formulated as;

DPV = R/(1-i)n , or (1-i)n = R/DPV.

If the present economic "use value" of a particular tourism resource, i.e., water or coral reefs is $100 million, how should this resource be valued by the present generation if we have kept the same amount of resource without using it up to now? The valuation depends on two variables, the length of time (n = year) and discount rate (i). As is shown in FIGURE 8-12, the longer the time horizon and higher the discount rate, the lower will be the present value of the resource.

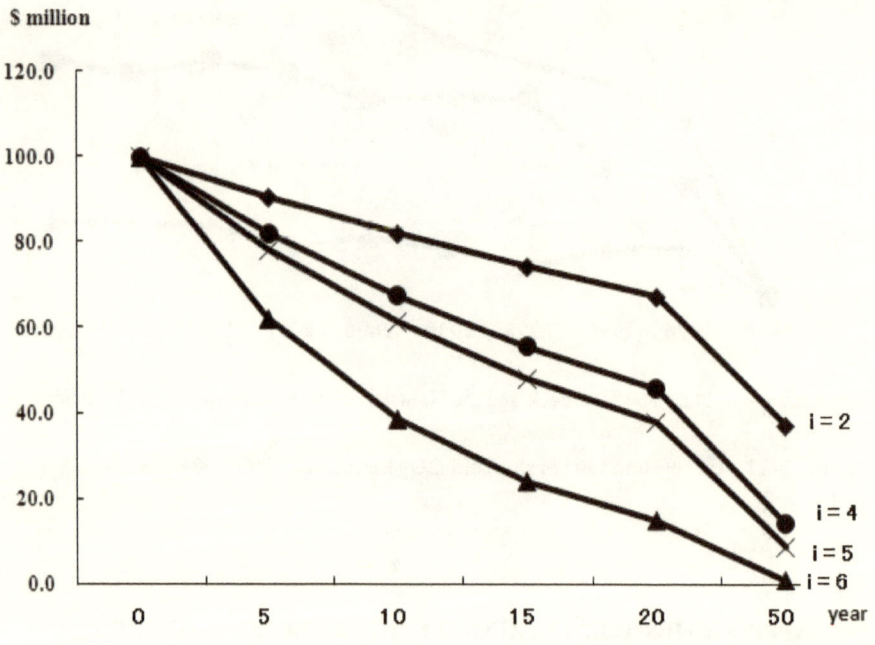

Source: Constructed by H. Kakazu.

FIGURE 8-12. A Hypothetical Example of Present Value of Future Tourism Resources.

The present value of a future (n=5-year) $100 million will be worth $90 if we discount the amount by 2% per annum. The present value will become only $37 in fifty years (n=50). If we discount the amount with 6% for fifty years, the present value will be almost zero. This will clearly suggest that the value of an environmental resource such as pristine, unspoiled coral reef will be worthless for poor fishermen presently if their living standards are not improved without utilizing it. The discount rate of a particular economic resource will be higher the lower the living standards.

Contingent Valuation Method (CVM) and Value of Corals

The CVM method has been used widely in recent years to evaluate the economic value of tourism resources such as landscapes, coral reefs, flora and fauna and amenities which are not easily valued through market transactions. The CVM method involves asking people directly about how much they would be willing to pay (WTP) for specific value of environmental services, or how much they would be willing to accept (WTA) in compensation for giving up specific environmental services. Therefore the method is contingent on a specific hypothetical scenario and questions asked (see more detail in Kakazu, 2007). Of course there are many limitations and assumptions we need to be aware of before we apply the method.

FIGURE 8-13 demonstrates the basic concept of the CVM method using a conventional diagram. The vertical axis indicates costs or income a consumer should pay in order to improve its environmental quality (EQ) which is drawn on the horizontal axis. S1 and S2 indicate the level of consumer's satisfaction or "utility function" if you wish to use economic jargon. Of course S2 gives greater satisfaction than S1, and any point on the same curve gives precisely the same level of satisfaction which is called "indifference satisfaction curve." The willingness to pay (WTP) can be defined as the difference between S2 and S1 (S2 − S1) because the level of consumer satisfaction has not changed from A to D despite the consumer having to pay environmental costs (C2 − C1) in order to improve its environmental quality from EQ1 to EQ2. Thus (C2 − C1) or BD in the figure can be considered as "compensating surplus" or the maximum amount of cost or income forgone in order to obtain EQ2 level of environmental goods.

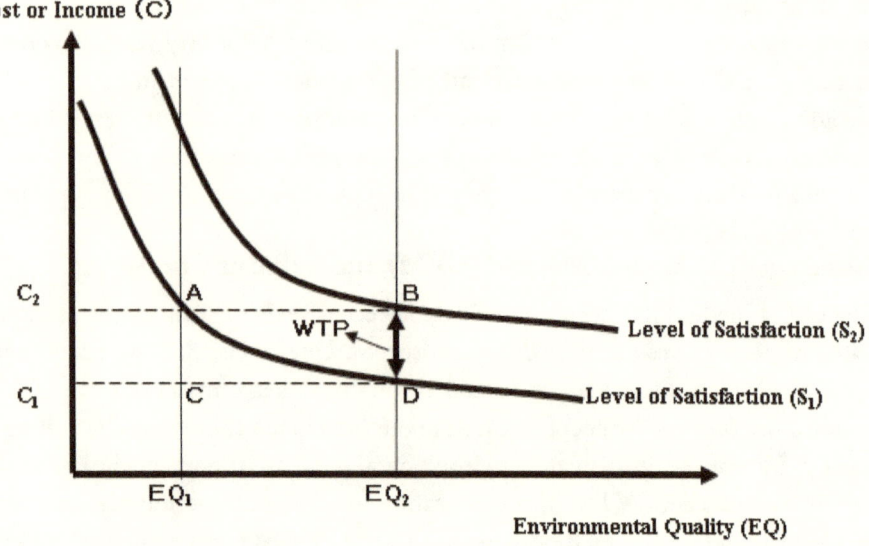

Source: Kakazu, H. (2007).

FIGURE 8-13. A Concept of Contingent Valuation Method.

TABLE 8-5 shows an interesting result of the CVM application on Okinawa's coral reefs. Tourists in Onna village are willing to pay 12,209 yen to conserve its coral reef, while visitors to Kerama islands and Naha citizens will pay 10,762 and 6,982 respectively. The study demonstrates that the value of environments will differ greatly by place, incomes, interviewees, age, sex and probably the way a survey is conducted. The CVM method needs a lot of refinements and improvements to be usefully applied to a particular project and situation.

TABLE 8-5. Willingness to Pay for Conservation of Okinawa's Coral Reefs :2003
(person, yen)

	Kerama Island (visitors)	Onna Village (visitors)	Naha (citizens)
Sample persons	142	639	674
Average amounts	10,762	12,209	6,982
Standard deviations	2,147	1,091	663

Source: Sukpil Oh, *A Study on Coastal Conservation and Utilization Valuations on Coral Reefs and Ecosystem of the Kerama Islands* Naha: Research Institute of Subtropics (March 2003), p.30.

The United Nations Environmental Programme (UNEP) released an interesting report in January 2006 on the value of coral reefs. According to the report, the total economic value of coral reefs is estimated at between $100,000 and $900,000 per square kilometer per year. The value of coral reefs critically depends on the incomes generated through utilizing costal zones. Since the tourism industry in most small island economies including Okinawa almost entirely depend on coastal resources, we need to assess the costs and benefits of preserving the coral reefs. The report says "close to a third of corals have gone, with 60% expected to be lost by 2030" (UNEP, 2006).

Social Carrying Capacity (SCC) of Tourist Sites

Carrying capacity of island tourism has been widely discussed in recent years (see references cited by Choi and Sirakaya, 2005). Social carrying capacity (SCC) of tourist sites can be defined as socially determined maximum number of tourists which are tolerated by local communities. The SCC is usually analyzed both from the local residents and tourists standpoints. The latest study by Brandolini and Mosetti (2005) concluded that the residents' SCC is lower than the visitors' SCC, and the site SCC is the result of a compromise between these two aspects of the SCC. Brandolini and Mosetti suggested two approaches of measuring SCC. One is conventional cost-benefit analysis (CBA) based on the maximization of individual preferences; the other approach is to let local residents determine the maximum number of acceptable tourists through the majority vote rule.

FIGURE 8-14 illustrates tourism social carrying capacity (TSCC) applied to Okinawa. The vertical axes and horizontal indicate costs and benefits or tourists' expenditures, and the number of tourists from 1995 to 2015 respectively. The vertical axis downward also indicates the number of employment generated directly and indirectly by tourists' expenditures. We do know these figures except the private as well as social costs of accepting tourist. The total net benefit from tourism activity (TNB) is defined:

$$TNB(N) = Private\ Net\ Benefit\ (N) - Cs(N) - Ce(N)$$

where Cs and Ce stand for the social costs such as noise, pollution and stress from crowding, and the value of environmental losses, respectively. N stands for the number of tourists per day. The maximum number of tourists which are tolerated by local communities can be determined by the following utility maximization rule:

Net marginal benefit = social and environmental marginal cost including environmental marginal costs.

This is where the social cost (SC) curves intersect with the private net benefit curve (PNB) in FIGURE 8-14.

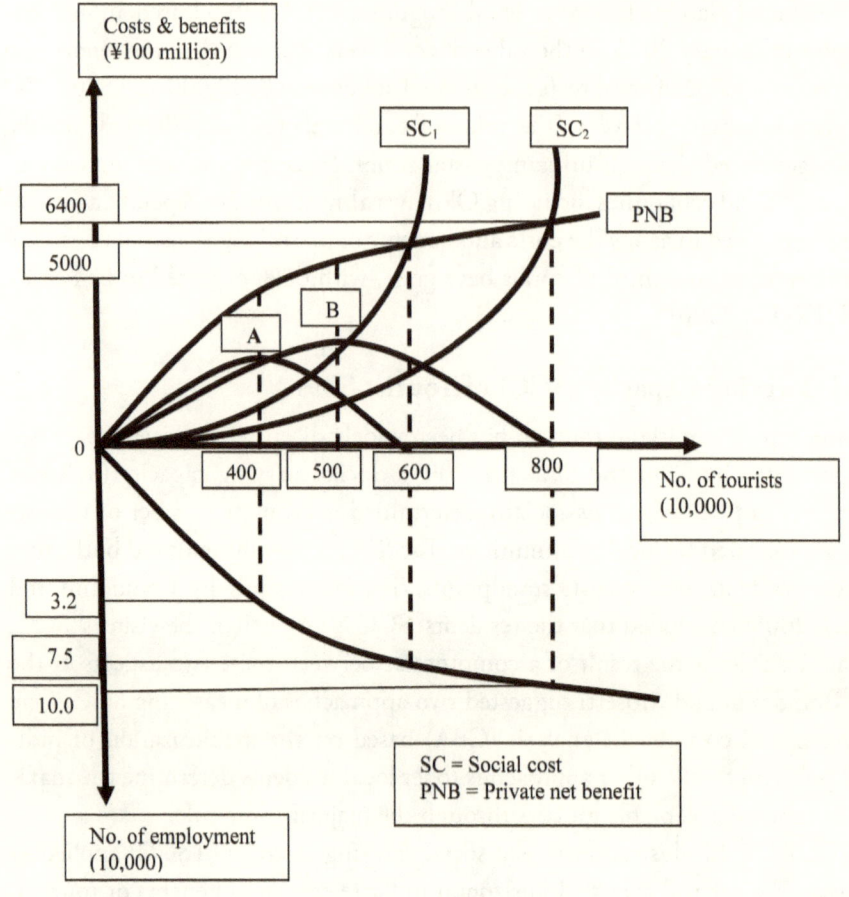

Source: Hiroshi Kakazu (2007).

FIGURE 8-14. An Illustrative Concept of Okinawa's Tourism Social Carrying Capacity.

The net marginal benefit is the additional net benefit generated from the additional number of tourists. Social marginal cost is the additional cost per tourist arrival in Okinawa. If we assume Okinawa's utility (satisfaction) curve from tourism rises as the number of tourists increases, and declines as a result of overcrowding and environmental disruptions, then we can draw utility function like the shapes A and B in the FIGURE 8-14 depending on the degree of tolerance. Obviously, the shape B is more hospitable to tourists than the shape A.

If the shape A is the genuine utility or tolerance curve, then Okinawa's optimum TSCC is determined at the intersection of SC1 and PNB where 6 million tourists with ¥500 billion tourists' expenditures and 75,000 local employment are maximum social net benefits Okinawa can generate from tourism activities.

Okinawa will experience net social loss if tourist arrivals exceed six millions. On the other hand, if the tolerance curve is the shape like B, the optimum number of tourists will be 8 million where SC2 intersects with PNB in FIGURE 8-14.

The optimum TSCC depends on the number of geographical, socio-economic, ecological, cultural, administrative and political factors on which reliable data are not always available.

CONCLUDING REMARKS: TOWARDS OKINAWA'S SUSTAINABLE TOURISM DEVELOPMENT

Future Prospects based on a SWOT Analysis

Okinawa's tourism industry faces challenging issues to be resolved. This author has made a preliminary SWOT analysis on Okinawa's future tourism by sending questionnaires to 30 selected researchers, policy makers and business leaders in Okinawa. **SWOT,** which stands for **S**trengths, **W**eaknesses, **O**pportunities and **T**hreats, has been widely and effectively used to identify and assess competitiveness and future opportunities as well as external threats to one's business environment. The SWOT framework offers a simple yet powerful tool to craft a business strategy. Here we will just introduce an outline of the analysis. Just think about answers to the following questions about tourism in Okinawa.

Strengths:

*What are the **comparative advantages or strengths** of Okinawa's tourism industry?
*How well has the industry performed in recent years?
*Is Okinawa endowed with enough resources to realize its comparative advantages?
*Would a third party favorably evaluate Okinawa's advantages?

Weaknesses:

*What are the **comparative disadvantages** within Okinawa's tourism industry?
*How far can stakeholders in the tourism industry take risks in an ever-changing business environment?
*What are the sources of business confidence in Okinawa's tourism industry?

Opportunities:

*Are Okinawa's comparative strengths in tourism sustainable taking into account the expected future changes to the tourism environment, such as demand, new technology and competition?

*What are the "sellable" resources to meet future business opportunities?

Threats:

*What are the immediate problems facing Okinawa's tourism industry?
*How do stakeholders assess their competitors' strengths?
*Are changing demand, technology and financial environments threatening Okinawa's future tourism industry?

The following table summarizes the results of the survey.

TABLE 8-6. A SWOT Analysis of Okinawa's Tourism

Conditions	Main Results
Strengths	Semi-tropical, warm weather with pristine, beautiful beaches and marine resources Abundant islands' floras and faunas which have been praised as the "Galapagos of the Orient." Rich cultural heritages and unique historical experiences with stable socio-political environments Warm-hearted, hospitality, courtesy-minded peoples Geopolitical center in the Pacific Ocean flanked by rich, emerging East Asian economies World's longest life expectancy with various healthy foods and healing environments Diversified accommodations and tourist facilities Others?
Weaknesses	Occasional typhoon visits in summer and cool and bad weather in winter Insularity and remoteness requiring high transportation and communication costs Isolated and unconnected tourism facilities Over dependency on Japanese tourists Lack of infrastructure and supply of utilities inviting traffic congestion and occasional water shortages Lack of globally active human resources
Opportunities	High reputation and brand name as resort and healthy islands Constant and continuing improvements on tourist facilities Expected rising inbound tourist demand from East Asia, particularly from China and Korea A center of international exchanges of academic, cultural and sports activities Relatively rich young population with higher education Relatively clean, unpolluted natural environments Appeal of "healthy islands"
Threats	Keen competition from the similar islands' resort destinations such as Guam, Hawaii, Saipan, Bali Geopolitical risk of having large military bases Limited islands' carrying capacity and environmental sustainability Declining trend of population in the long-run Declining image of "healthy islands"

Source: H. Kakazu (2005).

A Casino Controversy

Okinawa Governor, Mr. Hirokazu Nakaima, who was elected to the post in 2007 by a wide margin, announced an important message with regard to Okinawa's future tourism development. He proposed to introduce legalized gambling or land-based casinos which are now prohibited by the national law. The message caused a wave of controversy among residents. The governor's intention was to increase tax revenues, per capita tourist consumption and foreign tourists which declined in the past years. Those opposed to the idea typically argue that legalized gaming or casinos are associated with negative impacts such as higher incidence of crime, pathological gambling, and other social problems which are difficult to quantify.

Even if quantifiable positive economic and fiscal impact data are presented, they may not fully convince the local people to introduce the casinos. Hawaii once studied the economic impacts of shipboard gaming and pari-mutuel horse racing when its tourism industry stagnated in the early 1990s (Hawaii Department of Business, Economic Development, and Tourism, 1996). The study concluded that net economic and fiscal impacts on Hawaii's economy were uncertain mainly because of substitution effects of tourists' spending. That is to say these forms of gambling will not attract new dollars, but will cause a shift in spending patterns which will ultimately hurt existing domestic businesses. After careful study, Hawaii decided not to introduce the casinos. Hawaii and Utah are the only U.S. states that do not host the casinos.

In addition to social costs and substitution effects, we need to question whether or not casino tourism is compatible with Okinawa's clean and healthy island image. We also need to examine whether or not Okinawa can compete with well-established casino destinations such as Macao and Las Vegas.

Tourism and Offshore Finance

The Okinawa Special Financial Business Zone (SFBZ) was established together with the Special Information and Communication Business Zone (ICBZ) in 2002 in order to promote offshore as well as onshore financial businesses. The SFBZ and ICBZ allow various incentives including a tax break of 26% for ten years to companies which move their headquarters to the zones. Among other regulations, a new company in the zones is required to employ at least ten local workers.

As discussed in Chapter 1, the burgeoning offshore financial centers (OFCs) such as the Caribbean islands of Bahamas, Bermuda, Cayman and the British Channel Island Jersey are all tourism dependency economies, and they enjoy high per capita incomes. Tourism and OFCs share prerequisites, including favorable location, good transport and communications links, and above all political stability. These island OFCs are mostly located in the pleasure periphery of the developed economies (Turner and Ash, 1975).

> *The largest OFCs lie 2-4 hours flying time from large countries, particularly the Caribbean and European clusters. Thus despite information and communications technology that could spell the "end of geography," face-to-face meeting remain a prerequisite. Therefore, good transport and communications links are fundamental for both tourism and finance. The development of tourism in many islands has generally preceded offshore finance, providing opportunities for the latter to free-ride on pre-existing infrastructure (Hampton and Christensen, 2007).*

If the above observations hold true, Okinawa meets all prerequisites for OFCs because it lies two hours flying time both from mainland Japan and dynamic Shanghai. As discussed, Okinawa is the most favorable island tourist destinations for mainland Japanese with well-furnished infrastructures and political stability. A financial planer such as Naoki Togashi argues that Okinawa can be a Bahamas in the East China Sea if the Japanese government allows Okinawa equivalent incentive systems as Bahamas enjoys (Togashi, 2004). Togashi particularly emphasizes financial businesses including private and global asset or trust management for wealthy individuals using a variety of options, captive insurance, and offshore funds. Of course Okinawa has to avoid demerits such as a "crowding-out" effect of having dynamic OFCs which tend to deprive of limited island's human resources and capital funds from the tourism industry.

The Tourism Satellite Account (TSA)

In concluding this chapter, we need to touch on the Tourism Satellite Account (TSA), proposed by the World Tourism Organization (WTO), the Organization for Economic Cooperation and Development (OECD), and the Statistical Office of the European Communities (Eurostat). The TSA was approved by the United Nations Statistical Commission (UNSC) at its thirty-first session in March 2000.

The TSA is a new approach to understanding the economic impacts of tourism:

> *From an economic perspective, the increasing efficiency in collecting information relative to the activities of people during trips abroad and domestically, in places outside their usual environment, is commensurate with a growing desire to analyze tourism economic impacts on the overall economy in respect of goods, services and employment. This approach, in considering visitor activity, is underpinned by its consideration as a consumer activity, in the broad sense of the term. However, in order to perform economic analyses of tourism, it is not only necessary to identify the goods and services*

consumed by visitors but also the resources these visitors use in the course of their trips, hence the need to identify the economic units that supply each type of product consumed by visitors. Accordingly, both the demand and supply side of tourism are equally relevant to the consideration of tourism impacts." (WTO, 2001).

The proposed TSA will provide a variety of information on tourism activities ranging from tourism's contribution to the economy of a given region or country and its ranking relative to other sectors and in comparison with other regions or countries. This statistical information is crucial for Planners and entrepreneurs.

Compared to Europe, particularly to Spain and France, Japan's system of tourism statistics is still at its infant stage. Even current basic statistics on tourism such as the number of inbound and outbound tourists, per capita spending, and the length of stay are not satisfactory. Per capita tourist expenditure of Okinawa, for example, declined from \92,000 in 2000 to \85,000, or 7.6% in 2001 due largely to the change in the survey method from "postcard questionnaires" to "in-flight passenger questionnaires" (see FIGURE 8-15). A small change in per capita spending makes a big difference in the aggregate amount. The economic impacts of tourism on sectoral GDP, employment, balance of payments and taxes, which we derived based on Okinawa's input-output tables, were subject to the number of strong assumptions with insufficient statistical information. The TSA will be a useful tool to analyze tourists' behaviors both quantitatively and qualitatively. A task team should be established through the joint initiatives of the Okinawa Prefecture and concerned researchers to study Okinawa's TSA.

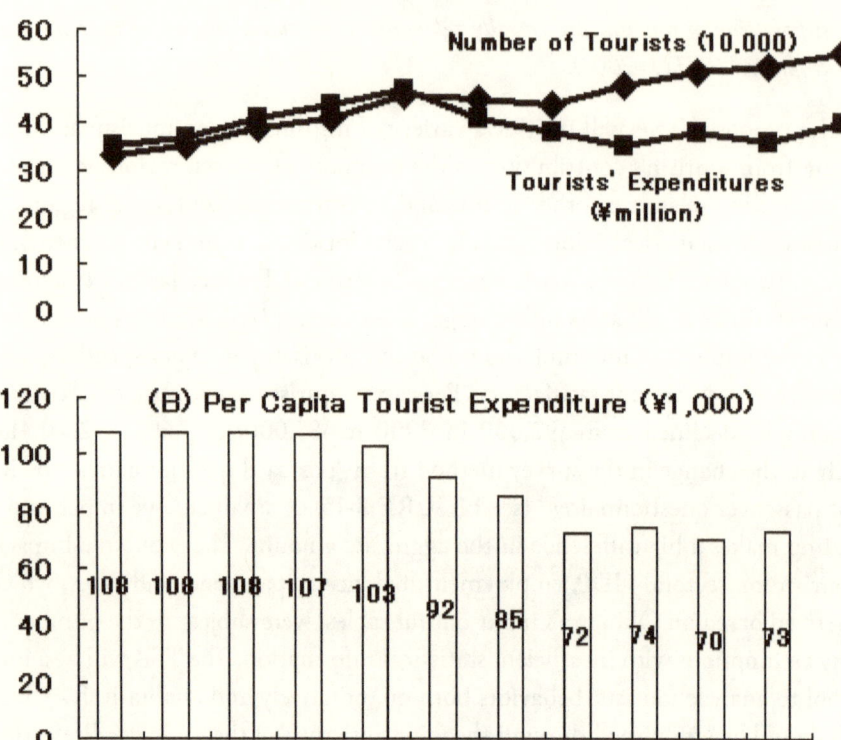

(A) Statistical Discrepancy Due to the Change in Estimating Method

Number of Tourists (10,000)

Tourists' Expenditures (¥million)

(B) Per Capita Tourist Expenditure (¥1,000)

108 108 108 107 103 92 85 72 74 70 73

1995 1996 1997 1998 1999 2000 2001 2002 2003 2004 2005

Source: See APPENDIX TABLE 8-5.

FIGURE 8-15. Okinawa's Tourism Statistics.

APPENDIX TABLE 8-1. World Tourist Arrivals by Region: 1990-2020

| | Tourist Arrivals (million) | | | Changes | | Shares (%) | | |
| | Actual | | Forecasts | Actual | Forecasts | Actual | | Forecasts |
	1990	2004	2020	04/90	020/04	1990	2004	2020
World	441	763	1,561	1.7	2.0	100	100.0	100
Europe	265	416	717	1.6	1.7	60.1	54.5	45.9
Asia-Pacific	58	153	416	2.6	2.7	13.2	20.1	26.6
Americas	93	126	282	1.4	2.2	21.1	16.5	18.1
Africa	15	33	77	2.2	2.3	3.4	4.3	5.0
Middle East	10	35	69	3.5	2.0	2.3	4.6	4.4

Source: UN World Tourism Organization.

APPENDIX TABLE 8-2. World Tourist Arrivals in Asia : 1990-2020

| | Arrivals (million) | | | Changes | | World Shares (%) | |
	1990	2000	2004	2000/1990	2004/1990	1990	2004
North-East Asia	26	58	79	2.2	1.4	0.1	11.3
China	10	31	42	3.1	1.4	0.0	6.0
Hong Kong (China)	6	9	14	1.5	1.6	0.0	2.0
Taiwan	2	3	3	1.5	1.0	0.0	0.4
Japan	3	5	6	1.7	1.2	0.0	0.9
Korea, Re. of	3	5	6	1.7	1.2	0.0	0.9
ASEAN	21	43	48	2.0	1.1	0.0	6.9
Malaysia	7	13	16	1.9	1.2	0.0	2.3
Thailand	5	11	12	2.2	1.1	0.0	1.7
Singapore	5	7	6	1.4	0.9	0.0	0.9
Indonesia	2	5	5	2.5	1.0	0.0	0.7
Philippines	1	2	2	2.0	1.0	0.0	0.3

Note: 2004 figure for Singapore is for 2003.
Source: UN World Tourism Organization.

	(US$, billion)			Changes		Shares (%)			GDP Shares
	1990	2000	2004	2000/1990	2004/2000	1990	2000	2004	2004
World	273	484	633	1.8	1.3	100.0	100.0	100.0	100.0
Europe	146	232	329	1.6	1.4	53.5	47.9	52.0	35.5
Asia–Pacific	47	91	128	1.9	1.4	17.2	18.8	20.2	23.7
Americas	69	131	132	1.9	1.0	25.3	27.1	20.9	36.5
Africa	6	11	19	1.8	1.7	2.2	2.3	3.0	1.2
Middle East	5	19	25	3.8	1.3	1.8	3.9	3.9	3.0

Source: UN World Tourism Organization.

APPENDIX TABLE 8-4. World Tourist Receipts in Asia: 1990–2020

	(US$, billion)			Changes		World Shares (%)			GDP Shares
	1990	2000	2004	2000/1990	2004/2000	1990	2000	2004	2004
North-East Asia	23.0	46.0	64.0	2.0	1.4	8.4	9.5	10.1	18.6
China	2.2	16.2	25.7	7.4	1.6	0.8	3.3	4.1	4.1
Hong Kong (China)	5.0	7.5	9.0	1.5	1.2	1.8	1.5	1.4	0.5
Taiwan	1.7	3.7	4.1	2.2	1.1	0.6	0.8	0.6	0.8
Japan	3.6	3.4	11.3	0.9	3.3	1.3	0.7	1.8	11.5
Korea, Re. of	3.6	6.8	6.0	1.9	0.9	1.3	1.4	0.9	1.7
ASEAN	14.5	26.2	32.1	1.8	1.2	5.3	5.4	5.1	1.8
Malaysia	1.7	5.0	8.2	2.9	1.6	0.6	1.0	1.3	0.3
Thailand	4.3	7.5	10.0	1.7	1.3	1.6	1.5	1.6	0.4
Indonesia	2.1	5.0	4.8	2.4	1.0	0.8	1.0	0.8	0.6
Singapore	4.9	5.1	5.2	1.0	1.0	1.8	1.1	0.8	0.1
Philippines	1.3	2.1	2.0	1.6	1.0	0.5	0.4	0.3	0.2

Source: UN World Tourism Organization.

APPENDIX TABLE 8-5. Main Indicators of Okinawa's Tourism

	Unit	Actual Performance					Targeted	
		2002	2003	2004	2005	2006	2007	2011
Number of tourists	10,000	483	508	515	550	565	580	650
Foreign tourists		18	10	13	14	NA	25	60
Per capita tourist spending	¥1,000	72	74	70	72	77	80	109
Tourism receipts	¥ 100 million	3,466	3,754	3,631	3,984	4,104	4,800	7,085
Average length of stay	day	3.8	3.9	3.7	3.4	3.9	4.8	7.1
Rate of repeater	%		62		69	69	NA	NA
Number of hotel rooms	room	25,423	27,533	28,303	31,238	NA	31,200	33,500
Room capacity utilization	%		75	73	74	NA	NA	NA
Number of study tours	1,000	286	336	393	426	NA	NA	NA
Cruise ship visits		72	47	71	NA	NA	90	200
Resort weddings	pairs		2,500	3,500	NA	NA	7,500	10,000
Number of conventions		486	687	649	NA	NA	730	650
International conferences		31	23	35	NA	NA	45	50
Sports conventions		146	174	192	NA	NA	220	240

NA = Not Available.
Source: Okinawa Prefectural Government, Statistics on Tourism.

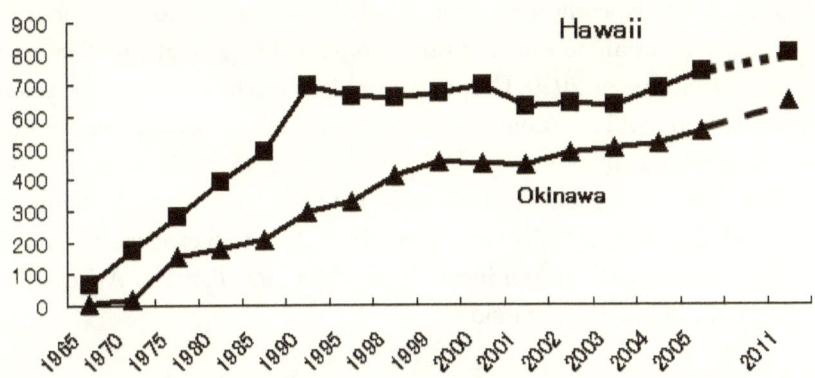

(A) Inbound Visitors, Okinawa & Hawaii: 1965-2011

1.0000 visitors

Hawaii

Okinawa

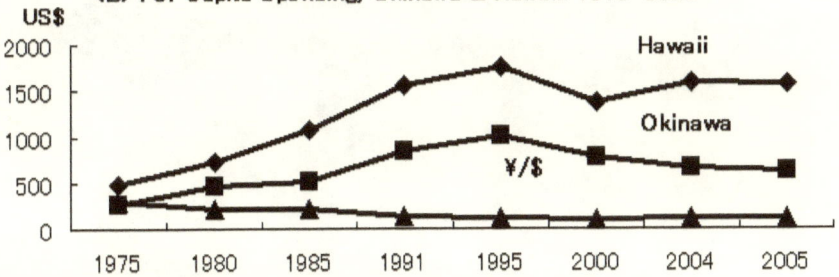

(B) Per Capita Spending, Okinawa & Hawaii: 1975-2005

US$

Hawaii

Okinawa

¥/$

Sources: See Appendix Table 1, Japan's _White Paper on Tourism_ and Hawaii's Department of Business, Economic Development & Tourism
Figures for 2007and 2011 are targeted numbers in the "Tourism Promotion Action Plans."

APPENDIX FIGURE 8-1. Tourism Development of Hawaii and Okinawa.

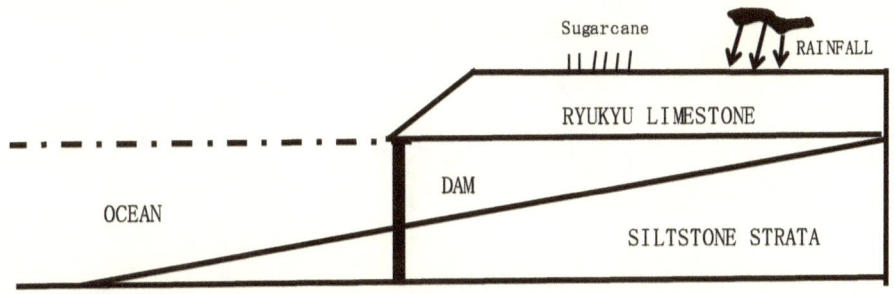

Source: H. Kakakzu (2006).

APPENDIX FIGURE 8-2. Structure of the Subsurface Dam of Miyako Island.

APPENDIX FIGURE 8-3 presents a grand macro view on Okinawa's economy from the past (1972), present (2005) and future (2020). The diagram shows important variables including GDP, population, per capita income, labor force, unemployment, public expenditure and tourism development. The tourism industry, Okinawa's most important leading industry, is projected to grow about 50% in terms of the tourism income by 2020. Despite various issues to be resolved, the expansion of tourism industry will contribute to Okinawa's self-reliant development through creating employment and reducing a heavy dependency on fiscal transfer expenditure.

This three-dimensional model can be applied to any island economy and can be expanded to include many related variables. If we feed exogenous variables into the hidden equations, we can instantly obtain a PPF diagram. Anybody wish to challenge for improving the model?

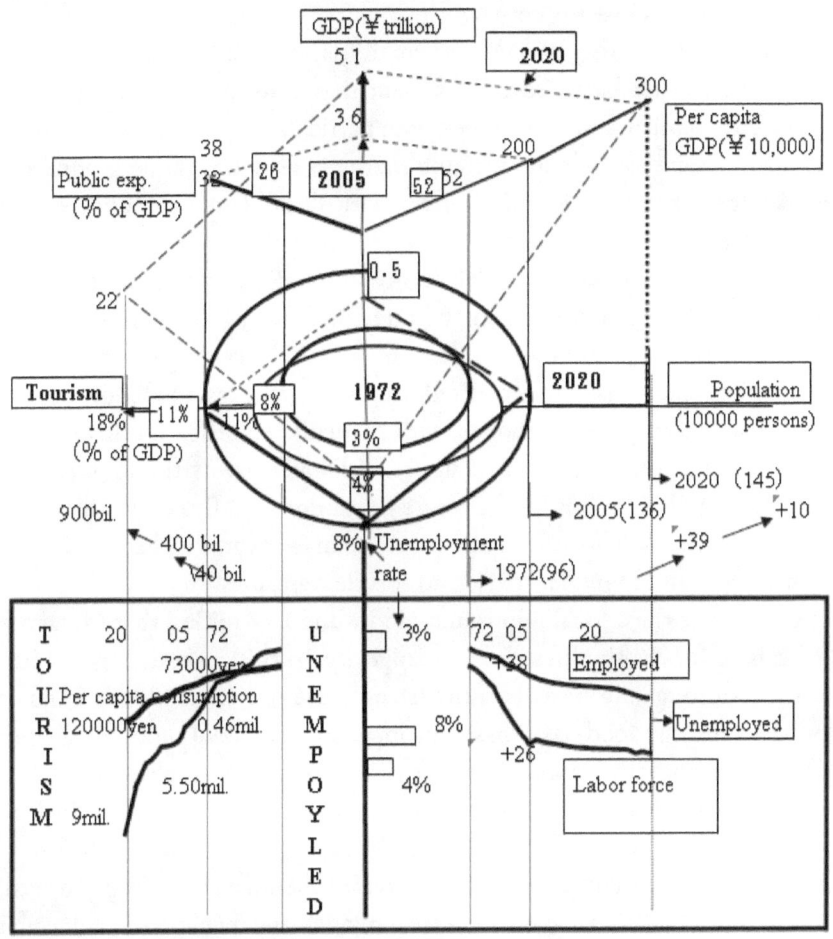

Source: Constructed by Kakazu, H.(2005).

APPENDIX FIGURE 8-3. A PPF Analysis of Okinawa's Tourism Economy.

APPENDIX 8-4. The Miyako Declaration on "Island Biodiversity and Sustainable Livelihoods"

Based on the proceedings of the International Small Island Studies Association (ISISA) Experts Meeting on "Island Biodiversity and Sustainable Livelihoods" held on Miyako Island, Okinawa on September 2, 2005 as part of the Islands of the World IX Okinawa Preconferences, 1-3 September, 2005, the participants hereby affirm the critical importance of developing appropriate long-term models for the promotion of sustainable island livelihoods and governance based on the combination of the sustainable use of small island ecosystems and biodiversity and the best mix of modern and traditional knowledge, research, education, communication and resource-use systems.

We also recognize that Miyako is a small island, with limited and fragile resources. This requires balanced development that takes into account economic, social and environmental sustainability, with particular emphasis on the conservation and sustainable use of coral reef and marine ecosystems, underground freshwater resources, coastal and inland forests, agricultural lands and our settlement and infrastructure.

We recognize that the terrestrial, freshwater and marine ecosystems of Miyako are very closely interconnected and attempts must be made to maintain the quantity and quality of groundwater resources, to protect our waters and island from pollution and to use the terrestrial, freshwater and marine biodiversity as a foundation for sustainable livelihoods, with particular emphasis on the promotion of sustainable tourism, fishing, agriculture and water use as the foundation for sustainable island livelihoods for the future generations of Miyako. In this context, Miyako dedicates itself to sustainable waste management and becoming a zero emission society and to reduce, reuse and recycle wastes.

We recognize the critical importance and world recognition that Miyako and Okinawa have for healthy lifestyles and longevity. In this context, Miyako Island dedicates itself to remaining a "Healthy Island" through the production and consumption of healthy foods as a basis for long life and the promotion of sports, physical fitness and other appropriate activities that will ensure the physical and mental wellbeing of our residents and treasured visitors to our island, including the famous Triathlon.

In relation to all small islands, we recognized the unique challenges related to small size, isolation, fragmentation, resource limitation and fragility, and vulnerability to natural disasters and outside economic and political events beyond their control.

It is also recognized that small islands offer great opportunities for the development of appropriate models for sustainable development and the conservation, sustainable use and equitable sharing of biodiversity and island resources.

As such we make the following recommendations to the international community, national leaders and policy makers, non-government organizations, private enterprise and local communities and others who have a role to play in the promotion of the sustainable development of small islands nations and communities.

- That greater emphasis be placed on the exchange of students, information and communication technologies as a basis for strengthening relationships, building capacity and developing models for socially, economically and environmentally sustainable development for all small island nations and communities.
- That increased emphasis be placed on awareness raising and education,

with particular emphasis on the involvement of school children, as our future leaders, and on the involvement of older members of the communities who are the custodians of traditional knowledge of island cultures and environments.

- That research and education be more field-based as a means of making these to activities more relevant to small islands and their local communities.
- That research and education be more closely linked to policy formulation.
- That there is a critical need for the marriage of the most up-to-day modern day research findings and communication technologies with traditional knowledge and systems of information dissemination.
- That there is a critical need to improve the content of our educational messages and materials in parallel with the rapidly expanding information and communication technology to make it more relevant to the needs of small island communities.
- That environmentally and culturally sustainable tourism offers one of the best long term options for sustainable small island development and collaboration between small islands
- That this declaration and the deliberations of this meeting be carried through and built upon as the basis for a vision of truly sustainable livelihoods for small island nations and communities throughout the world.

NOTES

Brundtland, H.G. (1987), p.5.
Miwa, N., Yamauchi H. and D. Morita (1988), p.124.
UNEP (2006), p.5.
Brandolini S.M. and Mosetti R. (2005), pp.1-10.
Hampton, M.P. and Christensen, J. (2007), p. 1001.
World Tourism Organization (WTO, 2001), p.1.

REFERENCES

Association for Tourism and Leisure Education. 2007. "Sustainable Tourism," at http://www.gdrc. org/uem/eco-tour/eco-tour.html ttp://www.gdrc.org/uem/eco-tour/eco-tour.html.

Brandolini S.M. and Mosetti R. 2005. *Social Carrying Capacity of Mass Tourist Sites: Theoretical and Practical Issues about its Measurement*. Milano: Social Science Research Network Electric Paper Collection, pp.1-10.

Brundtland, H.G. 1987. *Our Common Future: Report of the World Commission on Environment and Development*. Paris: UNESCO.

Choi Hwan-Suk and E. Sirakaya. 1995. "Measuring Residents' Attitude toward Sustainable Tourism: Development of Sustainable Tourism Attitude Scale." *Journal of Travel Research*, SAGE Journals Online, May, pp.380-394.

Hampton, M.P. and Christensen, J. (2007). "Competing Industries in Islands: A New Tourism Approach." *Annals of Tourism Research*, vol. 34, no.4, pp. 998-1020.

Hawaii's Department of Business, Economic Development, and Tourism (DEBEDT), and Tourism. 1996. *The Economic Impacts of Shipboard Gaming and Pari-Mutuel Horse Racing in Hawaii*. Honolulu: pp.1-127.

Kakazu, H. 2007. "Sustainable Island Tourism: The Case of Okinawa." A paper presented at the 21st Pacific Science Conference. Okinawa: Okinawa Convention Center, June 12-18, 2007.

_____. 2007. "Text on Quantitative Methods of Tourism Study." The Department of Tourism Sciences. Okinawa: University of the Ryukyus, pp.1-49.

_____. 1994. *Sustainable Development of Small Island Economies*. Boulder: Westview Press.

_____. 2002. "The Challenge for Okinawa: Thriving Locally in a Globalized Economy." In: Hsin-Huang Michael Hsiao, *et al* (eds.). *Sustainable Development for Island Societies: Taiwan and the World*. Taipei: Academia Sinica, pp. 201-232.

_____. 1998. "Sustainable Tourism Development: The Case of Small Islands." A paper presented at the Inter-island Cooperation in Asia: Tourism Policy in Island Area, The Busena Resort, Okinawa: 24 July.

_____. 1997. "Tourism Development and Cultural Heritage." In: A Study of Human Resources and Development Needs in Asia. Nagoya: Nagoya University, pp.1-12.

_____. 1996. "Effects of Tourism Growth on Development in the Asia-Pacific Region: The Case of Small Islands." A paper presented at the UNESCO Conference on Culture, Tourism, and Development: Crucial Issues for the XXI Century, 26-27June. Paris.

Ministry of Land, Infrastructure and Transport, *White Paper on Tourism*, various issues. Tokyo.

Miwa, N., Yamauchi H. and Morita D. 1988. *Water and Survival in an Island Environment: Challenge of Okinawa*. Honolulu: University of Hawaii.

Togashi, N. 2004. "A Development Potential of the Okinawa Financial Special Zone: Establishment of a Marine Resort cum Offshore Financial Center." In: *A Report of Okinawa Financial Expert Meeting*. Naha: Okinawa Times, pp. 86-101.

Turner, L. and Ash J. 1975. *The Golden Hordes: International Tourism and the Pleasure Periphery*. London: Constable.

Sinclair, M.T. and. Stabler M. 1997. *The Economics of Tourism*. London: Routledge.

Sukpil Oh. 2003. A Study on Coastal Conservation and Utilization: Valuations on Coral Reefs and Ecosystem of the Kerama Islands. Okinawa: Research Institute of Subtropics.

Umemura, T. 2004. "The Prospect of Okinawa Tourism from a Viewpoint of Global Trend." Unpublished paper. Okinawa: University of the Ryukyus, pp.1-20.

UNEP-WCMC 2006. *In the front line: shoreline protection and other ecosystem services from mangroves and coral reefs*. Cambridge: UNEP-WCMC, pp.1-33.

World Tourism Organization (WTO). 1995. *Global Tourism Forecasts to the Year 2000 and Beyond*. Vol.1. Madrid: WTO. Also see WTO, Compendium to Tourism Statistics. 2007 Edition (Data 2001-2005).

World Tourism Organization (WTO). 2001. *Tourism Satellite Account (TSA): Implementation Project—the Tourism Satellite Account as an Ongoing Process: Past, Present and Future Developments*. Madrid: WTO.

Chapter 9

Okinawa: Champuru Culture and Its Prospects

Introduction

Culture, which has its root meaning "to cultivate" is commonly defined as "the set of distinctive spiritual, material, intellectual and emotional features of society or a social group, and that it encompasses, in addition to art and literature, lifestyles, ways of living together, value systems, traditions and beliefs" (UNECSO, 2002). Culture is a way of living that is closely attached to a given land or society, whereas civilization could be considered the institutions and functional apparatus of living that can be utilized universally beyond land and society (see Masuda, 1992). These cultural traits are transmitted from generation to generation through the socio-economic impacts of endogenous as well as exogenous forces, and they change over time.

Okinawa or Ryukyu has undergone three major cultural transformations (see Watanabe, 2002). The first was from 14th to 19th century when the Ryukyu Kingdom was a tributary state of China. Through trade and cultural exchange, Okinawa prospered economically and culturally. Many Chinese customs and practices were introduced, in areas such as ancestor worship, court ceremonies, lifestyle, industrial and construction skills, crafts, education, the lunar calendar system, *harii* (dragon boat races), food, education and entertainment.

The second transformation took place after the Japanese government forcefully dismantled the Ryukyu Kingdom and created Okinawa Prefecture in 1879. Japanese cultural influences actually began much earlier when the Lord of Satsuma invaded the Ryukyu Kingdom in 1609. However, from 1879 direct Japanese rule resulted in active assimilation in the areas of education and language. In order to fully integrate Okinawa into the Japanese system, Okinawan children were forbidden from speaking local language or *uchinaguchi* in school for many decades.

The third transformation of Okinawa took place after the Battle of Okinawa in 1945. Okinawa fell under direct U.S. military occupation for twenty-seven years, during which it was subject to different institutional systems from that of Japan proper. Additionally, the American way of life penetrated deeply into the island lifestyle. Each external influence served to shape Okinawa's cultural heritage into a *champuru* culture, or mixed culture as is schematically depicted:

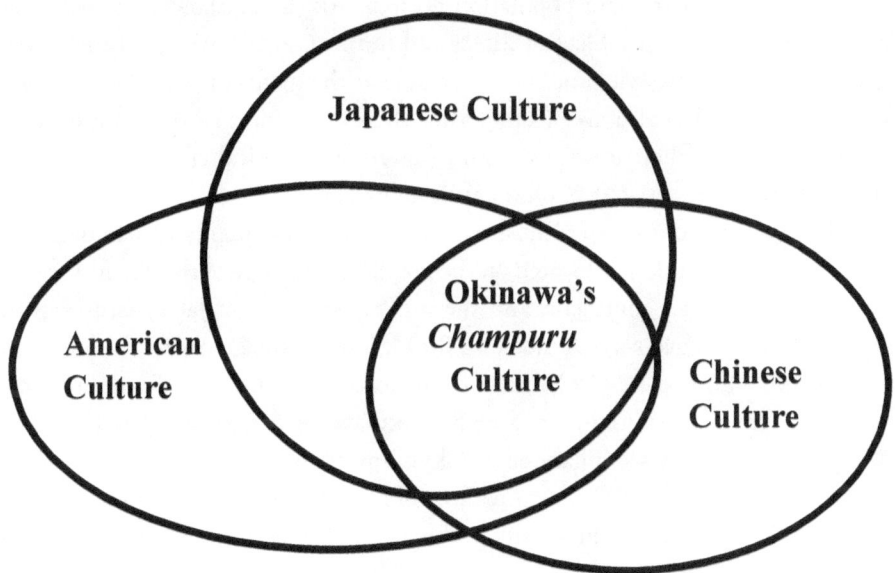

Source: Kakazu, H.

FIGURE 9-1.   A Concept of Okinawa's Mixed Cultures.

Okinawan ideas and values such as *champuru, icharibachode* (once we meet, we are like brothers and sisters), *chimugurisan* (someone's pain is my pain), *yuimaru* (reciprocity) and *nuchidotakara* (life is the most precious thing in the world) developed out of a long, dynamic historical process of island life. This rich, diverse cultural heritage is today appreciated within and beyond Okinawa, particularly on mainland Japan. It may be appropriate to quote Professor Haruo Misumi: "Okinawa is a place where its art culture has surpassed that of Japan and has grown to the scale encompassing the whole of Asia" (Misumi, undated). This chapter examines the formation of Okinawa's unique *champuru* culture and its future prospects.

HISTORY AND CHARACTERISTICS OF OKINAWA

As we have discussed in Chapter 1, small island societies including Okinawa possess some common characteristics because of their small, remote and oceanic topographic characteristics with strategic cross-border locations which to a certain extent determine the ways of living of island peoples. Small islands are not only extremely vulnerable to natural disasters such as typhoons, tsunami, earthquakes, global warming, but they are also vulnerable to outside interventions such as war, invasion, trade embargo and population growth. All single island nations in the Pacific which have been subject to direct and indirect colonization or rule by foreign powers. Their lifestyles and identities were at the mercy of politico-economic exercises of the colonial powers. Long after their independence they still have to depend heavily on their former suzerain powers for political stability as well as trade and economic assistance. Okinawa is an example.

Okinawa, the southwesternmost part of Japan with a total land area of 2,265 square km (874 sq. miles), is located on the northwestern edge of the Pacific Ocean, just east of the Asian continent, and the southwestern tip of Japan (see Map in FIGURE 9-2). It covers a distance of 1,000 kilometers (622 miles) from east to west and 400 kilometers (248 miles) from north to south. The Ryukyu archipelago, the pre-modern Chinese name for Okinawa encompasses more than 160 islands, of which forty are inhabited. Ryukyu limestone, found throughout the archipelago, is the product of many millennia of coral accumulation. Okinawa is the only Japanese prefecture to lie wholly in the subtropical oceanic climatic zone. The average annual temperature is 22.4 degrees Celsius, and average annual precipitation is 2,037 millimeters. Except for occasional typhoons during the summer, no natural disasters have been reported in recent years. Okinawa with its abundant flora and fauna, including world-renowned species such as the Iriomote wildcat, Pryor's woodpecker and Okinawa rail, has sometimes been called the "Galapagos of the Orient."

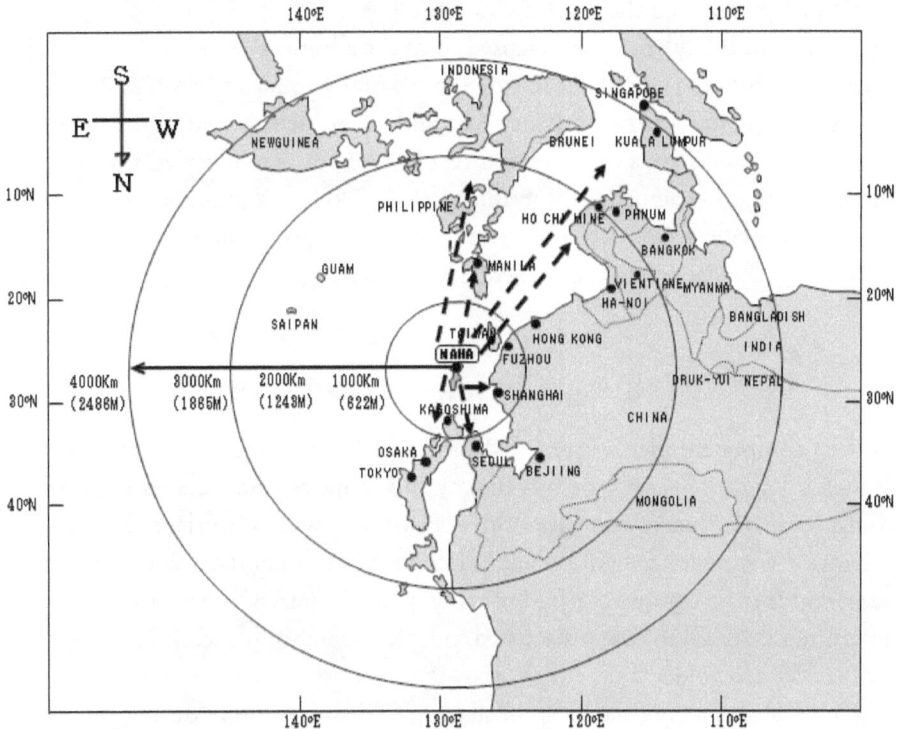

— — ▶ Trade routes of the Ryukyuan Kingdoms (NAHA = Capital).

Source: Hiroshi Kakazu (2000).

FIGURE 9-2. Ryukyus: At the Heart of the South Seas.

Okinawa possesses few economically significant natural resources to be exploited. The most important natural resources are coral reefs and beaches which attract millions of tourists every year. There are 350 varieties of coral in Okinawa alone accounting for nearly half of the world's varieties.

From the late 14th century to the late 16th century, the Ryukyu Kingdom maximized its geographic advantage by engaging in multilateral trade with its East and Southeast Asian neighbors (see the map above). For the kingdom, trade was not only the engine of growth, but it also brought rich cultural assets.

On the other hand, the Battle of Okinawa in 1945 resulted in the tragic loss of some 125,000 civilian lives, constituting approximately one-third of Okinawa's total population at that time. The war destroyed virtually every visible asset including priceless cultural heritage, buildings and artifacts, and engraved deep psychological scars on the minds of the islanders. The peace monuments erected in the southern part of Okinawa Island symbolize a tragic by-product of Okinawa's strategic location which was utilized as a stepping stone for the U.S. advance toward mainland Japan during the Pacific War.

More than thirty years have elapsed since the administrative reversion of Okinawa, or the Ryukyu Islands, from the United States to Japan in 1972. This postreversion period in Okinawa's history is roughly equivalent to that from 1945-1972 when the Ryukyu Islands were under direct United States military administration. Despite significant changes in the international politico-economic environment in the Asia-Pacific region since reversion, Okinawa's geo-military position as the 'Keystone of the Pacific' has remained almost unchanged.

CHINESE CULTURAL INFLUENCES

The first component of *champuru* culture came from China and Southeast Asia through a long, proud, prosperous history of Okinawa's interactions with neighboring countries during the 14th-16th centuries in what historians described as Okinawa's "trade-induced golden age" (Takara, 1998; Akamine, 2006). This glorious period is still very much alive for many contemporary Okinawans. Whenever the future role of Okinawa is discussed, people nostalgically recall this self-generated, self-owned golden era.

China played a dominant role in shaping Okinawa's culture during the period not only in materialistic dimensions such as the introduction of sugarcane and sweet potato cultivations, handicraft and traditional dances which became major assets of Okinawa, but also in the practices of education and spiritual belief systems. Although the Chinese system of education was totally displaced by the Japanese system particularly after the annexation of Okinawa by mainland Japan in 1879, "ancestor worship" and related rituals are still firmly rooted in Okinawa's spiritual life. Family altars, tombs, *obon*, and *eisa* are all related to ancestor worship which combined with Okinawa's ancient belief of animism, Buddhism and Taoism. The Chinese zodiac and the lunar calendar system still play important roles in Okinawa's major rituals and festivals. Several important Chinese cultural legacies are highlighted.

Ancestor Worship: Okinawan Religion?

"Okinawan religious beliefs may be characterized as animistic, for all things, animate and inanimate, are conceived as possessed of indwelling spirits." (Lebra, 1966). Animism was formally transformed into ancestor worship in Okinawa through the influence of Chinese Buddhism. Ancestor worship is a strong tradition close to the status of religion. For in sharing their happiness and healing their despair with their ancestors, they expect the cenotaph tables of their forefathers to protect them. Ceremonies and styles of ancestor worship are observed in Okinawa's daily life and typically on the occasion of special festivals. One symbol is the family altar, called

Totome, small wooden plaques located on step-like shelves in the central room of the house, which is inscribed with the names of family ancestors.

(*Totome* =Alter)   (Prayers before *Totome*)

Another visible example of Chinese influence is found in the style of Okinawan tombs. Visitors from mainland Japan are surprised to see such large tombs located near residential areas. The shape of these tombs symbolizes the woman's womb from which babies are born and to which the dead should return. These tombs, which were initially introduced by a Chinese Fujian Buddist priest, symbolize the ancestor worship of Okinawa which came from China many generations ago. In the early period of Ryukyuan history, the deceased were buried in caves on hillsides and along the seashore. These "turtle-back" style Chinese tombs were used as hiding places or shelters during the Battle of Okinawa.

(Old OkinawanTomb)   (Chinese Turtle-back style Tomb)

Obon (*Bon*), the most important yearly religious ritual and festival to honor the dead, is held in August according to the Chinese lunar calendar in Okinawa. The festival is celebrated to welcome the spirits of ancestors to the family altar. Relatives offer food and gifts, and they pray and talk with their ancestors. During the *Obon* season, people enjoy listening to the sounds of *eisa* drums and folk songs, and they also feast their eyes on *eisa* or bon dances performed in the streets and various open fields by the youth. The traditional, colorful costumes of dancers are worn under the full moon.

Eisa dances are unique to Okinawa. Passed on from generation to generation in a manner of cultural innovation and creativity, the dances have changed, in part, due to outside influences such as entertaining tourists. The very nature of *eisa* dance is an ethnic phenomenon or a diasporas performing art which is deeply rooted in Okinawan cultural heritage (see Yamamoto, 2002).

(*Eisa* dance)

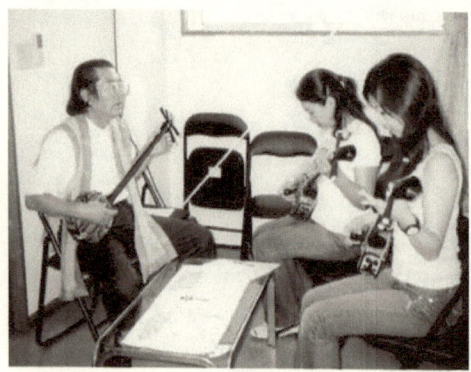

(*Sanshin* lesson)

Dragon Boat Race (*Harii* or *Hare*)

Harii or *hare* (in Itoman), which was introduced from China, was traditionally linked to the *Kaijin-sai* (*Unjami*) or fisherman's festival to give thanks to the sea god and pray for the safety of fishermen and good catches. Nowadays, harii is one of the most popular, lively festivals in Okinawa during the late spring and summer period. Among many *harii* in Okinawa, the most popular ones are the Naha *harii* and Itoman *hare*. Itoman is a southern community village with a long history of fishing for its livelihood. The Itoman *hare*, which is held on the fourth day of the fifth month in the Chinese lunar calendar, symbolizes the end of the rainy season and the beginning of summer in Okinawa.

(Naha Harii)

Architecture: Shuri Castle

Shuri Castle, the home of twenty five Ryukyu kings from King Sho Hashi (1407-1469) to King Sho Tai (1866-1879), is a living symbol of the prosperous Ryukyuan Kingdom as well as a symbol of the architectural mix of Chinese, Korean and Japanese styles. Shuri Castle was said to have been patterned on the Forbidden City or the Palace Museum built during the Ming dynasty. Shuri Castle was bombed during the Battle of Okinawa and the wooden structure burned to the ground. Part of the castle was reconstructed and opened as Shuri Castle Park in 1992. It has been designated a UNESCO-protected World Heritage site.

(Palace Museum)   (Shuri Castle in 1935)   (Shuri Castle in 1992)

Ishiganto and *Shisa*

Almost on every busy street corner in Okinawa, you may come across a stone marker with the following Chinese characters: 石敢當 *(ishiganto).*

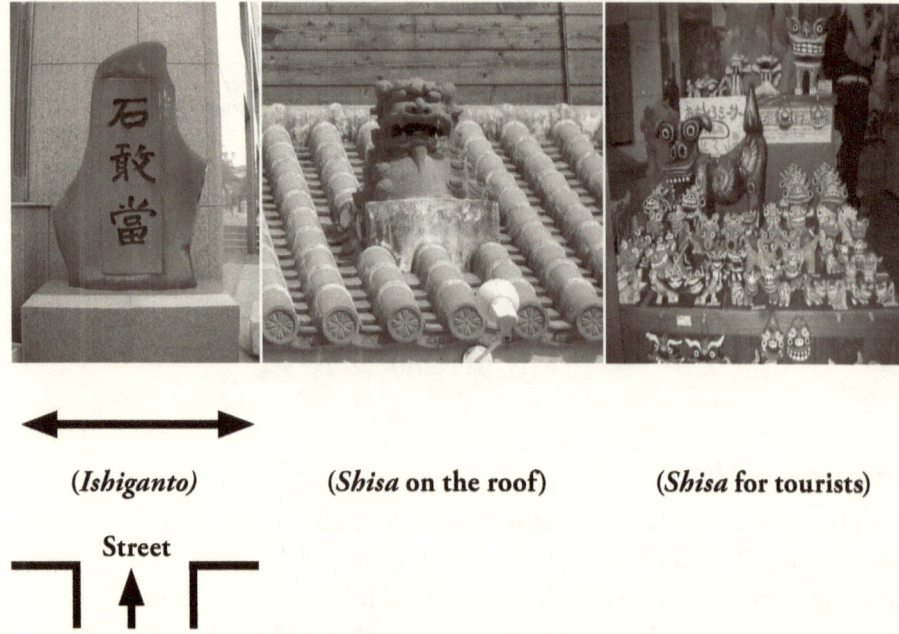

(*Ishiganto*)   **(*Shisa* on the roof)**   **(*Shisa* for tourists)**

Street

According to Kodama (1999), the *ishiganto* (石敢當), a symbol of old Chinese beliefs, was introduced to Okinawa from China around the early 18th century to ward off evil spirits from entering into a house. The *ishiganto* is erected at an intersection or a dead end street because of the belief that evil cannot turn at corners.

The most popular symbol of Okinawa is a lion-dog statue called a *shisa* which was introduced from China around the 14th or 15th century to ward off or deflect bad spirits. *Shisa* can typically be found at the entrance to main streets, buildings and the roofs of houses. It is unlikely that you can walk along any Okinawan street without encountering strange looking, ferocious, yet various shaped humorous *shisa* figures. Similar *shisa* statues can be seen in Asia and mainland Japan, but the statue fits more comfortably in Okinawa than in any other country in the world because it is an essential part of Okinawa's spiritual life. Furthermore, the *shisa* is the most popular souvenir for tourists. This is a good example that Okinawa's cultural assets can be commercialized.

Language

After the unification of the Okinawa Island by the Chuzan Kingdom based at Shuri in the 15th century, the Shuri dialect became the standard language of Okinawa. According to Iha (2000), the father of Okinawa *gaku* (Okinawaology), and Hokama (1971), the best-known living linguist on Okinawa, the Shuri dialect is a sister language of old Japanese. The Shuri dialect, however, evolved into a unique and independent language system influenced by the interactions with China and

Southeast Asia. We can still trace a lot of Chinese words currently used in Okinawa such as *unche* (雲菜), *sanpin* (香片), *sunshi* (筍子), *tauchi*(闘鶏), *tari* (大人), *chinsuko*(金楚糕), *popo*(餑餑) (see more details in Higa, 1983). *Chinsuko* is Okinawa's top-selling cookie.

Why is there no Chinatown?

Despite a long, pervasive history of Okinawa's interactions with China, Okinawa does not have its own Chinatown. Contemporary history books tell us about "thirty-six Chinese families" (a term which means "many") settled in Kume Village, present-day Naha City in the late 14th century (see Kerr, 2000). They were mostly specialists in arts, crafts, administration and agriculture. "Of the Chinese customs introduced at this time and taken over into Okinawan life many became so well assimilated to local tradition and custom as to be indistinguishable today" (Kerr, *ibid*.). If we think of flourishing Chinatowns in mainland Japan and Southeast Asia, it is a great mystery why there are no remnants of a defined Chinatown. One explanation is Okinawa's *champuru* culture totally absorbed Chinese culture.

JAPANESE CULTURAL INFLUENCES

There is much evidence that Okinawa had socio-cultural, economic exchanges with Japan long before Satsuma's troops invaded Okinawa in 1609. The Okinawan dialect, for example, is considered to be a part of the Japanese language system (see Iha, 2000). The Okinawan dialect contains numerous expressions of old-style Japanese. There are also a lot of common cultural heritages between Okinawa and mainland Japan including animism and ancestor worship. Okinawans, however, are often distinguished from the mainland Japanese by their physical traits of "hairy, dark, big eyes and friendly smile."

The Japanese influence on Okinawan culture, however, has become apparent particularly in the areas of education and socio-economic systems since the annexation of Okinawa in 1879. After several decades of a "hands off" policy towards the new Okinawa prefecture, the Meiji government implemented various unification policies. In the name of "modernization" and creating good "imperial subjects," the old communal practices were abolished, and the Japanese school system was introduced. Introduction of nation-wide compulsory education was probably the most important tool in the assimilation of Okinawa into Japanese society.

The Japanization of Okinawa reached the peak of its intensity in the 1930s under the rising influence of Japan's military power. The Standard Japanese Enforcement Movement was instituted in 1939 as a part of national spiritual mobilization campaign. All school children were expected to speak fluent Japanese from the primary school level. In order to achieve this objective, a pupil who spoke Okinawan dialect or *hogen* on school premises was punished by means of *hogen bura* (方言札) or a dialect tag teachers hung from the necks of offending students, which could only be gotten rid of by passing it on to other students slipping into the tabooed language. "The hapless student who was still tagged at the end of the day had to go home earning the badge of humiliation. Sometimes, in desperation, an offender would hit unsuspecting classmates in the hope of eliciting an exclamation, which, naturally would come in dialect rather than in standard Japanese" (Field, 1991). I vividly remember that the *hogen bura* was practiced long after my childhood in the postwar period (see a photo below).

Most of the Okinawan elite supported the forced assimilation policy believing that Okinawans were discriminated against by mainlanders mainly because they could not speak proper Japanese. If Okinwans spoke standard Japanese, then they would not suffer discrimination. "Okinawan elites employed to minimize fundamental cultural differences with the mainland" (Smith, 1999). According to Higa (2003), the practice instilled in the mind of younger generation a sense of cultural inferiority. The late governor of Okinawa Prefecture, Junji Nishime used to say that Okinawans wished to be good Japanese since the late nineteenth century onward, but we could not make it. "There is still a pervasive anxiety about speaking 'correct' Japanese. Language is the most elusive, because subtle, traitor. If all visible difference between peoples could be effaced, speech would still threaten to betray cultural difference, too easily thought to have a genetic, and therefore racial, origin. The waves of programs to eradicate this difference in the Okinawan prewar continued into the postwar" (Field, 1991).

(Dialect tag in 1952)   (*hoanden* in the 1930s)

Prior to Okinawa's annexation in 1873, the Japanese Ministry of Education declared that all Okinawans as new "imperial subjects" must follow the national educational policy. The essence of the policy called *kokutai* (literally nationality) was to install absolute loyalty to the emperor who was a "living god" in all subjects. Okinawa's schools established *hoanden* in particular which housed the emperor's photograph. The *hoanden* (see a photo above), together with the Rising Sun flag was intended to unite "children and their teachers throughout Japan in a common discipline and served to instill belief in the sacred being of the emperor and to promote the instinct for obedience to his wishes (Field, 1991).

AMERICAN CULTURAL INFLUENCES

America, or more precisely, the United States Department of Defense at the Pentagon ruled Okinawa for twenty-seven years from 1945-1972. Huge U.S. bases remain including Kadena Airbase, the largest airbase in the Far East. The American influence on Okinawan culture came mainly through military base activities. American bases gave birth to "Okinawa rock music" which became a brand name of Koza (current Okinawa) city located near Kadena Airbase. The rock music, combined with traditional Ryukyuan music and *shimauta* (island songs), produced a unique music culture in the postwar period. Okinawan popular singers such as Namie Amuro, Kiroro, Da Pump, Speed, Max, Shokichi Kina, Orange Renge to name a few, gained enormous popularity in Japan and Asia.

Okinawans also picked up American food habits. The first fast food franchise introduced in Okinawa and Japan was "Papa Burger" with root beer, a product of A&W, long before McDonald's became popular in Japan. Okinawa is still the only place in Japan which houses A&W fast food restaurants. American food culture definitely adversely affected Okinawa's proud history of world-renown longevity as will be discussed later in this chapter.

One of most important cultural legacies of American occupation of Okinawa may be "anti-war culture." Since the end of WWII, Okinawa has been the "Keystone of the Pacific" for the defense of the U.S. and Japan. The San Francisco Peace Treaty, concluded between the United States and Japan in 1951, mandated huge military bases on Okinawa. As we have discussed the U.S. bases have been the most controversial socio-political and economic issue since the inception of the U.S. occupation of the island.

(Kadena Airbase)   **(Rock Music)**   **(American Fast Foods)**

The U.S. bases also gave birth to new professions such as garden boys, house-maids, dry-cleaners, and drivers and prostitutes who also bore biracial children. Biracial children were called *konketsuji* (mixed blood children) or *ainoko* (half-breed children). They suffered discrimination and prejudice in the Okinawan community partly because people tended to connect them with the sex entertainment industry that catered to American soldiers in Okinawa. These terms, however, have evolved into *hafu* (half) or *daburu* (double) to be positively used in Japan today to describe all racially mixed people. The term Amerasian (children fathered by U.S. service-men on the island of Okinawa), which was coined by Pearl Buck, the first American woman to win the Nobel Prize for Literature, has been frequently used today (see Murpy-Shigematsu, 2002). Although they still face discrimination and hardships in Okinawa, their social status has remarkably improved due to their exceptional talents particularly in the areas of music, sports and performing arts. According to Suzuki, there are about 2,000-3,000 Amerasians in Okinawa (Suzuki, 2003).

The U.S. presence has greatly influenced Okinawa's economic activities. U.S. military expenditures used to account for 30-40% of Okinawa's GDP in the 1960s. If we take into account the Japanese government transfer payments to Okinawa as ODA to support the U.S. bases, the percentage today remains at the same level. Field (1991) described the Okinawan economy as a "prostitution economy." Iha (1942) also described Okinawan mentality as "unintended prostitutism" citing Okinawa's old proverb: "a person who provides food is our Lord."

It is interesting to note here, despite the U.S. occupation of Okinawa including the use of the U.S. dollar as Okinawa's legal currency, Okinawa never picked up the custom of tipping. Compared with Hong Kong, Singapore and the South Pacific which were under British and American colonial rules, Okinawa's overall English proficiency is lower. It also never surpassed that of mainland Japan which was occupied by the Americans for seven years.

Even after thirty-five years of Okinawa's reversion to Japan, Okinawa still hosts 75% of all U.S. military bases in Japan, and the bases are continuously a hot socio-politico-economic issue. Although the majority of islanders are against the presence of the U.S. bases, they are fully aware of the economic consequences of the base withdrawal. Researchers have just begun to investigate how the presence of U.S. bases, which is an enclave zone in Okinawa, intertwine with the local culture and shaped Okinawa's lifestyles positively as well as negatively (see Yamazato, 2005). It will take time to untangle the complex knots of cultural influence and confluence.

Prospects for *Champuru* Culture

The Virtuous Circle of Culture

Even "traditional" culture is subject to change over time, and quite often it changes without notice by the indigenous people. As we have seen, Okinawan culture has changed gradually, due to external interventions as well as by self-generating endogenous forces. For a small island society in particular, external forces can render significant changes. The following diagram shows how indigenous culture changes through interactions with external influences.

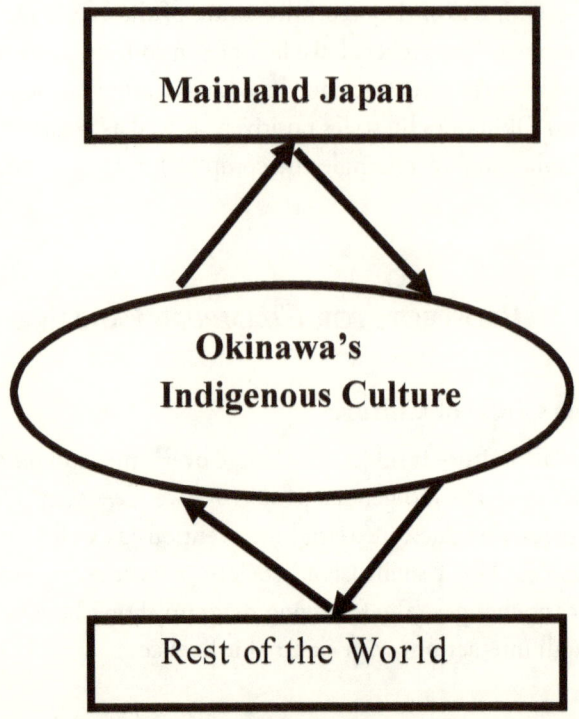

Source: Kakazu, H.

FIGURE 9-3: A Possible Process of Cultural Influences.

For many years, Japanese looked down upon Okinawan culture, language and food (pork); however, recently Okinawa and Okinawan products have become popular on the Japanese mainland and abroad. "The third party appreciation" of the Okinawan culture has provided the Okinawan people with enormous pride in their culture and identity, and it encouraged the promotion of local cultural activities such as traditional music, dances, karate, arts, healthy foods including pork dishes and even *uchinaguchi* (Okinawan dialects) which were considered as an inferior language in the past. This is what I call a "cultural virtuous circle."

The virtuous circle is typically demonstrated by the activities of overseas Okinawans, or *Uchinanchu* in the local dialect, who migrated to Hawaii, North and South America, Southeast Asia, the South Pacific and other areas. As we have discussed in Chapter 3, It is estimated that these overseas migrants and their descendants, excluding mainland Japanese, numbered about 300,000 in 2006. As they prospered in their settled lands, they remitted funds to their motherland.

Their practice continued until just after World War II. At one point, these remittances covered the entire trade deficit of Okinawa. It was only quite recently, however, that they actively organized or networked themselves to enhance their "*Uchinanchu* identity" beyond national boundaries. One active organization is the Worldwide *Uchinanchu* Business Association (WUB) which was inaugurated in Hawaii in 1997 for the purpose of creating businesses through a worldwide network of Okinawans.

As we have seen in Chapter 3, WUB has been organized across five continents and in the Pacific. It is ironic that during the early years of migration, around the turn of the last century, people were driven out of Okinawa by conditions of abject poverty and were regarded as *kimin*, or deserters, whereas today they have become valued catalysts in the networking of Okinawa with the rest of the world. It is interesting to note that the third and fourth generations of emigrants from Okinawa are increasingly more concerned and more appreciative of their ancestors' culture than their parents and grandparents. This is particularly so when the cultural value and lifestyle of Okinawa is highly appreciated by the world community. This coincides with Lowenthal's observations on emigrant communities:

> *Networks of obligation with homelands may persist for generations, as Cook Islanders in Newzealand and Paupans in Australia show. Diaspora communities like Guamanians in California and West Indians in Toronto retain or replicate so much island culture they can be said to replenish rather than diminish the home society. Indeed, emigrants whose education and economic success foster self-awareness assert their land identity more strongly in exile than those at home (Lowenthal, 1998).*

Yuimaru, Uchina Time, Slow Life

Yuimaru is an Okinawan dialect and means "reciprocity." It is the Okinawan concept that is rooted in old work-sharing practices where all villagers cooperated to help each other with financing, planting, constructing houses and irrigations, or harvesting crops. *Yuimaru* spirit is still vividly alive in Okinawa in various festivals, mutual finance system called *moai* and community activities. This is a social "safety net" system to prevent individuals or communities from collapsing. The value of *yuimaru* is also re-evaluated as globalization, or Americanization of lifestyles, a symbol of cut-throat competition and rigid individualism, prevails and affecting adversely Okinawa's lifestyles of health and sustainability (LOHAS). Okinawa is now a booming tourist resort for mainland Japan. A typical mainlander, who used to blame an Okinawan for his or her backwardness, and easygoing attitude towards work, is reported to say that "every nation and citizen can live in peace.

I am very proud of this original Okinawan idea and I would like to diffuse this *yuimaru* mind all over the world.

Okinawa's comparatively easygoing and time-loose lifestyle is also gaining popularity as a way to ease the various stress and pressures arising from workplaces and complex human relations. *Uchina* time (unpunctual Okinawan time), which was almost totally replaced by *Yamato* time (Japanese time) a long time ago, has also been gradually revived as a result of a general acceptance of "slow-life" and healing-oriented lifestyle reflecting partly Japan's rapidly aging society.

Okinawa: The Real Shangri-La?

According to George Kerr (1958), the best-known American historian on Okinawan history, the first Chinese emperor, Ch'in Shih Huang Ti (221-210 B.C.) sent several missions into the Eastern Sea in the direction of the Ryukyu Islands to search for the secrets of immortality. Thousands of years later, others are following in their footsteps. The latest book on *The Okinawa Program: Learn the Secrets to Healthy Longevity* by Willcox, Willcox and Suzuki (2001) became a best seller in the United States by scientifically proving the secrets of Okinawan world-renown longevity. They cited the ancient Okinawan proverb:

> *At seventy you are but a child, at eighty you are merely a youth, and at ninety if the ancestors invite you into heaven, ask them to wait until you are one hundred, and then you might consider it (Willcox, Willcox and Suzuki, 2001).*

A Shangri-la, the land of happy immortals sought by many Chinese as well as European emperors, is portrayed in James Hilton's best-selling book *Lost Horizon*. Willcox, Willcox and Suzuki used Shangri-la as a metaphor based on a painstaking investigation into Okinawan longevity:

> *There are more than 400 centenarians in a population of 1.3 million---about 34 per hundred thousand---many of them still healthy, active, and living independently. In the United States there are only five to ten centenarians per hundred thousand---a huge difference---and most older Americans are in far less robust health (Willcox, Willcox and Suzuki, 2001).*

Okinawans' longevity is, no doubt, the product of a complex combination of climate, culture, closely-knit social organizations, food and lifestyle and probably DNA. The above authors have discovered that food culture is particularly important for the healthy life. The most popular Okinawan dishes are the various *champuru* recipes, notably *goya* (bitter gourd) *champuru*. *Goya* and its products have become best selling health foods in Japan in recent years.

Tourism and Cultural Heritage

Impacts of tourism on cultural heritage and change have been intensively discussed in recent years (see Gusti Ngurah Bagus, 1992). Tourism is all about selling dreams to those who wish to escape from the dull and daily treadmill into a wonderful, exciting and challenging world. Tourism is not so much about travel, accommodation, and destinations, all these are merely the means to another end, it is to do with the attractions which are deeply related to cultural identity.

"Cultural identity is the expression of one's place in the world" (Schouten, 1996). Both the host and the tourist carry their cultural identity on which they base their communications to find not only inspirations, excitements, but also underlying conflicts through which local culture is gradually eroded and exposed for a constant change for better or worse to the extent that even the local peoples no longer remember their authentic culture. A good case in the point can be found in the Bali dances and other cultural performances which have been modified and made into packages of entertainment solely for tourists. They are quite different from the original ones (see Michel Picard, 1983). The similar phenomenon can be found in Okinawa where more than 90% of tourists are from mainland Japan. Okinawan traditional dances, music, folk arts, foods have been increasingly Japanized in recent years.

We may call this phenomenon "commercializing culture" in a vulgar term or "a dynamic nature of culture" in a more positive term, if we define culture as an ever-evolving source of inspiration. "Ever-evolving" means a constant cultural touch with the changing world reality, both external as well as internal. We quite agree with Schouten's following verdict on cultural dynamism:

> Culture is a phenomenon constantly in development, a living identity. Culture is a dynamic pattern and when it is forced into a static pattern it will cease to be a source of inspiration. When conservation of culture is turning into conservatism, the treatment will be worse than the disease and will eventually kill the "patient" (Schouten, 1996).

Therefore, if we frame tourism as a catalyst for internal socio-cultural and politico-economical changes driven by external factors such as tourist supply and international political relations, our approach is naturally that of inter-or trans-disciplinary with a "normative" connotation. That is to say, whether one calls mass-tourism or green-tourism or eco-tourism or cultural tourism, we need to start from recognizing the very fundamental idea and paradigm that all socio-cultural systems and their expressions are at parity; and at the same time, tourism must be carefully managed and sustained in terms of not only money making, but also in terms of conserving tourism resources, including marine, historical and cultural assets.

In this sense, the tourism industry needs to be conceptualized as a composite industry not as a mere market-oriented service industry. Such re-conceptualization of the industry will provide a development framework for culturally sensitive international tourist sites such as Okinawa and Bali.

Conclusions: Can *Champuru* Culture Save Ailing Japan?

Japanese society is, no doubt, ailing and aging. Japan's international status has been weakening in the 21st century due largely to its declining relative economic power, aging population, and above all its inward-looking culture and politics. Japan is the least open society among the OECD countries. This character is deeply rooted in its culture and in its racially homogeneous peoples who tend to reject cross-cultures. Despite more than a century of assimilation and Okinawa's painstaking efforts to be a part of Japan, "Japanese are not capable of accepting Okinawans as full-fledged members of the national family" (Smits, 1996).

As we have seen, however, there is an increasing number of mainlanders who favorably evaluate the Okinawan lifestyle and wish to live in Okinawa in recent years. There has been an interesting phenomenon in population flows in recent years. The indigenous population of Okinawa's outlying small islands have continuously emigrated to neighboring larger islands, while an increasing number of Japanese mainlanders have been attracted to the leisurely "island lifestyle." If such a trend in population dynamics continues, we may see the entire population of these islands being replaced by mainlanders in the future. Nobody can predict the socio-economic impacts of these cultural dynamics (Kakazu, 2006).

Okinawa's *champuru* culture represents not only cultural diversity which is a norm of international society, particularly in the Asia-Pacific, but also it empowers the local people through healthy lifestyle and warm *yuimaru* spirits. Okinawa is the only local prefecture in Japan whose population is still growing. There is a no nonsensical joke that Okinawans will be the last Japanese to survive in the 25th century if the current depopulation on the mainland continues.

The strength of *champuru* culture is its resilience and flexibility towards external shocks (see Oshiro, 1972; Okamoto, 1972; Tonaki, 1986). This strength has probably been nourished through its enduring history of ambivalence, war and colonial rule. At the same time, the *champuru* culture has bred a dependency syndrome culturally as well as economically. Okinawa has strived to achieve economic self-reliance for many centuries without success. It is an idle dream to achieve the goal unless a Manx-Gaelic motto of the Isle of Man in the British Isles is seriously pursued: "Wherever I'm thrown, I stand on my own feet."

Okinawa has almost everything that mainland Japan is lacking. Although

I do not have enough space to elaborate on this point, Okinawa will play a very important role in saving Japan in the future. I have found an influential Western "Okinawanologist" who argues that:

Japanese history could only be understood in light of the history of Ryukyu... it must not be understood as a 'minority' on an ethnical, cultural, or any other sense: Ryukyu and its culture as well as its language form one of two main equal pillars of support, standing side by side, which hold up the Japanese culture. Only the realization of this fact makes it possible to appreciate the immensely rich diversity of Japanese culture" (Kreiner, 2001).

Another world-class Ryukyuanist, Taira Koji has conceived of an independent for Okinawa:

A strong sense of self-reliance refined by increased interactions with the world at large will enable Okinawans to see Japan as just another country and see themselves deserving of their own nation and state on an equal footing with any nation-state. A long-awaited third golden age will then dawn on Okinawa (Taira, 2001).

In closing we would like to emphasize that although Okinawan *Champuru* culture is Japan's marginal culture in a marginal or peripheral region, it does contain a spirit of reciprocity or mutual help and stability which are also common cultural characteristics in Asia. This is why Asian visitors to Okinawa feel at home when they have discovered the Okinawan motto: *icharibachode* (once we meet, we are like brothers and sisters).

NOTES

Misumi, Haruo (Undated), p.1.
Lebra, William (1966), p.45.
Kerr, G.H. (2000), pp.448-449.
Ibid.
Field, Norman (1991), p.72.
Smith, Gregory (1999), p.151.
Field, Norman (1991), p.72.
Ibid., p.69.
Iha, Fuyu (2000, originally published in 1942 from Seijisha), p.14.
Willcox Bradley, Craig Willcox and Makoto Suzuki (2001), p.1.
Ibid., p.5.

Schouten, F. (1996), p.42.
Ibid., p.42.
Smits, Gregory (1999), p.154.
Kreiner, Josef (ed.) (2001), p.15.
Taira, Koji (2001), p.413.

REFERENCES

Akamine, Mamoru. 2004. *Ryukyu Ougoku* (The Ryukyu Kingdom). Tokyo: Kodansha.

Bagus, G.N. 1992. "Cultural Tourism and Religious Belief Systems in Bali." In: Wiendu Nuryanti (ed.). *Universal Tourism Enriching or Degrading Culture?* Yogyakarta: Gadjah Mada University Press, pp.68-74.

Field, Norman. 1991. *In the Realm of a Dying Emperor: Japan at Century's End.* New York: Vintage Book.

Hamamoto, Darrell.2006. "'Soft Colonialism': A *Nikkei* Perspective on Contemporary Okinawa." *The Okinawan Journal of American Studies*, no.3, pp.28-34.

Hokama, Shuzen. 1971. *Okinawa no Gengoshi* (A History of Okinawan Language). Tokyo: Hosei University Press.

Higa, M. 2003. *Okinawa kara Ajia ga mieru* (Asia is understood from Okinawa). Tokyo: Iwanami Shoten.

Higa, Seihan. 1983. "Okinawa no Gairaigo" (Foreign Words in Okinawa). *Gekkan Gengo*, vol.12, no.4, pp.76-82.

Iha, Fuyu. 2000. *Ko Ryukyu* (Old Ryukyu). Tokyo: Iwanami Bunko.

Kakazu, H. 2006. "Networking Island Societies under the Globalizing World: The Case of the Pacific Islands." *Journal of Island Studies,* no.6, pp.1-10.

Kerr, G.H. 2000. *Okinawa: The History of an Island People.* Revised Edition. Boston: Tuttle Publishing.

Kodama, M. 1999. *Ishiganto* (Stone Symbol). Naha: Ryukyu Shmpo Sha.

Kreiner, Josef (ed.). 2001. *Ryukyu in World History.* Bonn: Bier'sche Verlagsanstalt.

Lebra, William. 1966. *Okinawan Religion: belief, ritual, and social structure.* Honolulu: University of Hawaii Press.

Lowenthal, David. 1996. "Islands Today: Conservation and Innovation." A paper presented at Islands of the World Conference, Vancouver Island, pp.1-28.

Masuda, Seiji (ed.). 1992. *Japanese Systems: An Alternative Civilization?* Yokohama: Sekotac Ltd.

Misumi, Haruo. Undated. "The Performing Arts of Asia and Okinawa." *Mimeographed*, pp.1-27. Okinawa.

Murphy Shigematsu, Stephen. 2002. *Amerasian Children: An Unknown Minority Problem.* Tokyo: Shueisha.

Okamoto, Taro. 1972. *Okinawa Bunka Ron* (Culture of Okinawa). Tokyo: Chuo Koronsha.

Oshiro, Tatsuhiro. 1972. *Uchinaru Okinawa, sono Kokoro to Bunka* (Inside Okinawa: Its Minds and Culture). Tokyo: Yomiuri Shinbunsha.

Picard, M. 1983. *Community Participation in Tourist Activity on the Island of Bali: Environment, Ideologies and Practices.* Paris: UNESCO/URESTI-CNRS.

Schouten, F. 1996. "Tourism and Cultural Change." A paper presented at the UNESCO Conference on Culture, Tourism and Development: Crucial Issues for the XXI Century. Paris.

Smits, Gregory. 1999. *Visions of Ryukyu: Identity and Ideology in Early-Modern Thought and Politics.* Honolulu: University of Hawaii Press.

Suzuki, Marika. 2003. *Empowering Minority Youth in Japan: The Challenge of the AmerAsian School in Okinawa.* School of Education, Stanford: Stanford University, Monograph, pp.1-77.

Takara, Kurayoshi. 1998. *Ajia no Naka no Ryukyu Ogoku* (The Kingdom of Ryukyu in Asia). Tokyo: Yoshikawa Kobunkan.

Taira, Koji. 2001. "Okinawa in the Twenty-First Century." In: Kreiner, Josef (ed.), *Ryukyu in World History.* Bonn: Bier'sche Verlagsanstalt, pp.395-417.

Tonaki, Akira. 1986. *Okinawa no Bunka* (Culture of Okinawa). Naha: Hirugisha.

UNESCO. 2002. *Universal Declaration on Cultural Diversity.* Paris.

Watanabe, Yoshio. 2002. *Okinawa no Bunka no hirogari to Henbou* (Changes and Diversity of Okinawa's Culture). Ginowan: Youju Shorin.

Willcox Bradley, Craig Willcox and Makoto Suzuki. 2001. *The Okinawa Program: Learn the Secrets to Healthy Longevity.* New York: New York Times.

Yamamoto, Nari. 2004. "A Study of the Ethnicity of Young Okinawans in Hawai'i." A paper presented at the ISLANDS of the WORLD VIII Conference, 1-7 November 2004, Kinmen Island (Quemoy). Taiwan.

Yamazato, Katsunori. 2005. *Sengo Okinawa to America: Ibunka Sesshoku no sogoteki Kenkyu* (An Interdisciplinary Study of Postwar Cross-Cultural Contact between the U.S. and Okinawa). Okinawa: Faculty of Law and Letters, University of the Ryukyus, pp.1-367.

Chapter 10

OKINAWA'S CHALLENGES FOR SUSTAINABLE DEVELOPMENT

INTRODUCTION

Like many small-island economies, Okinawa's economy possesses general characteristics that have presented challenges for its economic development: (a) specialized rather than diversified economic activities; (b) a small domestic market; (c) a reliance on a limited number of primary products and tourism for export earnings, while at the same time being dependent on imports of consumer and capital goods; (d) chronic trade-balance deficits; (e) diseconomies of scale; (f) high transportation costs; (g) rising population pressures on a small arable land area, and; (h) a heavy reliance on government expenditures and activities as a major source of income and employment. These disadvantages for development have intensified in recent years as a result of the rapid globalization of the Japanese economy upon which Okinawa depends heavily.

Against the above background, this chapter focuses on Okinawa's post-reversion economic performance, and the problems and prospects for the 21st century. In so doing, the focus is on Okinawa's competitiveness within the context of the Japanese economy as well as the global economy more broadly.

How to measure competitiveness is rather elusive for Okinawa because it is now an integral part of Japan politically as well as socio-economically. Therefore, measuring Okinawa's competitiveness is based on domestic comparative advantage and international comparative advantage. Sugarcane, the main agricultural export crop in Okinawa, for example, possesses domestic comparative advantage. However, the crop has no international comparative advantage at all. The crop is heavily protected by the Japanese government. Therefore, the conventional index of "revealed comparative advantage (RCA)" to measure Okinawa's international competitiveness cannot be applied.

Okinawa's future industrial development depends on its international comparative advantages as well as its positive economic policies to shape these advantages. After briefly examining Okinawa's economic performance in the past three decades under the Government of Japan's (GOJ) Okinawa Development Special Measures Act, this chapter attempts to measure Okinawa's global strength through its strategic location, population and labor force, structural transformation, productivity, tourism, external trade, technology, human resources, conversion of U.S. military bases and various other impediments to successful development.

DEVELOPMENT PLANS AND THEIR PERFORMANCES: 1972-2005

Population and labor force

Since reversion in 1972, the Okinawa Prefectural Government (OPG) under the Okinawa Development and Promotion Measures Act of the central government has implemented four ten-year development plans. The latest fourth development plan (2002-2011) is in its mid-year review stage. The previous three plans focused on unification and catching-up with the levels of the mainland in terms of living standards and various socio-economic systems and infrastructures, while the current fourth plan aims at the self-sustainable development of socio-economic activities based on Okinawan self-help efforts and the full utilization of local resources. The goals and performance results are summarized in TABLE 10-1.

TABLE 10-1. Okinawa's Development Plans and Performance: 1972-2005

	Unit	Time of Reversion 1972	End of 1st Plan 1982	End of 2nd Plan 1992	End of 3rd Plan 2002	Latest Performances 2005	Goals of New 10-year Plan 2011	Changes 2004-5/1972
Population	10,000	96	113	124	134	136	139	1.4
Labor force	1,000	375	469	566	625	649	700	1.7
Employed	1,000	364	446	542	573	598	670	1.6
Unemployed	1,000	11	23	25	52	51	30	4.6
Rate of joblessness	%	3.0	4.9	4.3	8.4	7.9	4.3	2.6
Employment by industry	%	100	100	100	100	100	100	
Agriculture	%	17	12	9	5	5	5	0.3
Construction	%	12	13	14	13	12	18	1.0
Manufacturing	%	9	7	7	6	6		0.6
Tertiary	%	61	66	70	75	76	77	1.2
Services	%	25	23	29	40	41	NA	1.6
Tourism	million	324	1,656	2,802	3,466	4,061	5,379	12.5
No. of tourists	10,000	44	190	319	484	550	650	12.5
Per capita consumption	¥10	7,364	8,716	8,784	7,161	7,384	8,275	1.0
GDP annual growth rates	%		13.0	3.4	1.5	1.1	NA	
Per capita income	¥10,000	44	136	204	203	202	270	4.6
(% of national average)	%	60	74	69	71	70	NA	1.2
Fiscal dependency (% of GDP)	%	24	35	37	41	40	NA	1.7
(national average)	%	18	23	21	23	23	NA	1.3
Fiscal exp. of central gov't (national average)	¥100mil.	1,800	3,332	4,300	3,512	2,833	NA	1.6
Exp. for development plans	¥100mil.	760	2,000	2,700	3,112	2,478	NA	3.3
(Accumulated totals)	¥100mil.	760	12,879	16,118	14,125	78,464	NA	101.1
College enrollment	%	27	19	20	29	34	NA	1.3
(national average)	%	29	30	33	44	45	NA	1.6
Unit labor cost of mfg.	1973=100	NA	120	150	150	NA	NA	
(national average)		200	200	300	300	NA	NA	

Note: Unit costs = manufacturing incomes/no. of employed in manufacturing (nominal).
NA = not available.

Sources: Computed from Okinawa Economic Outline and Okinawa Statistical Yearbook, various issues.

The population increased more than planned from about one million in 1972 to 1.36 million in 2005. The average annual population growth rate during the post-reversion period was 1.3%, compared to 0.7% in Japan proper. Okinawa is the only Japanese rural prefecture whose population continues to rise. According to the latest projections of the National Institute of Population and Social Security Research, Okinawa's population will peak in 2025 with 1.43 millions or 5% more than 2005 in which year the national population declined for the first time in Japan's postwar history.

Amid the continuous depopulation of Japan, Okinawa will be the most important source of human resources for Japan's future development in the coming decades as it used to be during Japan's high economic growth period in the 1960s. Although Okinawa's population is aging rapidly, her younger population (age 14 and under) will still account for 28% of the total population compared to Japan's 10% by 2035 (FIGURE 10-1). In addition to the natural rate of population growth, Okinawa has experienced net social increases in recent years. In particular, Okinawa has become Japan's most popular rural prefecture in terms of being a retirement location (or place to spend the rest of one's life) amongst the so-called "postwar baby boomers."

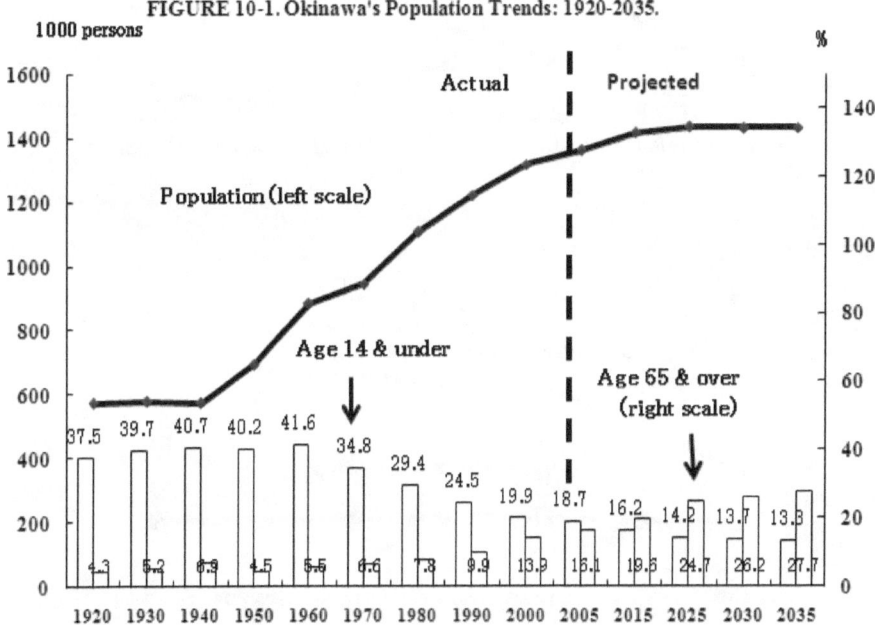

FIGURE 10-1. Okinawa's Population Trends: 1920-2035.

Notes: Figures for 1920-2005 are actual data. Figures for 2010-2015 are projected by the National Institute of Population and Social Security Research (2007).

Sources: Okinawa Prefectural Government, *Okinawa Statistical Yearbook*, various issues.

Okinawa's real gross domestic product (GDP) has grown on average by 5.4% annually over the post-reversion period (1972-2005). At the same time, however, the growth rate has declined continuously from 9.9% in the 1970s to 5.5% in the 1980s, 1.2% in the 1990s and 1.6% in the first decade of the 21st century (FIGURE 10-2). Real growth rates picked up during this latter period due mainly to declining GDP deflators. Although Okinawa's GDP performed better than Japan proper in the post-reversion period, growth rates have roughly synchronized with the national average particularly after the third and fourth development plans.

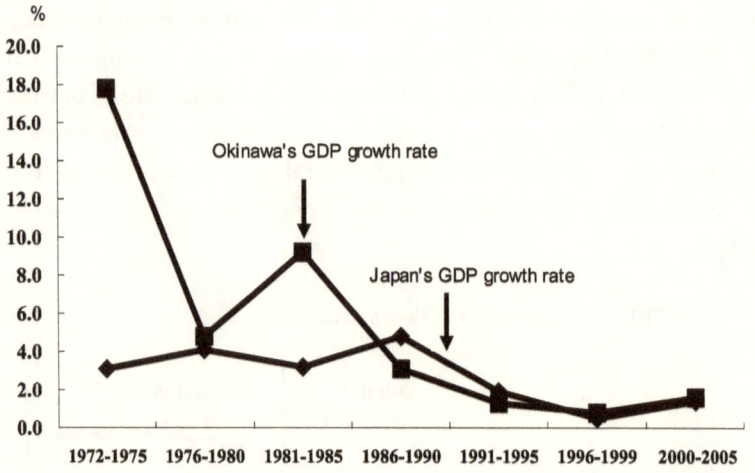

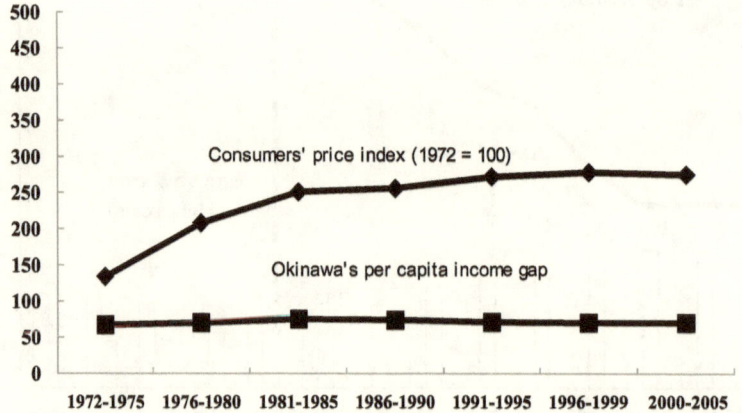

Notes: Income gap is defined: Okinawa's per capita income /Japan's per capita income (%).
Sorce: See FIGURE 10-1.

FIGURE 10-2 Okinawa's Grwoth Indicators: 1972-2005.

Okinawa's relatively higher economic growth than Japan proper, particularly during the 1980s, contributed to narrowing the gap (*kakusa zessei*) in living standards between the Japanese mainland and Okinawa. Okinawa's per capita income (PCI) increased from US$15,000 or 62% of the national Japanese average in 1972, to US$23,000, or 70% of national average in 2005, although it fell short of the targeted level of 80% during the first plan period. Okinawa's per capita income in terms of purchasing power parity (PPP) is now almost comparable with Japan's rural prefectures such as Nagasaki, Kagoshima, Aomori and Akita where populations have declined continuously and therefore contributed to the rise in per capita income.

Clearly, a pronounced disparity between Okinawa and Japan proper exists in the area of per capita income and per capita savings, Okinawa's PCI measured in nominal U.S. dollars, is almost comparable to the G-8 highly industrialized countries (FIGURE 10-3). One important indicator of a high-quality lifestyle, however, is demonstrated by the well-publicized longevity of Okinawans which has already been discussed in a previous chapter. The average life expectancy of women in Okinawa is eighty-six years, the highest in the world. There are many explanations offered for this longevity including food, water, climate, easy-going work habits, communalism, and even DNA. However, an in-depth study has not yet been conducted. In recent years Okinawa's lifestyles of health and sustainability (LOHAS) have attracted retirees from the mainland who wish to spend the rest of their lives in Okinawa.

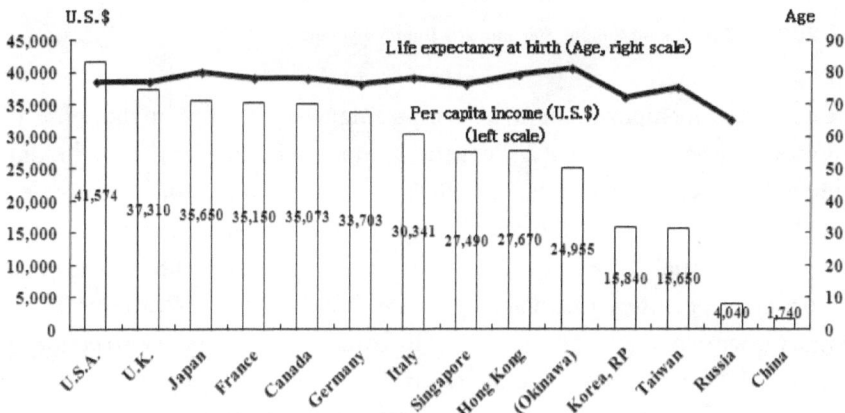

Notes: Per capita incomes are preliminaries. Life expectancies are for 2002.

Sources: IMF, International Financial Statistics Yearbook, 2006 and ADB, Key Indicators 2006.

FIGURE 10-3. Per Capita Income and Life Expectancy of the G-8 and Selected Asian Countries: 2005.

A rapid population increase after reversion, accompanied by a proportionally larger labor force, has generated a continuous labor surplus in Okinawa's job market. Over the post-reversion period (from 1972 to the present), the labor force has increased by 2.3% annually. Although local employment has also increased by 2% annually during the period, it has not been enough to absorb the increased labor force. Consequently, the jobless rate jumped from 3% to about 8%, which is twice as high as Japan proper (FIGURE 10-4). The creation of jobs has been the most important economic and political agenda in Okinawa since reversion.

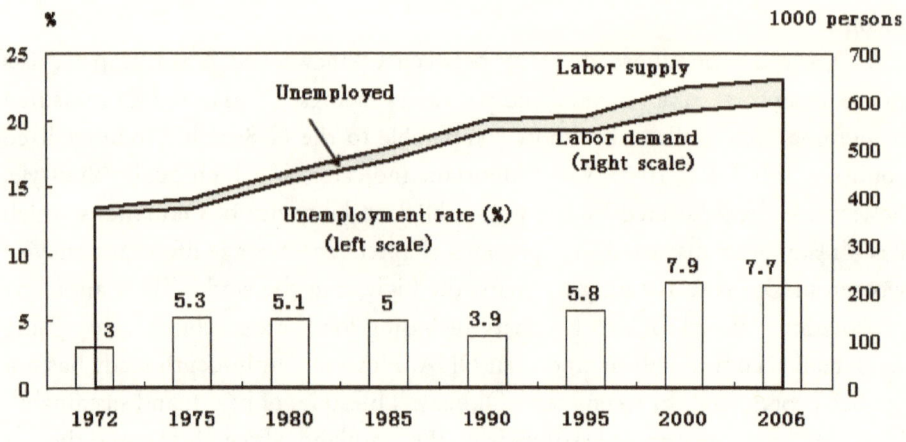

FIGURE 10-4. Labor Supply, Demand and Unemployment.

Okinawa's unemployment structure is unique nationally, in the sense that young people (those under age 24) constitute more than 30% of the total number of unemployed compared with only 20% in Japan proper. Young unemployed people have largely been supported by pooled family incomes and by an age-old *Yuimaru*, or mutual help system. This explains why there is little social unrest despite a high, persistent unemployment rate. We should note, however, that involuntary unemployment, created mainly by bankruptcies and the restructuring of companies through attrition, the increased use of part-time employees, and spin-offs, such as early retirement and the phenomenon of "*freeters*" (those who chose to work according to their convenience and lifestyles) have been on the rise in recent years. Okinawa's rising *freeters* are also reflected its highest rate of NEET (Not in Employment, Education or Training) population among Japanese prefectures.

In view of weakening family ties, a weakening social safety net or social capital, growing competition and an aging population, unemployment within Okinawan society will become increasingly more difficult to bear in the future. There is plenty of evidence that unemployment has many far-reaching effects other than loss of income, including psychological harm, loss of work motivation, skill and self-confidence, an increase in ailments and morbidity, disruption of family relations and social life, the hardening of social exclusion and the accentuation of racial tensions and gender asymmetries (see Basu, Pattanaik and Suzumura, 1995)

During the fourth plan period, the tourism, medical services and information and communication technology (ICT) industries have absorbed the growing labor force while traditional industries such as agriculture, construction and manufacturing have lost employment (FIGURE 10-5). The construction industry, which used to employ 14%-15% of all employees in the first plan period, now absorbs less than 13% of the total. In the past, the central government spent lavishly on public works programs for Okinawa so as to narrow the infrastructure gaps with the mainland as well as to maintain the U.S. bases on Okinawa. Yet the days of the construction boom are over. Okinawa has to look for alternative sources of employment. The goods-producing sectors, namely agriculture and manufacturing have also declined from 17% and 9% of total employment in 1972 to a mere 5% and 6%, respectively, in recent years. These sectors are not expected to grow to absorb future labor force increase. As we have seen already, tourism and tourism-related sectors, ICT and professional services are the most encouraging areas to focus on for employment creation.

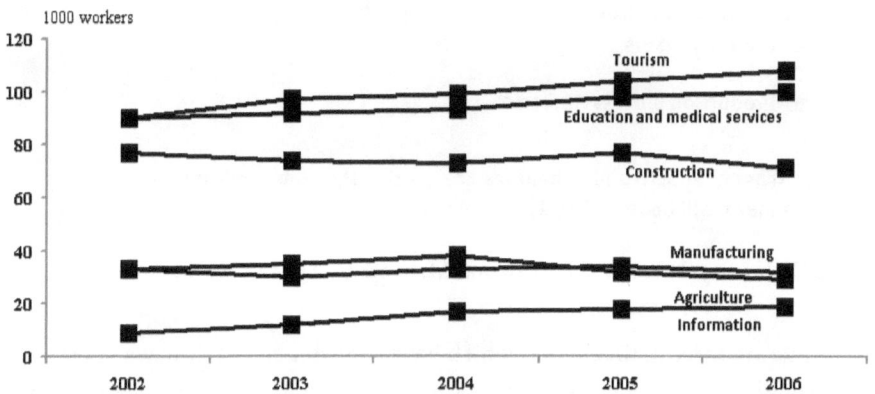

Notes: Agriculture includes all primary industries; Tourism includes other services
Information (2002-3 figures are estimated); Education and medical services include welfare.

Source: See FIGURE 10-5.

Okinawa's labor market is more complicated than it appears. There has been a growing "mismatch" between active job openings and applicants particularly in the young adult job market (FIGURE 10-6). The number of job openings has been greater than applicants for customer and professional services such as hotels, call centers, medical services, various tourism-related businesses and sales. Although tourism is the most promising and growth-oriented industry in Okinawa, the educated younger generation tends to look down on the industry due not only to its relatively low-pay and hard work, but also to its low social status compared with the public service sector. This is a general phenomenon in developing island societies where the public service sector dominates economic activities.

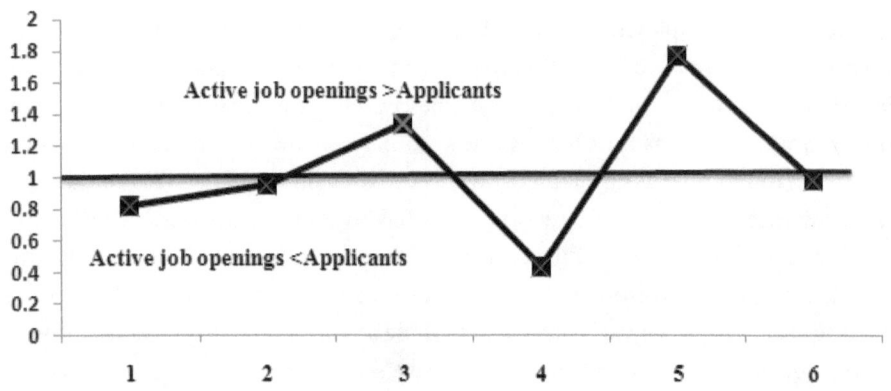

1 = Professional & technical workers Professional & technical workers
2 = Services
3 = Customer services
4 = Clerical workers
5 = Sales
6 = Production process workers

Note: Whenever active job openings are greater than job applicants,
the index will be less than 1.

FIGURE 10-6. Okinawa's State of Job Mismath by Type of Professions: 2005.

There are three main engines which have contributed to Okinawa's post-reversion growth rates. Public expenditure is the single most important item, accounting for 30% of Okinawa's GDP in recent years, followed by income generated from tourism (11%), and U.S. military base expenditure (5%) (FIGURE 10-7). Immediately after reversion, public expenditure, mostly in the form of fiscal transfers from the Japanese government, replaced U.S. military expenditures within the local economy as the main engine of growth. The relative importance of base expenditures, including the wages of civilian employees, base land leases, and base-related expenditures by U.S. forces and their dependents for local products and services, has declined from 25.6% of GDP in 1970 to 5% in 2005. The U.S. bases still generate 180 billion yen annually, and provide employment for about 8,000 local people. There are always more local job applicants for base employment than jobs available, owing mainly to the lack of stable and attractive job opportunities in the local market. Beyond that, a large chunk of Japanese central government transfers are directly and indirectly related to the maintenance of bases.

The second important economic growth factor is the tourism industry. The number of visitors to Okinawa has increased more than ten-fold, from 440,000 to 5.5 millions during the period 1972-2005, which constitutes an annual increase of 28% compared to a GDP growth rate of 2.5%. Direct income from tourism has also increased more than twelve-fold during the period.

Okinawa's self-sufficiency rates defined in the footnote of FIGURE 10-7 improved continuously after reversion until the 1980's, from 30% to over 60%, reflecting diversification and the expansion of the economy. After the collapse of the economic bubble and the ensuing globalization-cum stagnation in the 1990s, however, the sufficiency rates have flattened out.

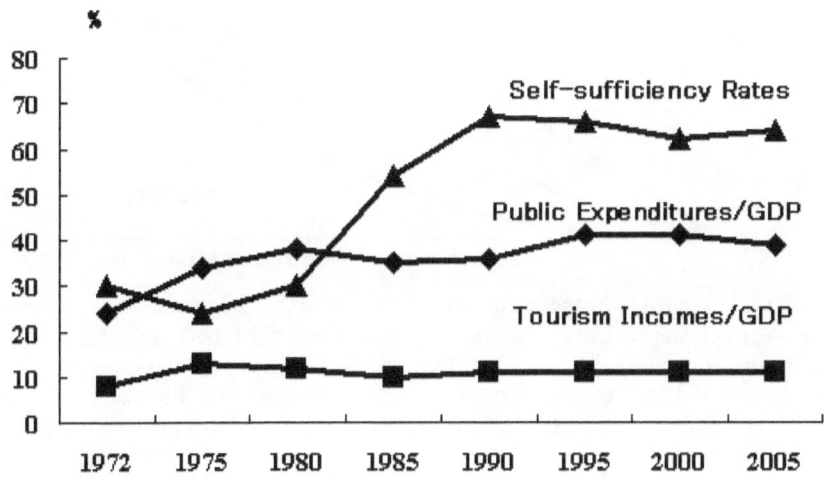

Notes: Self-sufficiency rate = 1 - Total imports/Total demand
2005 figures for self-sufficiency rate and GDP are preliminary.

Source: Statistics Bureau, Management and Coordination Agency.

FIGURE 10-7.Tourism and Self-reliant Development: 1972-2005.

High economic growth has inevitably been accompanied by environmental degradation, notably air and water pollution, as well as soil erosion that require comprehensive study and the adoption of serious measures. The widening income gap among households as measured by the Gini index is also of concern. Okinawa's Gini index rose from 0.3678 to 0.4026 over the past two decades (FIGURE 10-8). The Gini index of 0.4026 means that 70% of household income is earned by 30% of households. The index was the highest among Japan's 47 prefectures, with the national average at 0.3598. Two main factors can explain the relatively unequal distribution of household incomes in Okinawa. One is the widening gap in per capita growth between rural and urban areas. Per capita income of the northern rural areas of Okinawa Island, for example, grew much less than that of the prefectural average in the past decade.

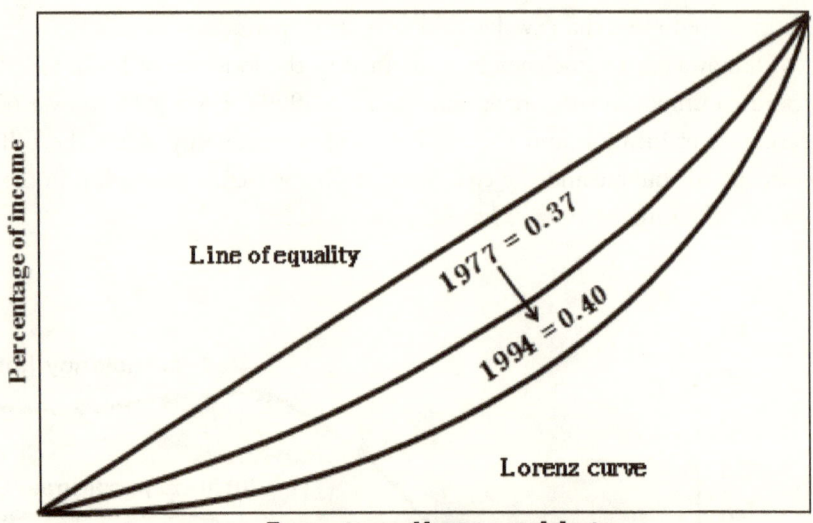

Notes: Gini indexes or coefficients can be obtained by calculating the ratio of the area between the diagonal and the Lorenz curve divided by the total area of the half-square in which the curve lies. The indexes are aggregate measures of inequality and can vary anywhere from 0 (perfect equality) to 1 (perfect inequality). The index on the order of 0.2 to 0.35 is considered relatively equal income distribution.

Source: Bureau of Statistics, Management and Coordination Agency.

FIGURE 10-8. Okinawa's GINI Index: 1977 and 1994.

Although the Gini index for Okinawa has not been estimated in recent years due to a lack of available data, there is evidence that the personal income gap has been widening. For example, Japan's Gini index, which includes Okinawa Prefecture, rose from 0.4983 in 2002 to 0.5263 in 2004 (*Japan Economic Journal,* 2007). Although the rise of Japan's Gini index is largely attributable to the aging population, inequality sentiment among the ordinary people has been intensifying in recent years (see Tachibana, 2006, for an excellent account on this issue).

Another evidence of economic hardship is found in the number of Okinawa's households on welfare assistance program which increased from 9,465 in 1995 to 15,245 in 2007. The number of recipients of unemployment insurance also doubled during the period reflecting increased unemployment (FIGURE 10-9). The increasing number of the so-called "working poor" has also contributed to the income gap. More than 40% of regular workers and about 60% of part-timers earned less than four million yen and one million yen, respectively, in 2000.

number of recipients

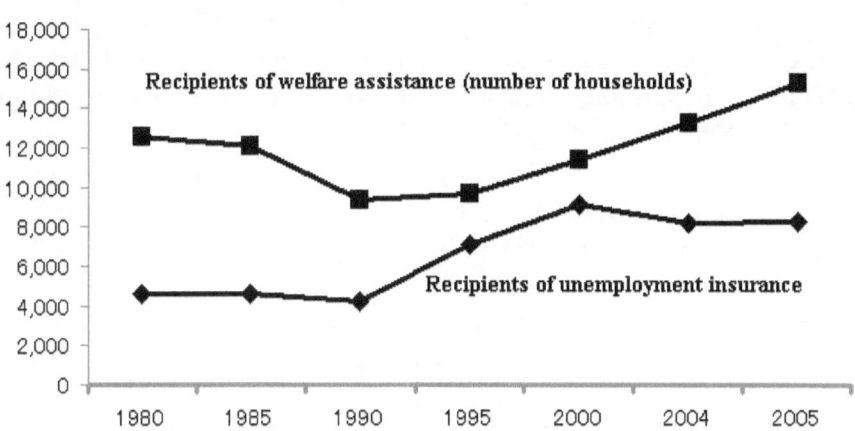

Source: *Okinawa Statistical Yearbook*, various issues.

FIGURE 10-9. Indicators of Social Safety Net: 1980-2004.

Transformation in Industrial Structure

The structure of the Okinawan economy is very similar to that of Hawaii's. In both cases, the service industry dominates economic activities. Agriculture, which was the dominant industry during the 1950s, now accounts for only 7.1% in terms of labor force and 2.4% in terms of income. An empirical law discovered by Kuzunets (1965) suggests that the agricultural sector tends to generate low incomes in part because of the low income elasticities of its products as a whole compared to those of other sectors; as the cost of producing farm products falls with technological progress, prices tend to fall as well. Moreover, the skills required for traditional agricultural production are less and do not demand extensive education as can be observed in many small island economies. Okinawa has followed this pattern more than any of Japan's other prefectures.

Although Okinawa's agriculture has been diversifying away from traditional sugarcane and pineapple cultivation to flowers, such as orchids and chrysanthemums, tropical fruits such as mangoes and citrus and healthy foods such as turmeric *(ukon)*, and bitter melon *(goya* or *nigauri)*, the relative contribution to Okinawa's GDP may continue to decline in the future as a result of increasing international competition, stagnant productivity gains, and aging farm workers.

The share of manufacturing income declined sharply from 11% of GDP in 1972 to 5% in 2005 which is very low compared with that of Japan proper (21%), Taiwan (23%) and Singapore (22%). The declined share of Okinawa's manufacturing industry is mainly due to relatively high-cost of economic structure in the world of increasing international competition. Only those local cottage industries such as *awamori* (rice wine), various health foods and protected agro-industries are surviving.

There is a consensus amongst policy makers and researchers that the development of a large-scale manufacturing industry in Okinawa is simply not viable, either now or in the future. Okinawa's local markets are small, fragmented and far away from major markets; wage and rental rates are far higher than those in neighboring Asian countries; and the levels of human resources and technology development are low. Okinawa's average monthly wage per manufacturing worker, for example, was US$2,591 for 2003, which was about twice as high as that in Taiwan and Hong Kong, where per worker productivity is higher than in Okinawa. That is to say, the unit labor cost in Okinawa (wage per worker/per worker productivity), which roughly determines international competitiveness, is more than three times higher than in the aforementioned countries.

The unit labor costs in Okinawa are high not only in comparison with its neighboring economies, but they have also rapidly increased in recent years. Okinawa's unit labor costs in the manufacturing sector have increased more than four times over the past two decades compared with less than two times in the case of Japan proper. This would indicate that Okinawa's domestic as well as international comparative advantage in the manufacturing sector has substantially weakened after reversion despite some protective measures by the government (FIGURE 10-10).

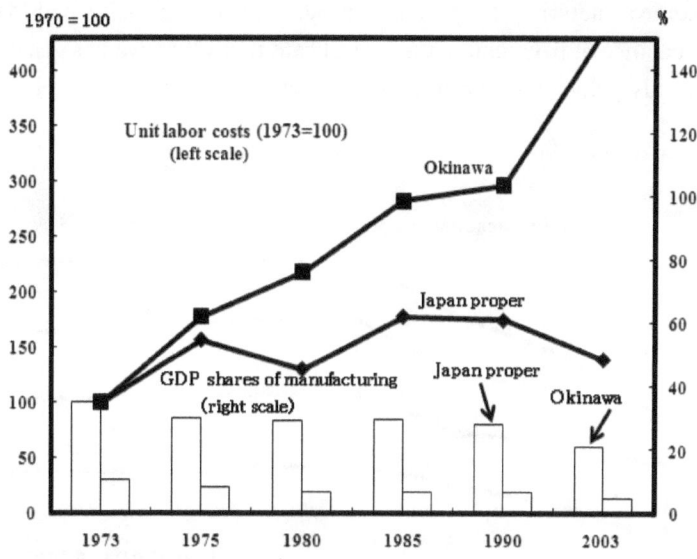

1970 = 100 %

Unit labor costs (1973=100)
(left scale)

Okinawa

Japan proper

GDP shares of manufacturing
(right scale)

Japan proper

Okinawa

1973   1975   1980   1985   1990   2003

Notes: "Unit labor cost" is defined as the index of per worker wages/the index of per worker productivity in the manufacturing sector. The GDP shares are in current prices.

Sources: Statistics Bureau, Management and Coordination Agency. Unit labor costs were estimated by Atsuo Wakugami for 1973-90 of the Okinawa International University.

FIGURE 10-10. Unit Labor Costs and GDP Shares of Manufacturing Activities: 1973-2003.

The construction industry accounts for 13% and 9%, respectively, of total employment and GDP, the highest among Japan's 47 prefectures. This reflects Okinawa's level of per capita public expenditure, also the highest in Japan. The easy entry into the construction industry has functioned as an "absorber" of unskilled, young unemployed labor. In contrast, the income share generated by the service industry, including trade, tourism, and various private as well as public services jumped from 67% in 1972, to 75% in 2005. This shows that while Okinawa, like many other small-island economies, has a comparative advantage in producing services, this is not the case for agricultural and manufactured goods which require economies of large-scale production and a large domestic market as well as advanced technologies.

External Trade

Although trade imbalances (deficits) persisted after reversion, the sources to finance the deficits have changed. Government transfers financed 51% of Okinawa's total external payments, including imports, for the latest fiscal year of record, followed by receipts from exports (34%), tourism (24%) and U.S. base-related expenditures (11%) (FIGURE 10-11). These add up to more than 100% because the external sources of finance exceeded Okinawa's trade deficits. That is to say, Okinawa's economy has recorded a sizable surplus in its current account balances, indicating that

it has become a "net capital exporter." Unlike many cash deficit small island economies, the balance of payments statistics indicate that Okinawa has generated sizable
"surplus funds" which have been used elsewhere if the statistics are reliable.

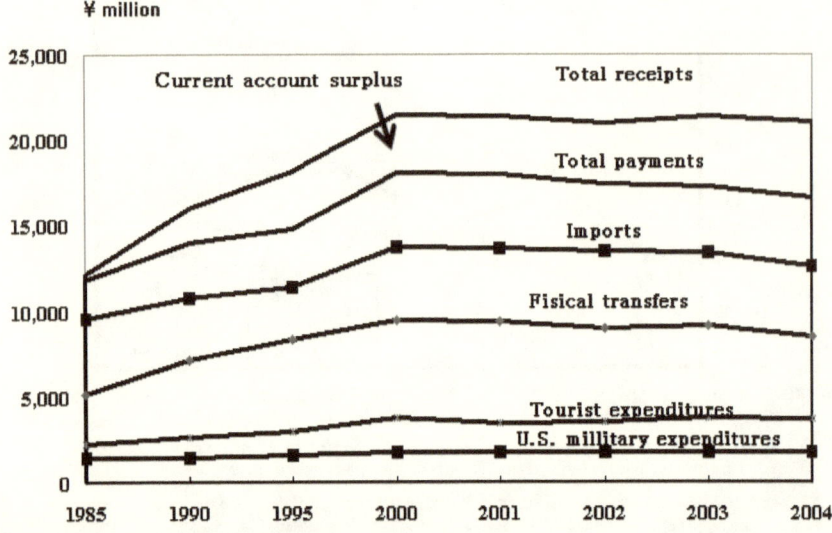

Sources: Okinawa Prefectural Government, Okinawa Statistical Yearbook, various issues.

FIGURE 10-11. Okinawa's Balance of Payments:1985-2004.

Okinawa imports almost all of its consumer goods and capital equipment. Its
major exports are petroleum products (refined on-island from imported crude oil),
sugar, tropical fruits, flowers, health foods, rice wine, and various craft products.
There is, however, no single export product that has hooked deeply into the domestic Japanese market, much less the international market. A special free trade
zone (SFTZ), which will be discussed later in this chapter, was created in 1998 to
promote exports of high-tech products consistent with Okinawa's relatively high
wage and resource costs. Unfortunately its performance is well below what planners expected.

Entrepreneurship and Human Resources

Despite the various incentives and preferential measures to promote industry over nearly three decades of implementing long-term economic development
plans since reversion, the Okinawan economy has failed to achieve self-reliant or
self-sustainable development, that is to say, financing its mounting trade deficits
through internally generated incomes.

Economists and policy makers have persistently pointed to the lack of entrepreneurship, that is, the lack of initiative, well-conceived plans, actions, self-assessment and calculated risk-taking on the part of the private business sector. Nurturing entrepreneurship is profoundly linked to human resource development. The subject has been a hot topic for many years because Okinawa, with limited natural resource endowments and with small markets, must pursue its development efforts through effective utilization of its relatively abundant human resources. Compared to Japan proper, where the population declined in 2005, Okinawa's population is expected to increase until 2025. This effectively means that Okinawa will be in a position to supply portions of the labor force for Japan's future development provided, of course, that this labor supply is well-educated and highly trained in the appropriate skills.

Currently, the potential of Okinawa's labor force is not even close to being maximized. This is chiefly the result of job mismatch, that is, the skill qualifications of job seekers is not matched to market demand. To resolve this mismatch, Okinawa's educational as well as professional training systems must be drastically overhauled. Okinawa's unemployed labor force tends to stay in Okinawa. The reasons for this are partly pragmatic, given the existence of Okinawa's traditional mutual support systems and various social safety-net systems; but cultural factors such as the easy-going lifestyle and strong sense of community identity compared with mainland Japan also enter into the equation.

One particularly worrying aspect of human resource development in Okinawa, however, is the close to stagnant trend in college enrollment rates (percentage of college and university enrollments against the number of high school graduates) which actually declined from 26.5% in 1972 to 22.9% in 1995. Although the enrollment rate picked up to 32% in 2005, it was much lower than Japan's overall 50% enrollment rate, itself a remarkable improvement from 29% in 1972. Educational quality is also a big problem. According to the latest nationwide tests on academic achievement in elementary school sixth-graders and third-year junior high school students, Okinawan school children achieved the lowest scores on all subjects including mathematics and Japanese writing and reading (*The Okinawa Times*, 2007). The survey also indicates that there are positive correlations between the level of household incomes and the test results.

DEVELOPMENT CONSTRAINTS

High Cost and Low Productivity

As we have already discussed, small island economies have been suffering from comparative cost disadvantages arising mainly from their smallness along with their isolated, fragmented location. Okinawa's locational advantage cannot be easily exploited unless transportation facilities connecting international business centers are adequately provided with competitive prices. The reality, however, is far from international standards. There are only seven international shipping routes in operation with most offering just one trip per week. As we have seen already, one-way, small-lot cargo traffic between Okinawa and international hub ports makes unit cargo costs very expensive compared with major hub ports. For example, transporting a 40-foot container from the U.S. west coast to Naha cost 1.9 times and 2.3 times more than to Yokohama and to Taipei, respectively, in 1998. Air routes are much less developed than sea routes, except for the Naha-Taipei route.

Limited Infrastructure and Carrying Capacity

In addition to the high cost of transportation, the inward-oriented economic structuresupported by inward-oriented incentive policies are major issues to be resolved for global competitiveness. Okinawa's exports account for just over 10% of its GDP compared to more than 150% for Hong Kong and Singapore in recent years. Additionally, more than 90% of Okinawa's exports are destined for mainland Japan.

There are also possible supply constraints of public utilities such as water and electricity which have increased more than Okinawa's economic growth rate since reversion. Although a severe water shortage has not occurred in recent years, the water supply is precariously dependent on rainwater. As discussed in Chapter 8, recent severe water shortages in the Zamami Islands, one of the most popular tourist destinations in Okinawa, indicates that there is a potential risk to island tourism arising from water supply which is the most important lifeline for isolated, small islands.

The major problem with electricity supply is the relatively high cost of power generation because of the existence of only small-scale, isolated operations compared to mainland Japanese companies where electricity can be mutually traded during peak demand seasons. Okinawa is not only far removed from the mainland market, but there are also about thirty very small, remote islands within the archipelago of Okinawa which make power generation a costly and risky operation.

In addition to the increasing demand for water and energy resources as the population and the number of tourists increase, the economy's carrying capacity and environmental disruptions will become serious constraints on future development. It is particularly serious for Okinawa where tourism, which depends on clean, sandy beaches, is the most important engine of the economy. There is already good evidence that Okinawa's world-renowned coral reefs are on the verge of extinction due largely to global warming, overfishing and various construction activities. It is particularly important to assess whether or not Okinawa's small, environmentally fragile islands can sustain their ever-increasing de facto population given their extremely limited capacity of renewable as well as non-renewable resources. Therefore, capacity as well as capability building towards sustainable island development are crucial for Okinawa's 21st century plan.

THE OKINAWA 21ST CENTURY PLAN

Okinawa is now implementing its fourth ten-year development plan. The plan, amongst other objectives, aims at creating development processes to strengthen Okinawa's self-help efforts or "ownership." As already discussed, although the per capita income level fell short of objectives, Okinawa's infrastructure and living standards have improved significantly under the previous three plans. In the development process, however, the economy's external trade imbalance and dependency on the public sector have deepened, leaving the ownership issue unresolved. As such, the plan's objective of achieving self-reliant development was carried over to the current 21st Century Plan (2002-2011). This basically follows the socio-economic trends anticipated for 21st-century Japan, including the development of a knowledge-based society, low birthrates and an aging society (declining birthrate), and globalization and environmental limitations.

Okinawa has many positive elements, or strengths, that could be exploited in the drive towards its future economic development. In this age of highly competitive and interdependent markets, easy and instant capital movements, and expanded global trade and investment opportunities, however, Okinawa must start to effectively highlight these strengths. Based on our preceding analysis, this author has proposed the following diversified development model which is consistent with the 21st Century Plan (FIGURE 10-12). The model is also consistent with Okinawa's strategic location, natural and human resources capacity and capability, and its aspirations.

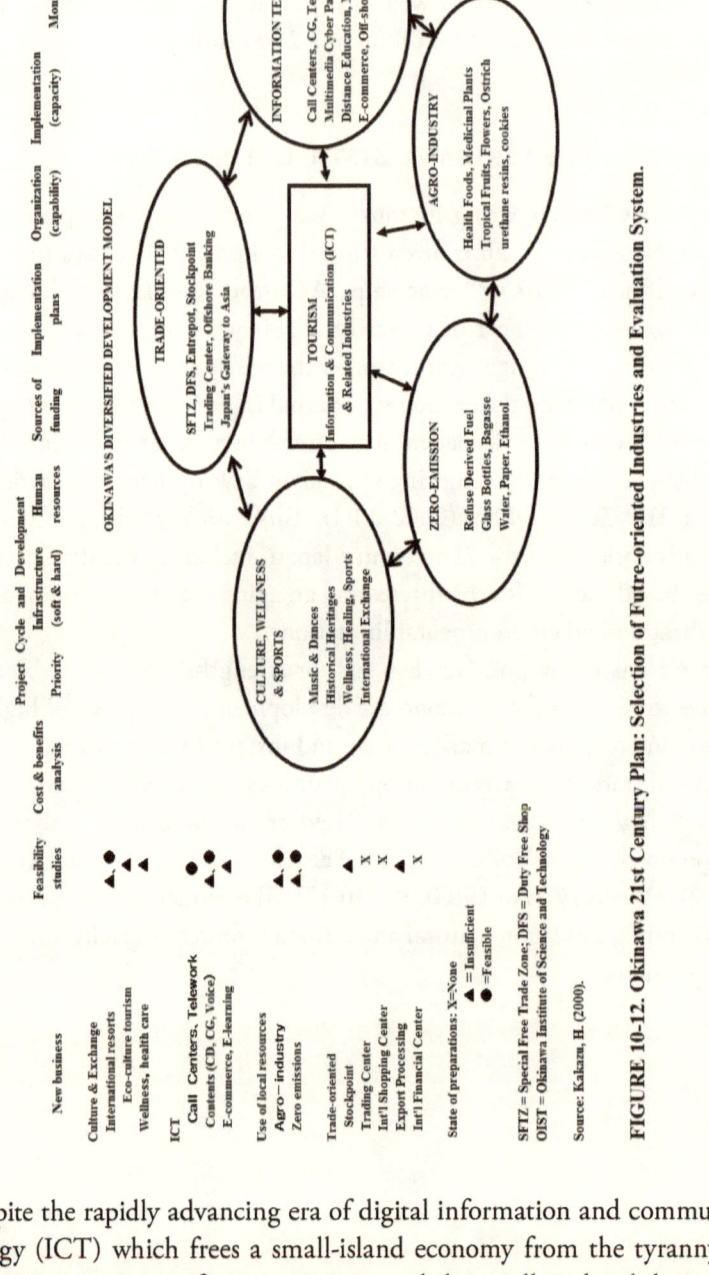

FIGURE 10-12. Okinawa 21st Century Plan: Selection of Future-oriented Industries and Evaluation System.

Despite the rapidly advancing era of digital information and communication technology (ICT) which frees a small-island economy from the tyranny of distance, comparative costs of transportation, and the small, isolated domestic market have discouraged any world-class or even national-class manufacturing companies from establishing a foothold in the islands. The proposed model is intended to make full use of Okinawa's available resources, both human and non-human, to compete internationally. The model can be competitive in the global market because it is designed to harness Okinawa's comparative advantages in tourism through promoting tourism-related "niche" industries such as health therapy and healing, health foods, sports, conventions, duty free shops (DFS), environmental conservation, zero-emission projects, e-commerce, ICT, and emphasizing the rich and varied array of culture to be found in the prefecture. Okinawan music, dance and, of course, karate, are already known. As we have already seen, the industry has expanded twelve-fold since reversion in terms of income derived. If we include all the various tourism-related industries, the impact of tourism on Okinawa's economy is much greater than the total of direct spending. It is natural and reasonable, therefore, that we project the future course of Okinawa's development as being based on tourism and its satellite industries.

Tourism as an Engine of Growth

Tourism is Okinawa's most competitive industry on both domestic and international scales. As discussed in Chapter 8, tourism has expanded about twelve-fold since reversion, mainly as a result of private sector initiatives. The industry generated an income of almost 400 billion yen or 11% of Okinawa's GDP and 38,000 regular jobs for a wide range of industries in 2005. The economy, however, could capture only 40% of total tourist spending through the sale of domestic services and goods. The rest leaked out on imports.

The model in FIGURE 10-12 illustrates that there are multifaceted ways to fill the gap between tourist spending and the economy's capacity to meet demand. Many surveys indicate that tourist spending on restaurants and souvenirs, which account for only 8.1% and 5.9% respectively, of total spending, can be expanded further since Okinawa is well-known for its longevity and health foods. In fact, health food products have grown so rapidly within Japan's major markets to the point where an "Okinawa brand" could be established.

Okinawa's tourism industry needs to diversify vertically through strengthening intra-industry linkages, and horizontally through geographical linkages including Okinawa's rural areas and cross-border areas such as the Ryukyu archipelago, Taiwan, Hong Kong, Shanghai and South Korea. Deepening the structure of tourism is the most effective measure that can be taken to address the recent declining trend of per capita tourism consumption. The average tourist in Okinawa spent 37% less than a tourist in Hawaii in 1997. "Cheap, Near and Short-stay" has been a recent slogan to attract mainland tourists to Okinawa. As a result, despite high hotel-room occupancy rates, per-room revenue has actually declined substantially. Such excessive competition by means of price-cutting may eventually damage tourism in Okinawa.

As we have already seen, Okinawa's economic ownership or self-sufficiency improved in the past, being supported mainly by the tourism-related industries. Fiscal transfers (mainly transfers from the central government) and U.S. military base incomes have been declining or have stagnated in recent years, and they are no longer expected to be growth engines in the future (FIGURE 10-13).

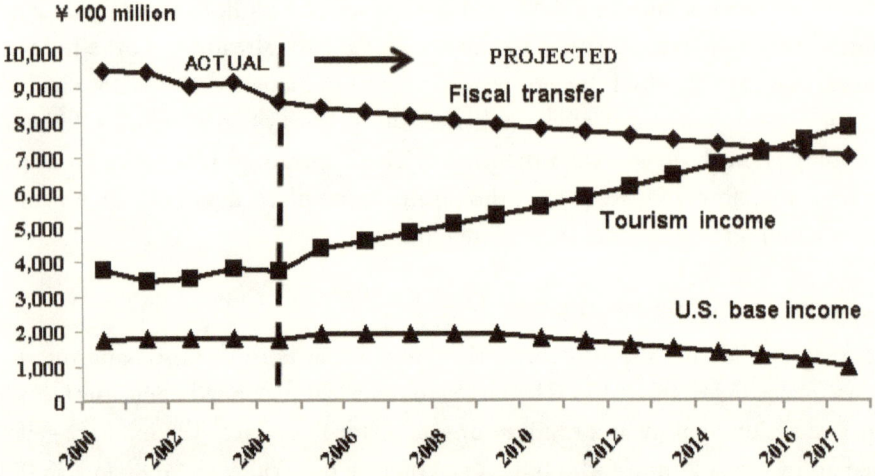

Sources: Okinawa Prefecture and Kakazu estimates for 2005-2017.

FIGURE 10-13. Tourism Is Okinawa's Leading Industry: 2000-2017.

One important condition for Okinawa's self-reliant development is to replace fiscal transfers and incomes from U.S. bases by self-generating economic activities mainly through promoting tourism and related industries. The following figure project that tourism income will replace fiscal transfers as the most important engine of growth by 2016, or twelve years from now, assuming that the number of visitors grows consistent with recent trends and per capita tourist spending increases from the current ¥70,000 to ¥100,000. This is not an overly optimistic projection. The Okinawa Prefectural Government (OPG) officially projected 10 million tourists with one trillion yen tourism income by 2017. In order to achieve this goal the Okinawa tourism industry has to overcome a variety of pending issues, as was discussed in Chapter 8. In particular, the pursuit of high-valued tourism in conjunction with its socio-economic sustainability will be the most important issue to be resolved.

Information and Communication Industry

The most important factor conspiring against Okinawa in establishing any viable international business is the small size of its economy, which is based in part to its isolated location from major markets. Information and communication technology (ICT), however, has begun to free Okinawa from its traditional constraints, particularly from the high costs arising from its smallness and isolation. In this sense, Okinawa, an island located in the center of the Asia-Pacific region, can be rediscovered not only as a strategic military keystone, but also as a keystone or a hub of ICT and training.

Since Japan's telecommunication giant, NTT, established its 104 telephone directory assistance call centers in 1998 in Naha and Nago with about 500 local employees, 41 call centers have been established with nearly 10,000 employees (FIGURE 10-14). These call centers absorbed one out every six of Okinawa's job seekers in the past decade. These call centers progressed not only in quantity, but also in quality, from NTT's so-called "white-belt" or low skill level call centers to high-level information and knowledge-intensive call centers such as customer services, software development, financial services, distance learning and back office operations. To cite some examples, CSK, a subsidiary of Sega Enterprise, started selling products, NEC began offering customer services, and Nomura Securities established a call center to sell financial services.

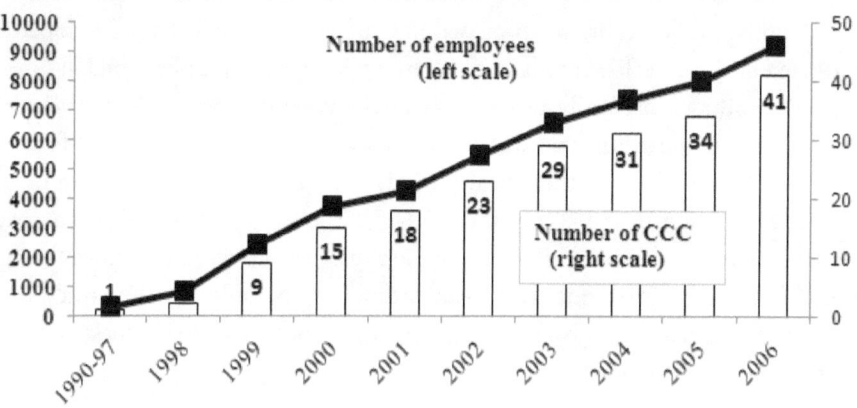

Note: CCC = Call Center Companies.

Source: Okinawa Prefectural Government.

FIGURE 10-14. Establishment of Call Center Companies in Okinawa: 1990-2006.

Call center businesses were introduced based on the OPG's Multi-media Island Plan which envisaged Okinawa as a hub of ICT in the Asia-Pacific region. Under the plan, the OPG initially subsidized 80% of the connection fees of call center businesses between Okinawa and the mainland. The Japanese government also provided incentives including wage subsidies and infrastructure development.

Along with these incentives, Okinawa has several advantages for information– intensive call centers such as a surplus, educated young labor force with lower wages than the mainland, a relatively stress-free working environment, and no record of major earthquakes which is an important condition for establishing back office operations in particular. The central government has a plan to establish a huge data center in Okinawa, mainly because it is a relatively earthquake-free area of Japan.

Health as an Industry

Okinawa is fast becoming a brand name connoting "health and longevity." Okinawa's longevity is the product of a complex combination of climate, culture, closely-knit social organizations, foods, and lifestyles. As the Greek physician Hippocrates said "let food be your medicine," so food is considered to be the most important factor influencing longevity. "There is certainly strong evidence that some of the compounds in the herbs and medicinal plants regularly consumed by Okinawans have powerful antioxidant and positive hormonal effects, and few ill effects have been associated with using them as foods, condiments, spices, teas, or home remedies" (Willcox, Willcox and Suzuki, 2001).

Okinawans are accustomed to consuming less salty, mineral-rich foods than mainland Japanese. As briefly discussed in Chapter 5, Okinawa has developed and marketed various healthy foods such as turmeric (*ukon*), and bitter melon (*goya* or *nigauri*) products, naturally processed salt, sea vegetable products (*mozuku, umibudo*), ostrich meat, and various deep-sea water products to name a few well-known examples. Sales of these health foods have jumped from \2 billion in 1995 to over \20 billion in 2004 (FIGURE 10-15). The sales of health foods exceeded the sales of sugar, the most important agricultural cash crop in Okinawa for many years. Sales of health foods have been promoted not only by Okinawa's world-renowned longevity, but also by Japan's enhanced health-consciousness stemming from its aging population.

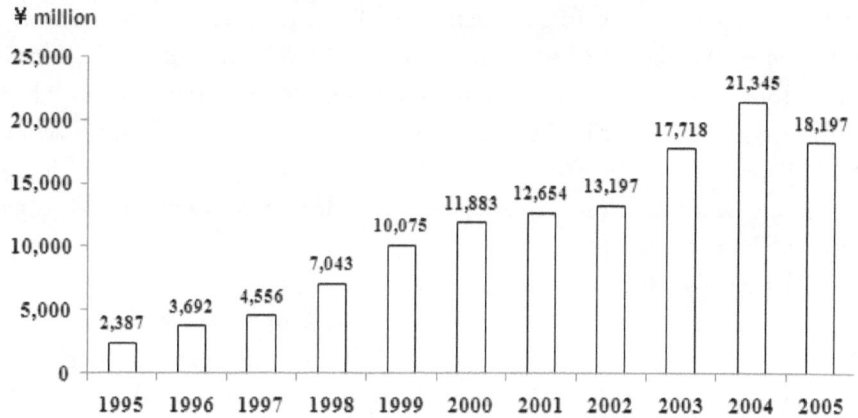

¥ million

FIGURE 10-15. Sales of Okinawa's Health Foods: 1995–2005.

Health foods possess comparative advantages in uniqueness of resource use and technology which can be developed on a small scale basis. Furthermore these products usually require more local inputs, including raw materials and labor, than conventional trading products. The OPG has been promoting "one island, one health food" because each island has its unique medicinal plants and herbs. Of course there has been keen competition in recent years among health foods producers.

Okinawa is also blessed with enormous untapped marine resources. One important area to be developed is deep-sea water for multi-utilization. Deep-sea water is defined as water taken from a minimum of 200 meters below the surface of the ocean, to which a negligible amount of light penetrates. Deep-sea water can be utilized for gradient power generation (OTEC), fish and sea vegetable cultivation and farming, processing new health foods such as mineral water, natural salt, soy sauce, ice, cosmetics, medicine and for water therapy including treatment of skin ailments. In Okinawa, on Kumejima Island, so-called *Thalassotherapie* (water therapy; *thalasso* means water in Greek) has been discussed with a view towards enhancing tourism and Okinawa's healthy image.

Special Economic Zones and Human Resource Development

As we have already discussed, the Special Free Trade Zone (SFTZ) was established in 1998 to attract trade-oriented companies. The zone provides various incentive schemes including taxes and subsidies. For example, Corporate SFTZ investors will receive a 35% deduction in their taxable income for a ten year period. Currently twelve companies, mainly of the trade-assembly type of manufacturing such as IC chips, golf clubs, shirts, cosmetics, acrylic panels and machine parts are operating at the SFTZ's 122 hectare site. The SFTZ has been under-utilized for various reasons that have already been discussed in Chapter 2. The SFTZ will be best utilized as a trade center in the Asia-Pacific instead of a site of low-skill assemblers. All Nippon Airways (ANA) has recently announced plans to establish its cargo base in the Asia-Pacific on Okinawa. This is a welcome step to make Okinawa into a trading hub in this region.

We have also discussed the Financial Special Zone (FSZ) which was created in 2002. The zone has not been performing well, primarily as a result of cumbersome regulations, lack of incentives and the lack of experts such as financial planners, international lawyers and public accountants to make the zone globally competitive and attractive. Offshore banking businesses, which have been successfully established in many small islands, can be one promising area to be pursed in the future. For this, we have to wait for the introduction of the federal system discussed in Chapter 7.

Okinawa has already demonstrated its relative advantages in training human resources. JICA's Okinawa International Center, for example, has been used as a model for similar training centers established on the mainland. The center has been particularly successful in computer-related and Japanese language training for people from more than 50 countries. The demand for information-related training has been rising in the Asia-Pacific region. A manpower shortage in this growing field is already apparent, and it could become a major bottleneck for further socio-economic development in this region in the coming decades.

The establishment of Okinawa Institute of Science and Technology (OIST) and the GOJ's latest announcement of the Asia Gateway Platform will give an added advantage to Okinawa as regards global human resources development. The OIST, based on the concept of "Best in the World," will become a leading intellectual hub (graduate institute) in Okinawa for the Asia-Pacific region by 2011 in the fields of bioscience, chemistry, computer and information science, engineering, mathematics and physics.

Technology and Innovations

Okinawa has developed various subtropical and island-based niche technologies and innovations which support the 21st Century Plan. Some important ones are listed below. Technologies such as fruit fly eradication, underground dams, deep-sea water utilization, fishing and environmental conservation are particularly noteworthy (TABLE 10-2).

TABLE 10-2. Major Technologies & Innovations Developed in Okinawa

Subtropical Base	Island Base
Fruit fly and sweetpotato weevil eradication	Transportation, communication & waste disposal systems
Tropical fruits & vegetables (mango, orange, papaya, goya, mozuku seaweed)	Water resources management underground dams multi-purpose dams
Tropical flowers (chrysanthemum, orchid)	desalination plants water tanks
Sugarcane cultivation	
	Energies
Aquaculture and payao (artificial fishing nests)	windpower solar
Deep-sea water utilization	ethanol from sugarcane
Environmental conservation coral reef mangrove rain forest	Coastal Sea Conservation soil erosion prevention & monitoring
	ITC technology
Grassroots public health and hygiene (medical support info. system for remote islands)	(call centers distance learning)
Subtropical & eco-tourism	Cummunity development (Yuimaru = mutual help
Studies on tropical biodiversity & longevity	Moai finance, one-island- one product network)
Amicable environments for education & training (i.e., JICA International Center, LEAD Program)	

Source: Kakazu, H. (2006).

CONVERSION OF U.S. MILITARY BASES

As discussed in Chapter 7, the conversion of U.S. military bases will be the single most important issue for Okinawa's future development plans considering the magnitude of the land use and the socio-economic impact on local economies. Major bases listed in TABLE 10-3 are scheduled to be returned to landowners by 2014 if the relocation of Futenma Air Station is completed by that time. Local governments such as Ginowan, where Futenma Air Station is located, Urasoe and Naha have already drafted ambitious development plans for the use of returned bases.

Past base conversion plans, however, met daunting and complicated obstacles including time-consuming consensus building with landowners, looking for viable projects and financing the projects. TABLE 10-3 lists the profiles of the main U.S. military facilities which are scheduled to return by 2014, except Kadena Air Base. The total base facilities provide rental incomes of $699 million for 33,258 landowners, 8,813 local employees and various base-related businesses. Local governments will also lose various financial support programs from the Japanese government after conversion plans are implemented.

TABLE 10-3. Main U.S. Military Facilities in Okinawa: 2005

	U.S. Base Area (ha)	Rental Payments ($million)	Number of Landowners (person)	Number of Employees (person)
Kadena Air Base	1,989	225	8,525	2,753
Camps Kuwae & Zukeran	711	86	4,297	2,420
Futenma Air Station	481	58	2,881	207
Makiminato Service Area	274	41	2,205	1,154
Naha Military Port	56	41	1,007	92
Other Facilities	20,160	248	14,343	2,187
Total	23,671	699	33,258	8,813

Source: Constructed from Okinawa Prefectural Government data.

Although the overall economic impact of U.S. bases on local economies are still important, base-related expenditures including base land lease payments, wages and off-base consumption and procurements of the U.S. forces and dependents declined from 26% of prefectural GDP in 1972 to less than 5% in recent years (FIGURE 10-16). It should be noted that payments for base land leases and local civilian employee salaries are financed entirely by the Japanese government.

Amid overall stagnation of U.S. military expenditures, base land rental payments increased sharply particularly in the 1990s (FIGURE 10-17). Mr. Masahide Ota, a staunch anti-base former university professor, was elected as the governor of Okinawa in 1990. The 1995 rape incidence of a school girl by three U.S. servicemen triggered island-wide resentment against the U.S. military presence. The increase of land rental payments coincides with these incidents

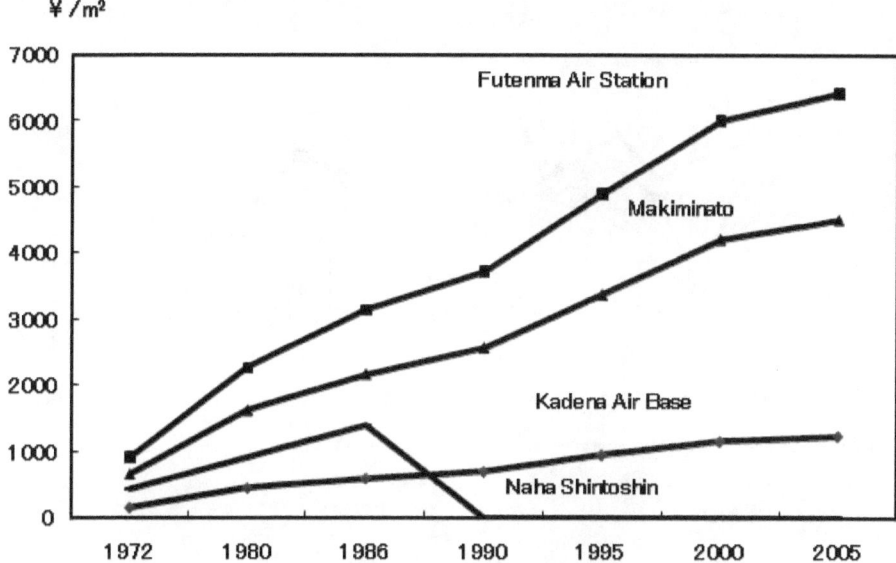

¥ / m²

Note: Shintoshin, formerly Makiminato Housing Area was returned to Okinawa in 1987.

Source: See FIGURE.10-12.

FIGURE 10-17. Military Land Rental Payments:1972-2005.

Since the rape incident, the Japanese government's base maintenance policy was strengthened through various types of financial support for cash-strapped localities which host U.S. bases. Base land rentals, which have become the largest single base-related expenditure since 1991, increased by more than Okinawa's nominal GDP growth rates and land prices in the 1990s (FIGURE 10-18).

Despite a sharp decline in land values after the collapse of asset inflation or "the bubble" in 1991, base land rentals increased 5.7% annually. This is because base lands are overvalued. Rental revenues would likely be much lower if they were determined by the market value of the lands. That is to say, the opportunity cost of the base lands, or the value of alternative use of base lands for landowners is much lower than the actual rental revenues derived from military bases. It is a well-known fact that land prices in Okinawa are the highest among Japan's rural prefectures due largely to the rising military land rentals which have been determined by military as well as political considerations.

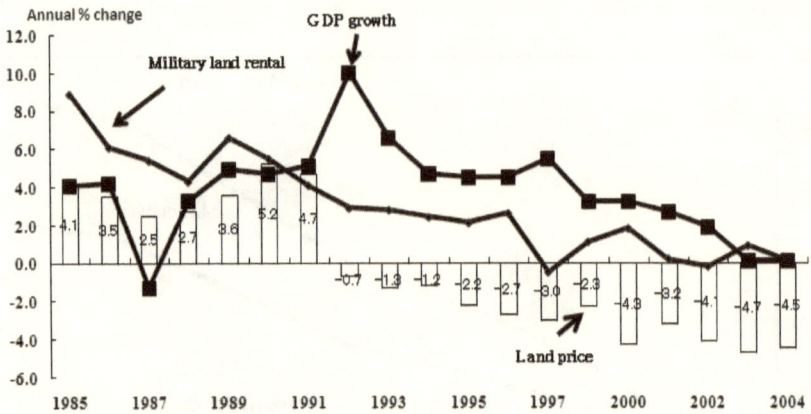

Notes: Annual changes are all in nominal prices. Land prices are simple averages for residential and commercial land use.

Sources: Okinawa Prefectural Government, *Okinawa Statistical Yearbook*, various issues.

FIGURE 10-18. Determinants of U.S. Military Land Rental, 1985-2004.

The socio-economic impacts of bases on local economies differ significantly by municipality. In Ginoza and Kin, for example, more than 35% of their total revenues are financed from base-related sources such as taxes on base land rentals and employment incomes and various government base support programs (FIGURE 10-19). Urban areas such as Ginowan, Urasoe and Naha, where the economic impacts of bases are as low as 5% of their total revenues, are likely to face less development problems than rural areas in terms of their base conversion plans and implementations.

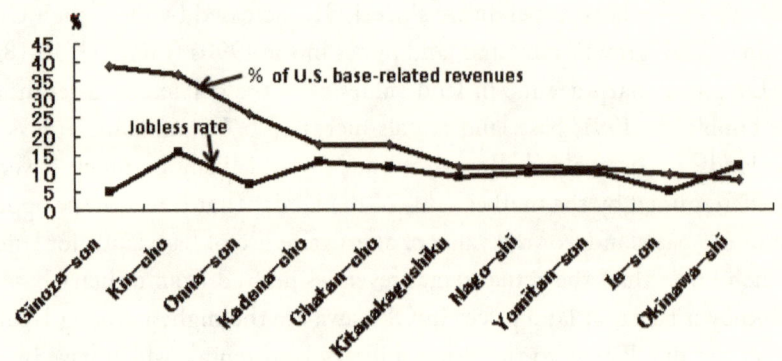

Notes: % of base-related vevenues = Base-related revenues/Total revenues (%).
Jobless rate = Total unempoyment/Total labor force (%).

Source: 2005 National Census and Okinawa Prefectural Government.

FIGURE 10-19. Base-related Revenues and Jobless Rate by Municipality: 2005.

An examination of the estimated shadow price or opportunity incomes of military bases located in Naha City for 1966-1977 revealed shocking findings (Kakazu, 1983). Even in the 1970s, opportunity incomes were about 15%-20% larger than military land rentals. Landowners in the Makiminato Housing Area (the present Naha *Shintoshin* area) requested that the U.S. and Japanese authorities return their lands as early as possible. The housing area was actually returned in 1987. After a tedious process of land re-registration, adjustments, consensus building and development planning that extended for the best part of a decade, the housing area was renamed as Naha *Shintoshin* (New Town) and various construction projects started in 1997. Now Naha *Shintoshin* has become the most bustling commercial center in Okinawa. Land prices in the area tripled over the past decade. *Shintoshin* is regarded as a success story in military land conversion along with the American village in Chatan village whose conversion started much earlier than *Shintoshin*.

Of course it is far too optimistic to assume that all military lands would be converted successfully into commercial use. The *Shintoshin* and American village models suggest that there must be at least a strong and enduring consensus among landowners as well as appealing and realistic development plans to attract development funds.

The author has estimated opportunity incomes for four bases, namely Kadena Air Base, Futenma Air Station (Ginowan), Makiminato Area (Urasoe) and Naha Military Port Area for 2005 (FIGURE 10-20). Opportunity incomes or incomes forgone due to military use were estimated through per hectare net income or value-added for each municipality. Military land rentals are the only incomes arising from the bases. Other incomes such as wages, taxes and other base-related expenditures are excluded due to the lack of information. Therefore military base incomes are underestimated. One important difference between military land use and commercial land use, however, is that the former does not directly generate goods and services which are exchanged in local markets, while the latter generates multiple economic activities.

Having said that, the opportunity incomes for Urasoe are seven times higher than the military base incomes followed by Naha, Ginowan and Kadena Air Base. Kadena Air Base is poised at the break-even point, namely incomes from land rental is on a par with incomes gained after the base conversion. The total net income generated from the conversion of the four bases amounted to about 200 billion yen, or four times larger than current base income. The net income effects roughly correspond to what the prefectural government estimated through inputs-outputs tables for the five bases located south of Kadena Air Base (see *Ryukyu Shimpo*, 2007).

Of course the estimates do not take into account social costs such as noise, crimes and environmental hazards arising from U.S. bases. The estimates also do not take into account the costs of conversion. From a landowner's point of view, it is also obvious that land conversion requires tremendous efforts and associated business risks compared to the steady military land rentals.

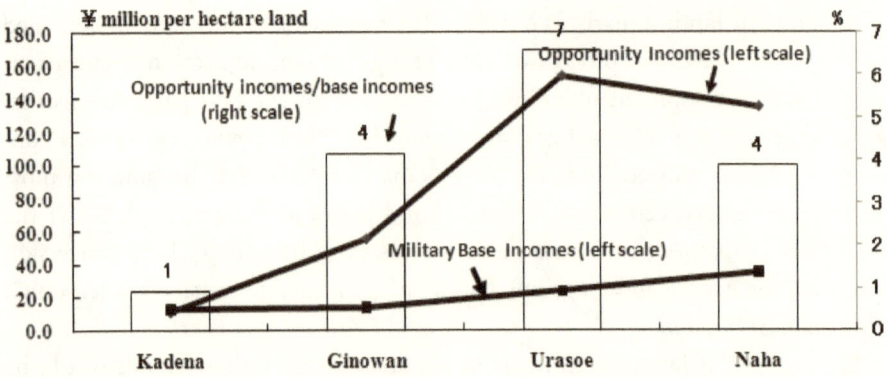

Notes: Opportunity incomes = Net municipal incomes generated if lands are used for non-military purposes. Military base incomes per hectare are for Kadena Air Base, Futenma Air Station (Ginowan City) Makiminato Service Area (Urasoe City) and Naha Military Port Area.

Source: See FIGURE 10-15.

FIGURE 10-20. Opportunity Incomes of U.S. Military Bases: 2005.

A huge amount of development funding is necessary for base conversion programs. How should these funds be raised? Even in the cases of American Village and *Shintoshin* where conversions were carried out successfully on a commercial basis, more than ¥200 billion of public money was spent on infrastructural developments. Futenma Air Station (480 hectare) alone will require ¥300-500 billion of pump-priming commercial funds. The conversion of Futenma Air Station is a daunting task considering the fact that it will take several years to clear thick concrete airfields and associated environmental hazards. Another development problem is that the area is located far from commercial centers making it difficult for developers to reap spillover effects experienced in the American Village and *Shintoshin*.

In the case of the large bases, like Futenma Air Station, the central government is obliged to restore the base lands in their original state and compensate landowners for five years after base withdrawal. As we have seen, even *Shintoshin*, where all conditions for commercialization were met, it took about twenty years to generate incomes after the return of the base. Therefore five years' compensation is too short and too little for base commercialization. Here I propose the set up of a "base conversion development fund" which should be financed by both the central and prefectural governments. The central government, in particular, is responsible for Okinawa's future development because Okinawa has contributed significantly to Japan's security without due compensation.

It is now a common understanding that Japan has spent only 1% of its GDP for its defense under the U.S.-Japan Security Pact which has been largely maintained by offering military bases in Okinawa (FIGURE 10-21). Normal countries such as NATO members, Australia and many Asian countries shoulder more than 2% of their GDPs for global security purposes. Japan needs to shoulder about ten trillion yen, or about 2% of its GDP to match her neighbors in protecting herself from unforeseen global threats.

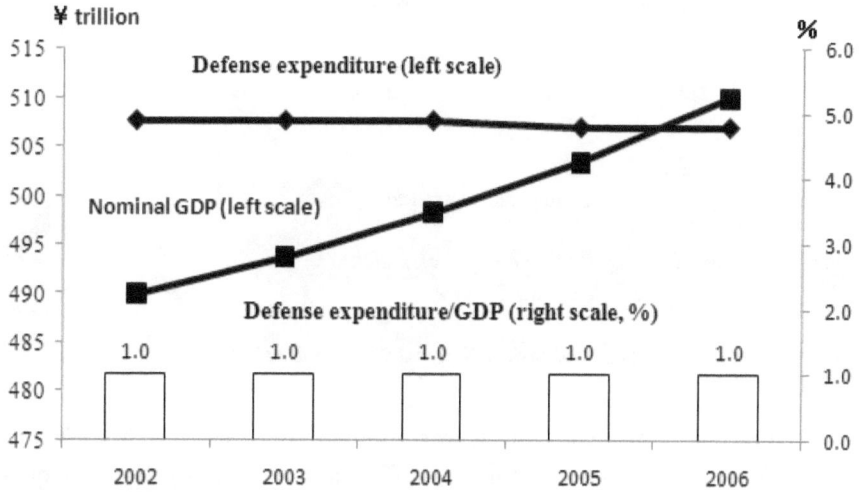

FIGURE 10-21. Japan's Defense Expenditure: 2002-2006.

This author calculated the costs of Okinawa's national security burden or contribution to Japan's global security based on a simple assumption that Japan needs to spend 2% of its GDP instead of the current 1% of GDP if there is no U.S. security umbrella. Since Okinawa keeps 75% of the U.S. military facilities located in Japan, Okinawa shouldered 3.6 trillion yen (\4.8 trillion defense expenditure x 0.75) in 2006 (FIGURE 10-22).

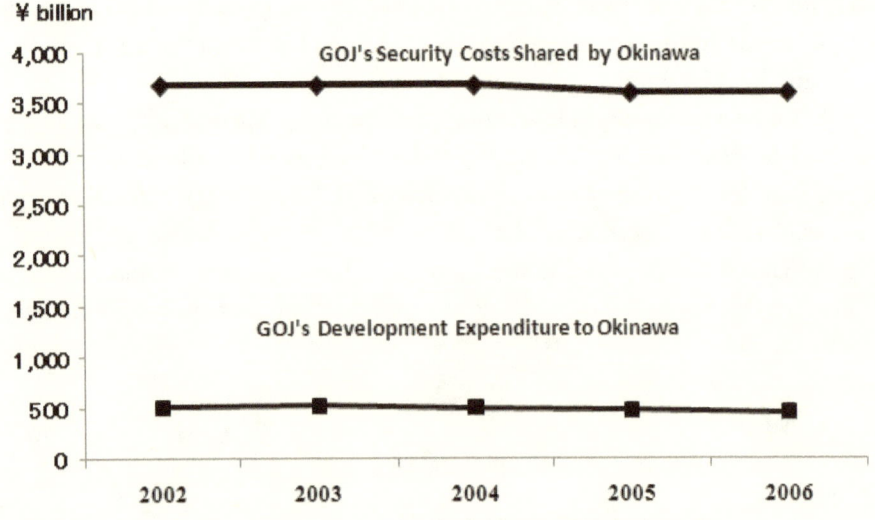

¥ billion

GOJ's Security Costs Shared by Okinawa

GOJ's Development Expenditure to Okinawa

Notes: GOJ = Government of Japan
Development expenditures by all government agencies.

Sources: Computed from Japan's *White Paper on Defense*
Cabinet Office, *Outline of Okinawa's Economy*.

FIGDURE 10-22. Costs of Okinawa's National Security Burden.

"The Keystone of the Pacific" is worth more than seven times the GOJ's current development assistance to Okinawa. Okinawa has never officially requested the cost of its security burden because such an action directly conflicts with her long-standing assertion that the U.S. bases should be relocated to mainland Japan or abroad. The creation of the base conversion fund will be fully justified if the GOJ truly intends to assist Okinawa's self-reliant development as clearly stated in the current development plan. On the contrary, the GOJ is now adopting a "stick and carrot" policy with regard to the relocation of Futenma Air Station to the northern part of Okinawa. New development projects will be funded according to the willingness of local people to cooperate with the government relocation program. The OPG and local governments are strongly against such a policy change. The GOJ's heavy-handed policy toward Okinawan development will, no doubt, affect adversely the stable maintenance of the U.S. bases on Okinawa as Mike Mochizuki, a well-known expert on security issues in the Asia-Pacific, has articulated:

The challenge facing Okinawa and the U.S.-Japan Security Alliance today is how to supplement the military hub Okinawa with an Okinawa that can become one of the dynamic nodes of the Asia-Pacific economy. To do so, Okinawa must become its own web weaver as well, and the United States and Japan must create a modicum of space for Okinawa to do so. Interestingly, the recent moves to strengthen U.S.-Japan defense cooperation during both global and regional security contingencies offer an excellent opportunity to explore creative ways for reducing the "quasi-permanent" U.S. military presence on Okinawa and to chart a more prosperous future for this island prefecture (Mochizuki, 2004).

CONCLUSIONS

Can Okinawa sustain its socio-economic activities in the future? The question has been asked repeatedly since Okinawa's first development plan in the 1970s. We have assessed Okinawa's economic performance and problems since reversion, and attempted to chart a possible future development path with strategies based on the archipelago's potential comparative advantages. What we have learnt from over three decades of economic performance is that, although Okinawa's standards of living, in terms of per capita income and infrastructural level, have improved remarkably, the economy's capacity to transform from a dependency structure to self-reliance has not been achieved successfully. More specifically, better GDP growth performance than that of Japan proper since reversion has been largely brought about by the massive inflow of public expenditures which simultaneously pushed up factor prices such as labor and land costs without improving labor productivity and the efficiency of capital. Apparently there are "perverse incentives": in the past, participants in business activities stood to gain by doing such things as politicizing the U.S. bases that helped obtain additional fiscal transfers and subsidies from the central and local governments.

Our estimates indicate that technological progress in the manufacturing sector was even negative in the past decades. This is precisely what Paul Krugman (1994) meant when he assessed Asian "miracle growth" as a myth. We should note that, despite overall positive effects of public expenditure on Okinawa's post-reversion economic development, our calculation indicates that it has generated a sizable negative multiplier effect on the trade balance. Specifically, one unit of public investment has induced 0.046 units of exports of goods and services and 0.459 units of imports, and, therefore, 0.413 units of trade deficits (0.459 - 0.046) (Kakazu, 2002). If we define self-reliant economic development as a process of reducing trade deficits on a sustainable basis, we need to reexamine the structural linkages between public expenditure, balance of payments and ecological balance so that public projects are designed to strengthen self-generating forces, development capabilities and environmental preservation.

In order to ride the cresting wave of such seemingly favorable trends, we must once again define the roles of the public and private sectors, and strike an appropriate balance between private and public actions in conducting economic activities. The private business sector, which has been fragile and inward looking, must play a crucial role as the engine of sustainable development. This is particularly true when all pubic sectors are suffering from heavy and deepening budget deficits.

There is no doubt that the urgency of integrating national as well as local economies into the international economy will be heightened in the coming decades. No region can afford to ignore an increasingly globalized, revolutionary, networked cyber world. As the Internet spreads and transport costs fall, companies are increasingly relying on international joint ventures, strategic relationships, and information-sharing partnerships.

Okinawa can fairly reap its comparative advantage in the coming age of globalization and global warming—in the areas of future-oriented tourism, health and foods, eco-businesses, sports and entertainment, small-scale industries and networking businesses including call centers, SOHO, entrepot trading and off-shore businesses. These activities are already visibly emerging through the initiative of the private sector with institutional support from local as well as central government. As we have discussed, of course, some of these activities are heavily subsidized by local as well as central government. It should be noted in particular that the "Internet age" does not necessarily bring equal opportunities and benefits to all regions and peoples. The so-called "digital divide," that is to say regional disparities in the use of personal computers and the Internet, which in turn cause regional income gaps, could be more serious in Okinawa than in mainland Japan considering Okinawa's characteristics as a peripheral and remote island community.

What is crucial in enhancing these locally-based, global activities is the availability of a highly flexible, skilled workforce. Okinawa has been experiencing a growing mismatch in the labor market arising from a rapid transformation of the economic structure and lagging human resource development. Despite the rising unemployment rate, which is not only an indicator of an underutilized labor force, but also an indicator of multiple deprivations such as social exclusion, loss of self-reliance, self-confidence and psychological and physical health, the emerging ICT companies are having a difficult time finding qualified workers.

This widening mismatch can be addressed by improved human resource development in targeted economic activities, namely tourism-centered and information-based activities. As noted earlier, Okinawa's quantity and quality of tertiary education, such as university and professional schools, lags far behind that of Japan proper. It is astonishing that, despite Okinawa's rapid advances on the mainland in terms of per capita income and the level of infrastructure, its college enrollment rates have not significantly improved in the past three decades. Investment in human resources is not only the top priority for Okinawa's industrial transformation towards higher value-added activities; but such investment also promotes opportunities for young Okinawans to venture into the global business world.

A drastic policy shift, from investments in hard and tangible infrastructure such as roads, bridges, ports and monumental buildings to investments in soft infrastructures such as human resource development, information networking and environmental preservation, is crucial and urgent in achieving the true ends of development, namely our choice and capability to lead the kind of lives we have reason to value. After all, development is "a process of expanding the real freedoms that people enjoy" (Sen, 1999). It should be clearly stated here that sustainable economic development and full employment are the only means to achieve these goals. What is required for Okinawa is probably toughness and discipline.

NOTES

Kakazu. H. (1983), p.27.
Mochizuki, M. (2004), pp.36-37.
Sen, A. (1999), p.36.

REFERENCES

Basu, K., Pattanaik, P. and Suzumura K. eds. 1995. *Choice, Welfare and Development.* Oxford: Clarendon Press.
Japan Economic Journal. August 25, 2007. "The highest Gini Index in the Past."
Kakazu. H. 2002. "The Challenge for Okinawa: Thriving Locally in a Globalized Economy." In:Hsin-Huang Michael Hsiao, *et al* (ed.). *Sustainable Development for Island Societies: Taiwan and the World.* Taipei: pp. 201-232.
———. 1998. "Sustainable Tourism Development: The Case of Small Islands," a paper presented at the Inter-island Cooperation in Asia: Tourism Policy in Island Area, The Busena Resort, Okinawa: 24 July 1998.
———. 1994. Sustainable Development of Small-island Economies. Boulder: Westview Press.
———. 1983. "Okinawa Keizai Jiritsu e no Michi" (A Path Towards Self-reliant Development of the Okinawan Economy). *Shin Okinawa Bungaku*, 56, pp. 2-53,

Krugman, P. 1994. "The Myth of the Asia's Miracle." *Foreign Affairs*, vol. 73, No. 6. November/December: 62-78.

Kuznets, S. 1965. *Modern Economic Growth and Structure*. New York: Norton.

Mochizuki, M. 2004. "U.S. Strategy in the Asia-Pacific: Alliances and Coalitions, Wheels and Webs." In: Hashimoto, A., Mochizuki, M. and Takara K. (eds.). *The Okinawa Question and the U.S.-Japan Alliance*. Washington, DC: The George Washington University, The Elliott School of International Affairs.

Okinawa Times. 25 October, 2007. "National Achievement Test: Shocking Results."

Ryukyu Shimpo. 27 July, 2007. "Economic Impacts of U.S. Base Conversion Located South of Kadena Air Base." p. 8.

Sen, A. 1999. *Development as Freedom*. New York: Anchor Books.

Tachibana, T. 2006. *Kakusa Shakai: Naniga Mondai Nanoka* (Unequal Society: Roots of Problems). Tokyo: Iwanami Shinsho.

Willcox B., Willcox, C. and Suzuki, M. 2001. *The Okinawa Program: Learn the Secrets to Healthy Longevity*. New York: New York Times.

CONCLUDING REMARKS

This volume has discussed a number of socio-economic issues that affect small Pacific islands, focusing on the sustainable economic development of Okinawa. Island economies, particularly small Pacific island economies, are facing the compound problems of development; in addition to the general problems associated with developing countries, they have economic and political disadvantages stemming from their insular nature, e.g., smallness, isolation from the major markets, and fragmentation within their own markets.

We have shown that despite such limited socio-economic opportunities compared to larger economies, some islands have succeeded in attaining sustainable island development through the use of niche resources and endogenous policies. Some islands have enjoyed a high level of per capita income within a global context. Unfortunately, the majority of independent Pacific islands have struggled to maintain even past standards of living amid population growth, environmental deterioration and globalization.

Bill Emmott's (1999) term "enlightenment optimism" means essentially that all problems are resolvable by reason. The development path and strategies suggested in this study might provide an answer to the seemingly eternal question for small islands: how can we achieve economic self-reliance? We have offered development models and approaches for sustainable island development through concepts of sustainable development, networking, economic partnership or alliance, special economic zones, social carrying capacity, safe-minimum standard, import-displacement, and international public goods (CO_2 emission trading).

It should be noted, however, that policy prescriptions derived from the present study may differ according to the stage of socio-economic development, natural resource endowments and the importance of the subsistence sector. The best available policy mix for each island economy cannot be found without addressing inter-related issues such as possible changes in technology, demographics and decision making processes at all levels.

For small island societies, globalization has provoked strong reactions, both positive and negative. Despite the new opportunities it brings, globalization is feared because it exposes local agriculture, workers and small enterprises to global competition. A typical example would be sugar and pineapple growers in Okinawa who are strongly opposed to Japan concluding a FTA with Australia where agricultural products have a greater comparative advantage. Many small islands, however, have faced dilemmas because open trade under globalization has also been the engine of growth. As we have discussed, many empirical studies support that, under a free trade regime, small island economies have enjoyed greater prosperity than larger economies by creating export opportunities as well as importing cheaper goods. At the same time, we have also demonstrated that open trade alone does not guarantee prosperity when considering impediments to labor mobility, global income redistribution and development finance.

We may argue about the relative pros and cons of globalization for small island economies, but open trade is an inevitable process. Indiscriminate protectionism is therefore likely to severely damage the long-run growth performance of island economies. Given this process and at the same time recognizing the trade-off between greater risk and uncertainty and the growth effects of their increased participation in the international economy, island economies need to seize growth opportunities brought about by globalization through endogenous policies that make use of strategic location, natural, cultural, human and diplomatic resources.

Although Okinawa is endowed with more politico-economic and locational advantages than most island economies in the Asia-Pacific region, including Japan's remote islands, it has thus far failed to fully utilize these valuable endowments in the self-generating development process. Ongoing megatrends within Japan and the Asia-Pacific, i.e., the importance of proximity to Asian growth centers, globalization, decentralization (or greater regional autonomy through localization), the aging population, the creation of a knowledge-based and environmentally conscious society, and NGO-based international cooperation are most definitely push factors for the future course of Okinawa.

The recent move of All Nippon Airways (ANA) to make Okinawa an Asian hub for its cargo operations by 2010 is an encouraging step to strengthen Okinawa's comparative advantage as an Asian center for commodities, parts procurement and exchange. Not that success necessarily follows. It will be remembered that Federal Express (FedEx), the largest cargo transport firm in the world, opened its cargo transport business in Okinawa in the late 1990s, but that the operation was a failure, primarily as a result of the island's small amount of cargo handling.

We are encouraged that ANA's planned approach is entirely different from that of FedEx. ANA starts with a stockpoint or warehouse business, as was discussed in Chapter 2.

According to ANA's *The Hub of the Asia* (2007) initiatives, Okinawa will be an Asia-Pacific distribution and commodity exchange center. Commodities such as flowers, fruit, rice, tea and other agricultural products are stored, priced and managed in Okinawa's Free Trade Zone (FTZ), together with local Okinawan products such as *awamori* and a range of health food, for marketing and timely distribution in the Asia-Pacific region. These ANA initiatives fit well into the original Okinawa FTZ concept which intended to promote out (foreign)-to-out transactions instead of current out-to-in (domestic) transactions. The Okinawa FTZ will also play an important role as an Asian-Pacific commodity exchange market where the demand for food and other commodities is expected to grow rapidly. For a particular commodity such as flowers, Okinawa can be a major trading center for both floor trade (open outcry) and electronic trade practiced in the Chicago Mercantile Exchange (CME) and the Singapore Exchange (SGX). The ANA initiatives may lead to further business opportunities such as CO_2 emissions trading which is already a multibillion-dollar business in Europe.

Introduction of the "Okinawa State Government (OSG)"

Although Okinawa is presented with a golden opportunity in the age of a locally-based global economy to take advantage of its strategic location in the Asia-Pacific as well as its historical legacy in activating the Okinawa FTZ and ICT & Financial Business Zones, there are obviously many problems to be overcome in the realization of these special measures for Okinawa. The thorniest issue probably revolves around regional politico-diplomatic-security relationships. Despite the enhancement of local autonomy in recent Japanese legislation, Okinawa is not in a position to negotiate with neighboring regions and countries to conclude trade related agreements. These are firmly within the realm of the Tokyo government.

In order to resolve these issues, the introduction of a Regional System (*Doshu-Sei*) is an essential first step. The Regional System has been intensively discussed at the Japanese Cabinet Office level as well as within academia. As we have discussed, in the context of its history, culture and geopolitical environment, Okinawa is a natural candidate for an autonomous regional government, tentatively called the Okinawa State Government (OSG).

It is important to realize, however, that the OSG will have to go beyond the current Okinawa special measure acts which allow local governments to set up various special zones under the guidance of the Cabinet Office. The OSG must guarantee a "One State, Two systems" that grants the OSG the ability to conduct its own economic diplomacy and internal affairs with all the attached risks and responsibilities. Clearly, several major issues must be dealt with in establishing the OSG. First and foremost is the constitutional question of erecting barriers to trade among Japanese states. Mainstream domestic scholars of the Constitution of Japan argue that tariffs or trade barriers between Okinawa and the other forty-six prefectures clearly violate Article 14-1 which states: "All of the people are equal under the law and there shall be no discrimination in political, economic or social relations because of race, creed, sex, social status or family origin."

According to this stipulation, a law discriminating against any people or region of Japan is unconstitutional. The special measures acts currently applied to Okinawa are temporary and there are many special measures acts in other parts of Japan. Those same scholars also argue that a heavy concentration of U.S. military bases on Okinawa does not violate Article 14 because such bases are also located in other areas within the Japanese main islands. As such, it is important to realize that whether or not the introduction of the Regional System would lead to an amendment to the Japanese Constitution, each state ought to have its own constitution which allows it to establish its own systems of governance. We need to carefully study and consider the history and experiences of other autonomous small island states such as Aland Islands, the Faroe Islands, Bermuda, Pueto Rico, the Isle of Man, the Azores, the Channel Islands and the State of Hawaii which are granted a special constitutional relationship with the central or federal government. As we have discussed, these island states have utilized their autonomy and jurisdictional muscles to build vibrant economic systems such as entrepot and offshore financial centers (see Warrington & Milne, 2007 for an in-depth study on island governance).

Although a favorable constitutional status guaranteeing the exercise of law-making rights and self-governing powers is critical to the success of the political economy of an island, it is not a sufficient condition for self-reliant development as demonstrated by many small South Pacific islands where independent, fully sovereign states have failed to sustain their socio-economic life. They have been increasingly dependent on unconventional development strategies such as selling sovereignty, passports, fishing licenses, stamps, Internet domain names, and military bases in addition to collecting foreign aid.

Okinawa is currently a long way away from satisfying the basic preconditions for establishing an OSG. First and foremost, the Okinawa Prefectural Government (OPG) has to balance its chronic fiscal deficit. The OPG was able to finance only 25% of its total expenditure (about $5 billion) from its own financial sources over the past five years. Subsidies have played the dominant role in financing OPG expenditures. The OPG should, at the very least, be required to finance 50% of its fiscal expenditures from self-generating financial sources. Second, although the number of Okinawa's municipalities decreased from fifty-three to forty-one in recent years through merger and consolidation, the number needs to be further reduced substantially. The current author previously suggested having three counties or cities, namely Okinawa, Miyako and Yaeyama in order to achieve area-wide high-quality public services with low costs for constituents.

Third, Okinawa needs to plot its own robust global strategy for sustainable development. So far Okinawa has been passive when it comes to designing new economic systems including free trade zones, financial business zones and global logistic systems. Like Singapore and the Bahamas, Okinawa should invite high-powered expertise on a global basis to realize the planned goals. Finally, as we have discussed, Okinawa's sustainable development may to a large extent depend on how it will make use of returned U.S. military base areas. In addition to consensus-building among all of the base stakeholders, the OPG has to take strategic initiatives to utilize the newly-available land resources.

Japanese society is, without doubt, ailing and aging. Japan's international status has continued to weaken during the early part of this 21st century due in large part to its declining relative economic power, aging population, and above all its inward-looking culture and politics. Japan is the least open society among the OECD countries. This character is deeply rooted in its culture and in its people who reject cross-culturalism, often rooted in their belief that the Japanese are racially homogenous. Okinawa's *champuru* culture, on the other hand, represents not only cultural diversity which is a norm of international society, particularly in the Asia-Pacific, but also it empowers the local people through healthy lifestyles and warm spirit of *yuimaru*.

Okinawa is the only local prefecture in Japan whose population is still growing. The strength of *champuru* culture is its resilience to and flexibility towards external shocks. This strength has probably been nourished through its enduring history of ambivalence, war and colonial rule. At the same time, the *champuru* culture has bred a dependency syndrome culturally as well as economically. Okinawa has strived to achieve economic self-reliance for many centuries without success. It is an idle dream to achieve the goal unless a Manx-Gaelic motto of the Isle of Man in the British Isles is seriously pursued: "Wherever I'm thrown, I stand on my own feet."

In closing we would like to emphasize that although Okinawan *Champuru* culture is marginal, coming as it does from a marginal or peripheral region of Japan, it does contain a spirit of reciprocity or mutual help and stability which are also common cultural characteristics in Asia. This is precisely why Asian visitors to Okinawa feel at home when they have discovered the Okinawan motto: *ichariba-chode* (once we meet, we are like brothers and sisters).

REFERENCES

Warrington E. and Milne D. 2007. "Island Governance." In: Baldacchino, G. (ed.), *A World of Islands*. Malta: Published by the Institute of Island Studies of Prince Edward Island, pp. 379-427.

Emmot, B. 1999. "Survey: The 20th Century." *The Economist*. September 11th-17th, pp.1-62.

ANA, *The Hub of the Asia*. 2007. Naha: pp. 1-6.

INDEX

ABOUT THE AUTHOR

 Hiroshi KAKAZU, currently Chairman of the Board of Trustees, Meio University, was born on the island of Okinawa. He received his Ph.D in Economics from the University of Nebraska. Since then, Kakazu has served as Visiting Research Fellow and Professor to the London School of Economics, the East-West Center (Fulbrighter), the University of Hawaii, the University of the Philippines (Japan Foundation) and others. He has also worked in positions as Economist of the Asian Development Bank, Professor and Dean of the International University of Japan, Professor and Chairman of the Graduate School of International Development at Nagoya University, Vice Governor (CEO) of the Okinawa Development Finance Corporation, Professor of the Colleges of Bioresources and Business Schools at Nihon University, Vice President of the University of the Ryukyus and Vice President of the Temple University of Japan Campus. He is the co-founder of the International Small Islands Studies Association (ISISA), Vice President of the International Scientific Council for Island Development (UNESCO-INSULA), Emeritus President of the Japan Society of Island Studies, and a member of the UNESCO panel of Experts on Culture and Tourism. He has served on various governmental panels including the Okinawa Development Promotion Council (currently Vice Chairman appointed by Prime Minister). *Nissology* (island study) is his lifework.

Recent publication of books includes *Island Sustainability: Challenges and Opportunities for the Pacific Islands in a Globalized World* (Trafford Publishing, Canada, 2009), *Growth Triangles in Asia* (co-editor, Oxford University Press, 1998), *The Structure of Okinawa's Economy* (Nagoya University, 1997), *Problems and Prospects of Asiatic Patterns of Development: Lessons of ADB's Thirty Years' of Experiences* (Nagoya University Press, 1997, The 10th Asia-Pacific Award), *Cross-border Growth Triangles in Asia* (Oriental Economist, 1995), *Sustainable Development of Small Island Economies* (Westview Press, 1994) and *Island Economies* (Hirugisha, 1985). In addition to the above listed books, he authored more than 100 articles on the Asia-Pacific economies for various academic journals.

www.ingramcontent.com/pod-product-compliance
Lightning Source LLC
Chambersburg PA
CBHW031824170526
45157CB00001B/178